HUMMEL ART II

John F. Hotchkiss

With Christine Cassidy

HUMMEL ART II

John F. Hotchkiss

First Edition, 1981
ISBN 0-87069-284-4 Hardbound
Copyright © 1981, John F. Hotchkiss

Art Director, Jann Williams
Editor, Liz Fletcher
Typesetting by Typeco, Inc.
Printed by McGrew Graphics, Kansas City, Missouri
Color by Art Lithocraft, Kansas City, Missouri

Published by

Wallace-Homestead Book Company
1912 Grand Avenue
Des Moines, Iowa 50305

How to Use This Book

The quickest way to obtain answers to your questions about Hummel art will be to look up a topic such as current figurines, rarities, reproductions, insurance, or where to buy and sell on the Contents page. If the topic is not listed there, turn to the Index on page 253 which has much more detail in alphabetical order.

To fully appreciate the ramifications of Sister Hummel's creations allow some time to go through the whole book page by page even though this might be limited to a quick skimming operation the first time. As in any field of art and collecting, the best informed person is the most successful collector.

The majority of readers will be interested in M.I. Hummel three-dimensional pieces which are covered in great detail. Information on each specific figurine — name, model number, marks, specifications, variations, history, sizes, age, etc. — accompanies its photograph in a comprehensive section entitled, "Photographs, History, and Production Records of the Collection" on page 34. If you know the model number, which is on the bottom of each piece, refer directly to that number in this section. If you know only the name of the figurine, turn to the "Alphabetical Guide to Model Numbers" on page 28, which will provide the model number for that name. In the event you do not know either the model number or the name, but have an idea of what it looks like, go through the photographs until you spot the piece you are looking for. The whole story except for the current value will be with the picture.

To obtain the present value refer by model number to the separate Current Price List of M.I. Hummel Figurines which is included with this book. This Price List will be revised annually, so be sure to have the one for the current year. If you go directly to the Price List, make it a point to also check the numerical model section for variations, rarities, and premiums due to design, color, size, or other attributes. The Price List alone will not provide all the information you need to make correct decisions.

Drawing #4642 courtesy Ars Sacra.

Drawing #4640 courtesy Ars Sacra.

Drawing #5900 courtesy Ars Sacra.

Contents

Drawing #5902 courtesy Ars Sacra.

Drawing #5618 courtesy Ars Sacra.

Introduction

The first objective of *Hummel Art II* is to provide quick, accurate answers to your questions and to satisfy your desire for more information on the art created by Sister Maria Innocentia Hummel. The many derivatives from it such as figurines, plates, bells, dolls, prints, cards, calendars, and needlework comprise an almost unending list of collectibles. Most collectors appreciate answers to at least three questions. Who made it? When was it made? How much is it worth? This book is designed to answer these and many more questions fully, quickly, and accurately.

Questions about where to buy or sell at the best prices, why you should insure your collection, how to use this book to make your own appraisal, who to consult for the proper type of insurance, where to get professional repairs made, why prices fluctuate, what current price is for ANY MODEL, SIZE, OR AGE Hummel figurine or collectible, what clubs you can join, how to spot reproductions, and what to do about defects are answered in detail. In short, a great effort has been made to cover every aspect that could make collecting M.I. Hummels more enjoyable, and perhaps more profitable, for you.

The two hundred thousand readers of *Hummel Art I* and *Supplements* will welcome the second objective in publishing this new book. *Hummel Art II* has been completely redesigned and reorganized to make it very easy to find the original, new, and changed information with little effort.

The third objective in the writing of this book was to organize and merge in one volume all the new information on Hummel art that has become available due to further research by the author, by the Goebel Company and the discoveries and fact-finding of such master connoisseurs as the Arbenzes, the Douses, Grandes, Markers, Millers, and over one thousand readers who have taken the trouble to share their knowledge with me and, subsequently, you.

Acknowledgments

More than one thousand individuals and organizations have made contributions in person and by letters to the author during the creation of this book. Some supplied generous amounts of time. Others contributed samples, pictures, unpublished information, counsel, and even leads to other sources. Our sincere thanks to all of them.

The author's right (write) and left hands were many. The "write" hands were Louise Young, Ellen Mulligan, and Christine Cassidy, chief editorial assistant, who assembled facts, figures, and pictures, as well as writing some sections. Jane Del Cour put unintelligible scribbling into legible form, along with others. Another hand, the "Guidance Council," was comprised of Robert L. Miller, Rue Dee Marker, Patrick T. Arbenz, and Dorothy Dous. Eileen Grande was instrumental in reviewing ideas and tables and providing an enormous amount of material in a way that only top echelon collectors and experts can do.

Drawing #14290 courtesy Ars Sacra.

Examples from the Gerald Busharts' comprehensive collection in Rochester, New York, appear in over half the photographs with Dorothy Dous and Hummelwerk supplying other important additions. Mary McCarthy's photography is responsible for the translation into color slides. Nancy Townsend, another assistant, provided the price compilations and analysis. Liz Fletcher is responsible for catching my many spelling and grammar discrepancies. Jann Williams used her artistic touch to create this beautiful book. The following list is not inclusive, but only a sampling of many hundreds of interested and helpful people.

Ars Sacra, Verlag, West Germany
Dorothy Andrews, Sanibel, FL
Patrick T. Arbenz, Sierra Vista, AZ
David W. Armstrong, Pomona, CA
Arnart Imports, New York, NY
Paul Atterbury, England
Marilyn Birmingham, Denver, CO
Barbara Barr, California
Alex Brown, England
Don Brown, Leon, IA
Jean Brunker, Berwyn, IL
Christine E. Cassidy, Rochester, NY
Collectors Showcase, Akron, OH
Nancy Condrey, Randolph, MA
James F. Coyne, Chicago, ILL
Joseph E. Cramer, Albany, NY
Mary Esther Croker, Grundy Center, IA
Jane DelCour, Rochester, NY
F. Desher, Delavan, NJ
Debbie Dickinson, Rochester, NY
Alex Douchette, Hingham, MA
Dorothy Dous, Yardley, PA
Robert Dous, Yardley, PA
Tammy Dous, Yardley, PA
Duane Dow, FL
Irving and Dorothy Dunckleman, Bolton, MA
Jean Evans, Lewistown, NY
Emil Fink, Verlag, F. Stuttgart, West Germany
Richard G. Fuller, Jr. New York, NY
Jolanta Geisel, Tarrytown, NY
The Goebel Collectors' Club, Tarrytown, NY
William Goebel, Rödental, West Germany
Jean Grady, Hot Springs, AR
Katherine Gullo, Rochester, NY
Helen Hall, Rochester, NY
Warren Hancock, Billings, MT
Harry's Gift Shop, West Germany

Ann Hotchkiss, Detroit, MI
Clayton Huber, Philadelphia, PA
Adolph Hummel, Massing, Germany
Viktoria Hummel, Massing, Germany
Sam F. Jackson, Tuscaloosa, AL
Aa Hyldgaard Jensen, Denmark
Ju Dee Kay's, Bremen, IN
Paula Keely, FL
James P. Kelly, Elmsford, NY
Fritz Kleber, Germany
Morris Kule, Elmsford, NY
Faith B. Lasher, Gaithersburg, MD
Ruth Laudien, Gary, IN
Jim Lerner, Tarrytown, NY
Leo's Gift Center, Wayne, MI
Library of Congress, Washington, D.C.
Ben Livingston, Columbus, OH
Marilyn Mallery, Rochester, NY
Else Marcy, Germany
Margaret Woodburg Strong Museum, Rochester, NY
Rue Dee Marker, Bremen, IN
Maxines, Des Moines, IA
Mary McCarthy, Rochester, NY
Jack McDermot, New York, NY
Rob McIntosh China Shop, Cornwall, Ont.
Robert L. Miller, Eaton, OH
Ruth Miller, Eaton, OH
Eric Moch, Lincolnwood, IL
Ruth A. Motsen, Philadelphia, PA
Mrs. Louise T. Mroczek, Dallas, TX
Ellen Mulligan, Sanibel, FL
National Potteries, Cleveland, OH
Jacques Nauer, Massappequa, NY
Marcel Nauer, Munich, West Germany
Herman Newhauser, Sarasota, FL
Niki's, Marietta, GA
Shirley Niz, Hinsdale, IL

Joan Ostroff, Tarrytown, NY
Lars Peterson, Belchertown, MD
The Plate Collector, Kermit, TX
Heidi Poag, Naperville, IL
Dr. Gotz M. Pollizien, Munich, Germany
Lillian G. Potter, Portland, ME
Schwester Radegundis, Germany
Chief Myron Raff, New York, NY
Carol Ramoudt, Sanibel, FL
Wayne Ranke, Mapleton, MO
Rankins, Green Bay, WI
Mrs. W. Robinson, Poway, CA
Rochester Public Library, Rochester, NY
Joel Sater, Marietta, PA
Paul A. Schmid, III, Randolph, MA
John Schmid, Randolph, MA
Barbara A. Schmidt, Hinsdale, IL
M. Schwartz, Lake Hiawatha, NJ
Scottsdale East, Scottsdale, AZ
Charles Shepherd, Rochester, NY
Shirley Ann-Tiques, Independence, MO
M.L. Sones, Newton, MA
Angelo Spadaro, Devon, PA
Charlotte Springer, Germany
Regina Steele, Wilmington, DE
Don Stephens, Rosemont, IL
Vera Stoof, Williamsburg, MD
Madeline Taylor, Providence, RI
Nancy Townsend, Rochester, NY
Tiffany's Treasures Ltd. Poway, CA
Tri-State Trader, Knightstown, IN
Terry Trotter, Pacific Grove, CA
U.S. Bureau of Census, Washington, D.C.
U.S. Department of Commerce, Washington, D.C.
University of Rochester Library, Rochester, NY
Pat Upton, Syosset, NY
Mrs. John Wallner, Manchester, VT
Mrs. John Walsh, Sanibel, FL
Randy Washington, West Germany
Joan Welch, Rochester, NY
Margaret Whitton, Rochester, NY
Bob and Ann Wilgus, NJ
Louise Young, Rochester, NY
David Zuckerman, Detroit, MI
Dorothy Zuckerman, Detroit, MI

1 *Original Hummel Art*

Drawing #14117 courtesy Ars Sacra.

Life of Berta/Sister Maria Innocentia Hummel

The work of artists, writers, poets, and philosophers who lived "between the wars" is known today as some of the most far-reaching work of the twentieth century. The genius evinced by that generation touched Berta Hummel, too. Her art, reproduced in the form of lithographs and figurines, is remembered and revered for its transcendence — a transcendence into the realm of idealized childhood. Who does not empathize with the praying child before his wooden horse? Or giggle with the tales one girl whispers into her friend's ear? Rainer Marie Rilke advised a poet in one of his *Letters to a Young Poet* (trans. M.D. Herter Norton, New York: W.W. Norton and Company, Inc., 1934), to "trust in childhood memories" when loneliness and solitude overcame the poet. In a confusing, contradictory world, Berta Hummel grasped the one life experience common to all people — childhood, in all its innocent joy. She allows us, in an equally confusing world, to free ourselves in her art.

Drawing #14728 courtesy Ars Sacra.

Viktoria Anglsperger Hummel gave birth to Berta Hummel on May 21, 1909, in Massing an der Rott in Lower Bavaria. She was the third child of six children in the Hummel household. Even at a young age, Bertl (the German diminutive of Berta) was a dynamic child and rightfully earned the nickname "Hummele," the "Bumblebee." She expressed her imaginative thoughts in sketches, in making doll clothes, and in dramatic performances with her siblings. As a pre-schooler, Berta Hummel designed postcards — forerunners, no doubt, of the cards she later created for friends.

In the midst of the First World War, Berta Hummel began school at age six. She attended the Catholic *Volksschule,* run by the School Sisters of Notre Dame. As Sister M. Gonsalva explains in *Sketch Me, Berta Hummel* (reprint edition: Eaton Ohio: Robert L. Miller, 1978), the *Volksschule* was the peasants' school. Berta Hummel was misunderstood in her first few years at school. However, in her fourth year at the *Volksschule,* one teacher, Sister Theresilla, recognized Berta's exceptional talent and freely encouraged the young artist. Friends and relatives of friends asked for and received sketches Berta had made. "Sketch me!" classmates cried, and Berta, always eager to draw, sketched with increasing skill. To her father at the front lines of the war, Berta sent postcards and colorfully illustrated letters.

In 1921, when Berta was almost twelve years old, she entered Simbach, a girls' boarding school directed by Englischen Fraulein teaching nuns. Berta was active at Simbach, expressing her creativity in a variety of ways. Sister M. Gonsalva relates how Berta, working like a

Opposite: HU-1, Sister M. I. Hummel Bust, 15" high, TMK-4, designed by Gerhard Skrobek in 1965. Discontinued by Goebel (date unrecorded). Now highly valued, as there are relatively few examples available.

Serious conference between Sister Maria Innocentia and several of her students photographed in the early Thirties. Girl with bow in her bobbed hair and thoughtful little boy bear a striking resemblance to a number of M. I. Hummel figurines.

Drawing #5324 courtesy Ars Sacra.

"veteran stagehand," donated her artistic skills to the many dramatic activities at the school. Sister Stephanie, Berta's art teacher, suggested to Berta that she attend the Art Academy in Munich.

After her graduation from Simbach in 1926, Berta traveled fifty miles from Massing to the Academy of Applied Arts in Munich. Munich, a cultural melting pot, opened new wellsprings of interest for Berta. Particularly, she came in contact with other artists and their work. Two women, Sister Laura and Sister Kostka, proved to be strong role models for Berta Hummel. Their lives as nuns and as artists showed Berta that it was possible to enjoy the creation of art while in religious service. After she graduated first in her class, from the Art Academy in 1931, Berta told her parents of her religious vocation and her desire to enter the convent.

Religion had always been a part of Berta Hummel's life. She grew up in a Catholic family in a Catholic town. She attended Catholic schools, and, in Munich, she lived in a boarding convent. As a child, Berta actively participated in religious and folk holidays; as a woman, she also took part in religious and non-religious festivities. Perhaps the influence of Sister Laura and Sister Kostka played a large role in Berta's realization that an artist could also be a nun.

By 1931 Berta Hummel's drawings were well received among her peers and among her instructors. Each of her four teachers at the Art Academy had hoped Berta would pursue advanced studies with one of them. Although Berta dreamed of traveling to southern Europe to view the works of the masters, she chose instead a life of religious dedication.

After two years as a novitiate, Berta Hummel took the veil in August, 1933, at the Siessen convent of the Sisters of Saint Francis, an order she selected for its egalitarian philosophies. A young nun, employed in the garden because she was not as well educated as some of the other nuns, once remarked, "Sister Innocentia . . . loves us simple sisters better than the rest." Indeed, through an artist's eyes, people and objects are often seen with different perspectives.

Sister Hummel's world was filled with children, art, and devotion to God. She taught art to pupils at the convent school and drew and painted in her small studio. Her daily life consisted of convent duties, prayer, and time to draw. Her work was exhibited at art shows which the Mother Superior allowed her to attend.

In 1934, Franz Goebel learned of Sister Hummel's gifted work through a young sculptor, Arthur Möller, at the Goebel Porzellanfabrik in Oeslau. After meeting with Franz Goebel, Sister Hummel and the convent entered into an agreement with the Goebel Company that permitted her drawings to be made into three-dimensional figurines. In 1935, at the Leipzig Trade Fair, the first few Hummels, each bearing Sister Hummel's facsimile signature, were shown to the public. Recognition of Sister Hummel's talent spread, and visitors streamed to the convent to greet the artist.

In 1935 Sister Hummel again returned to study at the Academy of Applied Arts in Munich. Her health began to fail in the fall of 1936 and she went back to Siessen. An order to evacuate the convent came from the Nazi government late in 1940. Reluctantly, Sister Hummel returned to her home in Massing. She was permitted to re-enter Siessen early in 1941, a time when the convent was used as a refugee camp. She stayed until 1944, when she became ill with tuberculosis.

After a stay at a sanatorium during part of her illness, Sister Hummel journeyed back to Siessen in September, 1946, where she died a month later on the sixth of November. The war years had taken their toll of Sister Hummel. However, her artwork was beginning to achieve international recognition and acclaim. Thirty-five years later, we are fortunate to share Sister Maria Innocentia's gifted vision which lives on in the reproductions of her art.

Berta Hummel Art — Pre-Convent Years

The term original Hummel art refers to the creations of Berta Hummel as a child, as a young girl in southern Bavaria, and throughout her foreshortened life in the Franciscan Convent at Siessen as Sister Maria Innocentia Hummel. These original works of art, broadly classified as graphics, are in the form of early untutored sketches evidencing great promise on through her accomplished drawings and paintings of later years. Hundreds of creative works by her hand are scarcely known in their original form in this country, as only a very few examples have been displayed publicly. However, in her native Germany, Berta Hummel was a recognized and published artist by the time she was twenty-one, even before she finished her formal training at the Academy of Fine and Applied Arts in Munich. This amount of recognition is accorded to very few artists of that young age. Having her work published as cards, prints, and books, so that it could be enjoyed by the masses rather than having the original hung in a place frequented by the elite was a primary goal of this talented artist. This expressed desire has been reiterated by both her mother and the convent a number of times when reviewing her work.

The great body of her original work still exists in the form of drawings done in pencil, charcoal, crayon, and in paintings in watercolor and oil. Of all of these, her favorite medium, according to the late Dr. Elizabeth Dubler head of Verlag Ars Sacra, her early publisher in Munich, was charcoal and crayon, individually or used together.

Only infrequently did she use watercolor or oils, because they took too long to dry and, therefore, impeded the impetuous speed with which she worked. Dr. Dubler said that when Sister Hummel was at the Academy in Munich (she was there both before and after she became a nun), Dr. Dubler's father would discuss a project with her in the morning and by afternoon the completed work would be in his hands.

"The River Rott in Massing," 1929, oil, 17½" by 13". Described as *"the most mature and professional artistic statement of Berta Hummel's pre-convent years."* The parish church that Berta attended is in the background.

"Hungarian Girl," 1928, watercolor, 10½" by 7", subject costumed in the manner of gypsies who roamed Central Europe during Berta's childhood.

"Child in Farm Wagon," crayon and charcoal, 27½" by 21¾", of a village child hurtling down a hill outside Massing in a ladder wagon. Courtesy Schmid Bros., Inc.

The best assessment of her artistic abilities has been made by Dr. James F. Plaut, distinguished art critic and author who said: "The artist's eye can be sharper than the surgeon's scalpel in stripping away the surface covering and reaching in the 'vital center.' There is a pictorial and spiritual essence in each of Berta Hummel's works, an inner center clearly perceived and simply depicted. Indeed, clarity and simplicity are perhaps the most rewarding qualities of her art, and they are arrived at naturally and honestly, without pretense or affectation."

Later he summarized by saying, "It is surely the fresh innocence of Berta Hummel's vision that is the most endearing feature of her artistic testament."

The work that she produced before she entered the convent in 1931 is largely in the possession of the Hummel family in Massing. A traveling exhibit was selected from this early period and is now touring museums in the United States and will continue to do so through 1982. This provides an unequalled opportunity for the collector and Hummel enthusiast to obtain a deeper appreciation of the development and capabilities of the artist, which will certainly enhance their satisfaction in owning any derivatives of Sister Hummel's art.

Whether one sees the exhibit or not, the superb color catalog, *The Formation of an Artist: The Early Works of Berta Hummel*, that has been produced for this exhibit should not be missed. Fully illustrated, it contains a critical assessment of the various works which include a unique, appliqued wall hanging called *Old Massing* which Berta did at the age of twenty-one. This catalog offers further documentation of the achievements of this talented artist that most collectors will want to refer to long after the exhibit is safely back in the historic home of the Hummel family in Massing, West Germany. Further details on the exhibit will be found in the section on Berta Hummel art by Schmid Brothers, Inc., who organized this display with the cooperation of the Hummel family.

Sister Maria Innocentia Art — Convent Years

The great majority of her drawings done in the convent, numbering somewhat under four hundred, are in the hands of Verlag Ars Sacra of Munich. In the last fifty years, they have published most of this work as lithographic reproductions by the millions in the form of cards, notes, prints, calendars, and books. They have also supplied their graphics for use in decorating innumerable other collectibles such as plates, boxes, bells, and candles. Some of these were limited editions; some are either continuing series or open editions.

Another publisher who has under one hundred of her originals is Verlag Emil Fink in Stuttgart, who also prints a similar wide range of graphics taken from the originals and books with Hummel drawings.

The Franciscan Convent in Siessen also has an extensive collection of her work which fortunately has now been arranged in the form of a

Postcard #5436 published by Ars Sacra from one of the original Hummel drawings in their collection. Note the Ars Sacra monogram and the international copyright insignia, © in lower left corner.

permanent exhibit in a new museum located in a building devoted exclusively to Hummel art. Unique among all of the works she created is a very special display of three studies of the Infant of Krumbad. These are the only known three-dimensional works sculpted by Sister Hummel herself, and were executed in papier-maché. One of the three models is used at intervals in novitiate ceremonies. This museum is open to the public, and most of her published work in the form of postcards is offered for sale there.

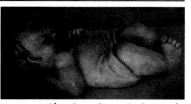

Papier-maché Infant of Krumbad, one of three studies executed by Sister Hummel. Believed to be the only sculptures created by her. Displayed in the museum at the Siessen Convent.

A few kilometers from Siessen, in the town of Salgau, is an interesting landmark named the Kleber Post Hotel. While Sister Hummel was in the convent she did a number of drawings for the Klebers that are still hanging in some of the bedrooms and public rooms. A duplicate original of her version of the Waiter is in the dining room. Another well-known one is the duplicate original of Stage Coach, or Mail Is Here, as it is also known. One that surprises Hummel collectors is an unpublished stagecoach scene which shows a rear view of this same coach leaving a stop with a tearful passenger waving auf wiedersehen from the rear window. These are not the only drawings in private hands. Sister Hummel did other duplicate originals as well as some portraiture, especially of children, on commission. The proceeds were always a welcome addition to the convent during the Great Depression years.

Unpublished companion drawing to "Mail Is Here," titled, in Sister Hummel's script, "Oh, It Was Just too Beautiful." Courtesy of the Kleber Post Hotel.

One of these was done as a favor to a surgeon who had helped her community. The study was of his young son. When one of her publishers saw the portrait he asked Sister Hummel to make a duplicate original from which prints and cards could be made and which is illustrated on this page. Recently the surgeon's son sold his original portrait to a collector in this country who now has a number of Hummel originals. Another original in this country is owned by a woman in St. Louis who appealed to Sister Hummel in the late Thirties to do a sketch of the young woman's auxiliary training group in Germany. It has been carefully preserved and treasured. In the last year, pictures and information about at least six more drawings that were for sale have been received for this author's comment or appraisal. A letter regarding one of these drawings was especially interesting.

Portrait of a young boy by Sister Hummel published by Emil Fink as graphic #800.

A man stationed with the U.S. Army in Germany wrote that he and his wife had stopped at a small flea market and had purchased a drawing that was signed in the lower right corner with the name Hummel. Having bought this on a gamble with a very minimum investment, he had doubts whether or not it was genuine. His investigation finally led him to Verlag Ars Sacra of Munich. There the firm's expert identified it as the original drawing from which they had published postcard #5943 — Die Jungbäuerin, and from which the Goebel Company sculptor adapted the figurine called Feeding Time, Hum. 199. The publisher was as surprised to see this original as the couple was pleased to know they had purchased a genuine Hummel. The company records had indicated that this drawing was destroyed along with several others in a fire at the plant during World War II. Later, officials of Verlag Ars Sacra wrote to say that the couple had agreed to sell them back the missing original. It is known that several more survived, so perhaps one of our readers may have the good fortune to discover one.

Postcard #5943 published by Ars Sacra from an original drawing lost during World War II and recently recovered.

A photograph of Sister Maria Innocentia and an example of how she signed most of her world-famous art. Courtesy Ars Sacra.

GÄNSELISL   HUMMEL

Courtesy Verlag Emil Fink.

How to Identify Original Hummel Art

Some of the early examples of Hummel art done while she was a student in the academy are signed with just the letter "H", and some are signed "B.H." Others are signed with the name "Hummel." One unusual signature on a watercolor used her first name diminutive, "Bertl Hummel." Actual examples of the methods and form she used in signing are shown on this page. Only two dated ones have come to the author's attention. The first one is an excellent oil painted at the age of twenty, while she was still at the Fine Arts Academy in Munich. The scene is her parish church with its reflection in the river Rott in Massing. This is signed "B. Hummel 29." (See photograph on page 11.) The other one is the original drawing from which the figurine, Stormy Weather, Hum. 71, was derived. The latter drawing is signed "Hummel 36," indicating that not all of her drawings done after she received her veil and religious name were signed in the familiar script M.J.Hummel. There seems to be no relation between the form of her signature on her secular work and the period of time it was accomplished. Apparently the use of her script signature was reserved for some of her religious works once she was given that name. While the middle initial in her signature looks like the letter "J", it is "I" for the first letter in Innocentia. The majority of her drawings of children are signed with only her last name.

The fact that a drawing of a subject done by Berta or Sister Hummel is signed in one of the above forms is no guarantee that the picture is a genuine original done by her hand. Copies by forgers of the fine art of popular artists abound. It is said of the famous nineteenth century French artist, Jean Baptiste Corot, that during his lifetime he completed some five hundred paintings and that more than four thousand of them are in the United States alone. Research of a purported Corot which was in an estate that this author was appraising disclosed that the actual original was hanging in the Louvre in Paris.

It is thought that copies (most of these are fakes — done with the intent of deceiving) were made of Sister Hummel's drawings after World War II, when G.I. interest in Hummel art exploded the demand for anything connected with her. While this is not an established fact, it behooves anyone interested, or offered an original drawing of Sister Hummel's, to remember, the old Roman expression, *Caveat Emptor* — Buyer Beware. A photograph of a supposed original painting of hers done in oil was received in the mail with an offer to sell. The original of this particular picture was done by Sister Hummel in crayon.

If offered a Hummel original work to buy, look at it under five or ten power magnification. Reject it if the image is made up of a series of different colored minute dots. It is a photomechanical copy. Should it pass this test, still do not buy until you have had a fine arts expert verify its authenticity.

A great many questions have been asked about the value of her original work. As in the work of any famous artist, the value depends to a large extent on which work it is, how well documented the example is and whether or not there were any duplicate originals. The value of most recognized artists' work is established in sales through well-known auction galleries in Paris, London, or New York. To date, there is no record of Sister Hummel's drawings having been sold at auction. A fully documented, authenticated original made and signed by Sister Hummel of a well-known subject probably would be valued from the mid to high four-digit figures if publicly sold. Some of her lesser sketches or work studies might be insured for several hundred dollars.

Courtesy Verlag Emil Fink.

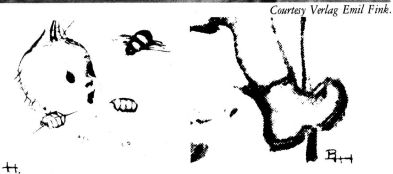

Courtesy Verlag Emil Fink.

Courtesy Verlag Emil Fink.

Courtesy Verlag Emil Fink.

Left: Imitation figurine, unmarked, possibly by Dubler. Right: Strolling Along, Hum. 5.

M.I. Hummel Figurines by Goebel

The best known adaptations of Sister Maria Innocentia Hummel's original work is in the form of three-dimensional ceramic figures which have been produced by the W. Goebel Company of Rödental, West Germany, since 1935 with the expressed individual approval of the Franciscan Convent at Siessen. The convent has licensed the Goebel Company as the exclusive producer in consideration for which the company has paid the convent royalties of several millions of dollars for about forty-five years. This company is the only one producing ceramic figurines and related decorative art that has the sole right to mark such articles with the facsimile of the Hummel signature as it appears here *M.J.Hummel*.

Some unofficial estimates place the number of persons who own one or more M.I. Hummel figurines at over two million. The Goebel Collectors' Club (see) has a membership of over two hundred thousand persons. Between ten and twenty thousand dealers are authorized to sell them in the United States. They are also distributed in innumerable other countries.

On the following pages is the complete story of how these figurines are numbered, named, marked, along with a color picture of each one, the sizes, and the trademarks that been used on each piece. A brief history of each model number is given from the time it was first made or copyrighted together with its status at this time. Current prices may be found by consulting the separate Price List which is included with this book.

Identifying Genuine Figurines

A hackneyed saying is, "Imitation is the sincerest form of flattery." Maybe so, but imitations of M.I. Hummel figurines are confusing to beginning collectors who are trying to identify pieces they own. The many reproductions and "look-alike" figurines that have been produced during the last forty-five years are fully covered in the later section, "Reproductions of Original Hummel Art." A positive way of ascertaining the authenticity of a Hummel figurine is to employ a short checklist used by advanced collectors and dealers, which will quickly separate the genuine M.I. Hummel figurine from a copy or another product. The five steps are:

- Look for the *M.J.Hummel* signature.
- Check incised model number against the master list.
- Determine the trademark classification.
- Examine each piece for damage.
- Check for overall quality.

For those who are already conversant with M.I. Hummel figurines, the above should suffice as a quick checklist to follow. For those who are not as experienced, a detailed explanation of what to look for and where to find it follows. Studying the information contained in the next few pages will help readers get more enjoyment and understanding of later sections of *Hummel Art II.* The wisest and happiest collector is often, not coincidentally, the most knowledgeable about all aspects of his or her collecting field.

Step 1 — Look for the M.J.Hummel Signature

Fortunately for collectors, Goebel did a superb job right from the beginning of marking the figurines they adapted from Sister Hummel's original drawings. The most important mark of all of them is the M.J.Hummel facsimile signature incised, usually, on the rear upper surface of the base or on the rear edge of the figurine. Look for it before buying any figurine that is offered as a genuine Hummel. It should be clearly visible.

There are very few exceptions to this statement. Some very small pieces, such as Girl with Sheet Music, Hum. 389, are so small that a label for the facsimile signature has to be used. A few cases have been reported where the M.J.Hummel signature does not appear on larger pieces. This might happen on very rare occasions in the production operation. Unless you are an advanced collector, pass up any of these. Insist on the incised facsimile signature.

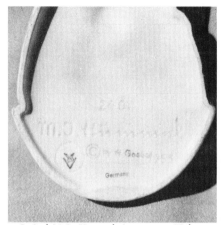

Incised M.I. Hummel signature on Holy Family Font, Hum. 246. Blue ink, TMK-2 Full Bee in incised circle. Incised ©; by W. Goebel stamped in blue; incised ©1955 (copyright year); with Germany stamped in black.

A high percentage of readers' letters state they have a figurine that is not included in the book, but they feel it is definitely a Hummel because it has a Full Bee (TMK-2) mark. What they are referring to is a company trademark that identifies Goebel as the manufacturer. Almost without exception the piece will be a Goebel product by another artist, not by Sister Hummel. Join the ranks of those who say, "Unless it is incised with the facsimile signature, I prefer not to consider it as genuine and only under exceptional circumstances do I want to invest my money in one that is not." When it comes time to dispose of an unsigned M.I. Hummel figurine, collectors have found that such relatively rare omissions are difficult to sell and bring less than the expected price.

Step 2 — Check the Incised Model Number

With the figurine facing to the front, turn the base up toward you. At the top of the base there should be an incised (indented) number which, for the series of M.I. Hummel figurines and related articles, should be between 1 and 400. Refer to the page where the chart, "The M.I. Hummel Pedigree," will further distinguish the model number location and what it looks like. Knowing the model number, refer to the section on page 30 titled, "Photographs, History, and Production Records of the Collection." The figurine being examined should match the picture shown for that model number. If the name is on a paper strip label on the figurine, it should also match the name shown in the book for that model number. In addition to the name and picture, the production record next to the picture will show what size that model number and size indicator should be. The height may not match exactly, as many older models varied from the current specified height. This table will also indicate what trademarks were used on this figurine by the letter

Whitsuntide, Hum. 163 with Incised Crown, TMK-1 and incised 163 (model number); printed black Germany. Also Full Bee, TMK-2 in black. Rare.

"P". The letter "P" means that this figurine has been produced with the trademarks shown, and that a price for the figurine in that particular trademark will be found on the separate Price List included with this book.

In addition to the statistical information for each model number, the historical information is given in as much detail as practical. This important story for each figurine will reveal whether or not there are any major variations, the relative rarity, the redesigns, and the existence of reissues that may affect the value.

Some collectors following this procedure will be disappointed because their figurine, even though incised M.I. Hummel, does not have an incised model number. The Goebel Company has offered to exchange any figurine with a missing number for a new one of that model and size provided it is incised *M.J. Hummel* and matches the photograph in the book. This might be advantageous to you if the figurine has the current trademark. If it has one of the old trademarks, it would usually be advisable to keep it, because an unnumbered old figurine is more valuable, even without the number, than a new one. Some old ones may be very rare.

If the model number does not match the one in the book, and there is no Goebel trademark, and the figure does not have the *M.J. Hummel* signature, it is *not* a genuine M.I. Hummel figurine. Possibly it might be one made in the 1940s by Herbert Dubler, Inc., in New York, or by the Beswick Company in England about the same period. For more information, see the section of the book pertaining to Dubler and Beswick figurines. It could also be a Hummel look-alike made by one of the countries in the Far East. More information on these is contained in the section titled "Reproductions of Original Hummel Art."

If the model in question has a Goebel trademark but no facsimile signature, and the incised model number is prefixed by one or more letters, it is a product of the Goebel Company, but inspired by another artist such as Robson (ROB) or Disney (DIS). It may have been an original creation by one of Goebel's staff sculptors and would be prefixed with an incised HM or other letters before the model number. These possibilities are fully explored in the section of this book titled "Goebel — Not Hummel" on page 182.

Step 3 — Determine the Trademark Classification

When considering any figurine, the Goebel Company trademark on the bottom should be compared to examples in this chapter.

For purposes of simplification, trademarks (TMK) have been divided into six broad groups for convenience in determining the approximate age, the date the figure was made, and the relative value. Each group has many minor variations. Most of the important ones have been pictured or described in the chart and in photographs of actual marks on the bottom of sample figurines shown later in this chapter.

Since the publishing of *Hummel Art I,* help from over a thousand readers, research by the Goebel Company, by advanced collectors, and by the author, has shed much more light on the variations in the trademarks and the span of years during which they were used. Probably the most important discovery is that the timespan in which each mark was used overlaps the timespan of the next earlier and later marks. There are no exact cutoff dates. Exceptions seem to be the rule. Secondly, the time period that each trademark was used has been verified as being much longer than previously thought. The best example of this is TMK-3, Stylized Bee. Examples have been documented that prove this mark was used as early as 1956 and as late as 1972. It overlaps the TMK-2 by two years and the TMK-4 by eight years.

Once the production process is understood, the reason for the overlap of trademarks is easily appreciated. Automobile companies shut down their assembly lines for months before a yearly model change, and when modifications are complete new models start coming off the line on a certain date each fall. All changes are made at once. Figurines are made in batches of various sizes and frequencies, depending on their popularity. A trademark change may be introduced provisionally to test a new design, method, or to get trade reaction. If successful, more batches are then made with the new identification. Finally, in months, maybe years, all batches of all models will have the same trademark. Some models may not be scheduled for production for many months or even years after a change is authorized. Sometimes small quantities of an old batch are discovered. Once in a while portions of a batch may be sidetracked and be released later with current ones carrying a newer trademark.

Compare the trademark on the figurine in hand to the marks shown on the chart and note the trademark group number. This establishes that it was made by Goebel, the relative age of the article, and indicates which trademark column to consult in the Production Record and in the Current Price List. The sub-class indicates alternate combinations that may further enhance the interest and value of the piece under consideration.

Step 4 — Carefully Examine Any Article for Damage

This step is becoming increasingly important and yet more difficult to execute in fact. While this is discussed in detail later in the book, be especially alert for repair materials that do not show up under black light, and an increase in the number of damaged pieces that have been professionally repaired. More and more of these repaired figures are being introduced in auctions where they are offered, "Where is, as is." So do a double take on Step 4. Ask an expert's opinion. Ask for privilege of return and refund if imperfections are discovered within ten days, or acquire a friend who has access to an X-ray machine.

For imperfections or repairs, a discount from the Current Price List figures of from 25 to 75 percent is in order. This is the price range reflected in actual sales. Broadly interpreted, allow a spread of 20 to 30 percent discount for minor nicks or touch-up not readily noticeable, advancing to about 50 percent for major portions broken, reglued, or

2A 2B
1950-1958

2C 2D 2E
1956 1957 1958

TMK-3
STYLIZED BEE MARK

1956-1960

3A Early Partial Stylized Bee, Stamped
3B Large Stylized Bee, Incised Circle
3C Large Stamped Stylized Bee, W. Germany
3D Small Stylized Transfer Bee, W. Germany

3A 3B
1956 1956-1960

W. Germany
3C
1960-1969

W. Germany
3D
1960-1972

TMK-4
THREE LINE MARK

© by
W. Goebel
W. Germany
1963-1972

4A Small Stylized Bee, Blue Transfer

Dates are approximate — earlier documented examples are known.

professionally replaced. Finally, allow from 70 to 90 percent discount from the Price List for "basket cases."

Step 5 — Check for Overall Quality

Hand assembly and hand decoration inherently produce minor differences in workmanship. In spite of rigid final inspection standards, for which Goebel almost invariably gets high marks, there will be an infrequent miss. Some collectors take great pains with this step and a few have unrealistic expectations. It is their money so they are entitled to the final decision. There is one isolated indication of substandard quality that is rarely found. It is customary in the ceramic trade to grind a diagonal line through the company trademark to identify substandard quality that is either to be sold at discount or broken up. The Goebel Company does not sell seconds. However, occasionally a Hummel piece is encountered in the secondary market with such a slash line that can be readily seen or felt by passing a fingernail across the trademark. These should be rejected by most dedicated collectors when found. They will always leave a nagging question in the owner's mind and are difficult to dispose of later.

Model Numbers and Size Indicators

Most of the genuine M.I. Hummel figurines or related articles that collectors will encounter are numbered between 1 and 400. The figurine numbers in catalogs and documents are preceded by the letters Hum in some form. The letters, of course, stand for the first three letters in the artist's name. When incising the model number on the base or back of any Goebel article, the number is usually prefixed by some combination of letters which identifies the artist who created the original work. For more information on this, see the section of this book, "Goebel — Not Hummel," on page 182. An important exception to note is that the prefix, Hum, is *not* incised with the model number on genuine M.I. Hummel figurines.

As shown in the accompanying pictures, this model number appears at the top of other information on the base or back of Hummel articles. These photographs also show that, in addition to the whole number, many examples may be identified by a device used by the Goebel Company to designate the relative size of one piece as compared to other sizes in the same model number. Not all models or motifs were made in more than one size. Many model numbers like Puppy Love, Hum. 1; Strolling Along, Hum. 5; and Begging His Share, Hum. 9, have only been produced in one official size for some forty-five years. Others like Apple Tree Girl, Hum. 141, and Infant of Krumbad, Hum. 78, have been produced in a range of sizes at different times since their introduction.

When a second size was introduced that was smaller than the one represented by the assigned model number, the smaller size was usually differentiated by adding a slash (/) mark and a zero (0) to the model number: i.e., 81/0. If the second size happened to be larger, the slash mark (/) was used with a Roman numeral I. The records indicate that sometimes when the second size was added, the original whole number would also be changed by adding either a zero or a Roman numeral if it were larger than the new added size. This may sound very precise and exact but there appears to be many deviations, as might be expected, over the years. Boots, Hum. 143, is an example that was first issued measuring about the 6½" with TMK-1 before 1950. In the early 1950s, Goebel decided to add a smaller version as well. This was incised 143/0 to indicate it was only somewhat smaller, about 5½" high. At about the same time, the 6½" size (previously marked only 143) was, from then on, marked 143/I. When Goebel added a second, smaller, 4¼" size to Happy Days (150/0 — 5¼" size), the new smaller size was marked 150/2/0. When Goebel added the larger, 3½" size to Infant of Krumbad (78/I — 2½"), the new larger size was marked 78/II. If the size change was a drastic one, Goebel skipped over some possible intermediate indicators. Apple Tree Girl, 141 V, is 10½" high. When her giant 32" sister was added, it was marked 141/X, leaving room for four more intermediate sizes (141/VI, 141/VII, 141/VIII, and 141/IX), if needed in the future.

Base of Umbrella Girl, Hum. 152 B with blue stamped Three-Line, TMK-4. Incised model-size indicator, 152/II B; incised U.S. copyright year, 1951.

On this page, is an example of one of the widest ranges of sizes that has been issued by Goebel — Apple Tree Girl, Hum. 141. While Apple Tree Girl presently is cataloged and produced in only four sizes, they range from 4" to 32" high. As shown in the distribution, they are 4", 6", 10", and 32", respectively.

So far there is no record of Hum. 141 ever being issued where dashes (—) are inserted. However, when first released before World War II, this model was marked 141, only, and was about 6½" high. This marking is found on the TMK-1 and TMK-2. Apparently, the whole number 141 marking was discontinued in favor of 141/I when the smaller size was added. It is evident that Goebel has provided plenty of open size indicators to take care of four more sizes between the 10½", 141/V, and the new 141/X, which was only introduced in the late 1970s.

Hum. No.	141/3/0	141/2/0	141/0	141/I	141/II	141/III	141/IV	141/V	141/X
Size	4"	—	—	6"	—	—	—	10"	32"

As mentioned before, there are variations in markings and their application. Not fully researched and published to date is the significance of the marking 141 (only) and 141. (decimal), both of which are usually found in TMK-1 and TMK-2. Another unexplained deviation is the substitution of the arabic numbering system for the Roman one. For example, 141/1 (arabic) rather than 141/I (Roman), for the 6" size, has been reported with TMK-2 and TMK-3. The use of the decimal after the whole model number and the substitution of the arabic numerals instead of Roman ones is used with many different model numbers and many different trademarks. They may have been optional or had some very definite meaning. In any event, they are of interest to collectors because there are fewer decimal marks and arabic numbers than "standard" whole number and Roman size indicators. Therefore, many collectors willingly pay a premium for alternate markings. Unfortunately, no

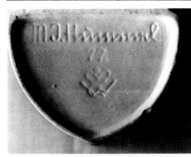

TMK-1A, Incised Crown with incised M.I. Hummel signature and model number 77. On base of Cross with Doves Font. Extremely rare example. Photograph courtesy Cheryl Trotter.

TMK-1B, Stamped Crown on base of Good Shepherd, Hum. 42/I. No model number, size indicator, country of origin, and no copyright year.

TMK-1C, Double Incised Crown on base of extremely rare Serbian Goose Girl, Hum. 947/0. Note partial glaze.

set percentage can be assigned. For some model numbers the decimal or arabic forms are not unusual, such as School Girl, Hum. 81. This is frequently found with 81. (decimal) so a modest 10 percent might be adequate in this case. Whereas if another model number previously unknown with an arabic marking suddenly appeared after all these years, some collectors might be willing to pay at least 25 percent more for such a rare example.

While the letters "Hum" are not incised with the model numbers, other incised indicators are used to distinguish certain types of articles. Bookends are sold as a pair. Apple Tree Girl, Hum. 141, and Apple Tree Boy, 142, become Hum. 252A and 252B, when mounted and sold as bookends. These are designated by incising an added letter after the model number. St. Joseph is incised 214/B in the small Nativity Set and 260 B in the large set. Angel Trio is a set of three figures, incised 238A, 238B, and 238C, respectively. Candy boxes are signified by a prefix of Roman III. The figurine Joyful, Hum. 53, is incised with just 53 on the base, while the candy box with this figure on top is incised III/53. Lamps are designated by the letter "M" preceding the model number. Apple Tree Girl, Hum. 141, when used as a portion of a lamp will be incised M229. Music boxes are marked in a reverse manner. The "M" appears after the model number. Thus, 388/M is the designation for the Little Band Music Box.

As mentioned before, the official catalog designation of any model number is preceded by the first three letters in Sister Hummel's name. Puppy Love is cataloged as "Hum. 1" but incised only with the number "1" on the base. Catalogs use other designations to further identify and distinguish differences in basic model design that will not necessarily be incised on the bottom of the actual article itself. One case is the suffix used after the catalog number to indicate one color from another. This is not incised on the figurines. The most common of these is a "W" to indicate that the piece is available in overglaze white (not glazed in colors). In the 1980 catalog, Flower Madonna is listed as Hum. 10/III/ W, indicating that this model/size is offered in a plain overglaze white 11½″ high for $165. Hum. 10/III/11 is the same size in hand-painted color for $200. "Hum.," the "W", or the "11", are not incised on the base of the actual piece.

Classification of Goebel Trademarks

Genuine M.I. Hummel figurines made only by Goebel have, in addition to the incised facsimile signature, another mark that is important to collectors. This mark answers three basic questions everyone wants to know about any of their possessions, be it a Hummel, a piece of barbed wire, or a sixteenth century oil painting. The questions are: "Who made it?" "When was it made?" and "How much is it worth?"

While Goebel products are among the best identified ceramic products, if not the best, one of the identification marks is of upmost importance to the Hummel owner. That mark is a sign, a symbol, a device, or a logo, but by any name, it represents and identifies the company that made the product. It says, "This product is made by the W. Goebel Company." Once this mark is properly registered around the world, the Goebel Company is the only one entitled to use it, in the same manner that they are the only one authorized to use the M.J.Hummel facsimile signature. Best of all this trademark answers the three questions uppermost in collectors' minds. "Who?" "When?" and "How much?"

The accompanying illustrations show six different marks that Goebel has used since the Thirties on all of their products, not just M.I. Hummel figurines. When any product bears one of these six classes of trademarks it is proof of "Who made it." Because the trademark has been changed at least six times in the last forty-five years, the design of the trademark indicates the approximate time period in which a piece with one of these marks was made. (More about how approximate this is is discussed later.) So any of the trademarks answer the second question, "When was it made?," fairly accurately. Since the value to collectors of any Hummel figurine is partially determined by its age, this all-important trademark gives one a preliminary indication of "How much it's worth." (See the section "Pricing of M.I. Hummel Figurines" for other factors that may be as important or more important in determining a fair market price.)

Going back again to "When was it made?", the Goebel Company, even if they wanted to, could not change from one mark to another on a given day. The changeover may have taken months, or years in some cases, before all models, are released bearing the newest trademark. It now appears that some marks such as TMK-3 and TMK-4 may have been used concurrently, with TMK-3 on some figurines and TMK-4 on others, during the period from 1965 to about 1972. This stands out quite clearly when reviewing posting of thousands of prices to each model card for each trademark. There are some models such as Whitsuntide, Hum. 163, and Forest Shrine, Hum. 183, that, as yet, have no entries for TMK-4, but have numerous ones for TMK-3.

The subject of trademark dates could be discussed at great length and when all the smoke clears, there would still be differences of opinion as to the date any one of the marks was first used. For example, at least one of the International Figurines has a TMK-2 on it, and yet these were made long before TMK-2 was adopted (now thought to be in 1950). Is this because the mark was actually used before WWII, or because a sample made then was not actually stamped until 1950 or later? According to Goebel records, the Nativity Set, Hum. 214, was designed in 1951 by Reinhold Unger and first sold in 1952 with TMK-2. How does it happen that a man from Buffalo, New York, touring Germany with a Lutheran youth study group bought a Hum. 214 Nativity Set with TMK-2 marks in 1949, which is a year before the mark was supposed to have been used, and, supposedly, three years before it was offered for sale? Could it have been an early prototype, a "trial balloon," or other, for reasons unknown?

After hearing of so many inconsistencies, it seems logical to assume that using trademarks to determine production dates is a very approximate yardstick, but it is so much better than no yardstick, that it should

TMK-1D, Incised and Stamped Crown on base of Puppy Love, Hum. 1. No model number, country of origin, or copyright year.

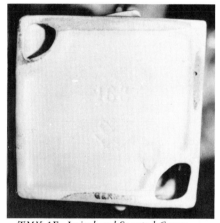

TMK-1E, Incised and Stamped Crown on base of Whitsuntide, Hum. 163. Stamped black Germany; no copyright year.

TMK-1, base of Globe Trotter, Hum. 79, without Crown mark; stamped US Zone and Germany; no copyright date.

TMK-1, Incised Crown and model number 58/0 on base of Playmates. Stamped U.S.-Zone (over) Germany. No year date.

TMK-2A, Incised Full Bee and TMK-2B, Stamped Full Bee on base of Umbrella Boy, Hum. 152. Unusual to find both on same figurine. Early incised © W. Goebel but no year; stamped black Germany.

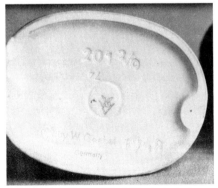

TMK-2B, Stamped Full Bee in incised circle; incised model number, 201 2/0, on base of Retreat to Safety. Incised © by W. Goebel and year, 1948; stamped Germany.

be used for what it is worth until something better comes along. It probably is accurate for more than 90 percent of the pieces produced during forty some years. The dates shown in the table as the span of years for any one of the six classes of trademarks seem to be realistic of present thinking. They should continue to be used until further research indicates the dates should be modified again, as they all have been during the past three years. Who knows, in another three years scientists may have developed dating by rays or chemical analysis to such a fine degree we may be able to distinguish whether a piece was made on the fourth or fifth of July, 1950.

Referring to the table of marks will show that they have been divided into six numbered groups for convenience and practicality and assigned numbers from 1 to 6: TMK-1 (Crown); TMK-2 (Full Bee); TMK-3 (Stylized Bee); TMK-4 (Three Line); TMK-5 (Goebel Bee); and TMK-6 (Goebel Only). Subclasses of the six are also shown and may be an important factor in pricing a specific piece, as will be explained.

TMK-1 (Crown) Premiums

The prices shown on the separate Price List are those for a single, incised, Crown TMK-1A. A double Incised Crown mark, TMK-1C, would be considered quite unusual and would double the price given. incised and stamped Crown marks, TMK-1D, would increase the single Crown mark value in the table by 50 percent. A single incised or stamped Crown mark which also had an added U.S. Zone mark would increase the basic value by about 50 percent. An Incised Crown and stamped Full Bee would be considered desirable with perhaps a premium of 10 percent over the single Crown.

TMK-2 (Full Bee) Premiums

The prices shown in the Price List are those for a large, stamped Full Bee, TMK-2B. Since there are less incised TMK-2A's than there are stamped ones, the prices in the table should be increased by 25 percent for an incised TMK-2A. Rather than complicate minor deviations, most collectors consider the later Full Bee marks (TMK-2, C, D, and E), at the same prices as shown for the regular TMK-2B in the Price List, or perhaps 10 to 20 percent less.

TMK-3 (Stylized Bee) Premiums

The prices shown in the Price List are those for Large Stylized Bee, TMK-3A, B, or C. Recently, collectors and dealers have been considering what they term the stamped "Large Stylized Bee" (TMK-3A, B, and C), as more valuable examples than the later, transfer-labeled Small Stylized Bee, TMK-3D. How much? That is still being negotiated by Mr. Supply and Mr. Demand. For now the smaller version might bring about 10 to 20 percent less than the values shown in the Price List, which are for the more scarce, Large Stylized Bee.

TMK-4 (Three Line)

This is the one mark that is pretty straight-forward and the prices reflect values for figurines having this mark, Three Line, TMK-4A.

TMK-5 (Goebel Bee) Premiums

Prices shown on the Price List are those for the overglaze Goebel Bee, TMK-5B. This recently superseded trademark now has three subclasses. One is the older underglaze label, TMK-5A. The other is in the newer overglaze method of application, TMK-5B. Here again, no uniform and distinct premium for the underglaze has emerged as definitive. Any indicated difference at this time would be in the area from 0 to 10 percent premium for earlier underglaze mark, TMK-5A. The easiest way to determine under or overglaze is to run a fingernail across the transfer label. If it feels perfectly smooth, it was applied before the final glaze was added. If unevenness is encountered from the printing, overglaze application is indicated. The prices given are for overglaze.

The newest classification, TMK-5C, is for those pieces that were hand-dated by the artist starting in 1979. At present there is insufficient data accumulated to indicate whether there is any great demand for them as compared to the undated examples. Therefore, the Price List can be used for TMK-5C at the present time. Future data may indicate a premium for year-dated pieces by the artist, which was begun in 1979.

TMK-6 (Goebel Only)

There is such a small interval between the introduction of this new mark and the publishing of this book that there is little or no difference between TMK-5 and TMK-6 noted at present. The same would apply to year-dated pieces in TMK-6A and TMK-6B. It is likely that a differential will emerge once the scarcity of either mark is known.

It is easy to visualize how clumsy and complicated any price list would be if all of the above variables, and many more not even discussed, were each shown in a separate column. More importantly, the circumstances under which premiums are paid and the amounts paid vary too much to record accurately. These variables represent a small portion of the total production and are of interest to only a small percentage of the collectors. Since it is already obvious that the six columns of prices, one for each trademark, are only a guide which has to be modified to suit the time, place, and individuals involved, slicing these figures any thinner would be a disaster.

A final comment is in order to indicate how little is definitely known about some of the variations in dates, designs, and values of such variations. Presently there are three pieces known that vary from the regular stamped TMK-1B, Crown mark. The marks on the pieces have been described as the "Roof Crown mark." Even the three are not alike, but a close representation of them is shown on this page. If Sketch A is a Roof Crown, then Sketch B would be Roof with Chimney Crown mark. The simple roof variation was submitted to several experts for comment. The explanation by some was that this was accidentally caused by a poor job of stamping the regular Crown mark. Other persons familiar with the process of stamping ceramics do not agree that such a "roof" or "roof with chimney" could have been caused by using a Crown stamp of conventional design. Anyone having more information or examples of this type of variation may be able to explain what appears to be another subdivision of TMK-1 Crown marks first noted by Heidi Poag and later by Barbara Schmidt.

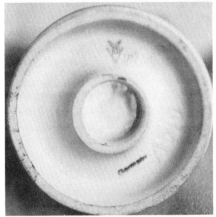

TMK-2B, Stamped Full Bee on base of Hear Ye, Hear Ye, Hum. 15/0. Has ® for registered mark, stamped black Germany, but no copyright year.

TMK-3A, Early Partial Stylized Bee stamped in incised circle with Western Germany stamped in black. Base of Volunteers, Hum. 50/0, with no copyright year or insignia.

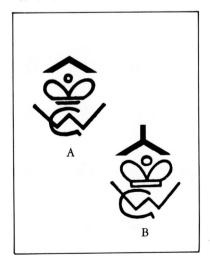

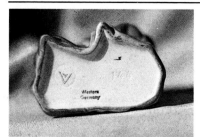

TMK-3B, Large Stylized Bee in incised circle and stamped Western Germany on base of Angelic Song, Hum. 144. No copyright date.

In addition to the table showing the classes, designs, and dates of the trademarks, photographs of some eighteen different figurine bases have been selected to give you an idea of how the trademarks vary, and how some may be faint or missing. The following pages will be a great help in determining the "pedigree" of any M.I. Hummel figurine.

Left: TMK-4A, Small Stylized Bee Three Line stamped in blue; KISS ME printed on base of Kiss Me, Hum. 311. Right: TMK-3C, Large Stamped Stylized Bee, W. Germany; incised 311 model number on base of Kiss Me with stamped W. Goebel in black.

TMK-3C, Large Stylized Bee and W. Germany stamped in blue on base of Umbrella Girl, Hum. 152/0. Incised year, 1957, and ©; by W. Goebel stamped in black.

TMK-4A, Small Stylized Bee Blue Transfer label on base of Umbrella Girl. Incised 152/II B with incised 1951 copyright year. W. Germany and company name in label.

TMK-5C, Blue Transfer Label overglaze, hand-dated, 79 on base of Just Resting, Hum. 112/I; incised 1938 copyright year.

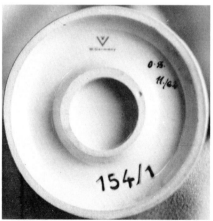

TMK-3D, Small Stylized Transfer Bee in blue on base of Waiter, Hum. 154/1. With unusual artist initials, "O.S." and date, "11/62." Incised model number filled in with black.

TMK-5, Special Foil Label, as base is too small for standard identification, on Girl with Sheet Music, Hum. 389.

TMK-6, Goebel (only) Blue Transfer Label overglaze; hand-dated, 79; on base of Spring Dance, Hum. 353/0 reissue.

The M.I. Hummel Pedigree

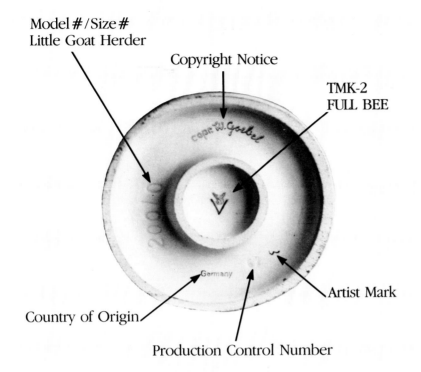

Model # / Size #
Little Goat Herder

Copyright Notice

TMK-2
FULL BEE

Country of Origin

Production Control Number

Artist Mark

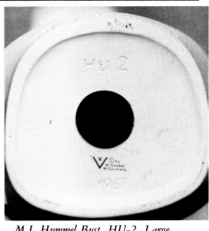

M.I. Hummel Bust, HU-2. Large. Stamped with Three Line, TMK-4, and incised year "1967." Designed by "SKROBEK"; year discontinued unknown. Superseded by small 5¾" bust in 1977 with TMK-5.

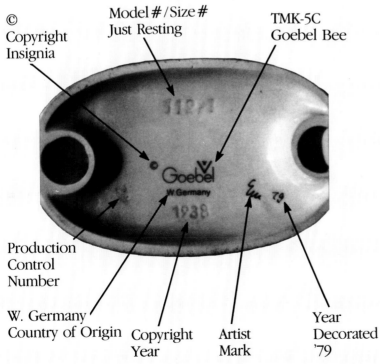

©
Copyright
Insignia

Model # / Size #
Just Resting

TMK-5C
Goebel Bee

Production
Control
Number

W. Germany
Country of Origin

Copyright
Year

Artist
Mark

Year
Decorated
'79

Three-dimensional prototype of TMK-2 derived from design by Sister Hummel. Photographed at the Hummel Home, Massing, West Germany.

Alphabetical Guide to Model Numbers

NAME	MODEL	CLASS	NAME	MODEL	CLASS	NAME	MODEL	CLASS
A FAIR MEASURE	345	F	Being Punished	326	PLQ	FEEDING TIME	199	F
ACCORDION BOY	185	F	BIG HOUSECLEANING	363	F	FESTIVAL HAR. W/MAN.	172	F
ADORATION	23	F	BIRD DUET	169	F	FESTIVAL HAR. W/FL.	173	F
ADORATION W/BIRD	105	F	BIRD WATCHER	300	F	FIDDLER, LITTLE	2 & 4	F
Advent Grp. w/Candle	31	CAN	BIRTHDAY CAKE	338	F	Flitting Butterfly	139	PLQ
Advent Candlesticks (3)	115-6-7	CAN	BIRTHDAY PRESENT	341	F	Flower Madonna	10	MAD
ADVENTURE BOUND	347	F	BIRTHDAY SERENADE	218	F	FLOWER VENDOR	381	F
Angel Cloud	206	HWF	Birthday Serenade	231	TLP	FLYING ANGEL	366	F
Angel Duet	193	CAN	Birthday Serenade	234	TLP	FOLLOW THE LEADER	369	F
ANGEL DUET	261	F	BLESSED EVENT	333	F	FOREST SHRINE	183	F
Angel Duet	146	HWF	BOOKKEEPER, LITTLE	306	F	FOR FATHER	87	F
Angel, Guardian	29	HWF	BOOK WORM	3	F	FOR MOTHER	257	F
Angel, Joy. News w/Trpt.	242	HWF	BOOK WORM	8	F	FRIENDS	136	F
Angel, Joy. News w/Lute	241	HWF	Book Worms (Boy & Girl)	14	BE	GABRIEL, LITTLE	32	F
Angel, Joy. News w/Lute	38	CAN	BOOTS	143	F	GARDENER, LITTLE	74	F
Angel, Joy. News w/Acdn.	39	CAN	BOY W/ACCORDION	390	F	GAY ADVENTURE	356	F
Angel, Joy. News w/Trpt.	40	CAN	Boy w/Bird	166	AT	Girl w/Fir Tree	116	CAN
Angel Lights	241	CAN	BOY W/HORSE	239 C	F	GIRL W/FROG	219	F
Angel Prayer (Left)	91 A	HWF	Boy w/Horse	117	CAN	GIRL W/DOLL	239 B	F
Angel Prayer (Right)	91 B	HWF	BOY W/TOOTHACHE	217	F	GIRL W/NOSEGAY	239 A	F
ANGEL SERENADE	83	F	BROTHER	95	F	Girl w/Nosegay	115	CAN
ANGEL SERENADE (Klng.)	214/D	F	BUILDER	305	F	GIRL W/SHEET MUSIC	389	F
ANGEL SERENADE (Klng.)	260 E	F	BUSY STUDENT	367	F	GIRL W/TRUMPET	391	F
Angel Shrine (Devotion)	147	HWF	Butterfly & Boy	139	PLQ	GLOBE TROTTER	79	F
Angel with Bird (Left)	167	HWF	Candlelight	192	CAN	GOAT HERDER, LITTLE	200	F
Angel with Birds (Right)	22	HWF	CARNIVAL	328	F	GOING HOME	383	F
Angel with Cross	354 C	HWF	CELESTIAL MUSICIAN	188	F	GOING TO GRANDMA'S	52	F
Angel with Flowers (child)	36	HWF	CHEF, HELLO	124	F	GOOD FRIENDS	182	F
Angel with Lantern	354 A	HWF	CHICK GIRL	57	F	Good Friends	228	TLP
Angel with Trumpet	354 B	HWF	Chick Girl	III/57	CBX	Good Friends & S.L.M.	251 A&B	BE
Angel Trio (A) (Sitting)	38, 39, 40	CAN	Chick Girl & Playmates	61 B&A	BE	GOOD HUNTING	307	F
ANGEL TRIO (B)			CHICKEN LICKEN	385	F	GOOD NIGHT	214 C	F
(Stng.)	238 A B C	F	Child in Bed	137	PLQ	Good Night	260 D	NAT
ANGEL, TUNEFUL	359	F	Child Jesus	26	HWF	GOOD SHEPHERD	42	F
Angelic Prayer	75	HWF	CHILDREN TRIO (A)	239 A B C	F	Good Shepherd	35	HWF
Angelic Sleep w/Candle	25	CAN	CHILDREN TRIO (B)	389	F	GOOSE GIRL	47	F
ANGELIC SONG	144	F	CHILDREN TRIO (B)	390	F	Goose Girl & Farm Boy	60 A&B	BE
Anniversary Plate — 1975	280	PLT	CHILDREN TRIO (B)	391	F	GROUP OF CHILDREN	392	F
Anniversary Plate — 1980	281	PLT	CHIMNEY SWEEP	12	F	Guardian Angel	29	HWF
Annual Bell — 1978	700	BL	CHRIST CHILD	18	F	Guardian Angel	248	HWF
Annual Bell — 1979	701	BL	CHRISTMAS ANGEL	301	F	GUARDIAN, LITTLE	145	F
Annual Bell — 1980	702	BL	Christmas Angels (3)	115-6-7	CND	GUIDING ANGEL	357	F
Annual Plate — 1971	264	PLT	CHRISTMAS SONG	343	F	HAPPINESS	86	F
Annual Plate — 1972	265	PLT	CINDERELLA	337	F	HAPPY BIRTHDAY	176	F
Annual Plate — 1973	266	PLT	CLOSE HARMONY	336	F	Happy Bugler (Tuneful		
Annual Plate — 1974	267	PLT	COMPANIONS	370	F	G/Night)	180	PLQ
Annual Plate — 1975	268	PLT	CONCENTRATION	302	F	HAPPY DAYS	150	F
Annual Plate — 1976	269	PLT	CONFIDENTIALLY	314	F	Happy Days	232	TLP
Annual Plate — 1977	270	PLT	CONGRATULATIONS	17	F	Happy Days	235	TLP
Annual Plate — 1978	271	PLT	COQUETTES	179	F	HAPPY PASTIME	69	F
Annual Plate — 1979	272	PLT	Cross with Doves	77	HWF	Happy Pastime	111/69	CBX
Annual Plate — 1980	273	PLT	CROSSROADS	331	F	Happy Pastime	221	CBX
Annual Plate — 1981	274	PLT	CULPRITS	56/A	F	Happy Pastime	62	AT
Annual Plate — 1982	275	PLT	Culprits	44 A	TLP	HAPPY TRAVELLER	109	F
Annual Plate — 1983	276	PLT	DADDY'S GIRLS	371	F	HEAR YE, HEAR YE	15	F
Annual Plate — 1984	277	PLT	Dealer's Plaque	187 C	PLQ	HEAVENLY ANGEL	21	F
Annual Plate — 1985	278	PLT	Devotion (Angel Shrine)	147	HWF	Heavenly Angel	207	HWF
Annual Plate — 1986	279	PLT	Display Plaque	187 A	PLQ	HEAVENLY LULLABY	262	F
APPLE TREE BOY	142	F	DOCTOR	127	F	HEAVENLY PROTECTION	88	F
APPLE TREE GIRL	141	F	DOLL BATH	319	F	Heavenly Song	113	CAN
Apple Tree Boy	230	TLP	DOLL MOTHER	67	F	HELLO	124	F
Apple Tree Girl	229	TLP	Doll Mother & Prayer B.B.	76	BE	HELPER, LITTLE	73	F
Apple Tree Boy & Girl	252 A&B	BE	Donkey	214/J	NAT	HELPING MOTHER	325	F
ARITHMETIC LESSON	303	F	Donkey	260 L	NAT	Herald Angels	37	CAN
ART CRITIC	318	F	DON'T BE SHY	379	F	HIKER, LITTLE	16	F
THE ARTIST	304	F	Dove (Holy Spirit)	393	HWF	HOLY CHILD, THE	70	F
AT THE FENCE	324	F	DRUMMER, LITTLE	240	F	Holy Family	246	HWF
AUF WIEDERSEHEN	153	F	DUET	130	F	Holy Family (Set)	214	NAT
AUTUMN HARVEST	355	F	EASTER GREETINGS	378	F	HOME FROM MARKET	198	F
Ba-Bee Rings (2)	30 A&B	PLQ	EASTER TIME	384	F	HOMEWARD BOUND	334	F
BAKER	128	F	EVENTIDE	99	F	HONEY LOVER	312	F
BAKING DAY	330	F	Eventide/Adoration	90 A&B	BE	Hum. Display Plq., Eng.	187	PLQ
BAND LEADER	129	F	FAIR MEASURE, A	345	F	English, Oeslau	211	
Band, Little	392/M	MBX	FAREWELL	65	F	English, Schmid	210	
BARNYARD HERO	195	F	Farewell	103	TLP	French	208	
BASHFUL	377	F	FARM BOY	66	F	German	205	
BE PATIENT	197	F	Farm Boy & Goose Girl	60 A&B	BE	Spanish	213	
BEGGING HIS SHARE	9	F	FAVORITE PET	361	F	Swedish	209	
BEHAVE	339	F	FEATHERED FRIENDS	344	F	"Hummel" Bust	HU-1	MIS

28   ABBREVIATIONS: AT-Ashtray; BE-Bookends; BL-Bell; CAN-Candleholders; CBX-Candybox; F-Figurine; HWF-Holy Water Font;

NAME	MODEL	CLASS
"Hummel" Bust	HU-2	MIS
"Hummel" Bust	HU-2C	MIS
I FORGOT	362	F
INFANT JESUS	214/A	F
Infant Jesus	260 C	NAT
INFANT OF KRUMBAD	78	F
JOYFUL	53	F
Joyful	111/53	CBX
Joyful	33	AT
Joyful & Let's Sing	120	BE
Joyous News	27	CAN
Joyous News w/Lute	38	CAN
Joyous News w/Accdn.	39	CAN
Joyous News w/Trmpt.	40	CAN
JUST FISHING	373	F
JUST RESTING	112	F
Just Resting	11/112	TLP
Just Resting	225	TLP
King (Standing)	214/L	NAT
King (Knlg. on one knee)	214/M	NAT
King (Knlg. on two knees)	214/N	NAT
King (Standing)	260 O	NAT
King (Kneeling)	260 P	NAT
KISS ME	311	F
Kneeling Angel	248	HWF
KNITTING LESSON	256	F
Lamb	214/O	NAT
LATEST NEWS	184	F
LET'S SING	110	F
Let's Sing	114	AT
Let's Sing	111/110	CBX
LETTER TO SANTA	340	F
LITTLE BAND	392	F
Little Band	388	CAN
Little Band w/Cndl.	288/M	MBX
Little Band w/o Cndl.	392/M	MBX
LITTLE BOOKKEEPER	306	F
LITTLE CELLIST	89	F
LITTLE DRUMMER	240	F
LITTLE FIDDLER	2	F
LITTLE FIDDLER	4	F
Little Fiddler	93	PLQ
Little Fiddler	107	PLQ
LITTLE GABRIEL	32	F
LITTLE GARDENER	74	F
LITTLE GOAT HERDER	200	F
Ltl. Goat Hrdr. & F'dng Time	250	BE
LITTLE GUARDIAN	145	F
LITTLE HELPER	73	F
LITTLE HIKER	16	F
LITTLE NURSE	376	F
LITTLE PHARMACIST	322	F
LITTLE SCHOLAR	80	F
LITTLE SHOPPER	96	F
LITTLE SWEEPER	171	F
LITTLE TAILOR	308	F
LITTLE THRIFTY	118	F
LITTLE TOOTER	214/H	F
LITTLE TOOTER	260 K	F
LITTLE VELMA	219	F
LITTLEST ANGEL	365	F
LOST SHEEP	68	F
LOST STOCKING	374	F
LUCKY BOY	335	F
LULLABY, HEAVENLY	262	F
LUTE SONG	368	F
Lullaby	24	CAN
Madonna	214/A	MAD
Madonna	260 A	NAT
Madonna (Wire frame)	222	PLQ
Madonna w/Child	48	PLQ
Madonna w/Child	243	HWF
Madonna, Flower	10	MAD
Madonna, Seated	151	MAD
Madonna w/Halo	45	MAD
Madonna w/o Halo	46	MAD
MAIL COACH	226	F
MAIL IS HERE	226	F
Mail Is Here	140	PLQ
MAN GOING TO MKT.	191	F
MAN READING PAPER	181	F
MARCH WINDS	43	F
MAX AND MORITZ	123	F
MEDITATION	13	F
Merry Christmas	323	PLQ
MERRY WANDERER	7	F
MERRY WANDERER	11	F
Merry Wanderer	92	PLQ
Merry Wanderer	106	PLQ
Merry Wanderer	263	PLQ
"M.I. Hummel" Plaque	187	PLQ
"M.I. Hummel" Plaques	205 +	PLQ
MISCHIEF MAKER	342	F
Moorish King	260N	NAT
MORNING STROLL	375	F
MOTHER'S DARLING	175	F
MOTHER'S HELPER	133	F
MOUNTAINEER	315	F
Nativity Set (Small)	214	NAT
Nativity Set (Large)	260	NAT
NOT FOR YOU	317	F
OFF TO SCHOOL	329	F
ON HOLIDAY	350	F
ON SECRET PATH	386	F
OUT OF DANGER	56/B	F
Out of Danger	44 B	TLP
Ox	214/K	NAT
Ox	260 M	NAT
PHARMACIST, LITTLE	322	F
PHOTOGRAPHER	178	F
PLAYMATES	58	F
Playmates & Chick Girl	61 A/B	BE
Playmates	111/58	CBX
POSTMAN	119	F
PRAYER BEFORE BATTLE	20	F
PROFESSOR, THE	320	F
PUPPY LOVE	1	F
Puppy Love & Serenade	122	BE
Quartet	134	PLQ
RELAXATION	316	F
RETREAT TO SAFETY	201	F
Retreat to Safety	126	PLQ
RIDE INTO CHRISTMAS	396	F
RING 'RND. T. ROSIE	348	F
RUN-A-WAY, THE	327	F
ST. GEORGE	55	F
St. Joseph	214/B	NAT
St. Joseph	260 B	NAT
SCHOLAR, LITTLE	80	F
SCHOOL BOY	82	F
SCHOOL BOYS	170	F
SCHOOL GIRL	81	F
SCHOOL GIRLS	177	F
Searching Angel	310	PLQ
SENSITIVE HUNTER	6	F
SHEPHERD, GOOD	42	F
SERENADE	85	F
Sheep (Standing) w/Lamb	260 H	NAT
Sheep (Lying)	260 R	NAT
SHE LOVES ME, S.L.M.N.	174	F
She Loves Me, She L.M.N.	227	TLP
She Loves Me & G. Fr'nds.	251 B/A	BE
Shepherd w/Sheep	214/F	NAT
SHEPHERD BOY	395	F
Shepherd Boy	214/G	NAT
Shepherd Boy (Kneeling)	260 J	NAT
Shepherd (Standing)	260 G	NAT
SHEPHERD'S BOY	64	F
SHINING LIGHT	358	F
SHOPPER, LITTLE	96	F
Shrine	100	TLP
SIGNS OF SPRING	203	F
Silent Night	54	CAN
Silent Night w/Bl. Child	31	CAN
SINGING LESSON	63	F
Singing Lesson	111/63	CBX
Singing Lesson	34	AT
Singing Lesson	272	PLT
SISTER	98	F
Sitting Angel (Angel w/Bird)	22	HWF
SKIER	59	F
SMART LITTLE SISTER	346	F
Smiling Through	690	PLQ
SOLDIER BOY	332	F
SOLOIST	135	F
SPRING CHEER	72	F
SPRING DANCE	353	F
Standing Boy	168	PLQ
STAR GAZER	132	F
STITCH IN TIME	255	F
Store Plaque	187 C	PLQ
STORMY WEATHER	71	F
STREET SINGER	131	F
STROLLING ALONG	5	F
SUNNY MORNING	313	F
SURPRISE	94	F
Swaying Lullaby	165	PLQ
SWEEPER, LITTLE	171	F
SWEET GREETINGS	352	F
SWEET MUSIC	186	F
TAILOR, LITTLE	308	F
TELLING HER SECRET	196	F
TENDERNESS	300	F
THE ARTIST	304	F
THE BOTANIST	351	F
THE BUILDER	305	F
THE FLORIST	349	F
THE HOLY CHILD	70	F
THE MAIL IS HERE	226	F
THE PROFESSOR	320	F
THE RUNAWAY	327	F
THRIFTY, LITTLE	118	F
TIMID LITTLE SISTER	394	F
Tiny Baby in Crib	138	PLQ
TO MARKET	49	F
To Market	101	TLP
To Market	223	TLP
Tooter, Little	214/H	NAT
Tooter, Little	260 K	NAT
TRUMPET BOY	97	F
TUNEFUL ANGEL	359	F
Tuneful (Goodnight) (Hpy. Bugler)	180	PLQ
UMBRELLA BOY	152 A	F
UMBRELLA GIRL	152 B	F
Vacation Time	125	PLQ
VALENTINE GIFT	387	F
VALENTINE JOY	399	F
VILLAGE BOY	51	F
VISITING AN INVALID	382	F
VOLUNTEERS	50	F
Volunteers	102	TLP
WAITER	154	F
Wall Vase Boy & Girl	360/A	WVS
Wall Vase Boy	360/B	WVS
Wall Vase Girl	360/C	WVS
WASHDAY	321	F
WATCHFUL ANGEL	194	F
WAYSIDE DEVOTION	28	F
Wayside Devotion	104	TLP
WAYSIDE HARMONY	111	F
Wayside Harmony & J. Rest'g	121	BE
Wayside Harmony	224	TLP
Wayside Harmony	II/111	TLP
WE CONGRATULATE	220	F
We Congratulate	214/E	NAT
We Congratulate	260 F	NAT
WEARY WANDERER	204	F
WHICH HAND?	258	F
White Angel	75	HWF
WHITSUNTIDE	163	F
W/ LOVING GRTNGS.	309	F
WOMAN GOING TO Mkt.	190	F
WOMAN KNITTING	189	F
WORSHIP	84	F
Worship	164	HWF

2 *The M.I. Hummel Collection by Goebel*

For dedicated Hummel collectors, this may well become the most dog-eared portion of this book. The purpose of this section is to include everything of interest to collectors about each M.I. Hummel figurine, candleholder, plate, plaque, etc. The only essential missing information is the applicable prices. Since retail prices and prices for older and rarer figurines change frequently (mostly up), a Current Price List, which is published annually, is included with your copy of *Hummel Art II.*

Since the Chinese proverb, "a picture is worth ten thousand words" is just as true today as when it was written, there is a photograph of every model that was available to use as the focal point of this section. The trademark of each piece pictured is indicated under the photograph to aid in comparing this particular version with that of any other trademarks. Searching for variations, deviations, rarities, unissued numbers, changes in design or color, add much interest and sometimes pleasant surprises for the collector of Hummels.

The small production record beside each photograph has six trademark columns, one for each of the six major classes of trademarks used by Goebel throughout the last forty-five years. This table gives a quick statistical synopsis of the production history of each model as far as is generally known today. Real progress has been made in filling in many missing statistics. Over one thousand readers have contributed documented facts about the previously unknown existence of certain sizes, model numbers, and trademark variations. The Goebel Company has furnished a great deal of new information about motifs that may be introduced in the future and has also revised some previously published information. Advanced collectors such as Arbenz, Dous, Grande, Marker, and Miller are also responsible for major additions and changes, many of which are being published here for the first time. The author has found old catalogs to be a fertile source of facts about older production models and is always interested in any old catalogs published prior to 1972.

The names, numbers, letters, and signs used in the production record next to the photograph need more explanation to be of optimum value to the collector. The left-hand column of the table lists the indicator model numbers for each figurine and related piece. The section of the book entitled "Model Numbers and Size Indicators" page 20, should be read in order to appreciate the diversity and meaning of Goebel's numbering system.

The next column is headed "Size." This is the height of the figurine or related piece in inches to the nearest ¼ inch. (Divide this figure by 2.54 to determine the height in centimeters.) The sizes are the ones used in the 1981 catalog published by Hummelwerk, one of three U.S. distributors.

Drawing #5940 courtesy Ars Sacra.

Drawing #14263 courtesy Ars Sacra.

Drawing #5545 courtesy Ars Sacra.

Opposite page: Blessed Event, Hum. 333, TMK-5, 5½" high, introduced in this country in 1964.

The height of a figurine can be measured by placing it on a table and holding a flat object (the blade of a table knife works fine) horizontally, just touching the highest point of the figurine. The distance from the table to the underside of the horizontal object is the height of the figurine. Variations in specified and actual sizes and their relation to values is covered in the model history, directly below the production record.

The next column to the right is headed "Status" to quickly indicate if such an example was ever made and identified. Several different letter symbols appear in this and adjoining columns. The legend at the beginning of this section lists these in alphabetical order with a definition of each one. The symbol most frequently found here is the letter "P". This indicates that the model/size number is currently cataloged by the Goebel Company and should be available from one of their authorized dealers. The letter "R" is shown for about forty items that were reissued or reintroduced in 1978 after having been uncataloged in the U.S. for some years.

The letter "D" means that this combination of model and size was at one time produced but has been discontinued and is not currently available. "C" in the Status column means the model is closed or cancelled. A few of these are known only as factory samples. For those numbers that have been assigned by Goebel to a specific motif, the letter "A" is used. None with this designation have been officially issued or announced. There are about twenty-two model numbers that have an "O" in this column which means the number is "Open." In other words, no motif has as yet been assigned to this number for design and possible production. The letter "U" is used to indicate that samples of certain cancelled numbers are unknown and even a factory sample is not available. It is also used to indicate that some sizes are unknown at present.

The next six columns, one for each class of trademark (TMK) used by Goebel on M.I. Hummel pieces, gives a shorthand history of approximately what years each model/size number was produced, if known. A column containing the letter "P" indicates that during the period represented by that trademark (see page 18) the particular model/size combination was produced, and verified examples are known to exist. This letter "P" also has a second meaning in the six TMK columns. If it was produced and is known to exist, a price has been listed in that same position in the Current Price List. This price is the most representative insurable value available based on sales tabulations.

Two other frequently used symbols in these six colums are the question mark (?) and the dash (—). The question mark simply means that at press deadline the author did not know of an example with this model/size combination in the trademark classification listed at the head of that column. Hopefully, someone else does know or will find out and let us know. Fewer question marks are present in this new book due to alert collectors and other sources who have documented the existence of previously questioned model/size combinations by the hundreds. The quantity of question marks remaining indicates the scope of unfinished

Drawing #5915 courtesy Ars Sacra.

Drawing #14286 courtesy Ars Sacra.

work ahead. It presents a challenge to all collectors and an invitation to advise the author if they can verify the existence of an example with that trademark. If not, keep looking for one. It could be a very unusual and rewarding discovery.

The other prominent mark is the dash (—) which indicates that it is unlikely (not impossible) that the model/size combination was ever produced in that trademark. This information is believed to be reliable, but has been proved wrong in numerous other instances in the last four years. Another four will not pass without readers or research improving the reliability of this designation which says "no" but sometimes means "probably not." Where there are many dash marks it is noticeable that the status column may have either a "D" or "R" which indicates that this model/size was once produced but was discontinued years ago (D); or that some discontinued models have been reintroduced (R).

The narrative history that accompanies the photograph of each model number and its production record has been gleaned from many sources, not all of which were always in full agreement. Old catalogs were a major source of availability, sizes, and names. Some intensive research by the Goebel Company during the last several years has been combined with similar efforts on the part of Robert Miller in order to publish the *Supplement* to *HUMMEL*. When there has been conflicting information to choose from, the Goebel Company suggested that the information in the *Supplement* would be the best information to use. Data from publications of the Hummel Collectors' Club and the Goebel Collectors' Club have been incorporated as are brief abstracts and paraphrases from columns in the *Plate Collector* by Pat Arbenz and from articles in *Collector's Editions* and *Collectors' News* by Robert Miller. A wealth of important information and discoveries, such as first knowledge of Cross with Doves, Hum. 77; the Serbian Goose Girl, Hum. 947; and the terra-cotta Madonnas all originated from letters to this author or discussions with readers and collectors. Over one thousand readers' letters offered fresh information and new ideas not previously incorporated in any publication. Information from auctions, sales, and lists were also compiled for this section. Research trips to Germany and various parts of the U.S. were responsible for new facts about Sister Hummel's original drawings, graphics, and other derivatives of her work. The U.S. Copyright Office contributed factual information and authenticated that some model numbers previously thought never to have been used had existed at least in the form of a prototype designs and tentative names.

This sounds like very impressive documentation for the following stories about each figurine, etc., but these individual histories are by no means complete or infallible. Hopefully, collectors will continue to write and point out omissions, commissions, and just plain everyday errors. The best possible supporting evidence for additional information or revisions of existing statements is a good color picture of the object and the same of the base (a good sketch is an adequate alternative for the base). However, information in any form will always be welcome and useful as long as it relates to the works of Berta or Sister M.I. Hummel.

Drawing #5863 courtesy Ars Sacra.

Drawing #5775 courtesy Ars Sacra.

1 **Puppy Love** *with bow tie, TMK-5, no copyright date.*

1 Puppy Love

Indicator	Size	Status	TMK-1	TMK-2	TMK-3	TMK-4	TMK-5	TMK-6
1	5″	P	P	P	P	P	P	P

For forty-five years this figurine has been made in this one size although the actual dimensions have varied. Oversize and undersize examples have been reported. When found, those pieces that deviate more than ¼″ should be valued at about 10 percent over the price for the standard 5″ size. Since 1936, the colors have become somewhat brighter. The model was restyled with some noticeable changes, probably in the 1950s; a bow tie was added and the fiddler now looks down at his right shoulder, rather than straight down the violin. This was one of the first ten models shown by Goebel at the Leipzig Fair in Germany in 1935. John Schmid bought a dozen at that time to be sold in the U.S. for approximately $1 each. To this day, these pieces are found without a copyright date. The early catalog listed this piece as "Little Fiddler with Dog" until about 1959. This corresponds to the German name *Geigerlein mit Hund.* It is the same figure as both models of Little Fiddler, Hum. 2 and Hum. 4.

2 **Little Fiddler,** *restyled, brown hat, TMK-5.*

2 Little Fiddler

Indicator	Size	Status	TMK-1	TMK-2	TMK-3	TMK-4	TMK-5	TMK-6
2/0	6″	P	P	P	P	P	P	P
2(.)	6″	D	P	?	P	—	—	—
/II	7½″	P	P	P	P	P	P	P
/II	10¾″	P	P	P	P	P	P	P
/III(3)	12¼″	R	P	P	?	?	R	R

While this figurine is almost identical to Puppy Love, Hum. 1, and to Little Fiddler, Hum. 4, Hum. 2 has some distinguishing characteristics. Hum. 2 has a brown hat and no dog. It is the only figurine of the three that was made in a range of sizes. Early catalogs list varying standard sizes. The largest size, 2/III, was not cataloged for some years but was reintroduced in 1978 in Canada for $525. The figurine has been reported with an arabic 3 in the earlier trademarks and an arabic 1 in TMK-1. The smallest size, 2. (decimal), has been found in both TMK-1 and TMK-3. It was restyled and newer models will appear with brighter colors. Until about 1960, this figurine was known as "Little Fiddler without Dog," which corresponds to German name *Geigerlein ohne Hund.* Verlag Emil Fink's postcard #203 is a reproduction of the original drawing.

3/1 **Book Worm,** *with book pictures in color, TMK-5.*

3 Book Worm

Indicator	Size	Status	TMK-1	TMK-2	TMK-3	TMK-4	TMK-5	TMK-6
3	5″	U	—	—	—	—	—	—
/I	5½″	P	P	P	P	P	P	P
/II(2)	8″	P	P	P	P	P	P	P
/III(3)	9″	R	P	P	P	?	R	R

This piece was adapted by Arthur Möller in 1935 from Sister Hummel's drawing. The two larger sizes were added at a later date. They have also been found with arabic size indicators. Hum. 3/III was absent from U.S. catalogs for some years but was reinstated in 1978. The only other name recorded so far is "The Bookworm" which is the translation of its German name *Der Bücherwurm.* This is the same figure as Hum. 8 which is made only in the smaller 4″ size. The same figure is used as one of a pair of bookends, Hum. 14 A. They can be distinguished in two ways. The book held in Hum. 14 A is not in full color and there is a stopper in the bottom so it can be weighted with sand. To date, there is no separate matching boy figurine, but the boy bookend, Hum. 14 B, forms the other half of the set and is of similar design.

4   Little Fiddler

Indicator	Size	Status	TMK-1	TMK-2	TMK-3	TMK-4	TMK-5	TMK-6
4(.)	4¾″	P	P	P	P	P	P	P

This is the same as Hum. 2 but is distinguished by having a black instead of brown hat. While issued in only one size, 4¾″ high, it has been reported as small as 4¼″ and as large as 6″ high. Thus it is possible to put together an ascending set of Little Fiddler figurines from about 4″ to over 12″ high. This figurine has also been reported as 4. (decimal) in the Crown mark. Hum. 4 also carries the German name of *Geigerlein ohne Hund.* (See Hum. 2 for further information on other forms of this motif.) Verlag Emil Fink produces a large graphic of the original drawing, #101A.

4 Little Fiddler, *black hat, 4¾″ high,* *TMK-5.*

5   Strolling Along

Indicator	Size	Status	TMK-1	TMK-2	TMK-3	TMK-4	TMK-5	TMK-6
5	4¾″	P	P	P	P	P	P	P

Here is another early adaptation, done in 1935 by Arthur Möller, master sculptor. The examples with TMK-1 and TMK-2 are reported with the boy gazing more to the rear. There are other minor color variations in the color of the dog. This piece is similar to Hum. 7 and to Hum. 11, Merry Wanderer, as its German name implies, *Wanderbub mit Hund* ("Wanderer with Dog" — dog rather than a satchel). No original drawing with a boy and dog has yet been located.

5 Strolling Along, *restyled version,* *TMK-5.*

6   Sensitive Hunter

Indicator	Size	Status	TMK-1	TMK-2	TMK-3	TMK-4	TMK-5	TMK-6
6/0	4¾″	P	P	P	P	P	P	P
6(.)	5″	D	P	?	—	—	—	—
/I	5½″	P	P	P	P	P	P	P
/II	7½″	P	P	?	P	P	P	P

This was originally introduced in the 4¾″ size in 1935 and was modeled by Arthur Möller. In the 1950s, it was the only size listed, but the other two sizes must have been added shortly after, as all three sizes are found in the trademarks and some of these have been reported as 6.(decimal). A 1959 catalog lists only the larger two sizes. The TMK-1 and 2 figurines are found with the lederhosen straps forming an "H" on the back. Sometime later, the model was restyled and the straps are now crossed in an "X" pattern in back. The prices shown in the list allow for the design variation. The shape and mottled coloring of the new hat is more pronounced. The German name is *Jägerlein* or "Little Hunter." Another companion hunter after the same game is Good Hunting, Hum. 307. This appears to be a variation of an original drawing owned by Verlag Emil Fink, from which they catalog a postcard #217. In this case, the hunter is gazing at a cricket.

6/1 Sensitive Hunter, *"X" straps,* *TMK-5.*

7/0 Merry Wanderer, *6" high,*
TMK-5.

8 Book Worm, *book pictures in color,*
TMK-5.

9 Begging His Share, *no candle*
socket, TMK-5.

7 Merry Wanderer

Indicator	Size	Status	TMK-1	TMK-2	TMK-3	TMK-4	TMK-5	TMK-6
7/0	6¼″	P	P	P	P	P	P	P
7	?	U	—	—	—	—	—	—
/I	7″	P	P	P	P	P	P	P
/II(2)	9½″	P	?	P	P	P	P	P
/III	11¼″	P	—	?	P	?	P	P
/X	32″	P	—	—	—	—	P	P

This must be the most widely publicized M.I. Hummel figurine. It appears in a ten-foot version to welcome visitors to the Goebel plant in Rödental. Another equally impressive replica is in front of the beautiful mansion in Tarrytown, New York, that has been converted into the headquarters of the Goebel Collectors' Club. It has appeared as the figurine symbol on the Goebel dealers' store plaques in several languages and in innumerable variations (see Hum. 187 and Hum. 205, 208, 209, 210, 211, 212, and 213). There are currently four sizes of Hum. 7 cataloged and two more of Hum. 11 which is also the same Merry Wanderer design. The same motif has also been used in plaques Hum. 92, Hum. 106, and Hum. 263, of which only the Hum. 92 is now in production. In addition to the six official sizes, process variations and model changes have produced a variety of sizes which is almost unlimited in the 4″ to 32″ range. Interesting collections have been made of nothing but height variations of Merry Wanderers. The Hum. 7/II size was issued in the early Seventies with the new textured finish restyled by Gerhard Skrobek, the present master sculptor for Goebel. The Hum. 7/III, out of production for some years, was restyled in similar manner and reintroduced at first in the German and Canadian catalogs in 1978. Hum. 7/I is known with a six-button vest, and 7/0 is known with a step-up base. The 7/X, modeled by Arthur Möller around 1950, may have been produced prior to 1976.

8 Book Worm

Indicator	Size	Status	TMK-1	TMK-2	TMK-3	TMK-4	TMK-5	TMK-6
8	4″	P	P	P	P	P	P	P

This figurine is the same as Hum. 3 (see). It is the smallest size produced and is listed in catalogs as early as 1947, and, of course, is found in all trademarks. It is unknown at this time why this smaller size was given a completely different Hummel number rather than the usual 3/0 marking. In this case the larger number represents the smaller size. Note that these two numbers, Hum. 3 and Hum. 8, are the first in the line to be made without a base. For other information on this motif, see Hum. 3.

9 Begging His Share

Indicator	Size	Status	TMK-1	TMK-2	TMK-3	TMK-4	TMK-5	TMK-6
9(.)	5½″	P	P	P	P	P	P	P

While this is found in all trademarks and was no doubt designed in 1935, it does not appear in a 1947 or 1950 U.S. catalog. Until it was restyled in the mid-Sixties, the large hole in the center of the cake served as a candleholder. After the mid-1960s it was issued with only a very small indentation in the center. The older models command a premium, as shown in the Price List. This figurine has been found with an incised 9. (decimal) in TMK-3, with and without the candleholder. The German name is *Gratulant,* or "The Well-Wisher." This forms another one of the group of figures sought after by dog owners, especially terrier owners. Verlag Ars Sacra produces postcard #14384 from an original drawing they own.

10 Flower Madonna

Indicator	Size	Status	TMK-1	TMK-2	TMK-3	TMK-4	TMK-5	TMK-6
10	8″	D	P	—	—	—	—	—
/I/II	8¼″	P	P	P	P	P	P	P
/I/W	8¼″	P	P	P	P	P	P	P
/III/11(3)	11½″	P	P	P	P	P	P	P
/III/W	11½″	P	P	P	P	P	P	P

According to factory records, this popular religious figure was adapted by another of Goebel's sculptors, Reinhold Unger, in about 1935. The earliest catalogs list the two sizes at approximately 8″ and 11″, although other size molds must have been used because of the wide range of sizes found. It has also been found in more color combinations and modifications of design than probably any other motif. The suffix /W and /II above refer to either white or color and are not part of the Hummel number 10 incised on the figure itself. The other known colors are an antiqued caramel color, an aqua with a burnished gold leaf halo, a pastel blue, a reddish brown, and a creamy ivory. There may be more out there since two of these were discoveries within the past year. Until about 1955, the halo was open in the back and is referred to as the "doughnut halo." The redesigned piece was introduced with a solid halo that has no opening in the back. Colors, except the current lavender blue and glazed white, are considered rare, with prices in the low to mid four-digit figures. Examples have also been found marked 10 (only) and 10/3 (arabic).

10/1 Flower Madonna *with flat halo,* *TMK-5.*

11 Merry Wanderer

Indicator	Size	Status	TMK-1	TMK-2	TMK-3	TMK-4	TMK-5	TMK-6
11/2/0	4¼″	P	P	P	P	P	P	P
/0	4¾″	P	P	P	P	P	P	P
11(.)	4¾″	D	P	P	—	—	—	—

Refer to Hum. 7, Merry Wanderer, for the complete story of this motif. Hum. 11 has been found with 11. (decimal) in TMK-1, and 11/2/0 is known with a six-button vest in TMK-2. The original drawings Sister Hummel did of this highly publicized motif is owned by Verlag Emil Fink, who has produced postcard #202 and print #101B from the original.

11/0 Merry Wanderer, *5″ high,* *TMK-5.*

12 Chimney Sweep

Indicator	Size	Status	TMK-1	TMK-2	TMK-3	TMK-4	TMK-5	TMK-6
12/2/0	4″	P	?	P	P	P	P	P
12(.)	6¼″	D	P	P	—	—	—	—
12/I	5½″	P	P	P	P	P	P	P

The popularity of this figure derives from the traditional continental belief that the chimney sweeps bring good luck. This figurine has been made since before World War II and is found in a wide variation of heights from the ones listed above. For example, in the 1950 catalog, "Smoky" and the German name *Schornsteinfeger* were listed as 14.5 cm or 6″ high for the 12/I size. This motif was also adapted by Goebel as a rubber doll in about 1954. The doll has been found with two style hats: one as shown on the figurine, and the other a broad-brimmed felt hat. Hum. 12 has been found marked 12 (only) in TMK-1 and 12/1 (arabic) in TMK-3. The original drawing, owned by Verlag Ars Sacra, has been published as postcard #14441. Goebel has also sold another Chimney Sweep figurine designed by a different artist which has confused some collectors because of similar company trademarks. All genuine Hummels are incised with the M.J.Hummel facsimile signature.

12/I Chimney Sweep, *TMK-4.*

13   Meditation

Indicator	Size	Status	TMK-1	TMK-2	TMK-3	TMK-4	TMK-5	TMK-6
13/2/0	4½″	P	—	—	U	P	P	P
13/0	5½″	P	P	P	P	P	P	P
13	6″	D	P	?	—	—	—	—
13/II(2)	7″	R	P	P	?	?	R	R
/V	13¾″	R	—	P	P	?	R	R

A collector's dream, this pensive motif is found in a number of sizes and design variations. It is known with all trademarks and an uncertain variety of copyright dates not indicative of the year of issue, in sizes from 4″ to 14″ high, and with a price range from two-digit figures to four-digit figures. One interesting variation was found marked $\frac{13}{0}$ (13 over 0), with only one bow on the right side of the head, in TMK-2. According to factory records, the 7″ size, Hum. 13/II, was restyled about 1962, which eliminated the flowers from the rear of the basket. However, the largest size, 13¾″, unavailable for some time, was cataloged again in 1978 with a full basket of flowers. The pigtails were also restyled. Because Hum. 13/V with old marks is very scarce, the reissues are snapped up on sight at premium prices. This larger size carries a 1957 copyright in some cases. It was once called "The Well Wisher," similar to the present German name *Die Gratulantin*. The original drawing owned by Fink is available in postcard #201.

13/0 Meditation, *no flowers in basket, TMK-5.*

14 A&B   Book Worm, Bookends

Indicator	Size	Status	TMK-1	TMK-2	TMK-3	TMK-4	TMK-5	TMK-6
14 A&B	5½″	P	P	P	P	P	P	P

The girl figure in this pair is similar to Hum. 3 and Hum. 8 (see), with two visible exceptions. The picture in the book which the bookend girl is holding is monochrome. It is in full color in the figurine. The bottom of the bookend has a hole (closed by either an older cork or a modern plastic stopper) for filling with sand or lead shot for weight to support books. The boy figure has no counterpart in separate figurines. The set is priced and sold only as a pair. The name used in the 1950 catalog, however, is "Learned Man and Bookworm" (*Der Gelehrte und Bücherwurm, beschwert*). In January, 1980, a motif similar to the bookend boy was introduced on the 1980 Annual Bell, Hum. 702, with modifications, such as the boy's legs being drawn up, his hair parted on the left side, and his left forefinger raised over a larger book. The bell is named "Thoughtful," a name formerly used for the boy portion of the bookends. For those collectors desiring matching figurines for their bells, this poses a problem. Perhaps Goebel will issue a similar figurine in the future.

14 A&B Book Worm Bookends, *no color in pictures, TMK-5.*

15   Hear Ye, Year Ye

Indicator	Size	Status	TMK-1	TMK-2	TMK-3	TMK-4	TMK-5	TMK-6
15/0	5″	P	P	P	P	P	P	P
15	?	U	—	—	—	—	—	—
/I(1)	6″	P	P	P	P	P	P	P
/II(2)	7″	P	—	—	P	P	P	P

This colorful and popular figurine designed in the 1930s was introduced in the smaller 5″ size before World War II as "Nightwatchman." It is listed in the 1947 catalog under that name at 5½″ high. Sometime before the 1959 catalog, it was produced in two larger sizes. As yet there is no report of the larger 7½″ size being found with the Crown or Full Bee trademarks. However, it has been found with TMK-1 in the two larger sizes marked arabic 1 and 2 respectively. Early trademarks have a baby blue metal blade versus gray. A 15 percent premium is added for an arabic marker. The figurine matches the bas-relief design on the 1972 Annual Plate, Hum. 265. The original drawing is owned by Verlag Ars Sacra. The postcard is #14350.

15/I Hear Ye, Hear Ye, *TMK-5.*

16   Little Hiker

Indicator	Size	Status	TMK-1	TMK-2	TMK-3	TMK-4	TMK-5	TMK-6
16/3/0	4″	D	—	P	—	—	—	—
/2/0	4½″	P	—	P	P	P	P	P
16(.)	5½″	D	P	P	—	—	—	—
/I(1)	6″	P	P	P	P	P	P	P

The important young man with oversize shoes has many other names such as "Happy Go Lucky," *Hans im Glück,* or "Hans in Fortune." First issued around the time of World War II, it was listed as being available in 16/2/0 and 16/I sizes as early as 1950. Sometime earlier, the 6″ size was produced as both 16 (only) and 16. (decimal). Other interesting trademark variations include a 16/3/0 with no trademark and stamped "Made in US Zone" and a 16/1 (arabic) in TMK-5. An Illinois collector has the figurine with a rare "roof" over the dot in the Crown mark, TMK-1. No major variations or redesigning have been reported to date. The original drawing by Sister Hummel is owned by Verlag Ars Sacra and issued as postcard #14832.

16/I Little Hiker, *TMK-3.*

17   Congratulations

Indicator	Size	Status	TMK-1	TMK-2	TMK-3	TMK-4	TMK-5	TMK-6
17/0	6″	D	P	P	P	P	P	—
17	6″	P	—	—	—	—	P	P
/I	?	U	—	—	—	—	—	—
/II(2)	8″	D	—	P	—	—	—	—

Currently produced only in the 6″ size and incised 17 only, it was originally found in this size marked 17/0. Three catalogs, one in 1950 and two different ones in 1959, list 17/0 as being 3¾″ high. To date, there is no record of an example, which, when and if found, should be worth at least double that of the larger size. At one time, this was produced in the 8″ size and marked either 17/II or 17/2 (arabic), and any example found should be valued in the high hundreds. These 8″ size and the older marks of the 6″ size are found without socks. Socks were added sometime in the early Seventies. Some Crown pieces have a handle of horn pointed toward the back of the figurine. The original drawing is owned by Verlag Ars Sacra, who produces postcard #14385 from the original drawing. The German name is *Ich Gratulier* or "I Congratulate."

17/0 Congratulations, *no socks,* *TMK-3.*

18   Christ Child

Indicator	Size	Status	TMK-1	TMK-2	TMK-3	TMK-4	TMK-5	TMK-6
18	2″ x 6″	P	P	P	P	P	P	P

The figurine on a pallet without a halo can be distinguished from Infant Jesus, Hum. 214/A/K, which has a halo, and from Infant of Krumbad, Hum. 78, which is not lying on a pad or pallet and also has no halo. Hum. 18 has been made in only the one size but the early catalogs show the size about ½″ larger in both dimensions. An uncataloged rarity is the same figure in white overglaze. An example found in this finish should be valued at two to three times the prices shown for the colored one in the Price List. The 1950 catalog not only lists this model as larger but refers to it as "Christmas Night," apparently from the assigned German name of *Stille Nacht, Jesuskind,* or "Silent Night, Baby Jesus."

18 Christ Child, *TMK-3.*

19   Cancelled

Indicator	Size	Status	TMK-1	TMK-2	TMK-3	TMK-4	TMK-5	TMK-6
19	?	U	—	—	—	—	—	—

A factory record suggests that this was similar to Prayer Before Battle, Hum. 20, done by master modeler Arthur Möller in 1935, but it was not approved by the convent and therefore never issued. No record of a prototype was found in the factory, nor have any been reported from other sources. If ever discovered, the value would be in the mid five-digit range.

20 Prayer Before Battle, *TMK-5.*

20   Prayer Before Battle

Indicator	Size	Status	TMK-1	TMK-2	TMK-3	TMK-4	TMK-5	TMK-6
20(.)	4½″	P	P	P	P	P	P	P

This model was adapted by Arthur Möller in 1935 from Sister Hummel's original drawing which is now owned by Verlag Ars Sacra. It was probably issued shortly after that in the late Thirties. A 1950 catalog lists the size as 4″ high while the current catalogs list it as 4½″. It is found in all trademarks and there seem to have been only minor variations over the course of the years. The demand for this piece usually appears to be in excess of the supply. The German name of *Der fromme Reitersmann* translates as "The Pious Horseman." The original drawing has been lithographed by Ars Sacra as postcard #1442. Prayer before Battle is also one-half of the pair of bookends, Hum. 76 A&B, with 76 A being Doll Mother.

21/I Heavenly Angel, *TMK-5.*

21   Heavenly Angel

Indicator	Size	Status	TMK-1	TMK-2	TMK-3	TMK-4	TMK-5	TMK-6
21/0	4¾″	P	P	P	P	P	P	P
/0/½	6″	P	P	P	P	P	P	P
21	?	U	—	—	—	—	—	—
/I	6¾″	P	P	P	P	P	P	P
/II	8¾″	P	?	P	P	P	P	P

This design is recognized by hundreds of thousands of collectors and dealers because it was used as the bas-relief design on the first M.I. Hummel Annual Plate, Hum. 264, in 1971. That year, Schmid Brothers, Inc., used the same design in transfer form on a similar plate. This figurine is now in great demand for its own merit and also as a companion piece to display in a shadow box along with the 1971 Plate. In a 1947 catalog, Hum. 21 was listed as "Advent Angel" at 4½″ high. In an early 1950s catalog, the figurine was listed in two sizes: 21/0 at 4″ and 21/0/1/2. The 21/0/½ is the only half-size indicator in the Hummel number series. The name in the 1950s catalog was "Little Guardian" or *Christkindlein kommt* in German. While the two larger sizes seem to have been introduced later, they have been reported with all trademarks. This figurine has been reported in white overglaze which would be valued at two to three times the corresponding standard colored one. This motif has also been used for Font, Hum. 207, by the same name. An original drawing of this motif is now owned by Verlag Ars Sacra and reproduced by them as postcard #4773. Verlag Emil Fink also produces a postcard #842 from another original (?) drawing. An interesting note in the same 1950 catalog states that by that time, 187 figurines had been adapted and issued from Sister Hummel's original creations.

22 Sitting Angel with Birds, Holy Water Font

Indicator	Size	Status	TMK-1	TMK-2	TMK-3	TMK-4	TMK-5	TMK-6
22/0	3½"	P	P	P	P	P	P	P
22(.)	4"	D	P	—	—	—	—	—

The title of this font has been expanded to accommodate both the original German name, *Weihkessel, sitzender Engel* and the name in the U.S. catalogs which refers to it as "Angel with Birds" because many fonts appear with only minor design modifications of small children or angels, some with wings and some without. Listed in the 1950 catalog in the two sizes detailed above, the larger size apparently was dropped from the line sometime after that. At that time, the 22/0 size was listed with the same dimensions as at present. Over the years, slight but not necessarily important changes have been made in color, design, and shape of the bowl.

22 Sitting Angel with Birds, *Holy Water Font, TMK-3; alternate name, Sitting Angel.*

23 Adoration

Indicator	Size	Status	TMK-1	TMK-2	TMK-3	TMK-4	TMK-5	TMK-6
/I	6¼"	P	P	P	P	P	P	P
/II(2)	7¾"	D	—	P	—	—	—	—
/III(3)	9"	P	—	?	P	P	P	P

The smaller size, 23/I, was listed as early as 1950 and at that time was only 6¼" high. Only one report is known of this motif in the 23/II size, which was marked 23/2 (arabic) and was 7½" high. It is valued in the low four-digit figures. No record has been received of 23/III in the Crown mark, but it has been noted as 23/3 (arabic), for which add 15 percent to the Price List figures. In TMK-2, 23/1 (arabic) has been found. Both 23/I and 23/III were made in rare, white overglaze and valued in the low four-digit range. In 1978, the large size was restyled in the modern textured finish, probably by Gerhard Skrobek. This large size was not cataloged in the 1974-76 U.S. catalogs. See Shrine Lamp, Hum. 100 for a very rare example of the model. The rare figurine, Adoration with Bird, Hum. 105, is a modification of this design which eliminates the shrine and substitutes a tree with a bird. Also see Bookend, Hum. 90 B, Adoration without Shrine. Hum. 23 has also been cataloged as "At the Shrine," "Ave Maria," and the German name of *Bei Mutter Maria, Marterl,* which translates as "At Mother Maria's." The original drawing is owned by Verlag Emil Fink. Postcard #839 is published by them as are prints #100A and #100G.

23/I Adoration, *TMK-5.*

24 Lullaby, Candleholder

Indicator	Size	Status	TMK-1	TMK-2	TMK-3	TMK-4	TMK-5	TMK-6
24/I(1)	3¼"	P	P	P	P	P	P	P
/III(3)	9"	R	—	P	P	?	R	R

This piece has been produced with two different diameter candles in the small and large sizes. Hum. 24 was found marked 24 (only). Lullaby was listed in the 1950 catalog in only the smaller size as "Cradle Song" which relates to the German name of *Wiegenlied mit Kerzentülle* or "Lullaby Candleholder." This same design was issued later as Heavenly Lullaby figurine, Hum. 262, without the candle socket and in the same size as 24/I. The rare 24/III was reinstated in 1978 in Germany and Canada. It immediately sold at premium prices. If this is left in production, the value of the rare old pieces is very likely to continue to decrease. The original drawing is owned by Verlag Emil Fink. Postcards #214 and #212 have been published by them from the original drawing.

24/III Lullaby, *Candleholder, TMK-3 (see 262).*

25 Angelic Sleep, *Candleholder, no trademark.*

26/0 Child Jesus, *Holy Water Font, rare blue gown.*

27/I Joyous News, *Candleholder, rare, TMK-1, Miller Collection.*

25   Angelic Sleep, Candleholder

Indicator	Size	Status	TMK-1	TMK-2	TMK-3	TMK-4	TMK-5	TMK-6
25	3½″	P	P	P	P	P	P	P

Another candleholder in the style of Lullaby but without the banjo. Apparently only found incised 25, even though some catalogs as recently as 1979 and 1980 list it as 25/I with the same dimensions. It has also been reported in white overglaze which is considered rare and would be valued at three to four times the prices shown in the Price List. This piece was believed to have been issued sometime in the 1940s. According to the German name of *Stille Nacht mit Kerzentülle,* this would have been still another group called "Silent Night," now used in connection with Hum. 31 and Hum. 54 candleholders. The original drawing is owned by Verlag Ars Sacra, who have published a postcard #5608. Verlag Emil Fink published copies of their original as card #211 and print #114.

26   Child Jesus, Holy Water Font

Indicator	Size	Status	TMK-1	TMK-2	TMK-3	TMK-4	TMK-5	TMK-6
26	?	U	?	—	—	—	—	—
/0	5″	P	P	P	P	P	P	P
/I	6″	D	?	P	P	P	—	—

When first issued this figure had a light blue gown (as shown in the photograph on this page). Later, the color was changed to the present dark red color. The date of this change has not been established. The two sizes, about 5″ and 6″ high, were listed as early as the 1950 catalog. Hum. 26/I has been reported only in trademarks 2 and 3, after which it was apparently discontinued. This larger size, 26/I, is scarce and difficult to find. A scalloped edge on the large bowl has been recorded and this would be valued in the high hundreds if found. This design has also been called "Christ Child." The German name is *Weihkessel, Christkindlein* or "Child Jesus, Holy Water Font." Postcard #14269 has been published from the original drawing owned by Verlag Ars Sacra.

27   Joyous News, Candleholder

Indicator	Size	Status	TMK-1	TMK-2	TMK-3	TMK-4	TMK-5	TMK-6
27/I	2¾″	D	P	?	—	—	—	—
/III(3)	4½″	R	P	P	?	—	R	R

Collectors are understandably confused by this model because it is also used for several similar Hummel numbers. The others of similar design are: Angel, Joyous News with Trumpet, III/40; Little Gabriel, a standing figurine, Hum. 32; and Angel with Trumpet, 238C, which is part of Angel Trio B. It also appears in the composite group, Herald Angels, Hum. III/37, a candleholder on a base. Hum. 27 was only available at high prices in the secondary market until 1978 when it was reinstated in the 27/III size as a figurine. The rare version 27/I, no longer in production, has a candle socket near the right or left thigh. Joyous News was found marked 27/3 with old coloring in TMK-5. It is still considered rare with TMK-1 or 2 and incised 27/3 (arabic). Beginning collectors should use caution in paying high prices in the secondary market because of the "lookalikes" and because the larger size has been reinstated. The German name of *O, du fröhliche* translates as "O, You Joyful One."

28   Wayside Devotion

Indicator	Size	Status	TMK-1	TMK-2	TMK-3	TMK-4	TMK-5	TMK-6
28	7″	U	—	—	—	—	—	—
/II(2)	7½″	P	P	P	P	P	P	P
/III(3)	8¾″	P	?	P	P	P	P	P

Even though there are no reports of factory prototypes, 28 has been listed as a possibility and if found would be valued at least in the low four-digit figures. The next size 28/II was listed as only 7″ high in the 1950 catalog. This has been reported in the arabic 2, as has the larger size in the arabic 3, each of which would be valued at 15 percent more than the Price List shows for the Roman numbers. Before 1950 this design was also used for a lamp of the same name, Hum. 104. There are no known examples or factory samples of the lamp. This design without the shrine is called Eventide, Hum. 99. It has also been referred to as "The Little Shepherd," and "Evening Song" which is the name used in German, *Abendlied, Marterl.* The original drawing is owned by Verlag Ars Sacra, who has published postcard #4971 as an exact reproduction.

28/II Wayside Devotion, *TMK-3.*

29   Guardian Angel, Holy Water Font

Indicator	Size	Status	TMK-1	TMK-2	TMK-3	TMK-4	TMK-5	TMK-6
29/0	5¾″	D	P	P	?	—	—	—
29(.)	6″	D	P	P	?	—	—	—
/I	6½″	D	P	P	—	—	—	—

This design was discontinued, probably in the late 1950s, and replaced by Kneeling Angel, Hum. 248. The unsupported wings of Hum. 29 were too easily damaged, so they were backed up and closed, as Hum. 248. It was still being listed in original form in a U.S. 1959 catalog and, therefore, should be found with the first three trademarks. The factory records show this as having been produced in the three sizes although examples are very scarce. One in unrestored mint condition should be valued in the upper hundreds depending on the trademark. The older catalogs refer to all of the fonts as merely "Holy Water Fonts" with no further descriptive name.

29 Guardian Angel, *Holy Water Font, scarce (see 248), TMK-1, courtesy W. Goebel Co.*

30A&B   Ba-Bee Rings

Indicator	Size	Status	TMK-1	TMK-2	TMK-3	TMK-4	TMK-5	TMK-6
30 A&B	4¾″	P	—	—	?	?	P	P
/0/A&B	5″	P	P	P	P	—	—	—
/1/A&B	6″	D	P	?	—	—	—	—

When these were originally issued as a left and right pair in the late Thirties, they were called "Hummel Rings" until the 1950s and, because the word "hummel" means "bumblebee" in German, thus "Bumblebee Rings." They are incised only 30 A and 30 B. The other sizes listed above are earlier marks. This change is believed to have been made sometime in the Fifties when the name was changed. The boy, 30 A, and girl, 30 B, rings are distinguished by the direction they face and the blue ribbon on the girl model. At one time the rings were made in red, and any found in this color would bring a premium in the low four-digit range as only one pair is known at present. What is believed to be the only known 30/I B in bisque color was reported by Arbenz in the *Plate Collector* in October, 1980. Such a rarity would also be valued in four figures. Their German name *Hui, die Hummel, Junge und Madchen, Wandringe* means "Oh, the Hummel boy and girl wall rings." The original drawing is owned by Verlag Ars Sacra, who has produced postcard #5207 from it.

30/A Ba-Bee Ring, *TMK-5.*

31 Advent Group with Black Child (Silent Night), *Candleholder, rare, TMK-1, incised and stamped.*

31   Advent Group with Black Child (Silent Night), Candleholder

Indicator	Size	Status	TMK-1	TMK-2	TMK-3	TMK-4	TMK-5	TMK-6
31	3½"	D	P	P	?	—	—	—

The research is still not complete on this rarity which may have been discontinued by order of the Nazi government. At present, an estimated four or five pieces have been found which show a black child at the left without shoes or stockings. The child also wears a gold earring in his left ear. When found incised "31" on the back, it would have an estimated value in the mid to high four-digit figures. It is not known to have been issued with a white child. Sister Hummel's original drawing shows two black children to the left, a white angel, and a white holy child. This print, #4531, is available from Verlag Ars Sacra, Munich. This is easily confused with Hum. 54 which is another candleholder that has recently been found with a black child in the same position but with shoes. As of now, this would be valued in the higher four to five-digit figures. Another similar group in the current catalogs is Heavenly Song, Hum. 113. It can be distinguished from the other two since the Christ Child has a halo and no clothing. When these similar motifs were first introduced has not been established. At this time, it is assumed that they all originated with modifications from the drawings done by Sister Hummel that are now located in Munich and for which there are cards and prints available from Verlag Ars Sacra, #4531, #4532, #4530, #4529.

32   Little Gabriel

Indicator	Size	Status	TMK-1	TMK-2	TMK-3	TMK-4	TMK-5	TMK-6
32/0	5"	D	?	P	P	?	P	—
32	5"	P	P	P	?	?	P	P
/I	6"	D	?	P	P	?	—	—

While current catalogs list this model as Hum. 32, factory records show that older models were originally produced as Hum. 32/0 about 5" high, and also as 32/1 about 6" high. The dates these were discontinued has not been established. Examples of the large size should be valued around three to four hundred dollars depending on the trademark. Recently, 32/0 has been reported in TMK-5. This standing figurine is similar to the seated ones called Joyous News, Hum. 27, and Hum. 238 C. Sister Hummel's original drawing was made of a similar standing figure and is located at Verlag Ars Sacra. The German name is *0, du fröhliche, Engel* or "Oh, You Joyful Angel."

32/0 Little Gabriel, *TMK-3.*

33   Joyful, Ashtray

Indicator	Size	Status	TMK-1	TMK-2	TMK-3	TMK-4	TMK-5	TMK-6
33	3½"	P	P	P	P	P	P	P

The numbering sequence indicates that this figure was used for the first ashtray introduced by Goebel in this line. In addition, this figure was used on the ashtray before it became the separate figurine, Joyful, Hum. 53, or the Candy Box, Hum. III/53. It was also used in the designs of two model numbers for which there is no record of production, Bookends, Hum. 120, and another design of Ashtray, Hum. 216. Some sources have indicated that this is a likely subject for the Annual Bell. Designed and issued before 1950, it is found in all trademarks with minor variations. The German name is *Ascher, Gesangsprobe,* or "Ashtray, Singing Rehearsal." Another reported name is "Boy with Mandolin and Bird." The original drawing for all of these related issues is owned by Verlag Ars Sacra. It is available in postcards as #14284.

33 Joyful, *Ashtray, TMK-3.*

34 Singing Lesson, Ashtray

Indicator	Size	Status	TMK-1	TMK-2	TMK-3	TMK-4	TMK-5	TMK-6
34	3½″	P	P	P	P	P	P	P

Was the second ashtray in the line and also produced before its companion figurine, Hum. 63. Both pieces were made before World War II. Hum. 34 is found in all trademarks with little variation in size, design, and coloring. A 1950 U.S. catalog refers to this piece as "Ashtray, Boy with Raven" which highlights the difference between the ashtray and the figurine, Hum. 63, the candy box, Hum. III/63, and the bas-relief of this motif used on the 1979 Annual Plate, Hum. 272. The ashtray is the only adaptation of this motif that shows a raven. All the others use a differently shaped yellow bird. When Sister Hummel made her original drawing, which is now owned by Ars Sacra, it was done with a yellow bird up in a tree as depicted on the 1979 Plate. Some minor variations may be encountered in comparing examples of different ages. The German name is *Ash, 's stimmt net,* or "It's Not Right." The original drawing was reproduced by Ars Sacra as postcard #14701.

34 Singing Lesson, *Ashtray, TMK-5.*

35 The Good Shepherd, Holy Water Font

Indicator	Size	Status	TMK-1	TMK-2	TMK-3	TMK-4	TMK-5	TMK-6
35/0	4¾″	P	P	P	P	P	P	P
35	5″	D	P	?	—	—	—	—
/I	5½″	D	P	P	—	—	—	—

Apparently, the first version of this font issued before World War II was incised with only the whole number, 35. This size was later cataloged as 35/I, also 5½″ high. By 1950, a smaller size, 35/0, 4¾″ high, was for sale at the same time. This motif was also used for the figurine Good Shepherd, Hum. 42, which in the smaller size also had a light blue robe but with slightly different pattern. For information on the original drawing and graphics available, see Hum. 42. Its German name, *Der gute Hirte,* translates the same as the English name. The original drawing is owned by Verlag Ars Sacra. Graphic postcards were produced as #14268.

35/0 The Good Shepherd, *Holy Water Font, TMK-5.*

36 Angel (Child) with Flowers, Holy Water Font

Indicator	Size	Status	TMK-1	TMK-2	TMK-3	TMK-4	TMK-5	TMK-6
36/0	4″	P	—	P	P	P	P	P
36(.)	4¼″	D	P	?	—	—	—	—
36/I	4½″	D	P	—	—	—	—	—

This font is usually cataloged and referred to as "Angel with Flowers," although it has also been recorded in German as *Kind mit Blumen* or "Child with Flowers" which is a more accurate name. Since the halo indicates spirituality, it has been listed as Angel and Child in this book, to minimize confusion. Some modifications in design, color, and size have occurred over the years. It appears to have been first issued as 36 (only) or 36. (decimal); later the piece was listed as 36/I for the 4½″ size and is still listed in current catalogs in the 36/0 size, 4″ high. In some cases, the rim of the halo is plain, in others ribbed. The shoes are either black or brown. These changes have not been associated with any trademarks.

36 Angel (Child) with Flowers, *Holy Water Font, TMK-1, incised and stamped.*

37 Herald Angels, *Candleholder,*
TMK-5.

37 Herald Angels, Candleholder

Indicator	Size	Status	TMK-1	TMK-2	TMK-3	TMK-4	TMK-5	TMK-6
37	2½"	P	P	P	P	P	P	P

This composite group of three angels on a common base is another pre-World War II issue. When first issued, the candle socket in the center was over 1" high. At some indefinite date, the height of the candle socket was reduced to about ½" high. Since this is a hand-assembled piece, the placement of the three figures may vary as may the dimensions and coloring. Any known deviations are allowed for in the Price List. There is a note in a catalog from the Fifties that no candle was furnished with this holder. At that time, candles were usually included. The similarity between the horn player and Joyous News, Hum. 27 is obvious. The three figures in Hum. 37 are sold separately without bases as Joyous News, Angel Candleholders (cataloged together as Angel Trio A), Hum. 38, 39, and 40 which follow. The German name for this Herald Angel group on a common base is *Adventsleuchter mid drei Engeln* or "Advent Candleholder with Three Angels." There are no other known forms of Hummel art of this composite group.

III/38/0 Angel, Joyous News with
Lute, *Candleholder, TMK-5, Trio (A).*

III/39/0 Angel, Joyous News with
Accordion, *Candleholder, TMK-5,*
Trio (A).

38 Angel, Joyous News with Lute

Indicator	Size	Status	TMK-1	TMK-2	TMK-3	TMK-4	TMK-5	TMK-6
I/38/0	2"	D	?	?	?	—	—	—
III/38/0	2"	P	P	P	P	P	P	P
III/38/I	2¾"	D	?	P	?	—	—	—

Since the inception of this model in the late Thirties, it has been issued in the two sizes shown, but not always concurrently. The early catalog shows the smaller size, 38/0, as 2" high, and the 1959 catalog shows this size as 2½". In the 1959 catalog 38/I, the large size, is 3" high. Note that the smaller size 38/0 was produced with two different sized candle sockets. The small size candle socket is 6 mm in diameter; the larger socket is 1 cm in diameter. This socket size difference is sometimes designated in catalogs with a prefix usually reserved for candy boxes. Roman numeral I is sometimes used to catalog the small candle socket; Roman numeral III is sometimes used for the larger socket, and only one is currently produced. The candle size I and III are not incised on the figurines. The differences between this figurine and Joyful, Hum. 53, are the candle socket, the wings, and the hair styling and coloring of the gown. This has also been known as "The Little Advent Angel with Lute" with the German name merely "Advent Angel with Lute" or *Adventsengelchen mit Laute*. Similar representations of this piece in other forms of Hummel art can be obtained by referring to Joyful, Hum. 53.

39 Angel, Joyous News with Accordion

Indicator	Size	Status	TMK-1	TMK-2	TMK-3	TMK-4	TMK-5	TMK-6
I/39/0	2"	D	?	?	?	—	—	—
III/39/0	2"	P	P	P	P	P	P	P
III/39/I	2¾"	D	?	P	?	—	—	—

The remarks about Hum. 38 pertain to Hum. 39, also, except for name and design. There are no other "lookalikes" for this one of the group called Angel Trio A, Candleholders. These three, Hum. 38, 39, and 40, are usually priced as a group, but sold separately at one-third of the total price. The only difference found in researching names is that the name of the instrument was called a "concertina" in the German name, *Adventsengelchen mit Bandoneon* and the similar English, "Little Advent Angel with Concertina."

40 Angel, Joyous News with Trumpet

Indicator	Size	Status	TMK-1	TMK-2	TMK-3	TMK-4	TMK-5	TMK-6
I/40/0	2″	D	?	?	—	—	—	—
III/40/0	2″	P	P	P	P	P	P	P
III/40/I	2¾″	D	?	?	—	—	—	—

See Hum. 38 and 39 for common remarks. It is important to note the difference between Hum. 40 and the very rare, discontinued Joyous News, Hum. 27/1. Besides the several thousand dollars difference in price, the candle socket in Hum. 40 is attached to the right hip, whereas in Hum. 27/1 it is attached at the left knee. That is quite a premium from right to left and hip to knee. Hum. 40 is also sold as part of a set and cataloged that way. The original drawing is owned by Verlag Ars Sacra. Graphics of the original were produced as postcard #14440 by them.

III/40/0 Angel with Trumpet, *Candleholder, TMK-5, Trio (A).*

41 Cancelled Number

Indicator	Size	Status	TMK-1	TMK-2	TMK-3	TMK-4	TMK-5	TMK-6
41	?	U	—	—	—	—	—	—

Recent research of the factory records by collector Robert Miller indicates that this number was provisionally assigned to a design similar to the ashtray Singing Lesson, Hum. 34, but, after further consideration, it was cancelled in October, 1935. No prototypes or examples have yet to be found. If the improbable discovery should happen, the value would be probably be somewhere in the low four-digit range. Since prototypes of other cancelled numbers (Hum. 77) have been found in private hands, someday an example of Hum. 41 may be available for illustrating.

42 Good Shepherd

Indicator	Size	Status	TMK-1	TMK-2	TMK-3	TMK-4	TMK-5	TMK-6
42/0	6¼″	D	P	P	P	—	—	—
42(.)	6¼″	P	P	?	?	?	P	P
/I	7½″	D	?	P	?	—	—	—

The German name *Der gute Hirte* translates essentially as "The Good Shepherd." This piece was designed in the mid-Thirties and issued before World War II. Examples of 42/0 have been found with a very light blue robe with TMK-1, TMK-2, and TMK-3. This version and the larger 42/I have both been inconsistently cataloged and finally discontinued with these size indicators probably in late Fifties. They are considered premium pieces, as shown in the Price List. They were superseded by the currently cataloged 6¼″ size as Hum. 42 without any size indicator and decorated in a golden rust colored robe. This same design and name is used for Holy Water Font, Hum. 35. Prints and postcards (#14268) of Sister Hummel's original drawing are now published and sold by Ars Sacra. The original drawing is also owned by the same publishing firm.

42 Good Shepherd, *TMK-5.*

43 March Winds, *TMK-5.*

44 A Culprits, *Table Lamp, TMK-2.*

44 B Out of Danger, *Table Lamp,*
TMK-4.

43   March Winds

Indicator	Size	Status	TMK-1	TMK-2	TMK-3	TMK-4	TMK-5	TMK-6
43(.)	5″	P	P	P	P	P	P	P

While this has been made in only one size, incised 43, since being designed in the mid-Thirties and issued somewhat later, numerous size variations are found due to mold growth or possibly mold redesign. When issued, it carried the German name of *Lausbub* for "Rascal," the name given to it by Sister Hummel. This piece is being produced in graphics as postcard #4780 from the original drawing which is now owned by Verlag Ars Sacra. A Dubler figurine made in the U.S. during World War II is similar to this motif, as is one of the "Our Children" series imported by Napco from Japan.

44 A   Culprits, Table Lamp

Indicator	Size	Status	TMK-1	TMK-2	TMK-3	TMK-4	TMK-5	TMK-6
M44/A	9½″	P	P	P	P	P	P	P

Numerous names have been employed since Culprits was first copyrighted in 1935 and issued a short time thereafter. Some of these are "Out on a Limb," which was used in U.S. copyrights GP1820 and GP1821 on October 6, 1950; "Boy in Tree" (1950 catalog), and *Apfeldieb Junge* for "Applethief Boy." This is the first number to be divided into a related pair (44 A, 44 B), and it is also noteworthy because it was the first lamp design and the lamp preceded the design of the figurine, 56/A. Recently Culprits has been found incised with 44 (only). This example is valued at 50 percent more than one incised 44 A. Speculation indicates that this lamp/figurine was issued prior to 44 B, Out of Danger. This is further supported by the 1935 copyright on 44 A and the 1936 date on 44 B. The original drawings have been reproduced in lithographs by Verlag Emil Fink in Stuttgart as postcard #223. The original drawing is also owned by Fink. Both the height and design of the lamps changed over the years.

44 B   Out of Danger, Table Lamp

Indicator	Size	Status	TMK-1	TMK-2	TMK-3	TMK-4	TMK-5	TMK-6
M44/B	9½″	P	P	P	P	P	P	P

The remarks about the other half of this pair apply except for the names which, in addition to "Out of Danger," were "Out on a Limb," "Girl in a Tree," and the German *In Sicherheit, Mädchen* for "Girl in Safety." This design carries an incised 1936 copyright date, a year later than 44 A. It seems likely that Sister Hummel made two similar originals of Culprits and Out of Danger as she did of other boys and girls such as Apple Tree Boy and Girl and Umbrella Boy and Girl. However, research for this book has failed to locate any drawing that resembles a girl having been chased up a tree by a dog that was close enough to have grabbed one shoe.

45 Madonna with Halo

Indicator	Size	Status	TMK-1	TMK-2	TMK-3	TMK-4	TMK-5	TMK-6
45/0/6	10½″	P	P	P	P	P	P	P
/0/13	10½″	D	?	?	—	—	—	—
/0/W	10½″	P	—	P	P	P	P	P
/I/6	12″	R	?	?	?	?	R	R
/I/W	12″	R	—	?	P	?	R	R
/III/6	16¾″	R	—	P	P	?	R	R
/III/W	16¾″	R	—	P	?	?	R	R

This piece has also been referred to as "Virgin with Halo," "Holy Virgin," and the German *Madonna mit Heiligenschein* equivalent to its present name. As would be expected of such a popular piece, Hum. 45 has been issued in an array of sizes and size variations since its introduction in the late Thirties. The numbers and letters following the size designator above of "6," "13," and "W" refer to color and finishing and do not appear as part of the model/size number incised on the bottom of each piece. The "13" indicates one decorated with a colored robe; "/W" indicates pieces finished in a white glaze; and "6" indicates current pastel color. Examples of this design have been found marked 45/1 (arabic), 45 (only), and 45. (decimal), and 45/3. Both Hum. 45 and Hum. 46 have been reported in pastel pink, ivory, and dark blue. Several examples mismarked as 46 are known to exist as well as some examples incised with both 45 and 46 on the same figure. Any madonna that is incised HM before the model/size designators is not a genuine M.J.Hümmel but rather a madonna made by Goebel and created by one of their sculptors. Refer to chapter, "Goebel — Not Hummel Figurines" for more information.

46 Madonna without Halo

Indicator	Size	Status	TMK-1	TMK-2	TMK-3	TMK-4	TMK-5	TMK-6
46/0/6	10¼″	P	P	P	P	P	P	P
/0/W	10¼″	P	—	P	P	P	P	P
/I/6	11¼″	P	?	P	P	?	P	P
/I/W	11½″	P	P	P	P	P	P	P
/III/6	16¾″	R	—	P	?	?	R	R
/III/W	16¾″	R	—	P	?	?	R	R

This version of the madonna created by Sister Hummel is most frequently referred to as Madonna without Halo which is the German name *Madonna ohne Heiligenschein,* also cataloged as "Praying Madonna." It is available in a similar range of sizes and color finishes as its counterpart, Hum. 45. In 1978 a very rare and unusual madonna in this design, made of terra-cotta or brick red material, was discovered by a very alert Hummel collector. It had been sent many years ago with an order of regular figurines to a dealer/wood carver who has treasured it for thirty-odd years. For some unknown reason, it was incised "18" on the bottom and inscribed M.J.Hümmel It is pictured on this page along with a very similar piece except for the added child. The right-hand piece was marked "Erphila" a contraction of Ebling & Reuss, Philadelphia, one of Goebel's distributors. These two ultra-rarities are now in the Robert L. Miller collection. This model has also been found with dual or reverse numbers, as was Hum. 45. The original drawings for these two of the many madonnas she created have not been located but are likely to be in the Siessen Convent, as none of the graphics published to date correspond to Hum. 45 or Hum. 46.

45/0 Madonna with Halo, *TMK-2.*

46/0 Madonna without Halo, *TMK-5.*

46 (L) Madonna without Halo, *incised M.I. Hummel, 18, stamped black "Made in Germany," rare terra-cotta. (R) Terra-cotta madonna and child, "HUMMEL" on bottom. Miller Collection.*

47/0 Goose Girl, *TMK-5.*

47   Goose Girl

Indicator	Size	Status	TMK-1	TMK-2	TMK-3	TMK-4	TMK-5	TMK-6
47/3/0	4″	P	?	P	P	P	P	P
/0	4¾″	P	P	P	P	P	P	P
47	5½″	D	P	—	—	—	—	—
/II(2)	7½″	P	P	P	P	P	P	P

The 5½″ size of this popular motif was listed as 47 (only) in the 1947 catalog and priced at $7.50, less than one-tenth of today's price. This model has been widely reproduced by various makers in the U.S., but WITHOUT the M.I. Hummel facsimile signature and not only in porcelain but also in glass. It appears as the motif on the 1974 plate and as one of the pair of bookends, Hum. 60 B. Some of the earlier issues were made with a projection between the two geese painted green and referred to by collectors as a "blade of grass." This commands a premium of 50 percent over the value in the Price List. Two extremely rare, perfect versions of Goose Girl in Serbian costume from the International Figurine Series with 947/0 incised on the bottom are known. One is in the collection of Robert L. Miller and the other is owned by an original owner. Other examples of this design are the lithographs from Sister Hummel's original drawing produced as postcard #220 by Verlag Emil Fink.

48/0 Madonna, *Plaque (see 222), TMK-3.*

48   Madonna, Plaque

Indicator	Size	Status	TMK-1	TMK-2	TMK-3	TMK-4	TMK-5	TMK-6
48	?	U	—	—	—	—	—	—
/0	4″	P	P	P	P	P	P	P
/II(2)	6″	R	P	P	?	?	R	R
/V(5)	10″	D	P	P	?	?	—	—

This bas-relief plaque is an adaption of Sister Hummel's well-known drawing called the "Madonna in Red." It has received a wide distribution as postcard #5204 by Verlag Ars Sacra. An original drawing is also owned by Emil Fink and was issued as #808 and #981. While the 48/0 size has been continuously available since World War II, the other two sizes were discontinued at some unknown time. The intermediate size, 48/II, was reintroduced in 1978 in Germany, Canada, and the U.S., with TMK-5. The older marks are still scarce. This has also been found as 48/2, with the arabic size indicator. It is reported to have been sold in white overglaze in the two smaller sizes. If found, these would be worth at least double the amounts shown in the Price List. See Hum. 222 for similar plaque with wire frame. These plaques have also been called "Virgin with Child" and *Madonnenbild* in German, or "Madonna Picture."

49/0 To Market, *TMK-3.*

49   To Market

Indicator	Size	Status	TMK-1	TMK-2	TMK-3	TMK-4	TMK-5	TMK-6
49/3/0	4″	P	?	P	P	P	P	P
/2/0	4½″	D	?	P	—	—	—	—
/0	5½″	P	P	P	P	P	P	P
49(.)	6¼″	R	P	?	—	—	R	R
/I	6¼″	R	P	P	—	—	R	R

So far only the 4″ and 5½″ sizes, 49/3/0 and 49/0 respectively, have been found in all marks. The 49/I, 6¼″, was discontinued at some time. Old mark examples are very scarce, and reinstated figures with TMK-5 are incised 49 instead of the old marking, 49/I. The To Market motif has also been used in two table lamps, Hum. 101 and 223. Hum. 49/3/0, the smallest size, is produced without a bottle in the basket. No original drawing or graphic in this exact design has been located, indicating that possibly two similar originals were combined to form this adaptation.

50 Volunteers

Indicator	Size	Status	TMK-1	TMK-2	TMK-3	TMK-4	TMK-5	TMK-6
50/2/0	5″	P	?	P	P	P	P	P
/0	5½″	R	P	P	P	—	R	R
50(.)	6½″	D	P	?	—	—	—	—
/I	6½″	R	?	P	P	—	R	R

Was the adaptation of this drawing inspired by the conditions in Germany when it was designed in the Thirties? An example with the early Crown mark incised with only 50. (decimal) has been reported. Of the three sizes currently offered, the two larger sizes, 50/0 and 50/I, were not available in the U.S. for some years. These two pieces were reintroduced in 1979 with the TMK-5, some of which were dated "79" by the artist. Depending on how many of these are made with this date mark, these reissues could also turn out to be scarce examples of this model. The German name for this motif is *Soldatenspiel* or "Playing Soldiers." The original drawing is unlocated at present.

50/2/0 Volunteers, *TMK-5.*

51 Village Boy

Indicator	Size	Status	TMK-1	TMK-2	TMK-3	TMK-4	TMK-5	TMK-6
51/3/0	4″	P	?	P	P	P	P	P
/2/0	5¼″	P	?	P	P	P	P	P
/0	6″	P	P	P	P	P	P	P
51	?	U	—	—	—	—	—	—
51/I	7¼″	R	P	P	?	?	R	R

Currently available in four sizes, of which the largest is Hum. 51/I, Village Boy was reintroduced in 1978 in Germany and Canada in a limited quantity after being unavailable for some years. It was listed in the 1947 catalog. The other sizes have been reported in all trademarks although they are not listed in all U.S. yearly catalogs. As with so many other motifs, this piece was restyled with more sculptured hair and brighter colors, as indicated by U.S. Copyright GF56, dated December 20, 1961. The new pieces are also incised with the 1961 copyright date. The German name for Village Boy is *Dorfbub*, and many of its companion pieces are listed in the paragraph about Hum. 49. This appears to be the boy on the right in graphic F665 published by Verlag Emil Fink from an original owned by them.

51/2/0 Village Boy, *TMK-5.*

52 Going to Grandma's

Indicator	Size	Status	TMK-1	TMK-2	TMK-3	TMK-4	TMK-5	TMK-6
52/0	4¾″	P	P	P	P	P	P	P
52(.)	6¼″	D	P	P	—	—	—	—
/I	6″	R	P	P	?	—	R	R

Another one of the pre-war designs that is currently produced in the two sizes listed. It seems likely that the 52. (decimal) was replaced at some period by the 52/I as both are about 6″ high. Unavailable in the U.S. in this size for many years, 52/I was reintroduced in 1979. Some examples may have the new artist's date, "79," and some may not. It still has the square base that was common to both old sizes. The small size, Hum. 52/0, was restyled and put on an oval base sometime in the Sixties, although there was no record found in the U.S. Copyright Office. The smaller size has always contained cookies or candy in a cone representative of a packaging method used at that time. The larger sizes appear to have an empty cone. The German name for this model is *Hausmütterchen* or "Housemother." The original drawing has not been found.

52/0 Going to Grandma's, *TMK-5.*

53   Joyful

Indicator	Size	Status	TMK-1	TMK-2	TMK-3	TMK-4	TMK-5	TMK-6
53(.)	4″	P	P	P	P	P	P	P

While Joyful apparently has been listed in catalogs as issued in only one size over the years, it is found smaller than the 3¾″ once cataloged and as large as 4¼″. When found as large as 4¼″ a 20 percent premium should be added to the prices in the Price List. Known earlier as "Banjo Betty," the German name is *Gesangsprobe* or "Singing Rehearsal." It also appears as a candy box (see), as one of the set of bookends, Hum. 120 (no known examples), and previously as Hum. 33, Joyful Ashtray. Hum. 53 is one of the motifs that has been considered as a possibility for the design on a future bell. Sister M. I. Hummel's original drawing is unlocated to date.

53 Joyful, *TMK-5.*

III/53   Joyful, Candy Box

Indicator	Size	Status	TMK-1	TMK-2	TMK-3	TMK-4	TMK-5	TMK-6
III/53	6¼″	P	P	P	P	P	P	P

This candy box, when first designed and released in the 1930s, was rounded in the form of a semisphere or bowl and the cover was slightly crowned and designed to fit inside and flush with the top edges of the bowl. In the early 1960s the box was redesigned, along with other candy boxes, in a cylindrical shape with vertical sides and a flanged top which was flush with the sides. The prices in the Price List include the old design for TMK-1 through 3. It is possible that there was some overlapping of the marks when the new design was being introduced.

III/53 Joyful, *Candy Box, new style box, TMK-5.*

54   Silent Night, Candleholder

Indicator	Size	Status	TMK-1	TMK-2	TMK-3	TMK-4	TMK-5	TMK-6
54	3¾″	P	P	P	P	P	P	P

This model can be and frequently is confused with Hum. 31 (see). The essential difference seems to be that the very few examples of Hum. 31 which have been found have a black child at the left of the group. This Hum. 31 child wears an earring but no shoes; his hair is smooth and less detailed than that of the same white children in Hum. 54. Sometimes these two model numbers are both referred to as "Silent Night" which further compounds the confusion. Since Hum. 54 is currently cataloged as "Silent Night," this book refers to Hum. 31 as "Advent Group (with Black Child)" to which the German name alludes. The German name for Hum. 54, however, is *Stille Nacht, Krippe mit Kerzentülle* or "Silent Night, Creche with Candleholder." An event in 1979 further stimulated questions when a reader reported an example of Hum. 54 with a black child. The incised 54 on the back was verified. The photograph on page 174 shows the black child with shoes and an earring. It has a Crown trademark. Pending further discoveries, both of the aforementioned Hummels with black children are very rare pieces which have a value somewhere in the upper four-digit figures. The original drawing is owned by Verlag Ars Sacra. They have published postcard #4532 from the original.

54 Silent Night, *Candleholder, trademark unknown.*

55 Saint George

Indicator	Size	Status	TMK-1	TMK-2	TMK-3	TMK-4	TMK-5	TMK-6
55	6¾″	P	P	P	P	P	P	P

This piece is often called the "most unusual Hummel" even though it is of definite religious origin. A representation of this mythical medieval English knight and patron saint of soldiers is frequently found in churches and may have been done by Sister Hummel in an unknown church, just as she did the drawing of St. Conrad in her own parish church. Saint George has also been reported in white overglaze which is so rare in most motifs that the value is usually at least double that of a similar, colored one that originally sold for more money. At least one of these figurines with early trademarks has been reported with dark red saddle. In addition to "Saint George," Hum. 55 has been called "St. George and the Dragon" and "Knight Saint George" after the German name *Ritter Heiliger Georg*. There is no lithographic reproduction of the drawing.

55 Saint George, *TMK-5*.

56/A Culprits

Indicator	Size	Status	TMK-1	TMK-2	TMK-3	TMK-4	TMK-5	TMK-6
56(.)	6¼″	P	P	P	P	P	P	P
/A	6¼″	P	P	P	P	P	P	P

This figurine was preceded by Hum. 44/A, essentially the same design in the form of the first numbered lamp, which was about 2″ taller. This was also introduced in the Thirties and listed in an early 1947 catalog as Apple Thief, Boy, which is also the translation of its German name, *Apfeldieb, Junge*. At that time it was listed for $9 and marked 56 only, indicating the companion Out of Danger was not listed until somewhat later in the Fifties. It has also been reported as 56. (decimal). In these earlier, smoother models the boy was not looking directly down at the dog as in later, restyled versions. A picture of this figure appears in the May, 1962, calendar. The original drawing is owned by Verlag Emil Fink, and graphics have been published by them as postcard #223.

56/A Culprits, *TMK-5*.

56/B Out of Danger

Indicator	Size	Status	TMK-1	TMK-2	TMK-3	TMK-4	TMK-5	TMK-6
56/B	6¼″	P	P	P	P	P	P	P

The same general comments on Hum. 56/B apply in this case to the lamp 44 B. This piece is listed in a 1959 catalog for $9. The apron seems to be flatter in the figurine than in some of the lamps. Examples of Hum. 56 B made in the Fifties showed the girl looking straight ahead (called eyes open by collectors). When restyled in a textured finish in the Sixties the girl was sculpted looking down at the dog (called "eyes closed" by collectors). This piece was illustrated in full color in the May, 1962, calendar. The original name was "Girl in Safety," which is the translation of the present German name, *In Sicherheit, Mädchen*.

56/B Out of Danger, *TMK-5*.

57/0 Chick Girl, *TMK-5.*

57   Chick Girl

Indicator	Size	Status	TMK-1	TMK-2	TMK-3	TMK-4	TMK-5	TMK-6
57/0	3½"	P	P	P	P	P	P	P
57(.)	4¼"	D	P	P	—	—	—	—
57/I	4¼"	P	P	P	P	P	P	P

This model, introduced in the Thirties and originally marked only 57 or 57. (decimal), was listed as 4″ high in the 1947 catalog. Later this designation was changed to 57/0 in a 1950 catalog for the 3¼″ size, and, at the same time, the larger size 57/I was listed at 4¼″. This larger size has three chicks in the basket instead of two as in the small first version. Presently 57/0 and 57/I are listed as 3½″ and 4¼″, respectively. An example of 57/0 has been verified without a chick near the girl's right foot and valued at a mid three-digit figure. This design is also used for the candy box, III/57, and as one of the pair of bookends, 61 B. It is scheduled to appear as the motif on the 1985 plate. The piece illustrated on this page is the smaller size with the TMK-5. "Little Chick Girl" was an earlier name, as was "Little Chick Mother," the translation of its German name, *Kükenmütterchen.* The original drawing is owned by Verlag Ars Sacra, and postcard #4951 has been published by them from the original.

III/57 Chick Girl, *Candy Box, new style box, TMK-5.*

III/57   Chick Girl, Candy Box

Indicator	Size	Status	TMK-1	TMK-2	TMK-3	TMK-4	TMK-5	TMK-6
III/57	6¼"	P	P	P	P	P	P	P

The Roman three (III) prefix is used to indicate that model 57 has been superimposed on a candy box. This was also an early issue at which time the shape of the box was curved in cup or bowl shape and the top was inset flush with the sides. In the early Sixties, the box was redesigned so that the bottom is now made with vertical sides with the cap-style cover in the same diameter and flush with the sides. The original drawing is the same one mentioned previously.

58/I Playmates, *TMK-3.*

58   Playmates

Indicator	Size	Status	TMK-1	TMK-2	TMK-3	TMK-4	TMK-5	TMK-6
58/0	4"	P	P	P	P	P	P	P
58	?	U	—	—	—	—	—	—
/I	4¼"	P	P	P	P	P	P	P

A companion piece to Hum. 57, Chick Girl, Playmates was listed in the 1947 catalog at 4″ high. The figurine has been reported with the marking 58/1 (arabic) at 15 percent premium over the regular model. One version of Hum. 58 is pictured with the ears of the farthest rabbit on the reader's left erect. The smaller size is styled with the ears more relaxed and separated. This design is now planned to be used on the Annual Plate for 1986. As with its companion, Chick Girl, it is paired on the bookends as 61A and also as the candy box listed next, III/58. One reader reported her 58/0 example had a deep diagonal scratch through the trademark, inviting speculation that a few "seconds" may have slipped out of the factory. "Just Friends" was an alternate name used in the 1947 U.S. catalog and "Rabbit Father" is the same as the German name, *Hasenvater.* A full-color picture of Playmates was used for the month of April in the 1974 calendar. The original drawing is owned by Verlag Ars Sacra, from which postcard #4950 was produced.

III/58　Playmates, Candy Box

Indicator	Size	Status	TMK-1	TMK-2	TMK-3	TMK-4	TMK-5	TMK-6
III/58	6¼″	P	P	P	P	P	P	P

See III/57, Chick Girl, Candy Box, for the story on marking and design changes in the box. So far there has been only one report of this candy box with the Crown mark, TMK-1. On the newer style box, the far right rabbit's ears follow the positioning of the ones in 58/0. Both shapes of boxes have been used on this as mentioned under III/57. The curved sided, bowl-shaped box usually has TMK-1, 2, or 3. The straight-sided cylinder design may have TMK-3 through 6. The original drawing is the same one used for Hum. 58.

III/58 Playmates, *Candy Box, new style box, TMK-5.*

59　Skier

Indicator	Size	Status	TMK-1	TMK-2	TMK-3	TMK-4	TMK-5	TMK-6
59(.)	5″	P	P	P	P	P	P	P

Another design from the Thirties, it is listed in the 1947 U.S. catalog as 5½″ high for $7.50. In present catalogs the size is 5″, although variations occur. These early models had wooden poles and wooden fiber disks. At an indefinite date, poles were changed to wooden with metal disks, then to metal or plastic poles. Any examples with the oldest trademarks should have original wooden poles. Since these are easily lost, they sometimes were replaced with small new wooden skewers. If the latest models, TMK-5 or 6, are found with wooden poles, these are not original and should be rejected or judged as such. The Price List values are only for figurines with poles that are original to the piece. A good picture of this model can be found on the December page of the 1978 calendar. The German name of *Ski-Heil* translates as "Hail, Skiing." The original drawing owned by Ars Sacra was used for a graphic produced as postcard #14259.

59 Skier, *no trademark.*

60 A　Farm Boy, 60 B　Goosegirl, Bookends

Indicator	Size	Status	TMK-1	TMK-2	TMK-3	TMK-4	TMK-5	TMK-6
60 A&B	4¾″	P	P	P	P	P	P	P

These two Bavarian country children are coupled as bookends and are sold only as a pair. These early-design bookends have the figures mounted directly on the wooden base, whereas the later ones such as Apple Tree Boy and Girl, 252 A, and 252 B, have the figurines on the normal integral ceramic base which is mounted and glued to the wooden bookends. For this reason, the trademark is on the wooden base itself, rather than on the figurine. Refer to Goose Girl, Hum. 47, and Farm Boy, Hum. 66, for more history. An early 1950s catalog indicates these were listed as only Hum. 60 at 6″ high compared to the present 4¾″.

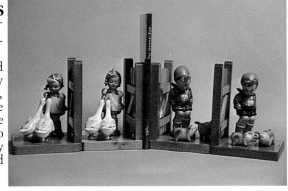

60 A&B Farm Boy and Goose Girl, *Bookends, TMK-3.*

61 A&B Playmates and Chick Girl,
Bookends, TMK-3.

61 A Playmates, 61 B Chick Girl, Bookends

Indicator	Size	Status	TMK-1	TMK-2	TMK-3	TMK-4	TMK-5	TMK-6
61 A&B	4″	P	P	P	P	P	P	P

Refer to the figurines Hum. 58 and Hum. 57 for further details. Like the preceding pair of Hum. 60 bookends, these figures were also mounted directly on the wooden bases rather than the composite figurine and base mounted on the wooden platforms as in the later designs. Again, these are trademarked on the back of the wooden base as were Hum. 60 A&B. In the 1950 catalog these also were listed as only Hum. 61 and, therefore, might be found marked that way. By 1965, the catalogs listed them with separate alphabetical letters. They were originally listed at 6″ high versus 4″ which is now the specified size.

62 Happy Pastime, *Ashtray,*
TMK-3.

62　Happy Pastime, Ashtray

Indicator	Size	Status	TMK-1	TMK-2	TMK-3	TMK-4	TMK-5	TMK-6
62	3½″	P	P	P	P	P	P	P

Another case where the motif was probably first used on a functional piece before it was introduced as the separate figurine, Happy Pastime, Hum. 69. Sister Hummel's original drawing shows the bird in an adjacent tree, somewhat as it is positioned in the 1978 Annual Plate which has the same motif in bas-relief form. An early catalog shows this piece as being only 8 cm high as compared to 9 cm or 3½″ high at present. First called "Ashtray with Knitter," other names are "Little Knitter," and "Knitting Liesl," the translation of the German name *Stickliesl.* It is reported that one of the early marks, TMK-1, had the incised facsimile signature on the back of the tray. The current models have the signature on the back of the figure. Such deviations and small changes that may have occurred in design are allowed for in the Price List. However, there is always the possibility of something not yet recorded. The figurine itself, Hum. 69, has been used for an illustration for the month of December in the 1969 calendar. Refer to Hum. 69, Happy Pastime, for further details.

63　Singing Lesson

Indicator	Size	Status	TMK-1	TMK-2	TMK-3	TMK-4	TMK-5	TMK-6
63(.)	2¾″	P	P	P	P	P	P	P

Some of the compromises that had to be made in adapting Sister Hummel's originals into three-dimensional figures can be seen by comparing the bas-relief motif on the 1979 Annual Plate, Hum. 272, with the photograph of Singing Lesson, Hum. 63. For the figurine, the bird had to be placed on the boy's toe rather than in the tree. Note that the birds on the plate, figurine, and candy box represent one species, while the bird on the ashtray, Hum. 34, is quite different and was referred to as a raven in the early catalog. This introduction in the Thirties was listed in the 1950 catalog as "Duet." It has been made with variations in size and also in the assembly of the components. Minor differences such as these, if significant, are allowed for in the Price List. Frequently this piece commands a premium at auctions and sales because it is often paired with the 1979 Annual Plate, Hum. 272, for display in shadow boxes. The figurine was pictured in the 1969 calendar for the month of May. The original drawing is owned by Verlag Ars Sacra, from which they produced postcard #4949.

63 Singing Lesson, *TMK-5.*

III/63 Singing Lesson, Candy Box

Indicator	Size	Status	TMK-1	TMK-2	TMK-3	TMK-4	TMK-5	TMK-6
III/63	6″	P	P	P	P	P	P	P

When the model number is preceded by the Roman three (III), this is an indication that the article is a candy box. See Hum. 63 for more details on the background of this design. As with other boxes, shape, when first introduced in the Thirties, was more spherical; design was changed later in the early Sixties to straight-sided. The positioning of the arms and head may vary in the assembly.

III/63 **Singing Lesson**, *Candy Box, new style box, TMK-5.*

64 Shepherd's Boy

Indicator	Size	Status	TMK-1	TMK-2	TMK-3	TMK-4	TMK-5	TMK-6
64	5½″	P	P	P	P	P	P	P

When first designed in the Thirties, this figure had somewhat different facial characteristics than the present model which also has brighter colors. It was probably restyled by Skrobek, perhaps in the Sixties. The catalogs show this with various sizes, at different times ranging from 5¼″ to 6½″ high. A 6″-and-over height would warrant a premium of 10 to 20 percent. This piece differs from Lost Sheep, Hum. 68, by having a second lamb standing in front of the shepherd. Other than that and a difference in coloring of the clothing, they are about the same. In an early catalog, they were both called "Shepherd's Boy" and distinguished by the description of the lambs. A very unusual counterpart of Shepherd's Boy was found in 1979. It was made by Beswick of England, which is now a subsidiary of Royal Doulton, famous maker of figurines and character jugs. The Beswick is marked on the bottom as follows: "Original Hummel Studios, Copyright (no year) (with a circular trademark), M. I. Hummel, Beswick England." It is incised number 914 and is signed on the top surface of the base in a script similar to Sister Hummel's signature. (See Chapter 5, " 'Hummel' Figurines by Dubler and Beswick.") A photograph in color of Hum. 64 is the month of April for the 1968 calendar. The original drawing belongs to Verlag Emil Fink. A lithograph of this in postcard form is #204/A.

64 **Shepherd's Boy**, *TMK-5.*

65 Farewell

Indicator	Size	Status	TMK-1	TMK-2	TMK-3	TMK-4	TMK-5	TMK-6
65/0	4″	D	?	P	—	—	—	—
65(.)	4¾″	P	P	P	P	P	P	P
/I	4½″	D	?	P	P	P	P	?

Currently cataloged as number 65 (only), 4¾″ high, Farewell was also listed in earlier catalogs as 65 (only), but later appeared as 65/0 for a short time with only a few examples known. Examples were also cataloged as large as 5½″ high and marked either 65 or 65/I in the Fifties. The ones marked 65/I have been reported in TMK-3 and in later marks. Such examples would carry a premium of about 25 percent over the same height marked 65 (only). However, an example of 65/0 would be insured for a very low four-digit figure. This motif was used in bas-relief for the Second Annual Bell in 1979 and also for Hum. 103 lamp. The 1969 calendar for September pictures the figurine. This is a sought-after piece to display with the 1979 Annual Bell, Hum. 701. The figurine was also called "Goodbye" and "Till We Meet Again." The original drawing is owned by Verlag Ars Sacra, who produced postcard #4770.

65 **Farewell**, *TMK-5.*

66 Farm Boy, *TMK-3.*

66 Farm Boy

Indicator	Size	Status	TMK-1	TMK-2	TMK-3	TMK-4	TMK-5	TMK-6
66(.)	5″	P	P	P	P	P	P	P

This piece has had a variety of names since being introduced in the Thirties. A 1947 catalog lists it as "Pig Boy," while a 1950 one called it "Three Pals." The German name *Schweinehirt* translates, obviously, as "Swineherd." While it has only been made in one size, about 5″ high, examples as late as TMK-5 have been reported as being marked 66. (decimal). This would now command a 20 percent premium. This was used with Goose Girl, Hum. 47, to form the pair of Bookends 60 A and 60 B. The 1947 catalog listed this as 5½″ high and the price as $8. Other catalogs list other minor sizes. No major design variations have been reported. The location of the original drawing is unknown at present. No graphics are currently cataloged by either Ars Sacra or Fink.

67 Doll Mother, *TMK-5.*

67 Doll Mother

Indicator	Size	Status	TMK-1	TMK-2	TMK-3	TMK-4	TMK-5	TMK-6
67(.)	4¾″	P	P	P	P	P	P	P

Originally called "Little Doll Mother" and listed in the early catalogs as being only 4¼″ high, it apparently has always been designated by only the whole number 67 and is currently 4¾″ high. However, two TMK-1 were found marked 67. (decimal). Any such example should be considered a premium piece with an insurance value of 20 percent more than 67 (only). It was restyled sometime ago and modifications were apparently minor but in line with the brighter palette and textured finish typical of Skrobek. A popular collector's item which frequently sells at premium prices at auctions and sales because it is a bridge to many pleasant memories in years past. Refer to 76 A for a picture of a rare factory prototype of this figurine as a bookend. The original drawing is owned by Ars Sacra, from which postcard #14412 is currently available.

68/0 Lost Sheep, *TMK-5.*

68 Lost Sheep

Indicator	Size	Status	TMK-1	TMK-2	TMK-3	TMK-4	TMK-5	TMK-6
68/2/0	4¼″	P	?	P	P	P	P	P
/0	5½″	P	P	P	P	P	P	P
68(.)	5¼″	D	P	P	P	—	—	—

This model is similar to Shepherd's Boy, Hum. 64, except that it has a single lamb and the colors of the jacket and pants are different and not always consistent. The pants color has vacillated between various mixtures of gray and even within the same TMK-2. One collector reports TMK-2 with gray pants and another with brown. While it was originally issued in just the plain 68 size, about 5½″ tall, by 1959 one catalog listed this as being 6½″ high which should command a 20 percent premium when found. At that time, it was also called "Shepherd's Boy," which is its German name, *Schaferbub.* When a new U.S. Copyright, GF98, was registered on January 1, 1963, the name used was "Lost Sheep." It has been reported with TMK-1 Crown mark and also 68. (decimal). By 1966, it was listed as 68/I, 6½″ high and 68/0, 4″ high. This appears to be about the year the 68/I was discontinued. This figurine adorns the April page of the 1968 calendar. The original drawing for the figurine, Shepherd's Boy, Hum. 64, is also thought to have been the inspiration for Lost Sheep, Hum. 68.

69   Happy Pastime

Indicator	Size	Status	TMK-1	TMK-2	TMK-3	TMK-4	TMK-5	TMK-6
69(.)	3½″	P	P	P	P	P	P	P

By referring to the picture of the 1978 Annual Plate, Hum. 271, one has an idea of how Sister Hummel's original drawing was modified. In making the three-dimensional figurine, the bird was placed at the side of the busy knitter instead of in a tree. Because of the correlation with the 1978 plate, the figurine frequently sells at a premium price in the secondary market. Although 69. (decimal) has been reported in TMK-3 and TMK-5, the figurine was only issued in this one designation and with minor size variations. The only major change is in name, from "Knitter" to "Happy Pastime," sometime after 1950. No major variations in design or coloring have been reported to date. This motif was also used on the Ashtray, Hum. 62. An illustration of the figure in color appears for December in the 1969 calendar. The original drawing is owned by Verlag Ars Sacra, and graphics from it are available from them as postcard #4948.

69 Happy Pastime, *TMK-5.*

III/69   Happy Pastime, Candy Box

Indicator	Size	Status	TMK-1	TMK-2	TMK-3	TMK-4	TMK-5	TMK-6
III/69	6½″	P	P	P	P	P	P	P

Refer to Hum. 69 for design notes on the figure. The candy box shape was redesigned in the mid-Sixties. (See notes on Joyful, III/53 for more details.) One interesting variation of this candy box, found with a pastel green rim on both the bottom and top of the old-style box, commands a 25 percent premium over the plain version. The original drawing was the same one that was used for the 1978 Annual Plate, Hum. 271 and the figurine Hum. 69.

III/69 Happy Pastime, *Candy Box, new style box, TMK-5.*

70   The Holy Child

Indicator	Size	Status	TMK-1	TMK-2	TMK-3	TMK-4	TMK-5	TMK-6
70	6¾″	P	P	P	P	P	P	P

This illustrates Sister Hummel's ability to depict serenity and piety in her religious drawings. Probably issued in the late Thirties, the later catalogs show a wide range of sizes for the same model number. Those 7″ high and over should bring a premium of 10 to 20 percent. In a ten-year span they ranged from 6¾″ to 7½″ high which indicates that all the size variations are not due to "mold growth." The later trademarks have the typical restyling with the textured finish, different facial features, and brighter colors characteristic of master modeler Gerhard Skrobek's work in the 1960s. The only other name recorded is the English translation of *Jeswein,* "Little Jesus." The location of the original drawing by Sister Hummel has not been determined, but it may be among the numerous drawings in the Siessen Convent. No indication of graphics published from the original were found.

70 The Holy Child, *TMK-3.*

71 Stormy Weather, *TMK-5.*

72 Spring Cheer, *TMK-3.*

73 Little Helper, *TMK-3.*

71 Stormy Weather

Indicator	Size	Status	TMK-1	TMK-2	TMK-3	TMK-4	TMK-5	TMK-6
71(.)	6¼″	P	P	P	P	P	P	P

Since being introduced in the Thirties, this figurine's appeal to a wide segment of the market was broadened even more with the use of its motif in bas-relief for the First Anniversary Plate, Hum. 280, in 1975. A comparison of the figurine and plate shows an entirely different treatment of the facial expressions of the children. The figurine portrays them with awe and fear, while the plate shows them with radiant smiles. Sister Hummel did two similar drawings for Ars Sacra who publishes two postcards, #5009 and #5008. These have been referred to as "Stormy" and "Clearing," respectively, indicating the reason for the change in mood. While the boy carries a staff in each Goebel adaptation, the cards show him with a staff only in #5008, the one with the smiles. In the 1950s this piece was cataloged as "Under One Roof," which agrees with the German name *Unter einem Dach.* While the catalogs indicate a spread of sizes, so do the actual pieces, which range from about 6¼″ to 7″ high. Those 6¾″ or 7″ high usually fetch a small premium at sales. Recently one piece sold at auction with both Crown and Full Bee marks and the model number was 71. (decimal), indicating the continual stream of new information being uncovered. This motif has been used in at least three calendars; for the covers of 1960 and 1972, and for the month of April, 1980. The original drawing is owned by Verlag Ars Sacra.

72 Spring Cheer

Indicator	Size	Status	TMK-1	TMK-2	TMK-3	TMK-4	TMK-5	TMK-6
72	5″	P	P	P	P	P	P	P

Another adaptation before World War II and at that time called "It's Spring," which corresponds to the present German name, *Fruhling ist's.* This is one model in which very definite changes were made when it was redesigned after 1960. Generally, examples with TMK-1, 2, and 3 have yellow dresses and no flowers in the right hand. Premium values for these examples are reflected in the Price List. The later marks, TMK-4, 5, and 6, are figures usually with two flowers in the right hands and green dresses instead of yellow ones. Since any change occurred over a period of time, there may be exceptions found in the trademarks. In the May, 1980, calendar, this figurine is well illustrated in a naturalized background. The specified catalog sizes range from 5″ to 5¼″. The original drawing at Verlag Ars Sacra was used by them to publish postcard #5010.

73 Little Helper

Indicator	Size	Status	TMK-1	TMK-2	TMK-3	TMK-4	TMK-5	TMK-6
73(.)	4¼″	P	P	P	P	P	P	P

One source indicates this has been in production from the mid-Thirties. In a 1955 catalog this was called "Diligent Betsy," but changed to the above before 1959. The German name indicates that this is referred to as "Busy Little Liesl" or *Fleissiges Lieschen.* A copyright was registered to use a bas-relief version of this figurine on the Annual Plate for 1984 and assigned Hummel number 277. It is interesting to note that the basket, which has been empty for at least fifty years, will be filled in the 1984 Plate version. Some size variations, ranging from 4″ to 4½″ high, have been found in examples and in catalogs. The months of July, 1978, and May, 1969, have interesting color photographs of Little Helper, as does September, 1980. The original drawing was used by Verlag Ars Sacra to produce postcard #4642.

74   Little Gardener

Indicator	Size	Status	TMK-1	TMK-2	TMK-3	TMK-4	TMK-5	TMK-6
74(.)	4″	P	P	P	P	P	P	P

This is one figurine that has had the same name in German (*Die kleine Gärtnerin*) and in English for over forty years. This is not true of its variations in color and design found from the same period. The color of the smock background has varied from the yellow side to the chartreuse side and the dots on it have been more accentuated in some cases. The only positive change related to time is the restyling that apparently took place in the Sixties with a change in the base and more modeling of the hair and costume. The round instead of oval base features a flatter flower which has not yet been revived by the watering can. Again, the sizes in examples and catalogs vary only from about 4″ to 4½″ high. Colored pictures of the later version appear in the calendars for May, 1969, and July, 1978. No original drawing or published graphic was found for this motif.

74 **Little Gardener**, *round base, TMK-3.*

75   Angelic Prayer (White Angel), Holy Water Font

Indicator	Size	Status	TMK-1	TMK-2	TMK-3	TMK-4	TMK-5	TMK-6
75	3¼″	P	P	P	P	P	P	P

Confusion exists here in names (both are listed in the Alphabetical Index). Their German name, *Weisser Engel,* translates as "White Angel" which is still used in Germany and in some publications. The 1980 catalogs for two of the U.S. distributors list Hum. 75 as "Angelic Prayer" which is in line with some other early catalogs. For these reasons it has been given preference here. When it was restyled, possibly in the Sixties by Skrobek, a hole was added at the top for hanging. Previously a concealed one was provided on the back. The location of the original drawing used for this adaptation is not known at present but may very well be in the Siessen Convent or unpublished by Ars Sacra or Fink.

75 **Angelic Prayer**, *Holy Water Font, new style with hole at top, TMK-3.*

76 A   Doll Mother,
76 B   Prayer Before Battle, Bookends

Indicator	Size	Status	TMK-1	TMK-2	TMK-3	TMK-4	TMK-5	TMK-6
76 A&B	4¾″	*	—	—	—	—	—	—

Illustrated for the first time in print through the courtesy of the Goebel Collectors' Club Museum in Tarrytown, New York, is 76 A, Doll Mother, half of this set of bookends. Factory records indicate that Doll Mother was not produced after 1938 and any other examples of either one would be a rare find, probably valued in the very high four-digit figures. This rare factory sample without the normal base is glued directly to the wood as are the similar, lower numbered bookends. The trademark and other identification are on the wooden base. Hopefully, some diligent collector will unearth a sample of the other half of the pair before the next edition of this book. Refer to Hum. 67, Doll Mother, and Hum. 20, Prayer Before Battle for further details on the figurines themselves.

*Factory sample of 76 A only.

76 A **Doll Mother**, *Bookend, c. 1937, TMK-1. Factory prototype courtesy of W. Goebel Co.*

77 Cross with Doves, Holy Water Font (CN)

Indicator	Size	Status	TMK-1	TMK-2	TMK-3	TMK-4	TMK-5	TMK-6
77	6¼"	C	P	—	—	—	—	—

Originally this number was listed by the factory as a Cancelled Number (CN); a term used only to identify a design or sample model that was never released for sale. The factory records indicate that this was closed "October, 1937." A surprising discovery by one of our readers who sent the accompanying picture for verification occurred in 1979. This is a rare find, indeed, with an insurable value of several thousand dollars. As far as is known, this is the only exception to the sample that is maintained in the factory archives. The German name is *Kreuz mit Tauben,* the same as the English translation. Original drawing does not appear to have been published in graphic form and its location has not been determined.

77 **Cross with Doves,** *Holy Water Font, only example known, TMK-1. Photograph by Cheryl Trotter.*

78/111 **Infant of Krumbad,** *TMK-5.*

78 Infant of Krumbad

Indicator	Size	Status	TMK-1	TMK-2	TMK-3	TMK-4	TMK-5	TMK-6
78/0/11	2"	U	—	—	—	—	—	—
/I/11	2½"	P	P	P	P	P	P	P
/II/11	3½"	P	—	?	P	P	P	P
/III/11	4½"	P	—	?	P	P	P	P
/V/11	7¾"	U	—	—	—	—	—	—
/VI/11	11"	D	—	—	P	—	—	—
/VIII/11	13½"	U	—	—	—	—	—	—

The figurine is a replica of the only known sculpture to have been done by the hands of Sister Hummel. There are three completed studies of this which are displayed in the public museum in the Franciscan Convent in Siessen, Germany. These were executed in papier-maché and have a twisted wire halo that is secured in two holes on the back. One of these models is used in the ceremonies involving novitiates at the convent. This piece has been adapted by Goebel into six official catalog sizes and at least three finishes. Only three sizes are currently available from U.S. distributors in the lightly tinted beige bisque. It may be found in other sizes and finishes in Germany. A 1950 catalog listed 78/0, 78/3, 78/6, and 78/8 sizes, ranging from 2¼" to 14" long, with no reference to color, and called it "In the Crib." It has been produced in white bisque and also in full color in Germany. One authority suggests that a mold change occurred in the Full Bee time period; the U.S. Copyright GF375 says July 7, 1966; another source has reported a regular Incised Crown plus an unknown stamped Crown with a "roof mark," similar to a "V" inverted. For more information on this mark variation, see the chapter on marks. More research is required to fully document when, where, and what sizes and colors were made. Verlag Ars Sacra has published postcard #14757 of this sculpture.

79   Globe Trotter

Indicator	Size	Status	TMK-1	TMK-2	TMK-3	TMK-4	TMK-5	TMK-6
79	5″	P	P	P	P	P	P	P

This appears to have had several names, such as "Stepping Out," "Happy Traveller," (now assigned to Hum. 109), and "Out into the Distance," for the German name, *Hinaus in die Ferne*. It has been made with two distinctive styles of woven basket. The older version is woven with a double parallel strand using an over-and-under crisscross weave. The newer version which has been restyled in other less pronounced ways has a basket of the same weave but executed in single strands. The price differentials are included in the Price List. The exact time of the change has not been pinpointed but may have spread over more than one trademark, probably TMK-3 and 4. Old catalogs list sizes from 4¾″ to 5¼″ high. The present standard is 5″. Its former popularity was given a big boost when it was used as a bas-relief design on the plate for 1973, Hum. 266 (note differences in treatment). It was also illustrated in the calendar for May, 1976. The original drawing is owned by Verlag Ars Sacra who have published it as postcard #5219.

79 Globe Trotter, *single weave basket,* TMK-5.

80   Little Scholar

Indicator	Size	Status	TMK-1	TMK-2	TMK-3	TMK-4	TMK-5	TMK-6
80	5½″	P	P	P	P	P	P	P

Catalogs for a number of years show the height as 5″, while the current standard is 5½″ high. Another source shows this figurine as having been found up to 5¾″ high which would merit a 10 percent premium. When this piece was restyled at an undetermined date (possibly the Sixties), the shoe color was changed from brown to a grayish black. The German name of *Erster Schulgang, Junge,* means "Boy's First Trip to School." The fact that the model number 81 has the same name for the girl indicates that these two were probably planned as a pair. The nonchalant "School Boy Truant," Hum. 82, became "School Boy" and paired with School Girl, Hum. 81. Little Scholar is illustrated in calendars for September, 1968, and for the same month in 1975. The original drawing is owned by Verlag Ars Sacra, who have published replicas as postcard #5223.

80 Little Scholar, *TMK-5.*

81   School Girl

Indicator	Size	Status	TMK-1	TMK-2	TMK-3	TMK-4	TMK-5	TMK-6
81/2/0	4¼″	P	P	P	P	P	P	P
/0	5″	P	P	P	P	P	P	P
81(.)	5½″	D	P	P	—	—	—	—

Available now from U.S. distributors in two sizes as listed, it was carried in some early catalogs as 81. (decimal) or 81 (only) at 5½″ high which warrants a 20 percent premium. The 1947 listings show the price in this size at $6. This marking and size was superseded by 81/0 at 4¼″ (11 cm) and 81/2/0 at 3¼″ (8.4 cm) by 1956, when it was called "Little Scholar." One School Girl figurine was found with the unusual marking 81.\0 (decimal and left-handed slash); another piece was found with the "O" directly under the "81." While the school girl's basket is empty in the 81 and 81/0 marks, the basket is full in the smaller sized 81/2/0. The Annual Plate for 1980, Hum. 273, also shown on the 1980 *Supplement* cover, enhances the demand for this popular figurine. Note that the 1980 Annual Plate reveals the basket with knitting in it. The original drawing is owned by Verlag Ars Sacra, who published postcard #5222 from it.

81/2/0 School Girl, *TMK-3.*

82/2/0 School Boy, *TMK-3.*

82   School Boy

Indicator	Size	Status	TMK-1	TMK-2	TMK-3	TMK-4	TMK-5	TMK-6
82/2/0	4″	P	P	P	P	P	P	P
/0	5″	P	P	P	P	P	P	P
82(.)	5½″	D	?	?	P	—	—	—
/II(2)	7¾″	R	?	P	?	—	R	R

Although the German name *Schulschwänzer, Junge* is still in use today, by 1947 "Schoolboy Truant" had changed to "School Boy" and was listed in one size only, 5½″ high, for $6. The 82/II or 82/2 (arabic) was available and listed in 7¼″ size and called "School Days" in a 1956 catalog. In the 1959 catalog, all three sizes shown above were listed but the large size had been dropped by 1966. This large size remained out of production and was considered rare until it was reintroduced in limited quantities overseas in 1978 and immediately zoomed in price. At the present price of several hundred dollars, the demand may cool off somewhat and resemble the price differentials that now exist for older marks. No significant changes in design or color have been recorded over the years. The original drawing's location has not been ascertained and no graphics were located.

83 Angel Serenade, *rare, TMK-3. Reissued.*

83   Angel Serenade

Indicator	Size	Status	TMK-1	TMK-2	TMK-3	TMK-4	TMK-5	TMK-6
83	5½″	R	?	P	P	—	R	R

This has been in the line since the Thirties and was produced without appreciable size variations until the Sixties, when it was no longer available. Thus it became a high-priced rarity until 1978 when it was reintroduced in the same 5½″ size at a fraction of the price old marks were commanding. It is too early to tell what will happen to the prices for the old marks; this will depend on Geobel's production policies to a great extent. Originally called "Pious Melodies," or "Devout Tunes" after the German *Fromme Weisen*, the figurine appears in modified form, the angel kneeling and without the lamb, as 214/D in Nativity Set, Hum. 214, and is called "Angel Kneeling" or "Angel Serenade." It is also 260 E in the large set and called "Angel Serenade." The original drawing has not been located at this time, nor likewise any graphics.

84/0 Worship, *TMK-5.*

84   Worship

Indicator	Size	Status	TMK-1	TMK-2	TMK-3	TMK-4	TMK-5	TMK-6
84/0	5″	P	P	P	P	P	P	P
84(.)	5¼″	D	P	?	—	—	—	—
/V(5)	12¾″	R	P	P	P	—	R	R

This model was first called "At the Wayside," after the German *Am Wegesrand, Bildstökl*, in the Thirties. The 1947 listing shows this model 6″ high as 84 (only) at a price of $7. It is more recently cataloged as 84/0/; the large size 84/V has been reported marked 84/5 (arabic). At present, there is no record of this being available in the TMK-4, and for that reason it has been listed as a reintroduction. One of the smaller sizes has been found in white glaze and valued in low four-digit figures. To date, there are no reports of sizes 84/III or 84/IV having ever been made. The original drawing is owned by Verlag Ars Sacra, who used it to publish postcard #14247.

85　Serenade

Indicator	Size	Status	TMK-1	TMK-2	TMK-3	TMK-4	TMK-5	TMK-6
85/0	4¾″	P	P	P	P	P	P	P
85(.)	5″	D	P	P	—	—	—	—
/II(2)	7½″	P	—	P	P	P	P	P

The earliest catalog entry located, 1947, shows this as being produced in the 5″ size marked as only 85, possibly 85. (decimal), either of which should bring a premium of about 20 percent over the current 85/0, the replacement. One list reported the existence of an 85/1 at 6½″ high but this has not been verified. If true, this would be rare and valued in the low four digits. The fingers of the "Flutist" (its early name) are found up or down with apparently no correlation to date of issue, as some very old ones have two fingers extended and some of the newer ones do, too. The 85/II or 85/2 (arabic) was cataloged as early as 1950 at 7″ high. Other size variations have been recorded in each size. This figurine is sometimes used in assembling a Hummel orchestra of musicians and singers, which makes quite an impressive grouping. A photograph of this piece is used as an illustration for January of the 1973 calendar. "Boy Serenading with Flute" is the translation of the German, *Ständchen, Junge mit Flöte.* The original drawing is owned by Verlag Ars Sacra who used it to publish postcard #4640.

85/0 Serenade, *TMK-3.*

86　Happiness

Indicator	Size	Status	TMK-1	TMK-2	TMK-3	TMK-4	TMK-5	TMK-6
86	4¾″	P	P	P	P	P	P	P

Another design from the Thirties and first called "Wandersong" after the German name, *Wanderlied, Mädchen* ("Hiking Girl Song"). Only reported in this one size with minor variations. This happy, hiking girl, strumming a banjo as she strolls, is a particularly appealing example of the carefree innocence and joy which Sister Hummel conveyed so dramatically in her art. The figure was used for the August, 1974, calendar page. The original drawing from which this was adapted with some artistic license depicted two girls striding in step, the far girl carrying a staff and the closest one as shown here with a banjo. This has been published as postcard #14248 by Ars Sacra who own the original.

86 Happiness, *TMK-3.*

87　For Father

Indicator	Size	Status	TMK-1	TMK-2	TMK-3	TMK-4	TMK-5	TMK-6
87	5½″	P	P	P	P	P	P	P

Sometime before 1950 this figurine was called Father's Joy; it has probably been made since the Thirties and is found in all trademarks ranging from 5″ to 5½″ high. Some collectors report a premium for an example with red-orange turnips (radishes). The German translation, "For the Little Father, Radish Boy," from *Fürs Vaterle, Rettichbub,* suggests the possibility that the boy is pretending to be his father. In either case, it is one of the popular models and makes a nice companion piece with the figurine, For Mother, Hum. 257. For Father is the subject of the October picture in the 1980 calendar. The original drawing is owned by Verlag Ars Sacra who used it to produce postcard #5233 which has more detail than is practical to incorporate in a ceramic adaptation.

87 For Father, *TMK-2.*

88/I Heavenly Protection, *TMK-5.*

89/I Little Cellist, *eyes down, TMK-5.*

88   Heavenly Protection

Indicator	Size	Status	TMK-1	TMK-2	TMK-3	TMK-4	TMK-5	TMK-6
88(.)	9¼″	D	P	P	P	—	—	—
/I	6¾″	P	—	?	P	P	P	P
/II	9″	P	—	P	P	P	P	P

In the early catalogs, this piece is referred to as "Guardian Angel," which is a good translation of the German name, *Schutzengel,* but perhaps too easily confused with the Holy Water Font, Hum. 29, Guardian Angel. Early pieces are found incised with either model number 88 (only) or 88/II, both around 9″ high. The smaller size 88/I is listed in the 1966 catalog, but must have been issued before that time, probably in the early 1960s. A U.S. Copyright, GF53, was issued on July 17, 1962. The figurine is not in the 1950 or 1959 catalogs. The two children must have been modeled from Hum. 94, Surprise, and combined with one of the numerous protective angels drawn by Sister Hummel, since no composite drawing or graphic was located resembling the figurine. One surprising reproduction made years ago in Japan is almost identical except the girl carries flowers instead of a basket — and, of course, it does not have the all-important facsimile signature incised on it.

89   Little Cellist

Indicator	Size	Status	TMK-1	TMK-2	TMK-3	TMK-4	TMK-5	TMK-6
89(.)	7½″	D	P	?	—	—	—	—
/I(1)	6¾″	P	P	P	P	P	P	P
/II(2)	7½″	P	—	P	P	P	P	P

When introduced, probably in the Thirties, the size ranged from 5¾″ high to about 6″ and was called "Cello Boy" before 1950. So far there are no reports or catalogs of any examples marked either 89 (only) or 89. (decimal). Early catalogs do list 89/I—5¾″. The larger size 89/II was introduced sometime before 1959, and is about 7½″ high. To date, no examples have been reported in this size with Crown or Full Bee marks, although one example of 89/2 (arabic) was found in TMK-2. A distinct variation exists in this motif. At first the Little Cellist looked directly at the viewer as he plodded along. In the newer style he is paying more attention to where he is going by looking down. The base of the newer example has rounded or chamfered corners. There are also color differences of lesser import. Prices in the Price List reflect these differences. A picture of this figurine was used on the January, 1971, calendar page. The Little Cellist is another member of the Hummel orchestra. The original drawing is owned by Verlag Ars Sacra who produced postcard #5329 from it.

90   Cancelled Number

Indicator	Size	Status	TMK-1	TMK-2	TMK-3	TMK-4	TMK-5	TMK-6
90 A&B	?	C	*	—	—	—	—	—

Here is a challenge to dedicated flea "marketeers" and possessors of "atticana." Research by Robert Miller and the Goebel factory has established that this number was assigned to a pair of bookends using the figurine Eventide, Hum. 99, and Adoration, Hum. 23 without the shrine, for design and prototypes for possible production. Both figures are mounted directly on the wooden base as were other early models. According to these records all work was discontinued in February, 1939, and only a factory sample is now known. There was no record of this number found in the U.S. Copyright Office. Any prototype or early model would be marked TMK-1. While it is extremely unlikely that other than a factory sample exists, such an authenticated example would have an insurable value in the five-digit figures. It has happened before with other cancelled numbers.

*Factory sample only.

91 A&B   Angels at Prayer, Holy Water Fonts

Indicator	Size	Status	TMK-1	TMK-2	TMK-3	TMK-4	TMK-5	TMK-6
91 A&B	4¾″	P	P	P	P	P	P	P
91	4¾″	P	P	—	—	—	—	—

91 A&B Angels at Prayer, *Holy Water Fonts, with haloes and holes, TMK-5.*

Angel at Prayer (facing left) was reported incised with 91 only. The history of these pieces is obscured by the fact that some of the early catalogs called any font a Holy Water Font, regardless of the design and the numbering system. However, they are found with all trademarks indicating a good long production pattern. It appears that the model facing left was introduced first as one model with Crown mark incised and 91 (only). The one facing right was introduced later. They are presently listed as a pair in one current U.S. catalog. One publication refers to them as Angel Facing Left, 91 A, and Angel Facing Right, 91 B. Sometime in the Sixties, they were redesigned (as shown in the photograph) by adding the halo background and piercing a hole above the head for hanging. The Price List values allow for the change in design between TMK-3 and TMK-4, although the dividing line may not be this exact.

92   Merry Wanderer, Plaque

Indicator	Size	Status	TMK-1	TMK-2	TMK-3	TMK-4	TMK-5	TMK-6
92(.)	4″	P	P	P	P	P	P	P

Two U.S. copyrights, G33488 on December 31, 1938, and R400639 on December 15, 1968, indicate important dates that approximate introduction and revision. This plaque is known in all trademarks, and examples as large as 5″ x 5½″ with Crown marks have been reported. The Price List allows a premium for the larger pieces. If the plaque is signed on both the front and back with *M. J. Hümmel*, add 15 percent premium. These are not readily available in all marks in the U.S., and many of the early catalogs do not list the number. The German name, *Bild, Wanderbub,* translates as "Wanderer Boy." This is the same motif as used in the figurines Merry Wanderer, Hum. 7 and Hum. 11 (see for more details). It is used in two other plaques by the same name, Hum. 106 (extremely rare) and Hum. 265 (a bas-relief only, no frame).

92 Merry Wanderer, *Plaque, TMK-5.*

93   Little Fiddler, Plaque

Indicator	Size	Status	TMK-1	TMK-2	TMK-3	TMK-4	TMK-5	TMK-6
93	5″	P	P	P	P	P	P	P

This apparently was designed as a companion piece to Hum. 92, even though it was registered as G33489 in the U.S. Copyright Office on December 31, 1939, and not widely distributed in the U.S. The first U.S. catalog found that had this listed is a 1966 bi-lingual version. This plaque is intriguing because it was issued with two different backgrounds. The earlier design had only three houses. The present design was probably covered by U.S. Copyright R404879 on February 23, 1968, and shows six houses. If found with an older design, the value would be in the low four-digit range. The Hum. 107 (see) is believed even rarer at this time and can be distinguished by the wooden frame. The other related issues to this one are the figurines Hum. 2 and 4.

94 Surprise

Indicator	Size	Status	TMK-1	TMK-2	TMK-3	TMK-4	TMK-5	TMK-6
94/3/0	4″	P	P	P	P	P	P	P
/0	5″	D	P	P	—	—	—	—
94(.)	5¾″	D	P	P	?	—	—	—
/I	5½″	P	?	P	P	P	P	P

In addition to the name, there is plenty of variety for collectors of this model. There are three names, "Surprise," "The Duet," and "Hansel and Gretel," English translation of the same German name, *Hänsel und Gretl*. Many interesting incised model numbers have been reported. In addition to the ones shown above, there is a figurine with the 94. (decimal) incised over a previously incised number 82 in one case, and number 38 in a similar case. Both of these carry the Full Bee trademark, TMK-2. Sizes as large as 6″ and as small as 4″ have been measured. Another variation is one with TMK-3, incised 94/2/0, and measuring 4½″ high. A 94/3/0 on TMK-2, measuring 4⅛″ has been found. Older marks used either a rectangular base or a base with chamfered corners. Almost all later models are made with an oval base. For the present, it would be prudent to stay with the values assigned in the Price List, except for major deviations like the doubled over stamp which might be valued in the high hundreds. These children have been illustrated on the cover of the 1954 calendar and for July, 1968, and September, 1974.

94/I Surprise, *TMK-2*.

95 Brother

Indicator	Size	Status	TMK-1	TMK-2	TMK-3	TMK-4	TMK-5	TMK-6
95(.)	4¾″	P	P	P	P	P	P	P

While this piece was never called "Hansel," it appears identical to the boy with the German name in Hum. 94. It was also listed in a 1950 catalog as "Our Hero," and the German name, *Dorfheld*, translates as "Village Hero." Currently listed as 4¾″ high, it has been found in sizes ranging up to 5½″ in TMK-3. Examples 5″ and over would merit a premium of 10 percent or more. Minor color variations have been reported but the prices given in the Price List should encompass any of these. The location of the original drawing is unknown at present with the possibility that this may have been based on a figure that was part of a composite group. Variation in suspenders may be found, as Hum. 94 has been reported with no design on the cross strap and also with no strap at all.

95 Brother, *TMK-3*.

96 Little Shopper

Indicator	Size	Status	TMK-1	TMK-2	TMK-3	TMK-4	TMK-5	TMK-6
96	5½″	P	P	P	P	P	P

If number 95 is "Hansel," then Hum. 96 must be the "Gretel" in the figurine, Surprise, Hum. 94. This is verified by the German name which reads the same. There seems to be a discrepancy in sizes, as some catalogs list this at 4½″ or 4¾″ and others as 5½″ high, and yet all are marked just 96. Any found 5″ high or more would be worth 10 percent more. In the early catalogs this piece was called "Errand Girl." Some minor color variations have been reported which are to be expected with many different artists doing the decorating. Hopefully some reader will confirm examples as large as 5½″ high with TMK-1 or 2. There does not seem to be a separate drawing of "Gretel" or any graphics published from it.

96 Little Shopper, *TMK-5*.

97 Trumpet Boy

Indicator	Size	Status	TMK-1	TMK-2	TMK-3	TMK-4	TMK-5	TMK-6
97	4¾″	P	P	P	P	P	P	P

This figurine has always been incised with only the model number 97 on the back and no size indicators. However an analysis of seven different catalogs would make one think otherwise, as the specified sizes range from 4½″ high to 5½″ high in some of the older ones. Because of this difference any examples that are found 5″ or over should have 10 percent added to the prices in the Price List. Any that are 5½″ should be valued at about 20 percent more than indicated. This would be the approximate differential if size indicators had been used. This piece is called *Der kleine Musikant*, or "The Little Musician." No major variations in color or design have been reported. The location of the original drawing has not been documented, and no graphics copied from such have been found.

97 Trumpet Boy, *TMK-3*.

98 Sister

Indicator	Size	Status	TMK-1	TMK-2	TMK-3	TMK-4	TMK-5	TMK-6
98/2/0	4¾″	P	—	?	P	P	P	P
/0	5½″	P	—	P	P	P	P	P
98(.)	5¾″	D	P	P	P	—	—	—

It appears that this piece was issued with old marks as 98 (only) or 98. (decimal), about 5″ to 5¾″ high, and later superseded by 98/0 in about the same size range. When Hum. 96 was called "Errand Girl," about 1950, Hum. 98 was known as "Little Shopper." Variations in color and design seem to have been insufficient to create any price differential, and there is no record in the U.S. Copyright Office of any restyling either. Some have been reported with a 1962 copyright date indicating a renewal, which was also recorded as GF96 in the U.S. Copyright Office on January 4, 1963. This motif appears to be the same as the girl in To Market, Hum. 49. The original drawing has not been located to date or any graphics.

98/0 Sister, *TMK-3*.

99 Eventide

Indicator	Size	Status	TMK-1	TMK-2	TMK-3	TMK-4	TMK-5	TMK-6
99	4¾″	P	P	P	P	P	P	P

See Wayside Devotion, Hum. 28, from which this figurine was apparently created by eliminating the shrine. In a 1947 catalog, Hum. 28 was called "Evening Song," the translation of the German name, *Abendlied*. In older models, the girl appears to be looking up at the shrine, rather than straight forward as in the newer trademarks, which would indicate some restyling. This piece has been found in a white overglaze, a very rare example valued in the mid four-digit figures. A similar version of Eventide also appears as Hum. 90 A, paired with Adoration (without shrine) as 90 B, bookend. Sister Hummel's original drawing, which includes the omitted shrine, is owned by Verlag Ars Sacra, who have reproduced it in postcard #4971. The white overglaze examples like the one above are usually in catalogs and are considered rare.

99 Eventide, *TMK-5*.

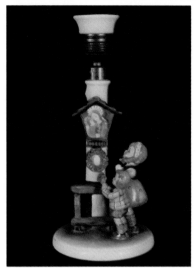

100 Shrine, *Table Lamp, rare,*
TMK-1. Grande Collection.

100   Shrine, Table Lamp

Indicator	Size	Status	TMK-1	TMK-2	TMK-3	TMK-4	TMK-5	TMK-6
100	7½″	D	P	—	—	—	—	—

This lamp is a modification of the figurine, Adoration, Hum. 23, substituting the lamp column for the upright post to which the shrine and wreath are attached. Hum. 100 is listed in the Goebel records as a Closed Edition (CE), so very few examples have been located. Two verified examples have TMK-1, and one unverified lamp has both TMK-1 and TMK-2. When found and verified with a Crown and Full Bee marks, this rare piece would be valued in the low four-digit figures. The original drawing of the roadside shrine from which this table lamp was adapted is owned by Verlag Emil Fink, who publish postcard #839 and prints #100A and 100G as exact replicas of the original drawing.

101 **To Market,** *Table Lamp, rare,*
superseded by Hum. 223, TMK-1.
Grande Collection.

101   To Market, Table Lamp

Indicator	Size	Status	TMK-1	TMK-2	TMK-3	TMK-4	TMK-5	TMK-6
101	7½″	D	P	P	P	—	—	—

This 7½″ lamp was created by using the figurine To Market, Hum. 49, on a larger base for stability and by adding a formal white column for the lamp. The factory records list this as a Closed Edition as of April, 1937, so any examples are very rare indeed. One Australian collector reported an example with a Full Bee trademark, and another report has been verified with a Stylized Bee (TMK-3) mark. Some years ago the model was redesigned as Hum. 223, substituting a tree trunk for the formal column. Hum. 223 is currently cataloged in the 9½″ size only. No U.S. copyright was found. An early model of Hum. 101 would be valued in the low four-digit figures, depending upon which trademark was incised.

102 **Volunteers,** *Table Lamp, unique,*
TMK-1, Miller Collection.

102   Volunteers, Table Lamp

Indicator	Size	Status	TMK-1	TMK-2	TMK-3	TMK-4	TMK-5	TMK-6
102	?	U	—	—	—	—	—	—

One example of this rare lamp exists today in the collection of Robert Miller. Hum. 102 was discontinued in 1937, as were Hummel lamps 101 and 103. Until recently, no known examples existed, not even a factory sample. According to Mr. Miller, the lamp was purchased by a dealer for $14 at a thrift shop in Seattle, Washington. Upon verification of the lamp's markings, Mr. Miller purchased this rare piece valued in the mid four-digit range. The lamp is marked with an incised number 102, a Double Crown (incised and stamped), a black stamped Germany, and an artist's mark. The underside of the base is doughnut-shaped; the lamp standard is white porcelain with a brass receptacle. Hum. 50, the figurine Volunteers, is quite similar in design to the figurine on the lamp 102. Is there still another example awaiting discovery and verification?

103   Farewell, Table Lamp

Indicator	Size	Status	TMK-1	TMK-2	TMK-3	TMK-4	TMK-5	TMK-6
103	?	U	—	—	—	—	—	—

The factory records show this lamp as being a Closed Edition at the same time as the two before, April, 1937. Since there is not even a factory sample available for illustration, it is likely that the first example found would be valued at least in the high four-digit range. The hunt for this rare lamp has been in progress for some time. Those joining the hunt should be looking for the motif as used in Farewell, Hum. 63, superimposed on a larger base of a lamp which may have a white porcelain column similar to 101.

104   Wayside Devotion, Table Lamp

Indicator	Size	Status	TMK-1	TMK-2	TMK-3	TMK-4	TMK-5	TMK-6
104	?	U	—	—	—	—	—	—

This is the fourth lamp in a row that is listed as a Closed Edition by the Goebel factory. This one was discontinued in 1938 with no existing samples known. Presumably, the post for the shrine in Hum. 28 was replaced by a circular column as in Hum. 100, or a column resembling a tree trunk as used in current models. The change in design is not too significant, but the change in value between the figurine Wayside Devotion, Hum. 28, and its counterpart as a lamp, Hum. 104, is from four to ten times greater than the price for the comparable figurine. If a reader is fortunate enough to find one, send us a letter with a good color photograph of the lamp and also one of the base showing all the marks on the bottom.

105   Adoration with Bird

Indicator	Size	Status	TMK-1	TMK-2	TMK-3	TMK-4	TMK-5	TMK-6
105	4¾″	D	P	—	—	—	—	—

The first examples of this figurine, which has also been referred to as Bird Lovers, were only recently found and are considered extremely rare. Further research of the factory records indicates that this piece was classified as a Closed Edition in 1938, so it is unlikely that many examples will be discovered. If so, one would be valued in the mid four-digit range. By observing Hum. 23, Adoration, the adaptation is quite apparent. The shrine that the children gaze at is replaced by a tree trunk with a bird holding the attention of the children. A slightly different version, closed out in the same year, was used in Hum. 90 B, one of a pair of bookends (see). There is no original drawing in this form done by Sister Hummel.

105 Adoration with Bird, *very rare, TMK-1.*

106   Merry Wanderer, Plaque

Indicator	Size	Status	TMK-1	TMK-2	TMK-3	TMK-4	TMK-5	TMK-6
106	6″	D	P	—	—	—	—	—

This piece is identical to Hum. 92 of the same name, with one important exception. This version is only a flat, bas-relief, tilelike piece which has been mounted in a wooden frame. Hum. 92 was molded with an integral, one-piece ceramic frame. This plaque is a Closed Edition, and it is not expected that any more will be made in this style. When and if more of these are located, the value would be in the higher range of the four-digit figures. Since the all-ceramic lookalike, Hum. 92, Merry Wanderer is still in production, a close inspection will reveal the difference in the frames of ceramic and wood, respectively. This plaque illustrates what Sister Hummel's original drawing looked like very well with all the background detail in place. (See Hum. 107.) Excellent prints and cards of the original drawing are available from Verlag Emil Fink as #202 and #101A.

107   Little Fiddler, Plaque

107 Little Fiddler, *Plaque, with wooden frame, unique, TMK-1.*

Indicator	Size	Status	TMK-1	TMK-2	TMK-3	TMK-4	TMK-5	TMK-6
107	6″	D	P	—	—	—	—	—

This plaque appears to have been made as a companion piece to Hum. 106. This version of the Little Fiddler has the same construction as its companion, being a flat, rectangular, ceramic bas-relief mounted in a wooden frame with a zigzag cloth backing. The first piece to be recorded was discovered in 1978 and is valued in the high four-digit range. It is now in the Robert Miller collection. This plaque appears almost identical to a scarce and early version of Hum. 93, Little Fiddler, which has an integrally molded ceramic frame. Another later version of Hum. 93 has a slightly different background, with peaks of six houses rather than three in the background. Prints and cards produced from the original drawing are available from Verlag Emil Fink. According to factory records, Hum. 107 was classified as a Closed Edition in 1938.

108   Cancelled Number

Indicator	Size	Status	TMK-1	TMK-2	TMK-3	TMK-4	TMK-5	TMK-6
108	?	U	—	—	—	—	—	—

This is another example classified by the company as a closed, or cancelled, number (CN), meaning that it will not be used again. The records indicate that the design was a plaque with an angel and two children. At present there are no known examples, not even a factory sample. Since others in this CN category have surfaced, there is always the remote possibility that at least one or more Hum. 108 will be found somewhere, sometime, by somebody — perhaps you.

109   Happy Traveller

Indicator	Size	Status	TMK-1	TMK-2	TMK-3	TMK-4	TMK-5	TMK-6
109/0	5″	P	?	P	P	P	P*	P*
109(.)	5″	D	P	?	—	—	—	—
/I	6″	U	—	—	—	—	—	—
/II(2)	7½″	P	P	P	P	P	P	P

109 Happy Traveller, *TMK-5.*

Old records going back to 1947 indicate this model has been made in the two sizes, about 5″ and 7½″ high, with minor variations. These have been marked with both 109 (only) and 109. (decimal), as well as the two size indicators listed. One example was found marked 109/2; however, there is no record to date of any example marked 109/I, which would probably be about 6″ high. Although cataloged earlier as 109/0, current examples are now marked only 109 without any size indicator. This piece at one time was called "Wanderer," and the German name, *Hinaus in die Ferne,* translates as "Out in Far Places." Note the similarity of this figure to Globe Trotter, Hum. 79, except for the missing basket. The original with the basket has been reproduced as postcard #5219 by Verlag Ars Sacra as was an interesting variation without basket or umbrella, #802, by Verlag Emil Fink.

*TMK-5 and 6 incised 109 (only) in this size.

110   Let's Sing

Indicator	Size	Status	TMK-1	TMK-2	TMK-3	TMK-4	TMK-5	TMK-6
110/0	3″	P	P	P	P	P	P	P
110	4″	D	P	P	—	—	—	—
/I	4″	P	P	P	P	P	P	P

110/0 Let's Sing, *TMK-5.*

Since this motif was used in bas-relief form on the First Annual Bell in 1978, Hum. 700, the price of this figurine in the secondary market has advanced disproportionately compared to similar figurines (sometimes as much as double). In addition to the sizes above, this piece has been reported found with 110. (decimal) with a Crown mark, 4″ high, and with 110 (only) with a Full Bee mark. The sizes cataloged and found have varied from the standards shown above. One variation reported was an example with feet apart. No other names were found except the German, *Heini, Bandoneonspieler,* for "Heini, the Accordion Player." This design was registered as G33487 on March 31, 1939, and again on February 23, 1967. This motif is also found as the Candy Box listed later; Ashtray, Hum. 114; and as a Closed Edition of Bookends, 120 B, copyrighted before 1940. A picture of this figure appeared on the July calendar for 1974. Verlag Emil Fink owns the original and has produced an exact likeness as postcard #816. Verlag Ars Sacra owns a very similar original, and postcard #14406 is produced from that version.

III/110   Let's Sing, Candy Box

Indicator	Size	Status	TMK-1	TMK-2	TMK-3	TMK-4	TMK-5	TMK-6
III/110	6″	P	P	P	P	P	P	P

III/110 Let's Sing, *Candy Box, new style, TMK-5.*

The Roman numeral III used as a prefix before the model number indicates that the article is a candy box. When first introduced before World War II, the shape of the base was spherical like a deep soup or cereal bowl, and the cover, which fitted inside, had a slight crown. This was redesigned in the Sixties so that the box now has straight sides and the cover laps over an internal lip and is flush with the sides. The diameter of the new design, while cataloged as being the same as the old style, is somewhat smaller.

111 Wayside Harmony

Indicator	Size	Status	TMK-1	TMK-2	TMK-3	TMK-4	TMK-5	TMK-6
111/3/0	4″	P	P	P	P	P	P	P
111(.)	5½″	D	P	P	—	—	—	—
111/I	5″	P	P	P	P	P	P	P

The name of this figure has almost as many variations as it has differences in sizes. A 1947 catalog lists this as "Boy on Fence." "Fence Duet," "Duet," and "Boy Just Resting" are other versions in addition to the German *Vaters G'scheitester* for "Father's Cleverest." This has been reported with a yellow shirt in 111/3/0 with TMK-2 and 3. When found add about 50 percent to figures in Price List. While this has been found with 111/1 (arabic) and 111. (decimal), with 1938 copyright date, no examples have been reported marked 111/2/0, even though the actual sizes have ranged from 3½″ to 5¾″ high. In 1980, a reader reported a unique example of this figurine with shiny, white overglaze. Verlag Emil Fink who owns one of the original drawings has produced at least two graphics, #703 and #815. Ars Sacra has issued a postcard #5194 from the one they own. The figurine itself is pictured on the July calendar page for 1971. Hum. 111 was introduced about 1938 and some examples are incised with that date. The U.S. copyright date is March 31, 1939. What is believed to be merely a renewal was registered as R404879 on February 23, 1967. Hum. 111 is also found as a lamp (listed next) and as lamps 224/I and 224/II.

111/I Wayside Harmony, *TMK-4.*

II/111 Wayside Harmony, *Table Lamp, 7½″ high. Rare, same design as Hum. 224, pictured. Dous Collection.*

II/111 Wayside Harmony, Table Lamp

Indicator	Size	Status	TMK-1	TMK-2	TMK-3	TMK-4	TMK-5	TMK-6
II/111	7½″	D	P	P	—	—	—	—

The Roman prefix II designates this as a table lamp created from figure 111. There are only minor differences in sizes. This 7½″ lamp was superseded at a later date by 224/I as the 7½″ size, and 224/II as the 9½″ size (see). The II/111 lamp is considered rare with a value in the high hundreds. To date it has only been reported with the Crown (TMK-1) and Full Bee (TMK-2) marks.

112 Just Resting

Indicator	Size	Status	TMK-1	TMK-2	TMK-3	TMK-4	TMK-5	TMK-6
112/3/0	4″	P	P	P	P	P	P	P
112(.)	5½″	D	P	P	—	—	—	—
/I	5″	P	P	P	P	P	P	P

While this is also known as "Girl on Fence" (1947), "Girl Just Resting," and in German, *Mutters Liebste,* for "Mother's Most Beloved," it is obviously a companion piece to Wayside Harmony, Hum. 111, and the pair makes an attractive display. The history of variations of sizes and backstamps is very similar to Hum. 111 (see). At least one report has been made of an example without the basket at the girl's feet. Such a sample would carry a 50 percent premium if it can be ascertained that it left the factory in that manner. Verlag Ars Sacra who own the original produced at least one graphic of it as postcard #5195. This figurine appears as the subject for the month of July in the 1971 calendar.

112/I Just Resting, *TMK-5.*

II/112 Just Resting, Table Lamp

Indicator	Size	Status	TMK-1	TMK-2	TMK-3	TMK-4	TMK-5	TMK-6
II/112	7½″	D	?	P	—	—	—	—

This 7½″ table lamp was superseded by 225/I and 225/II for the 9½″ size (see). It carries a 1938 copyright incised on the bottom and to date has only been reported with the Full Bee, TMK-2. It must have been made in very limited quantities in the very late Forties or early Fifties, as there are no known examples with a Crown, TMK-1. It is very rare and is hard to distinguish from 225/I, except for minor details such a the smoother bark on the tree of the early one, and, of course, the information on the base as mentioned. It has been found about 8″ high with the incised model number of 2/112/I. Any example of this lamp would be valued for insurance purposes in the low four-digit range.

II/112 Just Resting, *Table Lamp, 7½″ high. Rare, same design as Hum. 225, pictured.*

113 Heavenly Song, Candleholder

Indicator	Size	Status	TMK-1	TMK-2	TMK-3	TMK-4	TMK-5	TMK-6
113	3½″	R	P	P	—	—	R	D

This candleholder is similar to two others, Hum. 31, Advent Group with Black Child, and Hum. 54, Silent Night (see). This motif can be distinguished from the others by the halo on the child's head in this design. This also is rare with old marks. With a Crown mark, this piece is estimated to have a value in the low four-digit range. A search for this piece in past catalogs was unsuccessful back to 1947, indicating the possibility of this piece being made as a very special order. It was reintroduced in limited quantities in Germany in 1978, and was first listed in two U.S. catalogs in 1980. The German name *Stille Nacht, Adventsgruppe, Leuchter,* translates as "Silent Night, Advent Group Candleholder." During 1981 Hum. 113 was again discontinued. Whether or not any were made with TMK-6 is not known. It is very likely that any reissued pieces will be scarce, with widely fluctuating prices that may be in the high hundreds.

113 Heavenly Song, *Candleholder, recently discontinued; was always scarce, will become extremely rare. Miller Collection.*

114 Let's Sing, Ashtray

Indicator	Size	Status	TMK-1	TMK-2	TMK-3	TMK-4	TMK-5	TMK-6
114	3½″	P	P	P	P	P	P	P

This ashtray uses the same design as the figurine, Let's Sing, Hum. 110 (see for more details). Its popularity has jumped since the motif was used on the First Annual Bell, Hum. 700, in 1978. When found with the ashtray on the boy's right (viewer's left) and Crown mark, the value is estimated to be in the high hundreds. The ones with current marks have the tray on the boy's left (viewer's right). One interesting example has been found in the new style (ashtray on boy's left) but with TMK-2. Hum. 114 has been in the line since the late Thirties.

114 Let's Sing, *Ashtray, TMK-5.*

115, 116, 117 **Advent Candle-sticks.** *(L to R): 117, 115, 116, TMK-5.*

115 Advent Candlestick, Girl with Nosegay

Indicator	Size	Status	TMK-1	TMK-2	TMK-3	TMK-4	TMK-5	TMK-6
115	3½″	P	P	P	P	P	P	P

116 Advent Candlestick, Girl with Fir Tree

Indicator	Size	Status	TMK-1	TMK-2	TMK-3	TMK-4	TMK-5	TMK-6
116	3½″	P	P	P	P	P	P	P

117 Advent Candlestick, Boy with Horse

Indicator	Size	Status	TMK-1	TMK-2	TMK-3	TMK-4	TMK-5	TMK-6
117	3½″	P	P	P	P	P	P	P

These little children with the long names have a longer story. The tale begins in the 1930s, when Arthur Möller or Reinhold Unger sculpted three small Advent candleholders similar to Hum. 115, 116, and 117. However, Sister Hummel did not approve the molds for release. Goebel, therefore, took the last three letters of Sister Hummel's name, Mel, and marketed the small candleholders as Mel 1, Mel 2, and Mel 3. These pieces were called "The Christmas Trio," or *Weihnachts-Trio,* in an independently written and published catalog of the early 1950s. Sometime in the early 1960s, Gerhard Skrobek, the present master sculptor at Goebel, redesigned these candleholders and obtained the convent's approval of the figurines. Consequently, the Advent candleholders have been released as Hum. 115, 116, and 117. Goebel factory records indicate that at least eight "Mel" figurines were released. Happy hunting! Any "Mel" examples found would be valued in the high hundreds. The Hummel trio is also listed in current catalogs as a set of "Christmas Angels"; the individual names shown above are translations of the German names of these pieces. See page 214 for the complete story on Mel figurines.

118 **Little Thrifty, Bank,** *scarce, old model with heavy base, TMK-3.*

118 Little Thrifty, Bank

Indicator	Size	Status	TMK-1	TMK-2	TMK-3	TMK-4	TMK-5	TMK-6
118	5″	P	P	P	P	P	P	P

This figurine functions as a bank, and the slot at the top is actually for coins. It has a metal door on the bottom which locks with a key. While this is found with all trademarks, it was not listed in many of the early catalogs, which probably accounts for the scarcity of the model in TMK-1 and 2. The Price List allows for this difference in availability. The early models had a base that was almost 1″ thick. When it was redesigned, the thickness was reduced to about ¾″, as it is at present. There are height variations, such as the 5½″ version shown in the 1957 catalog. Verlag Ars Sacra owns the original drawing which shows some German words on the side of the bank. The publishers have reproduced this as postcard #14118.

119   Postman

Indicator	Size	Status	TMK-1	TMK-2	TMK-3	TMK-4	TMK-5	TMK-6
119	5″	P	P	P	P	P	P	P

While presently listed in one name and only one size, various old catalogs show the sizes as ranging from 4¾″ in 1956 to as much as 5½″ in 1966. The very large or very small sizes would merit a 10 percent premium. Probably designed before 1940 and introduced before the war, it was redesigned in the Sixties with the new, rougher, modeled or textured finish, with the cap tilted to the left rather than straight back as in the older models. The name used for this model in Germany is *Eilbote* or "Special Messenger." Sister Hummel's original drawing has been reproduced as postcard #5545 issued by Verlag Ars Sacra. The month of June, 1976, calendar shows a picture of this figurine. The motif is earmarked for the 1983 Annual Plate design.

119 Postman, *TMK-3.*

120   Joyful/Let's Sing, Bookends

Indicator	Size	Status	TMK-1	TMK-2	TMK-3	TMK-4	TMK-5	TMK-6
120	?	U	—	—	—	—	—	—

The Goebel Company records this as an edition that was closed in the late Thirties and states that there is no known example at the time this book was prepared, not even a factory sample. Any collector who is fortunate to own such a piece, and it is possible, should consider the value as being in the high four-digit figures. See Joyful, Hum. 53, and Let's Sing, Hum. 110, for more information and related originals and graphics.

121   Wayside Harmony and
Just Resting Bookends

Indicator	Size	Status	TMK-1	TMK-2	TMK-3	TMK-4	TMK-5	TMK-6
121	?	U	—	—	—	—	—	—

This pair was listed as a Closed Edition by the factory in the late Thirties, and there is no indication that any were made; there is not even a factory sample known. These, as are Hum. 120 and Hum. 122, are designed by placing the figures directly on the wooden base which carry the number and trademark. They represent another challenge to the well-informed and sharp-eyed collector to be the first to acquire such a set which would be valued in the high four-digit figures. It is likely that they would be glued directly on the wooden base (similar to Doll Mother, 76 A).

122 Puppy Love and Serenade, Bookends

Indicator	Size	Status	TMK-1	TMK-2	TMK-3	TMK-4	TMK-5	TMK-6
122	?	U	—	—	—	—	—	—

Another pair of Closed Edition bookends which use figurines Puppy Love, Hum. 1, and Serenade, Hum. 85; the factory sample indicates that the subjects were mounted directly on the wooden bookend bases and that a dog was used with Serenade to balance the one with Puppy Love. When and if any more are found they would be rare examples, indeed, as the record indicates these were discontinued in the late Thirties. The value of such a pair would be in the mid four-digit figures.

123 Max and Moritz, *TMK-5.*

123 Max and Moritz

Indicator	Size	Status	TMK-1	TMK-2	TMK-3	TMK-4	TMK-5	TMK-6
123	5″	P	P	P	P	P	P	P

These have retained the same identical name in both German and English since they were introduced in the Forties. Some of the early catalogs do not list them, but the catalogs that do show that the size ranged from the present 5″ high to 5½″ high in 1956. One reader sent a picture of this pair with their heads actually joined (TMK-1 and 2 marks), indicating the possible variables that can occur when the component parts are assembled by the "garnisher" at the factory. These are valued at a premium of 20 percent. The early figurines carry a 1939 copyright date, even with the TMK-3, but were restyled about that time (1960s). The prices given allow for any minor style and color changes. Both Fink and Ars Sacra have issued graphics of this pair from Sister Hummel's work. There is a postcard #103B by Fink and a similar #14264 by Ars Sacra which invites speculation that Sister Hummel may have produced more than one original, as she is now known to have done in some cases. A comparison between the original work and the three-dimensional adaptation indicates that the figurine adaptation appears to have produced more manageable youngsters than the drawing's unruly ones.

124 Hello, *TMK-5.*

124 Hello

Indicator	Size	Status	TMK-1	TMK-2	TMK-3	TMK-4	TMK-5	TMK-6
124/0	6¼″	P	?	P	P	P	P	P
124(.)	6¾″	D	P	P	—	—	—	—
/I	6¾″	R	P	P	P	—	R	R

This figurine, called *Der Chef* in German ("The Boss" in English), has had a long and varied history in size, color, and style since it was introduced (probably) in the Forties. Several different reports and a 1956 catalog in color indicate that the color of the trousers has progressed from a gray to a greenish gray to the present brown gray tone. Similar complementary color changes were made also in the vest and jacket. When first introduced, this figurine was incised with only the whole number 124 which represented the only size available, about 7″ high. Later a smaller size, about 6″ tall, was added to the line and designated as 124/0. In an early 1950 catalog, this is listed as follows: 124 — 17 cm or 6.9″ high, and 124/0 — 15 cm or 5.7″ tall. Later on, the designation 124/I was substituted for the larger size, but no record was found until the large size was reinstated in the 1978 catalog as 124/I — 7″ high. The prices given in the Price List allow for the color variations. The original drawing has been reproduced in card #5730 by Verlag Ars Sacra. The figurine itself was used for the January picture in the 1976 calendar.

125   Vacation Time, Plaque

Indicator	Size	Status	TMK-1	TMK-2	TMK-3	TMK-4	TMK-5	TMK-6
125	4¾"	P	P	P	P	P	P	P

Even though this plaque is not found in many of the catalogs from the 1950s, it is found with all trademarks. One way of distinguishing the early plaques from those of the later Sixties is by counting the number of pickets in the fence. Originally, there were six pickets, later plaques have only five pickets. In her original drawing, Sister Hummel had five pickets in front of the children. This drawing has been transferred photomechanically in Ars Sacra postcard #5325. A picture of the figurine appears in the July issue of the 1960 calendar. On the Price List, TMK-1 and 2 include the premium for the early design. In earlier catalogs this was called "On Holiday," and the German, *Ferienfreude, Bild,* reads, "Vacation Friends, Picture."

125 Vacation Time, *Plaque, known with six fence uprights (scarce), TMK-5.*

126   Retreat to Safety, Plaque

Indicator	Size	Status	TMK-1	TMK-2	TMK-3	TMK-4	TMK-5	TMK-6
126	4¾"	P	P	P	P	P	P	P

Issued before World War II, this plaque is not found in many early U.S. catalogs, as is the case with a number of plaques and other auxiliary articles. Some size variations of minor importance have been recorded. The English name has remained unchanged although the German name of *Bild, Angsthase* has the stronger derogatory connotation of "Coward." This is the same motif as the figurine of the same name, Hum. 201. (See for further details.) There is also some similarity between this very rare bas-relief plaque and the even rarer figurine, Little Velma, 219/2/0, which depicts a girl seated on the fence rather than a boy. This plaque was added to one U.S. catalog in 1978.

126 Retreat to Safety, *Plaque, TMK-5.*

127   Doctor

Indicator	Size	Status	TMK-1	TMK-2	TMK-3	TMK-4	TMK-5	TMK-6
127	4¾"	P	P	P	P	P	P	P

This meditative physician has been reported with his patient at various positions at his feet. Perhaps these variations are due to random placement of this extra piece by the "garnisher"; or maybe the standard location was altered when the figure was restyled with a rougher, textured finish, probably sometime in the Sixties. Since being introduced before 1947, there have been various sizes produced that have ranged from about 4¾" high to slightly over 5" high. One catalog may have been in error in listing it at 3½" as no examples have been reported this small. This piece has been reproduced extensively by several companies with striking fidelity. Be sure any piece acquired has the M.J.Hummel facsimile signature. The German name, *Puppendoctor,* or "Doll Doctor" is a somewhat more realistic name. The original drawing, owned by Verlag Ars Sacra, has been reproduced as postcard #5674. A picture of the figurine is shown for the January, 1960, and also the October, 1972, calendar pages.

127 Doctor, *TMK-5.*

128 Baker, *TMK-5*.

128 Baker

Indicator	Size	Status	TMK-1	TMK-2	TMK-3	TMK-4	TMK-5	TMK-6
128	4¾"	P	P	P	P	P	P	P

This figurine has been in the line since before 1946 without any record of important changes except for the restyling that many figurines underwent in the Sixties when Skrobek introduced a rougher textured finish and a brighter palette of colors. Over the years the size has varied from about 4½" high to 5" high compared to the present standard of 4¾". The German name is *Der Kleinge Konditor,* which means "Little Confectioner." Sister Hummel's original drawing, which is now owned by Verlag Ars Sacra and published as #5546, portrays the subject having somewhat more trouble with his confectionary creation than the figurine. The frosting appears to have been so soft it was dripping off the plate. The figurine itself is pictured for the month of April in the 1975 calendar.

129 Band Leader, *TMK-3*.

129 Band Leader

Indicator	Size	Status	TMK-1	TMK-2	TMK-3	TMK-4	TMK-5	TMK-6
129	5"	P	P	P	P	P	P	P

In production before 1946, this figurine was apparently made somewhat larger during the 1950s, since the sizes in the catalogs of that time range up to 5½" high, compared to the present standard of 5" high. Examples of this intense leader have been reported with the model number incised as 129. (decimal); another was reported with the music printed upside-down. Such would certainly be a premium piece (perhaps 50 percent over listed prices), but probably not to the extent of the well-known U.S. postage stamp with the upside-down airplane. This figurine had the same name as the German one of *Herr Kapellmeister.* In the early 1950s, it was sold as one of a group referred to as the "Hummel Orchestra" which consisted of Little Fiddler, Serenade, Band Leader, Duet, Street Singer, Soloist, Accordion Boy, and Sweet Music. These are, respectively, Hum. 4, 85, 129, 130, 131, 135, 185, and 186. The original drawing is owned by Ars Sacra who issued it as postcard #5731. The figurine is pictured on the January, 1972, calendar page.

130 Duet, *TMK-5*.

130 Duet

Indicator	Size	Status	TMK-1	TMK-2	TMK-3	TMK-4	TMK-5	TMK-6
130	5"	P	P	P	P	P	P	P

This appears in most of the early catalogs since 1947. In the 1947 catalog the price was $6. At that time, it was also known to have had the same name and size. The name is a contraction of the German, *Duett, Sangerpaar* ("Singing Pair"). Some minor variations in height along with slight deviations in color have been recorded. This pair appears to be the inspiration for both the Street Singer, Hum. 131, and the Soloist, Hum. 135. The figurine is well pictured in the calendars for April, 1960, the cover for 1968, and again for March, 1977. The original Sister Hummel drawing from which this motif was adapted actually portrays a nocturnal quartet in full voice using a streetlight to read their music. The nearest two figures were selected for use as this figurine. The other two are probably drawing unemployment pay. The original scene has been accurately shown in a postcard, #5432, published by Verlag Ars Sacra, owner of the original drawing.

131   Street Singer

Indicator	Size	Status	TMK-1	TMK-2	TMK-3	TMK-4	TMK-5	TMK-6
131	5″	P	P	P	P	P	P	P

A 1947 catalog refers to this as simply "Singer," Hum. 131, while a later catalog from the early Fifties carries the name "Soloist," which is now assigned to Hum. 135, which, at that time, was known as "High Tenor." The original German name, *Kammersänger,* would translate as "Chamber Singer." The sizes varied slightly on either side of the present standard of 5″. This figurine has been found in all trademarks, with some color differences not sufficient to affect the prices. It is pictured for the month of January in the 1973 calendar and appears as second singer from the right in Ars Sacra postcard, #5432.

131 Street Singer, *TMK-5.*

132   Star Gazer

Indicator	Size	Status	TMK-1	TMK-2	TMK-3	TMK-4	TMK-5	TMK-6
132	4¾″	P	P	P	P	P	P	P

Since at least 1947, this model has been trying to find a new constellation and was consistently called "Star Gazer" in both English and German *(Stern-gucker),* making it an exception to those that have had so many aliases. Many of the early catalogs in the Fifties and Sixties list this as 4½″, while the current standard size is 4¾″ high. The color of the shirt appears to have been more of a true blue than the reddish blue now used. One TMK-5 has been reported in white overglaze which makes one wonder whether some of these odd white pieces were possibly "lunchbox" samples that went out the employees' gate. Any price differential is included in the listed values. A picture of Hum. 132 is shown for November in the 1978 calendar. Sister Hummel's original work has been lithographed as a postcard #5547 by Ars Sacra who own the original drawing.

132 Star Gazer, *old model with blue shirt, TMK-5.*

133   Mother's Helper

Indicator	Size	Status	TMK-1	TMK-2	TMK-3	TMK-4	TMK-5	TMK-6
133	5″	P	P	P	P	P	P	P

This model is a favorite for feline fanciers because it is presently the only M. I. Hummel that includes a cat that would like playing with the yarn if her mistress did not have both feet firmly planted on it. This has not been consistently listed in all catalogs over the years, even though it is found with all trademarks and has been in the line since at least 1947. A similar figurine that may be released in the future was copyrighted as GP12634 on July 18, 1956, as "Mother's Good Helper" and assigned the number Hum. 325. From the latest editions of the book *HUMMEL* by Robert L. Miller and Eric Ehrmann, this appears to be almost identical to Sister Hummel's original drawing, which included a table and the cat positioned differently. Graphics include a large size poster, T29265, by Verlag Ars Sacra who own the original drawing.

133 Mother's Helper, *TMK-3.*

134 Quartet, Plaque

Indicator	Size	Status	TMK-1	TMK-2	TMK-3	TMK-4	TMK-5	TMK-6
134	6″	P	P	P	P	P	P	P

The group in this bas-relief plaque was adapted from an original by Sister Hummel that shows these four boys standing in a row entertaining on a street corner. It was published as graphics #5431 and #5432 by Ars Sacra from the original drawing in their possession. While only slight variations are found in the front, the back was redesigned so that the present plaques have a centered hole for wall mounting on a nail or patented hanger. Older marks are found with two holes for picture wire or cord, as most pictures were mounted this way years ago. This piece has also been called by the same name over the years with the similar German name of *Das Quartett, Bild,* and includes the two figures on the left in Sister Hummel's original who were omitted from Duet, Hum. 130.

134 Quartet, *Plaque, TMK-5.*

135 Soloist

Indicator	Size	Status	TMK-1	TMK-2	TMK-3	TMK-4	TMK-5	TMK-6
135	4¾″	P	P	P	P	P	P	P

When the companion piece, Street Singer, Hum. 131, was called "Soloist" in the early Fifties, Hum. 135, was called "High Tenor," which comes closer to the English translation of "Heroic Tenor" for the German word *Heldentenor,* a much more dramatic name. Known in all trademarks and currently specified as 4¾″ high, older catalogs indicate that the height has ranged from 4¼″ to 5¼″ over the last thirty years. Any example 5″ and over would warrant a premium of 10 to 20 percent. A full color picture of this figurine is in the 1972 calendar for the month of January. It is also the second figure from the right in Sister Hummel's original drawing and Ars Sacra graphic #5431 which was made from the original.

135 Soloist, *TMK-5.*

136 Friends

Indicator	Size	Status	TMK-1	TMK-2	TMK-3	TMK-4	TMK-5	TMK-6
136(.)	10½″	D	P	—	—	—	—	—
/I	5″	P	?	P	P	P	P	P
/V(5)	10½″	P	P	P	P	P	P	P

This piece has had the same name since 1947 which is the copyright date on the back of some of the smaller sizes. The smaller size, 136/I, had varied from at least 4¼″ to 5¼″ by 1966. The large size, 10½″ high, was listed as 136 (only) in the early 1950s; the 10½″ size is also known with 136. (decimal). No continuous record is shown for this piece, but later catalogs indicate this large size was marked either 136/V or 136/5 (arabic) in heights from 10½″ to 11½″. Add 20 percent for arabic 5. The larger size may have the copyright date 1954. A very rare version of Hum. 136 made of brick red terra-cotta and otherwise unfinished is known to exist. It is thought to have been available in this terra-cotta body at one time. An example found would be valued for insurance purposes in the low four-digit figures. The German name, *Gute Freunde,* meaning "Good Friends," is similar to the English one. A picture of this figurine is used for the month of March in the 1972 calendar.

136/I Friends, *copyright 1947,*
TMK-5.

137 A&B   Child in Bed, Plaque

Indicator	Size	Status	TMK-1	TMK-2	TMK-3	TMK-4	TMK-5	TMK-6
137	2¾"	P	P	P	P	P	P	P
/A	2¾"	U	—	—	—	—	—	—
/B	2¾"	D	?	P	P	?	?	?

This plaque was first issued in two versions differentiated by the markings 137 A and 137 B incised on the backs. When marked 137 A, the child was looking to the viewer's right. The other one of the pair, 137 B, showed the child looking at the ladybug and to the viewer's left. These could not have been sold in large quantities in the U.S. because they are not listed in the early catalogs. A 1959 U.S. catalog lists only the one version marked 137 (only), 3" in diameter. Apparently, 137 (only) superseded the former 137 B with the child looking at the ladybug. The other one, 137 A, must have been discontinued very early, as there have been no examples reported to date. If and when 137 A is found the value would be at least in the high hundreds. This has also been known as "Baby Ring with Lady Bug," but can be distinguished easily from the current Ba-Bee Rings, Hum. 30A&B, by looking closely at the insect on the ring. Ba-Bee Rings have bees; Child in Bed has a ladybug. The German name, *Bild, Kind im Bett,* means "Child in Small Bed."

137 Child in Bed, *Plaque, TMK-5.*

138   Tiny Baby in Crib, Plaque

Indicator	Size	Status	TMK-1	TMK-2	TMK-3	TMK-4	TMK-5	TMK-6
138	3"	C	*	—	—	—	—	—

In the first edition of this book, Hum. 138 was listed as "Unknown," and by the factory as CN for "Closed Number" never to be used again. Further search of the factory records resulted in locating a sample which shows an infant as titled. Since then a reader in Illinois has reported an example of this rarity which he purchased in Germany in 1951. This exciting discovery should be valued in the low four-digit figures, as the factory is of the opinion that this was never offered for sale.

*One example in Miller Collection.

138 Tiny Baby in Crib, *Plaque, TMK-2. Miller Collection.*

139   Flitting Butterfly, Plaque

Indicator	Size	Status	TMK-1	TMK-2	TMK-3	TMK-4	TMK-5	TMK-6
139	2½"	R	P	P	P	?	R	R

This piece may never have been distributed in the U.S. before 1959, even though it is known with all trademarks. The early marks show a smaller baby with a darker red dress with no dots and an open space behind the baby's neck. The new larger model, apparently redesigned in the Sixties, was introduced in the U.S. for the first time in all catalogs in 1980. Prior to 1980, examples of the redesigned model with TMK-5 were available only from German dealers. This piece continues to command a premium because of the scarcity.

139 Flitting Butterfly, *Plaque. (Left) reinstated, current design. (Right) old design, no dots on dress. Miller Collection.*

140 The Mail Is Here, *Plaque,*
TMK-5.

141/I Apple Tree Girl, *TMK-5.*

142/I Apple Tree Boy, *TMK-1.*

140   The Mail Is Here, Plaque

Indicator	Size	Status	TMK-1	TMK-2	TMK-3	TMK-4	TMK-5	TMK-6
140	4½″	P	P	P	P	P	P	P

In the Alphabetical Index, this plaque has been listed as above, but it is also known as "Mail Coach" by many collectors; the Goebel Company has used both names, sometimes almost interchangeably. This piece has not been consistently listed in catalogs throughout the years, but is still found in all trademarks listed above. This plaque has been reported to have been made in a plain white overglaze at some time. Any such piece would be rare and probably would be valued in the high hundreds if not a very low four-digit figure. About 1952, this design was released as a three-dimensional figurine, Hum. 226 (see for more information).

141   Apple Tree Girl

Indicator	Size	Status	TMK-1	TMK-2	TMK-3	TMK-4	TMK-5	TMK-6
141/3/0	4″	P	P	P	P	P	P	P
/0	5″	U	—	—	—	—	—	—
141(.)	6″	D	P	P	—	—	—	—
/I	6″	P	?	P	P	P	P	P
/V	10″	P	—	—	—	P	P	P
/X	32″	P	—	—	—	—	P	P

This figurine and its companion, Apple Tree Boy, Hum. 142, have been favorites with collectors since the Forties. The present English name and "Spring," a foreshortening of the German name, *Frühling, Mädchen im Baum,* were used in various early catalogs. First issued in the 6″ to 6½″ size and marked 141 (only) or 141. (decimal), the figurine was shortly thereafter issued as 141/I in the same size range of 6″ — 6½″ high. The 141/3/0 was listed in the early Fifties, and it has varied around 4″ high over the thirty or more years. Both 141/I and 141/3/0 have been found in TMK-1. In both of the early sizes, the base and tree trunk appeared as one. Later, a straight-sided base was uncolored and unrelated to the tree. These two sizes differed; the smaller 141/3/0 size being the only one issued without a bird in the top of the tree. One interesting piece, marked 141 (only), was discovered in white overglaze, the only one found to date. The next recorded size, 141/V, was introduced around 1970, and is found only with the last three trademarks. This was modeled by Skrobek who also restyled the other sizes. The giant size 141/X, which varies around 32″ high, was first available in the U.S. in 1976 in very limited quantities and priced at over $6,000.

142   Apple Tree Boy

Indicator	Size	Status	TMK-1	TMK-2	TMK-3	TMK-4	TMK-5	TMK-6
142/3/0	4″	P	P	P	P	P	P	P
/0	5″	U	—	—	—	—	—	—
142(.)	6″	D	P	?	—	—	—	—
/I	6″	P	P	P	P	P	P	P
/V	10″	P	—	—	—	P	P	P
/X	30″	P	—	8	—	—	P	P

The history of this companion piece is essentially the same. One difference is the time of year indicated by the ripe fruit on the tree, so this one was also known as "Fall," as the German name, *Herbst, Junge im Baum,* implies. Verlag Ars Sacra produces graphics of this pair from their originals as #5723 and #5724. These figurines appear in calendars for September, 1962, September, 1967, and May and October, 1974. The motifs are also used for the 1975 and 1976 Annual Plates, Hum. 269 and 270; Lamps, Hum. 229 and 230; and Bookends, Hum. 252 A&B.

143 Boots

Indicator	Size	Status	TMK-1	TMK-2	TMK-3	TMK-4	TMK-5	TMK-6
143/0	5½″	P	P	P	P	P	P	P
143	6¾″	D	P	P	—	—	—	—
/I	6½″	R	—	?	P	—	R	R

This piece has been reported with both Crown and Full Bee trademarks incised only 143, from 6½″ to 6¾″ high. Sometime in the early Fifties this whole number model was superseded by 143/I for figures in this height. This size has not been continuously available in the U.S. and was reintroduced in Germany in limited quantities in 1978; it is now available from U.S. distributors. The smaller size, Hum. 143/3/0, was listed in some of the early Fifties catalogs and called "Shoemaker." The listed sizes varied from 4½″ high to the present 5½″ high. The hobnails in the boots of some examples are much more pronounced than in others. This change most likely occurs between the time a new mold is placed in production and the time it is removed due to wear and subsequent lack of detail. The German name has no relation to the English one as it translates as "Mister Important" from *Meister Wichtig*. Ars Sacra has published an exact likeness of the original work in postcard #5769, and Goebel has used a picture of the figurine for their calendar pages of February, 1947, and August, 1967.

143/0 Boots, *TMK-5.*

144 Angelic Song

Indicator	Size	Status	TMK-1	TMK-2	TMK-3	TMK-4	TMK-5	TMK-6
144	4″	P	P	P	P	P	P	P

Introduced before 1947, a catalog of that year lists the name as "Singing Angel," 4¼″ high, for $5. The much more descriptive name of "Angel with Mandolin, Girl with Hymm Book," was used in the early 1950s. The German name is *Singendes Kind mit Engelein,* meaning "Singing Child with Small Angel." Aside from the small differences in height, other reported variations include some slight deviation in the blue flowers in the headband and a piece reported marked 144/I. This double figurine is pictured in the 1960 calendar for the month of November. The nearest graphic that has been found is Ars Sacra postcard #4439.

144 Angelic Song, *TMK-5.*

145 Little Guardian

Indicator	Size	Status	TMK-1	TMK-2	TMK-3	TMK-4	TMK-5	TMK-6
145	4″	P	P	P	P	P	P	P

The catalog history of this pair shows the height varying widely from as small as 3¾″ in 1950 to as tall as 4¾″ in 1959. Since the Price List reflects the current size of 4″, examples 4½″ and larger should be valued at a premium of about 20 percent, which would be in line for such a size were it made today. The headband on the kneeling child is also found with blue flowers instead of the more usual orange ones. When found with blue flowers, an example should be valued at about 25 percent more than one with orange flowers bearing the same trademark. The German name for this pair is *Betendes Kind mit Engelein,* which means "Praying Child with Small Angel." "Angel Pair" and "Girl Kneeling Beside Angel with Flowers" are other names used over the last thirty-five years. No original drawing by Sister Hummel with this motif has been located to date.

145 Little Guardian, *TMK-3.*

146 Angel Duet, Holy Water Font

Indicator	Size	Status	TMK-1	TMK-2	TMK-3	TMK-4	TMK-5	TMK-6
146	4¾″	P	P	P	P	P	P	P

Some of the older catalogs of the 1950s refer only to this piece as Holy Water Font, Hum. 146, slightly larger than the above listed size. The present name, Angel Duet, is confusing because it is also used for two other models which are not the same figures. One is a candleholder, Hum. 193, and another is a very similar figurine of two angels singing from a common hymnbook, Hum. 261. Hum. 146 is found in all trademarks and the later models have a palette of colors brighter than the earlier ones. German terminology is not much less confusing for these fonts. The location of Sister Hummel's original drawing for this motif has not been verified as yet.

146 Angel Duet, *Holy Water Font,*
TMK-4.

147 Angel Shrine, Holy Water Font

Indicator	Size	Status	TMK-1	TMK-2	TMK-3	TMK-4	TMK-5	TMK-6
147	5″	P	P	P	P	P	P	P

In *Hummel Art I,* this font was listed with the primary name of "Devotion" and the secondary one of "Angel Shrine." These have now been reversed, as only one catalog now lists this font as "Devotion." Some of the early catalogs referred to this as "Angel at Shrine" and the German name of *Engel* merely means "Angel." Although not listed in many catalogs, it was introduced by 1950, and it is found with all trademarks. The height listed varies from about 5″ to 5½″ high. Note how the tips of the wings join the shrine roof to reduce the hazard of damage to the fragile wings. The font has been found in TMK-2 with one extra flower to the left of the angel. The original drawing is owned by Verlag Ars Sacra who have faithfully duplicated it as postcard #4773.

147 Angel Shrine, *Holy Water Font,*
TMK-3. (Alternate name, Devotion.)
Dous Collection.

148 Cancelled Number

Indicator	Size	Status	TMK-1	TMK-2	TMK-3	TMK-4	TMK-5	TMK-6
148	?	U	—	—	—	—	—	—

According to *HUMMEL, Authorized Supplement* by Robert L. Miller, the factory records indicate that this number was not used after 1941 and may have been intended for some version of Farm Boy. While it is unlikely that a sample will ever be discovered in or out of the factory, there is always the slight chance that some diligent collector or researcher will find one which would be valued in the high four-digit figures.

149 Cancelled Number

Indicator	Size	Status	TMK-1	TMK-2	TMK-3	TMK-4	TMK-5	TMK-6
149	?	U	—	—	—	—	—	—

Factory records indicate that this number was not used after 1941 and may have been intended for a variation of the Goose Girl, also according to Robert L. Miller. While it is unlikely that any sample is extant, sometime, someplace, one may be ferreted out by a dedicated collector who will then have a prize possession valued at $5,000 or more.

150   Happy Days

Indicator	Size	Status	TMK-1	TMK-2	TMK-3	TMK-4	TMK-5	TMK-6
150/2/0	4¼″	P	?	P	P	P	P	P
/0	5¼″	R	—	P	P	—	R	R
150(.)	6¼″	D	P	?	—	—	—	—
/I	6¼″	R	?	P	?	—	R	R

This figurine has been produced with the four model/size indicators listed above, but not all simultaneously. The earliest listing found was in 1947. In the early 1950s, it was also incised with only the model number 150 at 15.5 cm. or slightly over 6″ high. A widely distributed, 1956 bilingual catalog in full color does not even show this model. By 1959, the 5″ size, 150/0, and the 4″ size, 150/2/0, were shown, but with no mention of the larger size. In 1966, only the smallest size 150/2/0 was listed as 4¼″ tall. Apparently this size has been continuously available from that date. The other two sizes marked 150/0 at 5¼″ and 150/I at 6¼″ (which superseded plain 150) were reintroduced in Germany in 1978 in very limited quantities. As this book went to press they are still being cataloged in all three sizes. Collectors should be wary of paying big prices for the older marks until Goebel's production policy is better known. This figurine is on the cover of the 1975 calendar and for the month of April in the 1962 issue. Verlag Ars Sacra has produced graphic #14409 and owns the original drawing.

150/2/0 Happy Days, *TMK-5.*

151   Madonna Holding Child

Indicator	Size	Status	TMK-1	TMK-2	TMK-3	TMK-4	TMK-5	TMK-6
151	12″	R	—	P	P	—	R	R
/II	12″	R	P	P	—	—	R	R

This figurine was known in the mid-Seventies as the very rare "Blue Cloak Madonna." Later, an example in white surfaced, and in 1977 a brown one was added to the well-known Robert and Ruth Miller collection. These were selling in the mid four-digit range until Goebel decided to reintroduce both the blue and the white versions in 1978 in Germany at a small fraction of the price. The present price for a Hum. 151, with TMK-5 or 6, is about one-tenth the price of an old one, but still expensive compared to a similar size Flower Madonna, Hum. 10. At present, other rare versions of this Madonna are known in a light blue cloak and in an ivory colored cloak. These two and the one in brown have not been reissued to date, but the possibility always exists. Collectors should be especially well informed when acquiring an old example of this model number as to what premium they are paying for an old mark on the bottom. There is always the chance of paying too high a price for even one with late TMK-5 or 6. Goebel's future production plans are the key factor. In an early publication, the picture used for this piece was that of the Flower Madonna, Hum. 10, which confused many collectors. The German name, *Sitzende Madonna mit sitzendem Kind,* translates as "Sitting Madonna with Seated Child."

151 Madonna Holding Child (*with blue cloak*), *TMK-5, courtesy W. Goebel Co.*

151 Madonna Holding Child (*with brown cloak*), *TMK-5, courtesy W. Goebel Co.*

152/A/0 Umbrella Boy, *TMK-4.*

152 A   Umbrella Boy

Indicator	Size	Status	TMK-1	TMK-2	TMK-3	TMK-4	TMK-5	TMK-6
152/A/0	4¾″	P	—	P	P	P	P	P
152(.)	8″	D	P	—	—	—	—	—
152A	8″	D	?	P	P	—	—	—
152/A/II	8″	P	—	P	P	P	P	P

The model was first produced sometime in the Forties and listed in a 1950 catalog as "Boy Under Roof," at 7¾″ high, incised only 152. In a 1956 catalog, this was then called "In Safety" and incised as 152A only, about 8″ high. The companion 152B, Umbrella Girl, was also listed in this catalog. By 1959, the smaller 4¾″ size had been introduced as an addition to the large 8″ size. At that time, they were designated 152/0 A and 152/II A, respectively. Crown marks would also be considered rare and in the low four-digit range. The U.S. Copyright Office shows registration date for GP3390 as January 17, 1951, with revisions in 1957 and again in 1972. The large size is usually found with TMK-2 through TMK-6, and the small size with TMK-3 through TMK-6. In German, the name is *Geborgen, Junge,* translated as "Sheltered Safe, Boy." This figure is already a very popular one and will become moreso when it appears in bas-relief on the 1981 Annual Plate, Hum. 274.

152 B   Umbrella Girl

Indicator	Size	Status	TMK-1	TMK-2	TMK-3	TMK-4	TMK-5	TMK-6
152/B/0	4¾″	P	—	P	P	P	P	P
152B	8″	D	?	P	P	P	—	—
152/B/II	8″	P	—	?	P	P	P	P

Since some of the early catalogs list only the number 152 for "Boy under Roof," it appears that this companion piece was introduced somewhat later, but before 1956. Otherwise, the remarks above about 152 A apply as well to Umbrella Girl. As mentioned, they were both restyled to reflect the more modern bright colors and textured or roughened surface. There are minor variations which happen in assembling the various parts prior to the first firing. Both 152 A&B have been produced in graphics by Ars Sacra as #5162 and #14386. Umbrella Boy figurine was on the cover of the 1954 calendar and the page for February, 1967. Umbrella Girl figurine was illustrated in the April, 1974, and January, 1969, Goebel calendar pages.

152/B/0 Umbrella Girl, *TMK-4.*

153   Auf Wiedersehen

Indicator	Size	Status	TMK-1	TMK-2	TMK-3	TMK-4	TMK-5	TMK-6
153/0	5″	P	?	P*	P	P	P	P
153(.)	7″	D	P	?	—	—	—	—
/I	7″	R	P	P	P	—	R	R

This boy and girl are a collector's delight with many variations and some unverified stories. First introduced in the Forties, it was called "Goodbye" and incised with only the model number 153 at about 7″ high. Sometime in the early Fifties, the name was changed in the English catalogs to the well-known German *Auf Wiedersehen.* About this time, a smaller size, 153/0, was introduced at about 5″ high, and the larger size was renumbered as 153/I. Some of these early small ones were made with the boy wearing a hat and not waving a handkerchief. They were marked with the large Full Bee trademark, TMK-2. These are scarce and are valued in the low four-digit range. The full story of this deviation has not been reconstructed as yet. One U.S. catalog dated 1959 lists the only size as 4″ high, but since there is no known example to date, this is believed to be in error. In any event, the large 7″ size was apparently uncataloged for years until it was reintroduced in limited quantities in 1977 in the U.S. Both sizes were restyled in the late Sixties or early Seventies. Many owners have a sentimental attachment to this pair, because it was often a memento received when emigrating to the U.S. The original drawing owned by Ars Sacra and issued as postcard #5617 was modified considerably for the figurine. The figurine itself has been pictured on Goebel calendars in July, 1972, and August, 1977.

*Some with hat.

153 Auf Wiedersehen, *TMK-5.*

154 Waiter

Indicator	Size	Status	TMK-1	TMK-2	TMK-3	TMK-4	TMK-5	TMK-6
154/0	6″	P	?	P	P	P	P	P
154	6½″	D	P	?	—	—	—	—
/I	7″	R	P	P	P	—	R	R

This model appears in a catalog of the late Forties when it was called by its present name. For a period of time in the Fifties it was called "Little Waiter," and incised with only the 154. The size ranged from 6″ to 6½″ high. When the smaller size, which is now 6″ high, was introduced, it was marked 154/0; about the same time the large one, now 7″ high, was introduced as 154/I. During the early period the Waiter had a gray jacket and striped gray pants. This was changed to a blue gray jacket and tan striped pants. It was recorded in the U.S. Copyright Office as R15212B on March 12, 1972. The label on the bottle of the current model carries the name "Rhein Wine," as have most examples in the past. The number of label variations are unknown, but there are several, including an illegible scrawl. Such variations in name would be valued at least 25 percent higher than a standard "Rhein Wine" with similar trademark. Sister Hummel made at least two originals of this drawing which has been reproduced as postcard #5771 by Ars Sacra who own one original. The other original was done for the Kleber Post Inn in Saulgau where it was still hanging in the dining room in 1979.

154/0 **Waiter,** *with brown pants, trademark unknown.*

155-162 Cancelled Numbers

Indicator	Size	Status	TMK-1	TMK-2	TMK-3	TMK-4	TMK-5	TMK-6
155-162	?	U	—	—	—	—	—	—

During a five-month period from May through October of 1943, these eight numbers were cancelled by the Goebel Company for unknown reasons. According to Robert L. Miller in his *Supplement* to the book *HUMMEL,* design studies were tentatively assigned to each as follows: Hum. 155, study of a Madonna; Hum. 156, wall picture of a seated woman and child; Hum. 157, boy with flower basket; Hum. 158, standing girl holding dog; Hum. 159, standing girl holding bouquet; Hum. 160, standing girl in tiered dress holding flowers; Hum. 161, standing girl with hands in pockets; and Hum. 162, standing girl with handbag. In the surprising event that one of these designs should surface, it would no doubt be valued in the four-digit range. It is not expected that these numbers will ever be used again.

163 Whitsuntide

Indicator	Size	Status	TMK-1	TMK-2	TMK-3	TMK-4	TMK-5	TMK-6
163	7″	R	P	P	P	—	R	R

The first two English names were assigned by someone other than a student of the bible. When introduced in the Forties, it was first called "Happy New Year." In the early Fifties, the name was changed to "Christmas." The German name, *Glockenturm mit Engeln,* which translates as "Bell Tower with Angels," is certainly more descriptive and accurate. This figure has not been consistently cataloged even though it may have been available on special order. So far it appears in all marks except TMK-4. It was reintroduced in very limited quantities in Germany in 1978 and appeared since then in U.S. catalogs. This reintroduction has lowered the price some collectors paid when it was available only in the older marks. Values in the Price List are tentative and may be subject to drastic change depending on Goebel's future production plans. The new version is easily distinguished, as it is only 6½″ high as compared to the older one that is about 7″ high. The angel on the base in the latest figurine is not holding a candle as some of the older ones did, but some examples with the Crown mark showed no evidence of a candle, either. If it were not for the fact that Hum. 163 was once rare, this piece would not have justified either the premium prices paid or the space taken by this essay.

163 **Whitsuntide,** *old design,* TMK-2.

164 Worship, Holy Water Font

Indicator	Size	Status	TMK-1	TMK-2	TMK-3	TMK-4	TMK-5	TMK-6
164	4¾"	P	P	P	P	P	P	P

At one time this model was called "Praying Girl Font." The older Crown and Full Bee styles are distinguished by a stippled coloring around the edge, compared to the shaded airbrush coloring on later models. The redesigned models also have an extension of the back beyond the semicircular bowl. This was probably introduced in the late Forties or very early Fifties. The German name, *Am Wegesrand,* translates as "At the Wayside." This design is entirely different than the figurine, Worship, Hum. 84, shown on page 64, which was also known as "At the Wayside." Postcard #14427 by Verlag Ars Sacra pictures the original drawing.

164 Worship, *Holy Water Font, TMK-5. Dous Collection.*

165 Swaying Lullaby, Plaque

Indicator	Size	Status	TMK-1	TMK-2	TMK-3	TMK-4	TMK-5	TMK-6
165	5¼"	R	P	P	P	—	R	R

For some years this was a very high-priced collectible when found with a Crown or Full Bee trademark. They could be obtained only in the secondary market. In 1978, Goebel reinstated production of this model in very limited quantities in Germany for about $35 U.S. It is now available through regular channels in the U.S. and the prices for old marks may drop considerably depending on the quantities being produced. Introduced around 1950, it was called, "Child in Hammock." The German names of *Kind mit Hängematte und Vogel* translate as "Child with Hammock and Bird." The inscription on the front means "Dreaming of Better Times." To date, no examples with TMK-4 have been reported. One of these would probably be valued in the high hundreds. A postcard, #5945, from the original, is published by Verlag Ars Sacra.

165 Swaying Lullaby, *Plaque, TMK-2, no copyright date. Miller Collection.*

166 Boy with Bird, Ashtray

Indicator	Size	Status	TMK-1	TMK-2	TMK-3	TMK-4	TMK-5	TMK-6
166	6¼"	P	P	P	P	P	P	P

While this has been found in all trademarks, it was not always cataloged, possibly due to low demand. The boy lying prone differs from Singing Lesson Ashtray, Hum. 34, in which the boy is seated as in the Figurine, Hum. 63, the Candy Box, Hum. III/63, and the 1979 Annual Plate, Hum. 272. The bird also varies in design and color. The German, *Junge mit Vogel* means "Boy with Bird." The original drawing is owned by Ars Sacra who have published a reproduction of the drawing as postcard #5862.

166 Boy with Bird, *Ashtray, TMK-5.*

167 Angel with Yellow Bird, Holy Water Font

Indicator	Size	Status	TMK-1	TMK-2	TMK-3	TMK-4	TMK-5	TMK-6
167	4¾″	P	P	P	P	P	P	P

This name has been modified since the font, Angel with Birds, Hum. 22, also has a seated angel with birds. In this case, the angel is facing to the left with no halo. In Hum. 22, the angel is facing to the right and has a halo. The early Full Bee, TMK-2 model of Hum. 167 does not have the hanging hole in the top of the font, and the edge of the bowl is stippled with no extension or protruding flange at the back of the bowl. At that time the width was only about 2″. As with other fonts, this has not been continuously cataloged although it has been produced with all trademarks.

167 Angel with Yellow Bird, *Holy Water Font, TMK-5.*

168 Standing Boy, Plaque

Indicator	Size	Status	TMK-1	TMK-2	TMK-3	TMK-4	TMK-5	TMK-6
168	5¾″	R	P	P	?	—	R	R

Another plaque that was a very rare and high-priced collector's item until 1978 when it was reintroduced in very limited quantities with TMK-5, continues in current production. The price of the old ones has already dropped and future prices will depend on how many of the recent production items are made. The German name, *Stehender Junge mit Herz und Flashe* ("Standing Boy with Heart and Bottle") is much more descriptive of the Valentine motif. This leads to the conclusion that this plaque and Hum. 399, Valentine Joy, which was the Goebel Collectors' Club limited edition for the 1980-1981 members, were adapted from the same Sister Hummel original which is now owned by Verlag Ars Sacra. An exact replica of this drawing has been published as postcard #5939 by Ars Sacra and shows how much more the plaque resembles the original than Valentine Joy does.

168 Standing Boy, *Plaque, original TMK-2 pictured. Miller Collection.*

169 Bird Duet

Indicator	Size	Status	TMK-1	TMK-2	TMK-3	TMK-4	TMK-5	TMK-6
169	4″	P	P	P	P	P	P	P

Since being introduced around 1950, the birds have changed their tune at least three, possibly more times based on the music that appears on the stand. This is only one of innumerable modifications in design, color, and height, some of which were due to general restyling in about 1961. With the Full Bee mark (early 1950s) the black baton was raised, as compared to the red baton at rest in the current version. In the German catalog spelling was once *Duett.* The German name deviates from this theme by calling it *Frühlingslied,* for "Song of Spring."

169 Bird Duet, *TMK-5.*

170/I School Boys, *TMK-5.*

170　School Boys

Indicator	Size	Status	TMK-1	TMK-2	TMK-3	TMK-4	TMK-5	TMK-6
170	10″	D	P	P	P	—	—	—
/I	7½″	P	—	—	P	P	P	P
/III	10¼″	P	—	—	P	P	P	P

This intently serious group was first issued around 1950 in just the large, 10″ size and incised only 170 on the base. Some of the catalogs of the mid-Fifties do not list this model at all. In a 1959 issue it was only listed as a special order item in the 9¾″ size. A smaller size, 7½″, was copyrighted in the U.S. on December 20, 1961, and from that time on it was incised 170/I. the larger 10″ size changed from only 170 to 170/III at about 9½″ to 10¼″ high. These continued to be listed in some catalogs as special orders and omitted from others. On March 14, 1973, Copyright GF1029 was registered in the U.S. for a restyling of the large 170/III size. The restyling may have been filed earlier in Germany, as the recent pieces are incised 1972 and the smaller ones are marked 1961. The German name of *Schwieriges Problem* ("Difficult Problem") captures the subject at hand very succinctly. A picture of the group was used for the month of September in the 1976 calendar, and Verlag Ars Sacra who own the original drawing published a postcard of it as #A5333. See School Girls, Hum. 177, for a companion piece.

171　Little Sweeper

Indicator	Size	Status	TMK-1	TMK-2	TMK-3	TMK-4	TMK-5	TMK-6
171	4¼″	P	P	P	P	P	P	P

Apparently, this was first called "Sweeper," after the German name, *Kehrliesl,* and then changed in the early Fifties to the descriptive phrase, "Girl with Broom," to distinguish it from "Mother's Helper (girl sitting on chair knitting), Hum. 133. Finally, before the end of the 1950s, the figurine assumed its present name. There have been no major changes reported in size and color except for the general restyling in the Sixties to brighter colors, a shinier finish, and a more "modern" look. A distinctive feature noted by one collector is that this is the only figurine which extends over the side and below the base. The original drawing is owned by Ars Sacra who published postcard #5673 from it. The figurine itself is pictured in the Goebel calendar for the month of February, 1973.

171 Little Sweeper, *TMK-5.*

172　Festival Harmony with Mandolin

Indicator	Size	Status	TMK-1	TMK-2	TMK-3	TMK-4	TMK-5	TMK-6
172/0	8″	P	?	?	?	P	P	P
172	10½″	D	P	P	—	—	—	—
/II	10½″	P	P	P	P	P	P	P

This impressive piece, like some of its contemporaries, was first issued about 10″ high, with a Crown mark, and incised with only the number 172. The design at that time, as illustrated, had the waist-high flower and bird arrangement in front of the angel. This was a special order piece and not listed in many of the early catalogs until 1959 or 1960. Prior to this time, it was redesigned showing only a plant with blossoms slightly above the hem of the gown and the bird resting on the mandolin (called "banjo" at that time). This version is found with the Full Bee mark. As with so many other figurines, this one was later restyled to reflect the brighter colors and rougher, textured finish. When restyled, the small blossoms were reduced to a point below the hemline. About this time a smaller size, about 8″ high in the new style, was introduced and incised 172/0 while the model number on the larger was changed to 172/II, instead of only 172, and is found usually in TMK-3, 4, and 5. The German name is *Adventsengel mit Mandoline*, "Advent Angel with Mandolin." Ars Sacra own the original drawing by Sister Hummel and currently publish a postcard replica #14552.

172/0 *(L)* Festival Harmony with Banjo, *TMK-1.*
172/0 *(R)* Festival Harmony with Mandolin, *TMK-5.*

173 Festival Harmony with Flute

Indicator	Size	Status	TMK-1	TMK-2	TMK-3	TMK-4	TMK-5	TMK-6
173/0	8″	P	?	?	?	P	P	P
173	10½″	D	P	P	—	—	—	—
/II	10½″	P	P	P	P	P	P	P

First issued with Crown mark in limited quantities as a twin to Hum. 172, it too followed the same progressive changes in design, apparently at exactly the same times through the Fifties and Sixties. The unavailability at certain periods, the introduction of the smaller size, and the change in model numbering followed in parallel. The flowers also made a similar descent to below the hemline of the angel's gown. The 1959 catalog called the instrument a horn instead of a flute, as it called the mandolin a banjo. Some collectors feel that this version is rarer than Festival Harmony with Banjo, Hum. 172. The German name, *Adventsengel mit Flöte,* means "Advent Angel with Flute." The original painting done by Sister Hummel is owned by Verlag Ars Sacra who used this drawing to publish postcard #14551.

173/0 Festival Harmony with Flute, *new style, TMK-5.*

174 She Loves Me, She Loves Me Not

Indicator	Size	Status	TMK-1	TMK-2	TMK-3	TMK-4	TMK-5	TMK-6
174	4¼″	P	P	P	P	P	P	P

Issued with a Crown mark in the late 1940s, 4¼″ high, but not shown in the 1947 U.S. catalog, this piece was modified before 1956 and again in the late Sixties. A premium is included in the TMK-1 price for the early model with a straight-ahead pensive stare, very small feather, and no blossom midway up the upright post on the left side. The TMK-2 version has a very prominent feather in the cap, a flower blossom about midway up the post on viewer's left, and straight-ahead gaze. Sometime after 1967, the piece was restyled by removing the midway flower and having the boy look down at a smaller daisy. Deeply sculptured hair and textured jacket (a la Skrobek) were also added. At one time, this piece was listed as "Boy Sitting Before Fence." The German name, *Liebt mich, liebt mich nicht,* is the same as the English.

174 She Loves Me, She Loves Me Not, *eyes down, TMK-5.*

175 Mother's Darling

Indicator	Size	Status	TMK-1	TMK-2	TMK-3	TMK-4	TMK-5	TMK-6
175	5½″	P	P	P	P	P	P	P

This model was called "Happy Harriet" in a late Forties catalog. The German name, *Markt-Christel* means "Market, Christine." The earlier TMK-3 examples had no polka dots in the head kerchief; also, the kerchief in her right hand had a pink background with blue polka dots, while the one in her left hand was a light aqua color with red polka dots. Furthermore, the polka dots in her dress had a touch of gold in them. The newer TMK-3 version has similar pastel blue backgrounds for each kerchief she is holding with no change in the dot colors, and white polka dots in the one on her head. The older version with TMK-3 should be valued at about 30 percent more than the newer. The other older marks have the allowance included. This figurine is pictured for April, 1971, calendar page.

175 Mother's Darling, *new colors, TMK-5.*

176 Happy Birthday, *TMK-5.*

176 Happy Birthday

Indicator	Size	Status	TMK-1	TMK-2	TMK-3	TMK-4	TMK-5	TMK-6
176/0	5½″	P	?	P	P	P	P	P
176(.)	5½″	D	P	P	—	—	—	—
/I	6″	R	P	?	—	—	R	R

When first issued before World War II, this figurine was incised either 176 (only) or 176. (decimal), about 5½″ high. A Crown mark example shows one girl's forefinger away from her mouth and raised polka dots in her dress. Both girls' shoes are the same shade of brown in this TMK-1 piece. When the smaller 5½″ high size, incised 176/0, was introduced on an oval base (probably around the mid-Sixties), the larger size was thereafter incised 176/I. The larger 176/I was sparsely produced until it was reintroduced in the 6″ size in Germany in 1978 for the equivalent of $63 U.S. Both sizes are currently cataloged and sold in this country. Verlag Ars Sacra, owner and publisher of the original drawing, issue a cropped version of it as postcard #5615. The figurine is shown in the 1976 Goebel calendar for October.

177 School Girls

Indicator	Size	Status	TMK-1	TMK-2	TMK-3	TMK-4	TMK-5	TMK-6
177	9½″	D	P	P	P	—	—	—	—
/I	7½″	P	—	—	P	P	P	P
/III	9½″	P	—	—	P	P	P	P

This group of three girls was introduced in the late Forties as "Masterpiece" which is the translation of its German name, *Meisterstück.* Examples have been found incised both 177 (only) and 177. (decimal) in TMK-1. One interesting piece in TMK-2 was found marked 177/0. Some of the catalogs in the mid-Fifties do not list this figurine. In 1959 it was listed as a special order item, 9¾″ high. A smaller size, 7½″ high, was copyrighted in the U.S. on December 20, 1961 (GF54). From that time on, it was incised 177/I while the larger size was incised 177/III instead of only 177. Both sizes continued to be listed in some catalogs as special order items and omitted from others. On March 14, 1973, Copyright GS1028 was registered in the U.S. for restyling of 177/III, the larger size. These are found incised 1972, possibly the year of the German copyright. Values for the larger piece with older trademarks can vary widely from those on the Price List. A picture of this group is on the cover of the 1967 calendar and Ars Sacra publish graphic #5332 from the original drawing in their possession. The girl knitting has been extracted from this group and is available separately as Hum. 255, Stitch in Time. She and the girl on her left have been adapted as the pair in Hum. 256, Knitting Lesson.

177 School Girls, *TMK-5.*

178 The Photographer

Indicator	Size	Status	TMK-1	TMK-2	TMK-3	TMK-4	TMK-5	TMK-6
178	5″	P	P	P	P	P	P	P

While some examples of the figurine are found incised with the year 1948, it may not have been introduced until sometime later. The piece was available only as a special order item. The U.S. copyright was registered on July 14, 1950. Early examples are listed as 4½″ high, while the present size is 5″. Other sizes due to mold variations are known. Like so many others, Hum. 178 was redesigned in the Sixties with brighter and shinier colors and minor modifications that do not materially affect the values. In some references, this is called "Photographer," so it is listed in the Alphabetical Index with and without the article "The." Verlag Ars Sacra own the original drawing and have produced a postcard of it as #4767. A picture of the figurine itself was used for the November, 1971, calendar page. The German name is *Der Fotograf.*

178 The Photographer, *TMK-5.*

179 Coquettes

Indicator	Size	Status	TMK-1	TMK-2	TMK-3	TMK-4	TMK-5	TMK-6
179	5″	P	P	P	P	P	P	P

An early catalog from the 1950s lists this as "Coquettes" (two girls on a fence in which there are holes for flowers). It is found in all trademarks and also incised as 179. (decimal) with a Crown mark. One variation has the girl on the viewer's right wearing a dark blue dress and holding flowers. This piece was also restyled and is found brighter and shinier in the newer marks. The figurine was pictured in the March, 1976, calendar. The German name of *Zaungäste* translates as "Fence Guests." The original drawing owned by Ars Sacra has been published as postcard #5861.

179 Coquettes, *TMK-5.*

180 Tuneful Good Night, Plaque

Indicator	Size	Status	TMK-1	TMK-2	TMK-3	TMK-4	TMK-5	TMK-6
180	5″	R	P	P	P	—	R	R

As with many other plaques, this heart-shaped piece was very infrequently listed in U.S. or bilingual catalogs. Ones with old marks are scarce and relatively high-priced. One verified old example had blue shoes and a very light blue dress. In 1978 the plaque was reintroduced in the German catalog and since 1980 it has been listed in the U.S. catalogs. The prices shown on the Price List are tentative and will depend on how many new marks are released by Goebel. In an early 1950 catalog this was listed as "Girl Sitting in a Heart," and it has also been called "Happy Bugler." Some of the TMK-5 examples having the painted year "79" on them may also attain collectors' special status. The German name is *Wandschmuck in Herzform, sitzendes Kind mit Trompete,* or in English, "Heart-shaped Wall Ornament, Seated Child with Trumpet." The original drawing has been reproduced as postcard #14305 by Verlag Ars Sacra.

180 Tuneful Good Night, *Plaque, TMK-1, no copyright date. Miller Collection.*

181 Old Man Reading Newspaper (Cancelled Number)

Indicator	Size	Status	TMK-1	TMK-2	TMK-3	TMK-4	TMK-5	TMK-6
181	6¾″	C	*	—	—	—	—	—

This figurine is a faithful adaptation of one of Sister Hummel's caricatures. The original drawing is now owned by Verlag Emil Fink who has published it as lithograph #657. As might be expected from her work as a student, Berta Hummel's mischievous mind sometimes used such caricatures to amuse her schoolmates. One attempt which backfired according to Ehrmann, was of her professor in the Art academy in Munich. After class he found a caricature of himself and put it back on her desk with the comment, "Pull out the lower drawer more," meaning that she had not exaggerated his protruding lower lip enough. The figurine is listed in Goebel's records as a closed number as of 1948. For further information as to why these were never put in regular production, see the remainder of this group, Hum. 189, 190, and 191.

*Only known example valued in the low five-digit figures.

181 Old Man Reading Newspaper, *prototype, incised M. I. Hummel, no trademark. Miller Collection.*

182 Good Friends, *TMK-5.*

183 Forest Shrine, *rare TMK-2, 9"*
high.

184 Latest News, *TMK-5.*

182   Good Friends

Indicator	Size	Status	TMK-1	TMK-2	TMK-3	TMK-4	TMK-5	TMK-6
182(.)	4"	P	P	P	P	P	P	P

At one time, this was called just "Friends," but since the earlier piece, Hum. 136, Girl with Fawn, was also called by the same name, this one was changed to eliminate the confusion. Examples have not only been reported with a Crown mark, but also as 182. (decimal) with TMK-1. When and if found, this scarcer version should be valued at a 20 percent premium. Throughout the Fifties, this piece was not listed in many of the catalogs, but since that time it has been consistently shown. It was recently (late Seventies) restyled by Gerhard Skrobek, Goebel's master modeler, with a more attractive facial expression and with his characteristic sculptured hair and textured finish. The German *Mädchen mit Böckchen,* is a descriptive name meaning "Girl with Kid." The original drawing is controlled by Ars Sacra who issued a print of it as #5859. The figure itself was pictured for October, 1975, and November, 1969, calendar pages.

183   Forest Shrine

Indicator	Size	Status	TMK-1	TMK-2	TMK-3	TMK-4	TMK-5	TMK-6
183	9"	R	P	P	P	—	R	R

Early catalogs used the more descriptive name of "Doe at Shrine." Always a very scarce collector's item, the figurine was not listed in U.S. catalogs for years until 1978 and had been considered discontinued by collectors. It was reintroduced first in 1977 in Germany in very limited quantities for the equivalent of $125 U.S. Beginning in 1980, U.S. catalogs listed the figurine for $260, but it was in very short supply. The high values shown in the Price List for TMK-1 through 4 are very vulnerable until it is more certain how many reissues will be produced. The reissued examples can be distinguished by the matt or dull finish on the doe, while the ones with early trademarks had a shiny, glossy finish. The German name *Waldandacht, Marterl* means approximately the same as the English, "Forest Shrine." The original drawing has been used by the owner, Verlag Ars Sacra, to publish postcard #5726.

184   Latest News

Indicator	Size	Status	TMK-1	TMK-2	TMK-3	TMK-4	TMK-5	TMK-6
184	5"	P	P	P	P	P	P	P

This has been in the production program since at least 1947 and is a collector's dream since it has been issued with a variety of different titles on the newspaper, some of which are very scarce or unique. *Das Allerneueste,* meaning "The Latest News," appears on some. *Munchener Presse* was used as early as the Full Bee mark. Robert Miller, in *HUMMEL, Authorized Supplement,* says that some catalogs listed O.S. (*Onne Shrift*) after the model number to indicate that it was also produced without lettering. In this way the buyer could have the name of his or her hometown paper added. Miller has one in his collection with the title "Register Herald" for the name of his hometown newspaper in Eaton, Ohio. Collectors Bob and Ann Wilgus have a display case filled with this figure reading eleven different newspapers. Redesigned in the 1960s, the current figurine is now on a square base with the boy looking down at the left-hand page. Formerly the base was round and the boy was peering over the top of the paper at the viewer. The original drawing, owned by Ars Sacra, has been used by them for publishing postcard #5728.

185   Accordion Boy

Indicator	Size	Status	TMK-1	TMK-2	TMK-3	TMK-4	TMK-5	TMK-6
185	5″	P	P	P	P	P	P	P

Issued in the late 1940s, several early catalogs list the name as "On Alpine Pasture," a slight variation of the German, *Bandoneonspieler* or "Accordion Player." In a 1950 price list, this piece was about 5½″ high compared to the present 5″ height. There are other variations due to mold growth and some minor deviations in color and style which do not affect the prices listed separately in the Price List.

185 Accordion Boy, *TMK-5.*

186   Sweet Music

Indicator	Size	Status	TMK-1	TMK-2	TMK-3	TMK-4	TMK-5	TMK-6
186	5″	P	P	P	P	P	P	P

This cello player is another number of the unofficial Hummel eight-piece orchestra of which Hum. 129 is the bandleader. Listed in an early 1947 catalog as "Sweet Music," it was called "Playing to the Dance" in at least two catalogs of the 1950s. Miller's *Supplement* to the book *HUMMEL* illustrates an interesting example with a Crown mark having striped instead of solid brown or black scuffs. This piece apparently was restyled to incorporate the newer, deeper colors as opposed to the old matt finish. The German name is *Zum Tanz*, or "To the Dance." Note: Hum. 186 was the highest number listed in an important bilingual, full-color catalog copyrighted in 1956. At that time there were 147 line items listed which included about 80 model numbers. Such old favorites as Puppy Love, Hum. 1, were not included.

186 Sweet Music, *TMK-3.*

187   Hummel Display Plaque (Store Plaque) (Dealer's Plaque)

Indicator	Size	Status	TMK-1	TMK-2	TMK-3	TMK-4	TMK-5	TMK-6
187	3¾″	P	P	P	P	P	P	P
187A	4″	P	—	—	—	—	P	P

An extensive collection can be made of this piece by itself; it has so many variations in design, coloring, and lettering. In addition to the three names listed above, it is also known as M.I. Hummel Collector's Plaque. See Hums. 205, 208, 209, 210, and 213, for related plaques in other languages and Hum. 211 which is also in English but is distinguished from Hum. 187 by also incorporating "W. Goebel Hummelwork, Oeslau, Germany." The earliest one was issued in the late Forties and carries a 1947 copyright (the U.S. copyright was issued in 1948). The early issue can be distinguished by the large bumblebee sitting on the top facing the Merry Wanderer figure at the right. In the Sixties, the design was altered by eliminating the bee and replacing it with a replica of the newly adopted Stylized Bee trademark (TMK-3). The next change was to substitute the Goebel Bee trademark, introduced in 1972 (TMK-5), for the TMK-3 design. These later plaques are incised with a 1976 copyright date. Within these three basic designs are innumerable variations of embossed and transfer-printed text. These variations are multiplied again by a multitude of color combinations with which the text was accentuated in black, blue, or orange. The most personalized and perhaps the rarest is the Australian TMK-5 plaque with the dealer's name "Carmosino's" added under the words "Authorized Dealer." (See page 106.) At least two others are known with different dealers' names. Any such individualized plaque would be valued in the low four-digit figures. The latest design plaque is now available for purchase by collectors as indicated in the Price List. This particular plaque is incised 187 A on the back and omits the words "Authorized Dealer." Other rarities include the French plaque, Hum. 208; the Swedish plaque, Hum. 209; "Schmid Bros., Inc. — Boston," Hum. 210; and a Spanish plaque, Hum. 213 (with umbrella handle turned down). Hum. 211 in white overglaze is also very unusual.

187 Hummel Display Plaque *with bee on top, TMK-2. Miller Collection.*

188 Celestial Musician, *TMK-5.*

189 Old Woman Knitting, *only example, incised M. I. Hummel, no trademark. Miller Collection.*

190 Old Woman Walking to Market, *only example, incised M. I. Hummel, no trademark. Miller Collection.*

188   Celestial Musician

Indicator	Size	Status	TMK-1	TMK-2	TMK-3	TMK-4	TMK-5	TMK-6
188	7″	P	P	P	P	P	P	P

This piece does not appear in all early catalogs even though it carries a 1948 incised copyright date. It was first copyrighted in the U.S. on July 14, 1950, as GP1813. The size has been listed as 7″ high throughout its history and there is no indication that this figurine has been restyled. The similarities between this model and the well-known Heavenly Angel, Hum. 21, are quite apparent and the German name of *Himmlische Klänge,* meaning "Heavenly Sounds" also bears out the relationship. Robert Miller reports that Hum. 188 was sold in white overglaze at one time. One such example would be rare and valued in the low four-digit figures. Verlag Ars Sacra own the original drawing and have used it to publish a faithful replica as postcard #4778.

189   Old Woman Knitting (CN)

Indicator	Size	Status	TMK-1	TMK-2	TMK-3	TMK-4	TMK-5	TMK-6
189	6¾″	C	*	—	—	—	—	—

Perhaps the sum total of Sister Hummel's artwork can be divided into three broad categories: children, religious, and the little known caricatures (cartoons or humorous exaggerations). Both the first two groups are well represented in the current line of M. I. Hummel figurines. Only the third classification is missing from the Goebel production line, mainly because the convent felt that the caricatures were not representative of Sister Hummel's love of children and her religious dedications, but rather indicated a lighter side of her artistic work. When Goebel submitted four adaptations of her originals in figurine form, Hums. 181, 189, 190, and 191, in the late 1940s, apparently after Sister Hummel's death, the convent did not approve the designs. Robert Miller discovered these four figurines and his research revealed that only samples were made for submission; these numbers were closed (CN) in the factory records in 1948. Since the examples are considered so unusual and are unique at this time they should be and probably are insured for values in the five-digit range. The original drawings were owned by Verlag Emil Fink who has published graphics in the form of postcards of these four subjects as #657, #658, #655, and #656.

*Only known example.

190   Old Woman Walking to Market (CN)

Indicator	Size	Status	TMK-1	TMK-2	TMK-3	TMK-4	TMK-5	TMK-6
190	6¾″	C	*	—	—	—	—	—

See Hum. 181 and Hum. 189 for information about this group of four similar figurines representing unusual caricatures by Sister Hummel.

*Only known example.

191 Old Man Walking to Market (CN)

Indicator	Size	Status	TMK-1	TMK-2	TMK-3	TMK-4	TMK-5	TMK-6
191	6¾″	C	*	—	—	—	—	—

See Hum. 181 and Hum. 189 for information about this group of similar figurines.

*Only known example.

191 Old Man Walking to Market, *only example, incised M. I. Hummel, no trademark. Miller Collection.*

192 Candlelight, Candleholder

Indicator	Size	Status	TMK-1	TMK-2	TMK-3	TMK-4	TMK-5	TMK-6
192	6¾″	P	P	P	P	P	P	P

This model was first copyrighted in Germany in 1948 and registered in the U.S. Copyright Office as GP1811 on July 14, 1950. At that time, the red ceramic candleholder in the angel's hands extended through her hands, almost to the tip of her shoe, and in the early catalogs the sizes ranged from 6¾″ to 7″ high. Sometime after 1960 (there was no U.S. copyright found) the figure was redesigned so that the candleholder was shortened to a red ceramic socket held in the angel's two hands. The Price List includes an allowance for and reflects the relative scarcity of the various trademarks because they were not always available in the U.S. except by special order. It was added again to one U.S. catalog in 1980, but still is in very short supply. The original drawing owned by Verlag Ars Sacra was lithographed and is listed in their current catalog as postcard #5260. The German name of *Engel mit Kerze, Leuchter* translates as "Angel with Candle, Candleholder."

192 Candlelight, *Candleholder, TMK-5.*

193 Angel Duet, Candleholder

Indicator	Size	Status	TMK-1	TMK-2	TMK-3	TMK-4	TMK-5	TMK-6
193	5″	P	P	P	P	P	P	P

The name Angel Duet has also been assigned to the very similar figurine, Hum. 261 (see), which features these same two angels both holding a common hymmbook but no candle. The early models carry the German copyright date of 1948 while it was not copyrighted in this country until July 14, 1950, as GP1806. Earlier models may be found oversize since they were cataloged in the 1950s as 5½″ high which would be valued at 10 percent more than the Price List shows. In those U.S. catalogs this figurine was listed as a special order item which may account for the fact that it is found in limited quantities in all trademarks. Robert Miller reports that this was made at one time in a plain white overglaze which is considered extremely rare. An example would be valued in the low four-digit range for insurance purposes. The German name of *Stille Nacht, Engelgrüppchen, Leuchter* translates as "Silent Night, Small Group of Angels." Sister Hummel's original drawing of this motif, owned by Verlag Ars Sacra, was lithographed and listed in their current catalog as postcard #5259.

193 Angel Duet, *Candleholder, TMK-4. (See 261.)*

194 **Watchful Angel**, *copyright 1948, TMK-5.*

194   Watchful Angel

Indicator	Size	Status	TMK-1	TMK-2	TMK-3	TMK-4	TMK-5	TMK-6
194	6½″	P	P	P	P	P	P	P

Not only did this model have numerous names such as the above, plus Angelic Care and Guardian Angel, but it has also been found in sizes ranging from about 6½″ to over 7½″ high with TMK-2. The interchanging of names between models of religious figures is a problem for collectors. One solution is to always accompany any name with the incised model number. While the first indication of a U.S. copyright is in 1950, many of these are found with a 1948 date incised which no doubt represents the German copyright date. *Schutzengel,* the German name, means "Guardian Angel," which is also used on the two styles of Holy Water Fonts, Hum. 29 and Hum. 248. A postcard, #5261, which is a lithograph from Sister Hummel's original, is available from Verlag Ars Sacra.

195/1 **Barnyard Hero**, *copyright 1948, TMK-5.*

195   Barnyard Hero

Indicator	Size	Status	TMK-1	TMK-2	TMK-3	TMK-4	TMK-5	TMK-6
195/2/0	4″	P	?	P	P	P	P	P
195(.)	5¾″	D	P	P	—	—	—	—
/I	5½″	P	P	P	P	P	P	P

A complete switch is evident here between the above name and the translation of *Angthase,* which is "Coward" in English. Perhaps the ironic implication of "Hero" adds a light touch to the English name. This piece was first issued with a 1948 incised copyright date, probably in the early 1950s in the U.S., which was about the time it was copyrighted here. It was available only in one size, 5½″ high, and incised 195 (only) on the underside of the base. Sometime later, the smaller size was introduced, 4″ high, incised 195/2/0; at that time 195/I became the indicator for the larger size. There is no indication to date that any intermediate size was issued as 195/0. In the early models of the small size, the boy's hands are on each side of the top rail. When this was restyled, probably in the 1960s, the boy's hands were placed one on top of the other. This figurine has been popular in calendar art, having been pictured in the annual Goebel calendars for November, 1954, August, 1962, and August, 1972. Sister Hummel's original drawing owned by Verlag Ars Sacra is issued as postcard #4782.

196/0 **Telling Her Secret**, *copyright 1948, TMK-5.*

196   Telling Her Secret

Indicator	Size	Status	TMK-1	TMK-2	TMK-3	TMK-4	TMK-5	TMK-6
196/0	5″	P	—	P	P	P	P	P
196(.)	6½″	D	P	P	—	—	—	—
/I	6½″	R	—	—	P	—	R	R

Copyrighted in the U.S. on July 14, 1950, as "Her Secret," this item carries an incised 1948 copyright date and was at one time incised only 196 or 196. (decimal) on the bottom. In the early 1950s, the smaller size, 5″ high, was introduced and incised 196/0. The larger size was then incised 196/I. Very shortly thereafter, 196/I was not cataloged but may have been produced in limited quantities. This vacuum was remedied with the reintroduction of the large 6½″ size in 1978. The listed prices for the older marks are vulnerable to the issue of large quantities of the new pieces with TMK-5 and 6. More documentation is needed on some trademarks. The girl on the right appears alone as Which Hand, Hum. 258. The German name is just *Das Geheimnis,* or "The Secret" in English. Sister Hummel's original drawing is owned by Verlag Ars Sacra and has been issued as a postcard #5834, while the figurine itself has been pictured for the month of February in the 1980 calendar.

197   Be Patient

Indicator	Size	Status	TMK-1	TMK-2	TMK-3	TMK-4	TMK-5	TMK-6
197/2/0	4¼″	D	D	D	D	D	D	D
197(.)	6¼″	D	P	P	—	—	—	—
/I	6″	P	—	P	P	P	P	P

The little girl feeding ducks was first copyrighted (GP1817) in the U.S. on July 14, 1950, although incised with 1948 and issued earlier. When first issued, the figurine was incised only 197 with TMK-1 and has also been reported incised 197. (decimal) with TMK-2. At that time, only the 6¼″ size was available. This designation was superseded some years later by the designation 197/I to distinguish it from the second size that was issued about 4½″ high and incised 197/2/0. There has been some color variation in the apron; one was reported with a pink apron, TMK-4, 4½″ high. More research is required before establishing premiums on any such variations. The German name of *Entenmütterchen* translates as "Little Duckling Mother." The location of the original drawing has not been determined, but pictures of the figurine itself have been used by Goebel in the March, 1962, and the August, 1971, calendars.

197/I Be Patient, *copyright 1948, TMK-4.*

198   Home from Market

Indicator	Size	Status	TMK-1	TMK-2	TMK-3	TMK-4	TMK-5	TMK-6
198/2/0	4½″	P	—	P	P	P	P	P
198(.)	5¾″	D	P	P	—	—	—	—
/I	5½″	P	—	P	P	P	P	P

When this piece was registered in the U.S. Copyright Office on July 14, 1950, it was assigned the name "Lucky Buyer." When first issued, it was incised with only the model number 198 on the base, was 5½″ to 6″ high, and was incised 1948. Late in the TMK-2 era, it was produced with 198. (decimal) incised on the bottom. Sometime before 1959 this size was changed to 198/I and was cataloged as small as 5″ high. This was done to distinguish it from the smaller size 198/2/0, around 4½″ high. One piece marked 198/I was found in the Full Bee (TMK-2). There is no record to date of any example incised 198/0 as an intermediate size. The German name of *Glück auf, Junge mit Schweinchen in Korb* translates in part as "Happy Purchase" in English. The present location of the original drawing by Sister Hummel is unknown but the figurine is pictured in the Goebel calendar for June, 1967.

198/I Home from Market, *copyright 1948, TMK-5.*

199   Feeding Time

Indicator	Size	Status	TMK-1	TMK-2	TMK-3	TMK-4	TMK-5	TMK-6
199/0	4¼″	P	—	P	P	P	P	P
199(.)	5½″	D	P	P	—	—	—	—
/I	5½″	P	P	P	P	P	P	P

This was registered in the U.S. Copyright Office as GP4386 on January 23, 1950. It was incised only 199 on the bottom, some with Double Crowns, and was about 5½″ tall. The girl had light golden hair. One Crown mark was found incised 199/I, indicating an early changeover in this large size because of the introduction of the smaller 4¼″ size. The smaller size was designated by an incised 199/0 on the bottom. Sometime in the early 1960s these were redesigned with a more alert expression, auburn colored hair, rougher surface texture, and brighter colors. The German name of *Im Hühnerhof* translates as "In the Chicken Run." One original Sister Hummel drawing is owned by Verlag Ars Sacra who used it to produce postcard #5943. To date, two original drawings of the Feeding Time design are known. Goebel used the picture of the figurine for their calendars in May, 1968, and May, 1975.

199/I Feeding Time, *copyright 1948, TMK-5.*

200 Little Goat Herder, *new style,*
TMK-5.

201/2/0 Retreat to Safety, *TMK-5*
(see 210).

200   Little Goat Herder

Indicator	Size	Status	TMK-1	TMK-2	TMK-3	TMK-4	TMK-5	TMK-6
200/2/0	4″	D	—	P	—	—	—	—
/0	4¾″	P	—	—	P	P	P	P
200(.)	5½″	D	P	P	—	—	—	—
/I	5½″	P	?	P	P	P	P	P

This is another model of the series that was copyrighted in the U.S. Copyright Office on July 14, 1950. However, the copyright date found on some examples is 1948, probably referring to the date of the German copyright. This figurine was incised 200 (only) or 200. (decimal) on the bottom when first issued in the large 5½″ size. This marking was changed to 200/I a few years later when a smaller 4″ size was introduced and marked 200/2/0. This 200/2/0 marking was later superseded by a 4¾″ size incised with marking of 200/0, which is still in production. The early model has what was known as a "piece of grass" between the hind legs of the kid in the foreground. This was probably eliminated in a restyling in the 1960s. The Price List values allow for this variation in TMK-1 and TMK-2. One 200/0 was found in a TMK-2 with only one goat, which would bring a premium of 50 percent. The German name of *Ziengenbub* means "Goatboy" in English. The original drawing by Sister Hummel has been issued as postcard #5942 by Verlag Ars Sacra who own the original. Goebel used a picture of the figurine in their calendars of October, 1967, and for June, 1974.

201   Retreat to Safety

Indicator	Size	Status	TMK-1	TMK-2	TMK-3	TMK-4	TMK-5	TMK-6
201/2/0	4″	P	?	P	P	P	P	P
201(.)	5¾″	D	P	P	?	?	—	—
/I	5½″	P	P	P	P	P	P	P

This apprehensive small boy is referred to more poetically in the German *In tausend Ängsten,* or "With a Thousand Fears." Note that this is the same little fellow who was having trouble with the goose in Hum. 195, Barnyard Hero. Originally issued only in the large 5¾″ size and incised with only the whole number 201, it was later changed to 201/I at the time the smaller 4″ size was issued and incised 201/2/0. When this model was restyled, the boy's hands were placed one on top of the other, whereas before each was placed on either side of the top rail. This is another figure from the group that was copyrighted in the U.S. on January 23, 1950, but on some examples 1948 is incised, presumably representing the earlier German copyright date. Verlag Ars Sacra who own the original drawing of Sister Hummel publish a graphic reproduction of it in the form of a postcard #4782. This figurine has been a popular subject, as it has been pictured two times in Goebel's calendars for August, 1969, and June, 1980.

202   Old Man Reading Newspaper, Table Lamp (CN)

Indicator	Size	Status	TMK-1	TMK-2	TMK-3	TMK-4	TMK-5	TMK-6
202	?	U	—	—	—	—	—	—

A sample of this lamp was made in the late 1940s but was not approved by the convent. Therefore, Hum. 202 was entered as a closed number (CN) in the factory records in 1948. See Hum. 181, 189, 190, and 191 for more background information.

203　Signs of Spring

Indicator	Size	Status	TMK-1	TMK-2	TMK-3	TMK-4	TMK-5	TMK-6
203/2/0	4″	P	P	P	P	P	P	P
203	5¼″	D	P	P	—	—	—	—
/I	5½″	P	P	P	P	P	P	P

Catalogs of the early 1950s indicate that this was first issued about that time in only the large 5¼″ size, which was incised with the whole number 203 on the bottom of the base, or in some cases 203. (decimal). Shortly after that, when the smaller size, 4″ high, was introduced and incised 203/2/0, the large size was changed to 203/I. There is no record to date of an intermediate size incised 203/0; one found as such would be considered unusual. A change in design in the smaller size was instituted by removing her right shoe so that, today, examples with TMK-2 are found with and without a shoe. Any figurines in this size found with TMK-2 with both shoes on would be very scarce and valued in the mid three-digit figures. A Double Crown, incised 203, 5¼″ high, was recently valued in this range. This piece was also copyrighted in the U.S. as GP4387 on January 23, 1950, and December 19, 1977. The German name of *Frühlingsidyll* translates as "Spring Idyll." A picture of the figure was used for the month of March in the 1967 and 1973 calendars produced by Goebel.

203/2/0 Signs of Spring, *one shoe, current model, copyright 1948, TMK-4.*

204　Weary Wanderer

Indicator	Size	Status	TMK-1	TMK-2	TMK-3	TMK-4	TMK-5	TMK-6
204	6″	P	P	P	P	P	P	P

The German title, *In Lauterbach hab i . . .* implies that a tired young girl is starting to tell of her long trip to the town of Lauterbach. And "Tired Traveler" was the name assigned at the time the copyright, GP1815, was issued to Goebel in the U.S. on July 14, 1950. Since many of the figurines are incised 1949, this is probably the year it was copyrighted in Germany. Older catalogs show that the size specifications changed from time to time, but it is only found with the whole number 204 incised on the bottom of the base. In fact, one old catalog from the early 1950s misnamed this piece as Merry Wanderer; one look at the subject belies that name. A well-known collector has reported a very rare version of this model with blue rather than the usual brown eyes. This blue-eyed piece would be valued at least 50 percent more than the Price List shows. A picture of this figurine was used by Goebel on calendar pages for March, 1976, and July, 1969.

204 Weary Wanderer, *copyright 1949, TMK-5.*

205　Hummel Display Plaque in German

Indicator	Size	Status	TMK-1	TMK-2	TMK-3	TMK-4	TMK-5	TMK-6
205	4″	D	P	P	—	—	—	—

The large bumblebee on top of this plaque suggests that it was issued in the late 1940s to serve as an indication in a store window or counter that M. I. Hummel articles were available for sale. It is similar in contour to the one in English, Hum. 187 (refer to this for more background). Like the Hum. 187 series of plaques, the coloring of the lettering varied as did the style of lettering in some cases. According to factory records this plaque was closed out in 1949, so the variations are limited. The availability of these plaques to collectors is also limited, as indicated by the high prices for TMK-1 and 2, the only marks found on the German version to date.

205 Hummel Display Plaque, *German, old style, scarce, TMK-1.*

206 Angel Cloud, *Holy Water Font,*
TMK-2. Hadorn Collection.

206   Angel Cloud, Holy Water Font

Indicator	Size	Status	TMK-1	TMK-2	TMK-3	TMK-4	TMK-5	TMK-6
206	4¾″	R	P	P	?	?	R	R

This font was listed in catalogs of the early 1950s merely as "Holy Water Font" with no descriptive name. In German, the name is *Kind auf wolke,* or "Child with Flower." The name "Angel Cloud" was assigned by the time this design was copyrighted in the U.S. on July 14, 1950, as GP1810. Some fonts are incised with the German copyright date of 1949. It may have been produced in Germany on occasions but was not listed in early U.S. catalogs. It was reintroduced in the U.S. in 1978 with TMK-5 at a small fraction of the old prices. It is unlikely that the high prices for early trademarks will remain at the present level if many of the newer ones are marketed. One dealer reports receiving three of these reissues in 1978 with a TMK-3 mark which would imply that they were made in the early 1960s. The design of the piece has changed over the years but the dates of restyling are uncertain. Note in the Price List the difference in prices between Hum. 206 and Hum. 207 due to scarcity.

207 Heavenly Angel, *Holy Water*
Font, no trademark, copyright 1965.
Dous Collection.

207   Heavenly Angel, Holy Water Font

Indicator	Size	Status	TMK-1	TMK-2	TMK-3	TMK-4	TMK-5	TMK-6
207	4¾″	P	P	P	P	P	P	P

This universally recognized design attained its renown when it was used in bas-relief form on the First Annual Plate, Hum. 264. Both of these bas-reliefs are adapted from the earlier figurine, Heavenly Angel, Hum. 21. (See for more detailed information and background.) When Hum. 207 was copyrighted in the U.S. as GP1809 on July 14, 1950, it was assigned the name, "Angel with Candle." The German name is far different; *Christkindlein kommt, Engel* translates, "The Little Christ Child Comes." When this font was redesigned, probably in the 1960s, the blind hole in the back for hanging was replaced by the pierced hole at the top of the present pieces. Other changes in the design of the bowl are typical of the changes previously described for fonts. This piece resembles postcard #4773, published by Ars Sacra who own one of the original drawings by Sister Hummel from which this font was adapted.

208 Hummel Display Plaque,
French, old style, rare, TMK-1.

208   Hummel Display Plaque in French

Indicator	Size	Status	TMK-1	TMK-2	TMK-3	TMK-4	TMK-5	TMK-6
208	4″	D	?	P	—	—	—	—

A notation in the U.S. copyright records indicates this plaque was copyrighted as early as 1947 and has the large bumblebee sitting on top. This out-of-production plaque is considered very rare as it was never made in large quantities and the scarcity is indicated by high prices that approach five digits. An example with TMK-1 or 2 would be valued in the very high end of the four-digit price range. Variations in lettering and punctuation have been reported, but any such variations would fall within the indicated price range already mentioned.

209   Hummel Display Plaque in Swedish

Indicator	Size	Status	TMK-1	TMK-2	TMK-3	TMK-4	TMK-5	TMK-6
209	4″	D	?	P	—	—	—	—

The large bumblebee on top indicates that this piece was probably designed and issued in the late 1940s. No copyright records were found in the U.S. Copyright Office. This was issued for Swedish dealers to display in their store windows or on their counters and is considered very rare and valued in the upper end of the four-digit range. There were at least three plaques that changed hands in 1979 but to date there is insufficient information on design and color variations, if any. It is quite likely that there are less than ten of these known, even with all the publicity and high prices.

209 Hummel Display Plaque, *Swedish, old style, rare, TMK-1. Grande Collection.*

210   Hummel Display Plaque in English

Indicator	Size	Status	TMK-1	TMK-2	TMK-3	TMK-4	TMK-5	TMK-6
210	4″	D	?	P	—	—	—	—

This differs from the other English language plaque, Hum. 187, in one unique respect. Embossed on the Merry Wanderer's satchel are the words "Schmid Bros., Inc., Boston." It was specifically made for this firm which was the first firm to import M. I. Hummel figurines into the U.S. in 1935. John Schmid discovered this design at the Leipzig Fair that year and ordered the first six dozen sold in the U.S. The plaque was probably not made before the late 1940s. For more information on the story of M. I. Hummel's introduction into the U.S., refer to the chapter about Berta Hummel art by Schmid Bros., page 193. Any example of this plaque would also fall in the extremely rare category and be valued in the very high four-digit or possibly very low five-digit figures.

210 Hummel Display Plaque, *English, Schmid, very rare, TMK-2, 1949 copyright. Miller Collection.*

211   Hummel Display Plaque in English

Indicator	Size	Status	TMK-1	TMK-2	TMK-3	TMK-4	TMK-5	TMK-6
211	4″	D	?	P	—	—	—	—

Another version of the early design of store window or counter plaque for M. I. Hummel dealers. Why this separate and similar version was made has not been determined. It can easily be distinguished from the other two "big bee" plaques, Hum. 187 and Hum. 210, by the lettering which is done in lowercase rather than uppercase letters and by the name of the town Oeslau, where the Goebel figurine factory is located. There were no copyrights found to show that this was registered in the U.S. Any example of this plaque would fall in the same rare company as its counterparts mentioned previously, but perhaps be valued in the very high four-digit range. One sample of this plague was reported in white overglaze finish. The one pictured here is from the Miller collection and may be one of only two known.

211 Hummel Display Plaque, *English, rare, TMK-2. Miller Collection.*

213 Hummel Display Plaque,
Spanish, rare, TMK-2, 1955 copyright.
Miller Collection.

187 Hummel Display Plaque,
TMK-5, very rare Australian version
personalized with dealer's name,
"Carmosino's."

214/A Virgin Mary and Infant
Jesus, *discontinued one-piece figurine.*
Miller Collection.

212   Cancelled Number

Indicator	Size	Status	TMK-1	TMK-2	TMK-3	TMK-4	TMK-5	TMK-6
212	—	U	—	—	—	—	—	—

According to factory records there is no information available on a design or sample with this number, and it is classified as a closed number (CN) never to be used again. Robert Miller, in *HUMMEL, Authorized Supplement*, believes that this may have been intended for grouping a number of existing, related figurines and selling them under Hum. 212 as an orchestra. This probability is enhanced by an entry in an English language catalog of the early 1950s which contained only numbers up through Hum. 187 but then finished with a listing with nothing in the number column but the name "Band Rehearsal (6 figures)" with the following Hummel numbers: 85 (illegible), 139, 130, 131, and 135. A 1959 Ebling & Reuss catalog lists "Orchestra, 5 pieces" with a different number series. Another catalog listing shows a picture of eight "orchestra" pieces: Hums. 85, 4, 186, 185, 129, 130, 131, and 135.

213   Hummel Display Plaque in Spanish

Indicator	Size	Status	TMK-1	TMK-2	TMK-3	TMK-4	TMK-5	TMK-6
213	4"	D	?	P	—	—	—	—

Another in the series of the big bumblebee plaques, probably designed in the late 1940s. This plaque, like the English, Hum. 211, and the Swedish, Hum. 210, are the only three that used lowercase letters instead of capitals in the wording on this long-discontinued, old style plaque. Any example that is found should be valued for insurance purposes in the high four-digit dollar range.

214   Nativity Set (Small)

Indicator	Size	Status	TMK-1	TMK-2	TMK-3	TMK-4	TMK-5	TMK-6
214 (12 pc.)		P	—	P	P	P	P	P
214 (16 pc.)		P	—	P	P	P	P	P
214 A&B/II	(3 pc.)	P	—	P	P	—	—	—
214 A&B/W		P	—	P	—	—	—	—
214/SI		P	—	P	P	P	P	P
214/A		D	—	P	?	—	—	—
214/A/M/II	6¼"	P	?	P	P	P	P	P
/A/K	3½"	P	?	P	P	P	P	P
214B/W	7½"	P	?	P	P	P	P	P
B/II	7½"	P	?	P	P	P	P	P
C/II	3½"	P	—	P	P	P	P	P
D/II	3"	P	—	P	P	P	P	P
E/II	3½"	P	—	P	P	P	P	P
F/II	7"	P	—	P	P	P	P	P
G/II	4¾"	P	—	P	P	P	P	P
H/II	4"	P	—	P	P	P	P	P
J/II	5"	P	—	P	P	P	P	P
K/II	6¾"	P	—	P	P	P	P	P
L/II	8¼"	P	—	P	P	P	P	P
M/II	5½"	P	—	P	P	P	P	P
N/II	5½"	P	—	P	P	P	P	P
O/II	2"	P	—	P	P	P	P	P
214/HX	8¼"	P	—	P	P	P	P	P

Many ardent M. I. Hummel collectors have one of these sets which is the focal point every year of their Christmas decorations, and just as essential as the tree. Other collectors without a set have one high on their "must" list. Others buy these figurines piecemeal at the rate of one a year. The U.S. Copyright, GF43014, issued June 21, 1952, to the Goebel Company for a sixteen-piece Nativity Set, suggests that it might have been first sold about that time in the U.S., even though some of the pieces are incised with a 1951 date (probably the date of the copyright in Germany). One set is known to have been purchased in Buffalo, New York, just prior to Christmas, 1949, with a TMK-2, or Full Bee trademark. There have actually been three different versions offered for sale since that time. For example, in 1959 one catalog listed a small stable and three pieces — Virgin Mary, Christ Child, and St. Joseph. It is known that originally the Virgin Mary and Child were made as one piece and when found today in color would be valued in the high hundreds. That is why, as individual pieces, they are still incised, today, the same way, 214/A. This catalog also offered a set of ten pieces and the stable for $84, or the ten individual pieces without stable for $70. Over the years, the individual pieces have not always been available but are now. In the latest edition, the sixteenth piece is Flying Angel, Hum. 366, which was added in the mid-1970s. At present, the stable is not included in the sixteen pieces and is sold separately for $50. It is also currently offered as a twelve-piece set which omits the following: 214/C Angel Standing ("Goodnight"), 214/D Angel Kneeling ("Angel Serenade"), 214/E We Congratulate, 214/H Shepherd Boy Kneeling ("Little Tooter"). Sometimes a camel is included which is marked HX306/0/6 because it was not designed by Sister Hummel but is available as an extra piece. The Nativity Set was once offered in an all-white finish and when found is a collector's item valued in the low four-digit figures. Presently, the three-piece set of Mary, Joseph, and Jesus is the only one available in white. Sets have been reported in all marks including TMK-1, the Crown mark. At one time, a star was used at the top of the stable instead of the present Flying Angel. The Goebel Company makes another Nativity set that confuses many beginning collectors since it is similar and sells at quite a discount from this M. I. Hummel set. Therefore, anyone buying a Nativity Set, whether or not in the secondary market, should be sure that each piece is incised 214 with the appropriate letter for the model as listed above, and that all the pieces bear the distinctive facsimile signature. Otherwise it is not a genuine M. I. Hummel set. The pieces in the other non-Hummel set have incised letters preceding the model number such as HA1 or HX. The picture of the M. I. Hummel set is shown in Goebel's calendar of 1967 for the month of December. See Hum. 260 for the larger size Nativity Set. (Note: No bases on the Hum. 214 Nativity Set figurines.)

214 Nativity Set with Stable, *TMK-3.*

Pictured below:

214 A Virgin Mary, Infant Jesus *(one piece).*

214/A Virgin Mary.

214/A Infant Jesus.

214/B Joseph.

214/F Shepherd, *standing with sheep.*

214/G Shepherd, *kneeling.*

214/H Little Tooter.

214/J Donkey.

214/K Ox.

214/L Moorish King.

214/M King, *kneeling, one knee.*

214/N King *kneeling on two knees.*

214/O Lamb.

366 Flying Angel.

215 Cancelled Number

Indicator	Size	Status	TMK-1	TMK-2	TMK-3	TMK-4	TMK-5	TMK-6
215		U	—	—	—	—	—	—

Two sources indicate different subjects were considered for this number, but apparently were never made. The number was classed as a closed number (CN) in 1951. Factory records indicate it was considered for a design of the Child Jesus. The U.S. Copyright Office lists a copyright November 5, 1964, for the design of a Madonna in Prayer as being number 215. This may have been a second design selected for this same model number at a later date. If an example that fits either description with this model number ever does appear it would be valued in the high four-digit figures.

216 Cancelled Number

Indicator	Size	Status	TMK-1	TMK-2	TMK-3	TMK-4	TMK-5	TMK-6
216		U	—	—	—	—	—	—

According to Goebel's factory records, this number was being considered for a variation of Joyful, Ashtray, Hum. 33, but for some unknown reason it was listed as a closed number (CN) in 1951. At present, there is no known example, but this situation may change as it has for other CN's, and the alert collector who locates one will have something valued in the mid four-digit range.

217 Boy with Toothache

Indicator	Size	Status	TMK-1	TMK-2	TMK-3	TMK-4	TMK-5	TMK-6
217	5½″	P	—	P	P	P	P	P

First found in the early 1950s catalog as 5″ high and with an incised copyright date of 1951. There was no record of the U.S. copyright found. A 1966 catalog lists it at its present height of 5″. During World War II, a poor quality reproduction of this called "Dentist Dodger" or "Bawling Bennie" was issued by Dubler in the U.S. Goebel catalogs have also listed this as just "Toothache." The original drawing by Sister Hummel, issued by Verlag Ars Sacra as postcard #5552 shows this bandaged boy standing at the dentist's office pulling a bellcord to announce his arrival. No major variations of design or color have been reported to date, but sizes vary due to changing specifications and mold usage. This boy is pictured in the calendars for January, 1967, and February, 1975. There are two known copies of this drawing. Sister Hummel made a second one for her dentist in Saulgau.

218 Birthday Serenade

Indicator	Size	Status	TMK-1	TMK-2	TMK-3	TMK-4	TMK-5	TMK-6
218/2/0	4¼″	P	—	P	P	P	P	P
/0	5¼″	R	—	P	P	—	R	R
218	5¼″	D	—	P	P	—	—	—

An interesting change in design was made in this pair of young musicians at the request of the convent for unexplained reasons in about 1954. The boy who had spent his first twelve years playing the horn was switched to playing the accordion, and the girl did the reverse, going from the accordion to the horn. While the first copyright was registered in the U.S. on July 31, 1953, large size pieces are incised 1952, even including the newly reintroduced pieces, Hum. 218/0 with the TMK-5 and 6, which now also have the boy playing the accordion and the girl the horn. The smaller sizes, first copyrighted in the U.S. on April 27, 1966, are incised with what is probably the year of the German copyright for this restyling, 1965. The small size, 218/2/0, is known in TMK-2 through TMK-4 with the old copyright date; some marked TMK-3 are known with the boy playing the horn and the girl playing the accordion. In making this change, the boy also acquired a slightly askew scarf around his neck. The calendars for May, 1967, and June, 1976, have good illustrations of this musical pair.

217 Boy with Toothache, *TMK-4.*

218/2/0 Birthday Serenade, *new design, TMK-5.*

219 Little Velma

Indicator	Size	Status	TMK-1	TMK-2	TMK-3	TMK-4	TMK-5	TMK-6
219/2/0	4"	P	—	P	?	—	—	—

This is the only M. I. Hummel figurine named by the authoritative collector, Robert Miller. He gave it this name in honor of the woman who first told him about the piece. Previous research indicated that this figurine, "Girl with Frog," might have been made in very small quantities but for some reason was discontinued. The number 219 was incorrectly listed as a closed number (CN) and never used. Even the U.S. Copyright Office record is incomplete, merely listing the Hummel model number. However, it does describe it as "Girl on Fence with Frog." Another mystery is why it was incised on the back 219/2/0, and not just plain 219 unless it was done to agree with its counterpart, Retreat to Safety, Hum. 201/2/0, in approximately the same size. As of now, somewhere between five and ten pieces of this extremely rare model have been reported. Any one of them would be insured for a figure in the mid four-digit range, which was the price received by a woman in Canada whose son had purchased it for her with $5 he earned on his newspaper route in the 1950s.

219/2/0 Little Velma, *very rare, TMK-2. Dous Collection.*

220 We Congratulate

Indicator	Size	Status	TMK-1	TMK-2	TMK-3	TMK-4	TMK-5	TMK-6
220/2/0	4"	D	—	P	—	—	—	—
220	4"	P	—	P	P	P	P	P

This figurine is essentially the same as the other ones by the same name, Hum. 214/E and Hum. 260 F, in the Nativity Sets, except that a base was added and two changes were made in design. The garland of flowers has been omitted from the girl and suspenders have been added to the boy. There is no record of a U.S. copyright, although 1952 is incised on some models. When first issued, the model number was incised 220/2/0 (a range of sizes may have been planned as this was only cataloged as 3¼" high). Later catalogs showed a gradual increase in the specified size until the current 4" high. At some later date the size indicator was omitted, therefore present models carry only the number 220. This has not been reported in a white overglaze finish as has Hum. 214/E without a base.

220 We Congratulate, *on base (see 214/E), TMK-5.*

221 Happy Pastime, Candy Box (CN)

Indicator	Size	Status	TMK-1	TMK-2	TMK-3	TMK-4	TMK-5	TMK-6
221	?	U	—	—	—	—	—	—

According to Robert Miller's *Authorized Supplement* to *HUMMEL*, this number was originally listed as "Unknown," as factory records indicated it as a Closed Number (CN). Hum. 221 was planned at one time to be a glamorized version of the present Candy Box, Hum. III/69. The main difference was the addition of flowers and blossoms on the top and sides of the box which would have been very vulnerable to damage. The bird was also positioned in front of the girl and her kerchief was without polka dots. This additional information is given in case you are the fortunate collector to have the only one known other than the factory sample and have it insured for a few thousand dollars.

222 **Madonna Plaque**, *wire frame, discontinued, TMK-2. Miller Collection.*

222   Madonna Plaque, Wire Frame

Indicator	Size	Status	TMK-1	TMK-2	TMK-3	TMK-4	TMK-5	TMK-6
222	5″	D	—	P	P	—	—	—

This plaque is based on a very popular and beautiful painting by Sister Hummel entitled "Madonna in Red." While she drew many madonnas, this one has received the widest acclaim. The original drawing is owned by Verlag Emil Fink who has published postcard #209 and thousands of lithographic prints in a number of different versions, some as large as 21″ by 26″, of this madonna. Their numbers are 981, 98LK, 98V, and 111. Verlag Ars Sacra also publish postcard #5204. The plaque itself is similar to Hum. 48. It also bears resemblance to the bas-relief, Hum. 249. When originally issued, Hum. 222 had an ornate black metal strap frame superimposed to hold the rectangular plaque. So far this has only been reported with TMK-2 and 3, many times without the wire frame. When found complete, the value would be in the low four-digit figures, and, without the frame, about 25 percent less. This value would only apply to those examples which have 222 incised on the back plus the dark brown border outlined in white.

223 **To Market**, *Table Lamp, trademark unknown.*

223   To Market, Table Lamp

Indicator	Size	Status	TMK-1	TMK-2	TMK-3	TMK-4	TMK-5	TMK-6
M223	9½″	P	—	P	P	P	P	P

This lamp is based on the figurine, To Market, Hum. 49, and is closely related to two other lamps, Hum. 101 and Hum. II/101, which should be referred to for more background. The principal difference between this lamp and the other two lamps is in size. Hum. 223 is 9½″ as compared to 7½″ for the other two. This also has a blossom on the tree trunk which II/101 does not have. The German name, *Brüderlein and Schwesterlein*, means "Brother and Sister," which these two figurines are called when they are listed separately as Hum. 95 and Hum. 98.

224 **Wayside Harmony**, *Table Lamp, trademark unknown.*

224   Wayside Harmony, Table Lamp

Indicator	Size	Status	TMK-1	TMK-2	TMK-3	TMK-4	TMK-5	TMK-6
M224	9½″	D	—	P	P	—	—	—
/I	7½″	P	—	P	P	P	P	P
/II	9½″	R	—	P	P	—	R	R

This adaptation of the figurine Hum. 111, by the same name, was apparently first issued incised only 224, 9½″ high. The 9½″ size was perhaps an alternative to Hum. II/111, the same lamp in the 7½″ size. In the 1950s, Hum. 224/I replaced the smaller, 7½″ size lamp. Concurrently, the markings on the 9½″ lamp were changed to 224/II. Hum. 224/II has been intermittently available in the U.S. market but was not cataloged by distributors until it was reintroduced in 1978.

225   Just Resting, Table Lamp

Indicator	Size	Status	TMK-1	TMK-2	TMK-3	TMK-4	TMK-5	TMK-6
M225		D	—	P	P	—	—	—
/I	7½″	P	—	P	P	—	P	P
/II	9½″	R	—	P	P	—	R	R

An ideal companion piece to Wayside Harmony Lamp, Hum. 224, and over the years has had much the same history of size, number, and size indicator changes. Hum. 225/II, also, has been infrequently available on the U.S. market, and was not cataloged by distributors until it was reintroduced in 1978.

225 Just Resting, *Table Lamp,*
TMK-5.

226   The Mail Is Here

Indicator	Size	Status	TMK-1	TMK-2	TMK-3	TMK-4	TMK-5	TMK-6
226	6″	P	—	P	P	P	P	P

This popular piece was originally copyrighted in the U.S. as "Stage Coach," GP6534, on January 22, 1954. Most of the pieces carry the German copyright date, incised as 1952. Some of the early catalogs also list this as "Mail Coach" and specify the size as 6¼″ high as compared to the present specification of 6″. The German name of *Trara — die Post ist da* translates in English as "Ta — dum, the Mail Is In." There are at least two original drawings done by Sister Hummel. From the one owned by Ars Sacra, a full-view postcard, #5549, has been published. The other original drawing is in the Kleber Post Inn in Saulgau. This old stagecoach inn may have been Sister's inspiration, as she sometimes waited at this inn to go to the nearby convent in Siessen. This drawing shows the coach from the rear as it is leaving the inn with a tearful woman waving her handkerchief out of the back window to her friends. Displayed together they make a very interesting pair. This popular scene appears in Goebel's calendars for October, 1962, the cover of 1969, and December, 1975.

226 The Mail Is Here, *copyright*
1952, TMK-4.

227   She Loves Me, She Loves Me Not, Table Lamp

Indicator	Size	Status	TMK-1	TMK-2	TMK-3	TMK-4	TMK-5	TMK-6
M227	7½″	—	—	P	P	P	P	P

This lamp and its companion piece, Hum. 228, Good Friends, have been made only in this 7½″ size. It has been reported in an example 8½″ high which could have been an error. No lamps have been reported in that size to date and this is the only mention of this size. If found at 8½″ high, it would be valued around 25 percent higher than Price List value with a comparable trademark. This adaptation of figurine, Hum. 174, has a flower on the left fencepost and eyes looking up (or straight at the viewer), as in some of the older figurines.

227 She Loves Me, She Loves Me
Not, *Table Lamp, TMK-5.*

228 Good Friends, *Table Lamp,*
TMK-5.

228   Good Friends, Table Lamp

Indicator	Size	Status	TMK-1	TMK-2	TMK-3	TMK-4	TMK-5	TMK-6
M228	7½″	P	—	P	P	P	P	P

Like its companion piece, Hum. 227, this lamp has been made only in the 7½″ size since its introduction in the 1950s. This lamp also was listed as being 8½″ high in the same 1959 catalog (no doubt in error) and would be valued about 25 percent more if found that large. Neither Hum. 227 nor Hum. 228 is known to date with the earlier Crown mark, TMK-1. Refer to the figurine of the same name, Hum. 182, for more information. Good Friends was matched with She Loves Me as one of a pair of Bookends, Hum. 251 A.

229 Apple Tree Girl, *Table Lamp,*
7½″ high, TMK-5. Miller Collection.

229   Apple Tree Girl, Table Lamp

Indicator	Size	Status	TMK-1	TMK-2	TMK-3	TMK-4	TMK-5	TMK-6
M229	7½″	P	—	P	P	P	P	P

This well-known figurine is a natural for a lamp because the girl is already sitting in the branches of a tree. Introduced about 1955 in the 7½″ high size, it was listed in a 1959 catalog as being 8½″ high, but an 8½″ lamp has yet to be found. This same model is also used in one of the pair of Bookends, Hum. 252 A. There is no record of this having been made in the larger 9½″ size as some other lamps have been. Refer to the figurine, Hum. 141, Apple Tree Girl, for more information.

230 Apple Tree Boy, *Table Lamp,*
7½″ high, TMK-5. Miller Collection.

230   Apple Tree Boy, Table Lamp

Indicator	Size	Status	TMK-1	TMK-2	TMK-3	TMK-4	TMK-5	TMK-6
M230	7½″	P	—	P	P	P	P	P

The same information applies to this lamp, as previously detailed for Hum. 229. This model was also used as part of the Bookends, Hum. 252 B, and the 1977 Annual Plate, Hum. 270, the year after the girl was used on a similar plate, Hum. 269. Both lamps, Hum. 229 and Hum. 230, were copyrighted in the U.S. in 1955, and both pieces are known in TMK-2 through TMK-6. See Hum. 142 for more information on Apple Tree Boy.

231 Birthday Serenade, Table Lamp

Indicator	Size	Status	TMK-1	TMK-2	TMK-3	TMK-4	TMK-5	TMK-6
M231	9½″	R	—	P	?	P	R	R

This lamp places the same musicians who comprise the Birthday Serenade figurine, Hum. 218, at the base of a tree trunk that forms the lamp standard. While the figurine has been in continuous production since 1954, the lamp was known only in TMK-2. In 1978, Hum. 231, was reintroduced with a TMK-5; however, one collector owns an example with a TMK-4. The original U.S. copyright date for this lamp was July 31, 1953, GP6995. Interestingly, the TMK-2 lamps are incised with a 1954 copyright date. On April 27, 1966, GF341 was registered in the U.S. Copyright Office for the redesigned version of Hum. 231. Refer to Hum. 218 for full details on the change in design made in the mid-1960s at the request of the convent. Hum. 234, a lamp similar to Hum. 231, differs slightly in size and design. Hum. 234 is 7½″ high and lacks the pink flower hanging above the boy's head. Hum. 231 also has a brass ferrule for attaching the lamp socket. As the Price List indicates, the lamp was considered rare until the reissue appeared in 1978. The price differential between old and new models may change, depending on how many reissues are produced. Prices also depend on the collector's willingness to pay steep prices for the old marks and design.

231 **Birthday Serenade,** *Table Lamp, 9½″ high, TMK-5. Miller Collection.*

232 Happy Days, Table Lamp

Indicator	Size	Status	TMK-1	TMK-2	TMK-3	TMK-4	TMK-5	TMK-6
M232	9½″	R	—	P	?	?	R	R

This 9½″ high table lamp utilizes the figurine by the same name, Hum. 150. The early models are incised with a 1954 copyright date which is apparently close to the date of issue since no examples have been reported with a TMK-1. At present, any examples of this lamp with a TMK-3 or TMK-4 would also be considered unusual. In researching available U.S. catalogs from 1954 on, no listing for this lamp was found until it was reissued in 1978 in Germany and later in other countries. No record of U.S. copyright registration has been located as yet. The TMK-2 examples were considered rare and usually sold in the high hundreds range. The price of these is liable to drop based on the number of reissues produced. The large 9½″ lamp is practically identical to the companion 7½″ model, Hum. 235, except that the larger version has a flower dropping from one of the branch stubs over the boy's head. The German name for this lamp is *Hausmusik, Kinderpaar,* which translates as "House Music by Pair of Children."

232 **Happy Days,** *Table Lamp, 9½″ high, TMK-5. Miller Collection.*

233 Cancelled Number

Indicator	Size	Status	TMK-1	TMK-2	TMK-3	TMK-4	TMK-5	TMK-6
233	?	U	—	—	—	—	—	—

Gerhard Skrobek, who is currently the master sculptor for Goebel, started to work there in 1954. In Robert Miller's *Supplement* to *HUMMEL,* Miller states that Hum. 233 was the first assignment Skrobek had of interpreting one of Sister Hummel's drawings as a figurine. The figurine was listed at that time in the factory records as being a boy feeding birds. For unknown reasons, it was never produced and not even a factory sample or original study has been reported. It is thought that this design was restyled and became Hum. 300, Bird Watcher, which was not issued until 1979. This restyling may have been done shortly after Skrobek's initial work on the figurine, because a U.S. copyright, GB12632, was issued on July 18, 1956, for Hum. 300 with the tentative name of "Friends of Animals." There is no U.S. record of a copyright for Hum. 233.

234   Birthday Serenade, Table Lamp

Indicator	Size	Status	TMK-1	TMK-2	TMK-3	TMK-4	TMK-5	TMK-6
M234	7½″	R	—	P	P	—	R	R

This 7½″ lamp is the smaller version of Hum. 231, with the older models carrying an incised 1954 copyright date. It was registered in the U.S. Copyright Office on November 2, 1955, and follows the same design as the figurine by the same name, which should be referred to for more details. The 7½″ version varies from the 9½″ version in that it has no flower in the branch stub above the boy's head. While this piece has been reported as having all trademarks starting with TMK-2, no listing could be found in the available U.S. catalogs from 1955 until 1978 when it was reissued in Germany and later in the U.S. Early models of the lamp were considered scarce and commanded a premium price. Early models are identified by the boy playing the horn and the girl the accordion. When reissued in 1978, the motif was restyled so that the boy plays the accordion and the girl the horn. Because of this design difference, the premium differential between the older trademark and the new reissues may fluctuate, depending on how many reissues are marketed and the collectors' demand for the lamps. The English name is the same as the German *Geburtstagsstandchen.*

234 Birthday Serenade, *Table Lamp, 7½″ high, TMK-2. Miller Collection.*

235   Happy Days, Table Lamp

Indicator	Size	Status	TMK-1	TMK-2	TMK-3	TMK-4	TMK-5	TMK-6
M235	7½″	R	—	P	?	—	R	R

Happy Days, Hum. 150, is essentially the same design that was used for this smaller 7½″ size and for Hum. 232, the 9½″ size, except that the larger model has a flower hanging down over the boy's head. Refer to Hum. 218 and Hum. 150 for more information. The date of issue was around 1954, the date of the incised copyright year on the bottom of the older model lamps. No examples have been reported with the early TMK-1. Examples with TMK-3 or TMK-4 would be unusual items, as catalog research indicates that this lamp was apparently out of production or not distributed in the U.S. until it was reissued in 1978. The new supply may adversely affect the prices of the older, scarce models. The extent of a weakening price differential will depend on how many of the newer versions are produced. The German name for this lamp is *Hausmusik, Kinderpaar,* which translates as "House Music by Pair of Children," which is also the German name of the figurine, Hum. 150.

235 Happy Days, *Table Lamp, TMK-2, copyright 1954. Miller Collection.*

236   Open Number

Indicator	Size	Status	TMK-1	TMK-2	TMK-3	TMK-4	TMK-5	TMK-6
236		O	—	—	—	—	—	?

A previous publication distributed by the Goebel Company indicates that this number was never assigned to one of Sister Hummel's drawings for adaptation into a three-dimensional object. Thus, number 236 remains available for assignment.

237　Cancelled Number

Indicator	Size	Status	TMK-1	TMK-2	TMK-3	TMK-4	TMK-5	TMK-6
237	?	—	—	—	—	—	—	—

The factory classified this number as "a number which has not been used and will not be used to identify 'M.I. Hummel' figurines," until Robert Miller conducted more research at the factory. It was then discovered that at one time this number was assigned to a wall plaque by the name of "Star Gazer." This might have been an intended adaptation of Hum. 132, Star Gazer, to add to the growing group of wall plaques. A sample in white overglaze apparently was made, but there is no record of any pieces being produced for sale, and the white sample has not been located. Since several cancelled numbers for which no examples were thought to exist have actually surfaced within the last few years, hope should spring eternal in the heart of the avid collector that she or he may be the one destined to uncover the only example of 237 ever made.

238　Angel Trio (B) (Set)

Indicator	Size	Status	TMK-1	TMK-2	TMK-3	TMK-4	TMK-5	TMK-6
238/A	2½"	P	—	—	—	P	P	P
/B	2"	P	—	—	—	P	P	P
/C	2½"	P	—	—	—	P	P	P

This Hummel number is used for three different, seated angels which are distinguished by the letter suffix, A, B, or C. "A" plays the lute (banjo); "B" plays the accordion; and "C" plays the trumpet. (Beginning collectors: If you are confused as to which is which and how they vary from Joyous News Candleholders, Hum. 38, 39, and 40; Joyous News Candleholders, Hum. 27/I and 27/II; and Little Gabriel, Hum. 32; plus Herald Angels Candleholder, Hum. 37; added to Little Band Candleholder, Hum. 388; plus Little Band Music box, M388, don't panic, don't get discouraged, don't give up. Almost every expert has had the same traumatic experience and still gets mixed up.) These angels are incised with the copyright date of 1967 which coincides with the three U.S. copyrights, GF516, GF517, and GF518 issued in December of 1967. They must have been released about that time according to the catalogs and supported by the fact that so far these have only been found with TMK-4, 5, and 6. No important variations of design, height, or coloring have been reported to date. These are usually sold as a set and priced in that manner.

238 A, B, C Angel Trio (B) Set. *TMK-4, 1967 copyright. Miller Collection.*

239　Children Trio (A) (Set)

Indicator	Size	Status	TMK-1	TMK-2	TMK-3	TMK-4	TMK-5	TMK-6
239/A	3½"	P	—	—	—	P	P	P
/B	3½"	P	—	—	—	P	P	P
/C	3½"	P	—	—	—	P	P	P

This group's name and number is used for three different figures cataloged and sold as a set by the above name. These are incised with a 1967 copyright date on the bottom of the bases and were registered in the U.S. Copyright Office on December 19, 1967, as GF521. Apparently they were issued just about that time, as so far they have only been found with the last three trademarks, TMK-4, 5, and 6. The three children are: 239A, Girl with Nosegay, 3½" high; 239B, Girl with Doll, 3½" high; and 239C, Boy with Horse, 3½" high. These have been adapted from Advent Candlesticks, Hum. 115, 116, and 117, candleholders, and are almost identical except that Hum. 239 figures have no candle sockets. Hum. 116, Girl with Fir Tree, carries a doll in Hum. 239 B. Refer to these other numbers for more information and how at once time they were issued as "Mel" figurines.

239 A, B, C Children Trio (A) Set.

239 A Girl with Nosegay, *TMK-5.*

239 B Girl with Doll, *TMK-5.*

239 C Boy with Horse, *TMK-5.*

240   Little Drummer

Indicator	Size	Status	TMK-1	TMK-2	TMK-3	TMK-4	TMK-5	TMK-6
240	4¼″	P	—	P	P	P	P	P

This figurine is listed in some catalogs as "Drummer," which agrees with the German name of *Trommler*. These models carry an incised copyright date of 1955 but there is no record of the design filed in the U.S. Copyright Office. So far no significant variations in conformation or color have been reported, although there are minor variations in height from the currently specified size of 4¼″. To date this piece has not been found with the early Crown mark, TMK-1. It was not listed in a widely circulated, multilingual catalog of 1956; however, it was found listed under the name of "Drummer," 4½″ high, in a 1957 U.S. catalog. This figurine was shown on the February page of the 1960 calendar.

240 Little Drummer, *copyright 1955, TMK-5.*

241   Angel Joyous News with Lute, Font (CN)

Indicator	Size	Status	TMK-1	TMK-2	TMK-3	TMK-4	TMK-5	TMK-6
241		U	—	—	—	—	—	—

241   Angel Lights, Candleholder

Indicator	Size	Status	TMK-1	TMK-2	TMK-3	TMK-4	TMK-5	TMK-6
241	?	U	—	—	—	—	—	—
241B	8⅜″	P	—	—	—	—	P	P

As stated before, no one expected that this number would be used for the release of an M. I. Hummel article. This candleholder group is a two-piece item with plate supporting an arch with an angel figurine in the design of Heavenly Angel, Hum. 21, with four candle sockets on the arch. It was introduced into the Hummel line in 1978 and was at first called "Angel Bridge." This was changed to the present name, Angel Lights, when it was found that another item made by Goebel had already used that name. When Hum. 241 was first issued some collectors only obtained the arch without the plate, but the two fit together to form the candleholder and should be purchased in this complete form. Originally, Hum. 241 was assigned to Font, Angel, Joyous News with Lute, produced as a sample, only. It is possible that Goebel will assign a new number to Angel Lights.

241 B Angel Lights, *Candleholder, TMK-5. Introduced in 1978; number assigned in error.*

242   Cancelled Number

Indicator	Size	Status	TMK-1	TMK-2	TMK-3	TMK-4	TMK-5	TMK-6
242	?	U	—	—	—	—	—	—

This number was initially assigned for an adaptation of Joyous News, Angel with Trumpet in the manner of either Hum. 27, Hum. 40, or Hum. 238 C. According to Robert Miller, only a sample was made and the number was cancelled in 1955. Since examples of similar cancelled numbers have shown up in the past few years (see Hum. 77), there is always the remote possibility that one or more of these will be discovered, perhaps at such an ordinary place as a flea market. Quite recently a letter from Germany related the writer's experience of finding an original painting by Sister M. I. Hummel in a German flea market. It was presumed by the owners to have been lost in a fire caused by a bombing raid during World War II.

243 Madonna and Child, Holy Water Font

Indicator	Size	Status	TMK-1	TMK-2	TMK-3	TMK-4	TMK-5	TMK-6
243	4"	P	—	P	P	P	P	P

Examples of this font are incised with a copyright date of 1955. It was registered in the U.S. on January 8, 1956, as GP12630. Since there is no record to date of an example with TMK-1, it must have been introduced shortly after the copyright date. However, distribution was very limited since no old U.S. or international catalogs available had this piece listed. The 1969 Hummelwerk catalog is the earliest U.S. listing found. This appears similar in style to Sister Hummel's well-known "Madonna in Red." This design was previously adapted by Goebel as Hum. 48 and Hum. 222. Both of these are referred to as merely, "Madonna, Wall Plaque"; the latter, Hum. 22, was encompassed by a wrought iron frame. The German name, *Madonna un Kind,* translates as "Madonna and Child."

243 **Madonna and Child,** *Holy Water Font, TMK-4.*

244 — 245 Open Numbers

Indicator	Size	Status	TMK-1	TMK-2	TMK-3	TMK-4	TMK-5	TMK-6
244		O	—	—	—	—	—	?
245		O	—	—	—	—	—	?

According to Goebel factory records, these numbers were never assigned for adaptation as figurines or other art form. This being the case, they have been listed as open numbers over the years and may at some future time be assigned to new Hummel products by the Goebel Company.

246 Holy Family, Holy Water Font

Indicator	Size	Status	TMK-1	TMK-2	TMK-3	TMK-4	TMK-5	TMK-6
246	4"	P	—	P	P	P	P	P

While this font carries an incised copyright date of 1955, it was copyrighted in the U.S. on April 27, 1956, as GP12631 with the name "Madonna with Jesus and Joseph." The font is found in all trademark periods except in the Crown period. The first available catalogs that list Hum. 246 are dated 1959; thereafter, this font seems to have been called "Holy Family." Verlag Emil Fink, owner of the original drawing, publishes it as postcard #210.

246 **Holy Family,** *Holy Water Font, TMK-5.*

247 Cancelled Number

Indicator	Size	Status	TMK-1	TMK-2	TMK-3	TMK-4	TMK-5	TMK-6
247	13″	C	*	—	—	—	—	—

In earlier publications, including *Hummel Art I,* Hum. 247 was listed as a Closed Edition which would never be used again. Thanks to some dedicated research by Robert Miller, we now know that this number was used for a crowned madonna. The tall (13″) figurine, adapted from a painting by Sister Hummel, carried the provisional name of "Standing Madonna and Child." She is distinguished from other madonnas by the star-topped crown, the yellow gown, the blue cloak, and the rosary draped over her left arm. The child also holds a rosary. Once a sample is known to the public, there is always the tantalizing thought that another might have been made. If so, it would be valued in the high four-digit figures.

*Factory sample only.

248 Guardian Angel, *Holy Water Font, TMK-4.*

248 Guardian Angel, Holy Water Font

Indicator	Size	Status	TMK-1	TMK-2	TMK-3	TMK-4	TMK-5	TMK-6
248	5½″	P	—	?	P	P	P	P
/0	5½″	D	—	—	?	P	—	—
/I	6¼″	D	—	—	P	—	—	—

This design was first copyrighted in the U.S. on February 17, 1959, GP20104, and is incised "1959" on the back of each piece. It apparently was issued about this time since it is found with TMK-3 through TMK-6. One unverified report claims an example with TMK-2, so the possibility of a TMK-2 is slight but not unreasonable. The purpose of this piece was to modify a similar font by the same name, Hum. 29 (see), that was discontinued in the late 1950s. For Hum. 248, the angel's wings are made an integral part of her head in order to lessen the possibility of breaking the wing tips, which must have been a problem with the first design. For some time it was made in two sizes, approximately 2¼″ by 5½″ and 2⅔″ by 6¼″, and incised on the backs 248/0 and 248/I, respectively. A search of the old catalogs indicates that this was not listed continuously and usually in only the smaller size that varied somewhat in quoted dimensions. It is now listed and marketed only in the smaller size which is incised with just the whole number, 248. The larger size 248/I is considered rare because of the limited number made since about 1959. These pieces are cataloged by Hummelwerk, a U.S. distributor, as "Kneeling Angel," which causes some confusion.

249 Madonna and Child, Plaque (CN)

Indicator	Size	Status	TMK-1	TMK-2	TMK-3	TMK-4	TMK-5	TMK-6
249	8¾″	C	—	*	—	—	—	—

When the first edition of *Hummel Art* was published in 1978, there was no information available on this model except that the Goebel Company considered this a closed number which would never be used again. As with some of the other closed numbers, careful research of the company archives by Robert Miller revealed that this number had been used for an unusual wall plaque of the original M. I. Hummel painting known as the "Madonna in Red." It differs from all other known wall plaques except Hum. 263, Merry Wanderer. All other plaques have bas-relief (semiraised) figures on a square or rectangular background with an integral ceramic frame. Hum. 249 has no background, only the bas-relief of the Madonna and Child as the entire piece. There is no integral ceramic frame. The only known piece is a factory sample.

*Factory sample only.

249 Madonna and Child, *Plaque, rare, designed by Skrobek, TMK-2, courtesy W. Goebel Co.*

250 A   Little Goat Herder, Bookend

Indicator	Size	Status	TMK-1	TMK-2	TMK-3	TMK-4	TMK-5	TMK-6
250/A	5½"	P	—	P	P	P	P	P

This half of a pair of bookends was produced by taking the figurine Little Goat Herder, Hum. 200, and securing it to a wooden base with a simulated slat fence for the book rest. The identification and trademark are shown on the wooden base because the base of the figurine is not visible. The restyled version of the figurine was used for this bookend, which was first issued and cataloged about 1965 at a price of $26.50 for the pair, Hum. 250 A&B. These bookends are normally found with TMK-3 through TMK-6. There is the possibility that one might have the earlier TMK-2 because of exceptions like this with other items by Goebel. For more information see Hum. 200.

250 B   Feeding Time, Bookend

Indicator	Size	Status	TMK-1	TMK-2	TMK-3	TMK-4	TMK-5	TMK-6
250/B	5½"	P	—	P	P	P	P	P

The figurine, Hum. 199, is permanently secured on a wooden base as described under Hum. 250 A. The two are usually cataloged as 250 A&B and now sold only as a pair at over five times what they retailed for in the mid-1960s. See 250 A for remarks about trademarks.

250 A&B Little Goat Herder, Feeding Time, *Bookends. TMK-5.*

251 A   Good Friends, Bookend

Indicator	Size	Status	TMK-1	TMK-2	TMK-3	TMK-4	TMK-5	TMK-6
251/A	5"	P	—	?	P	P	P	P

Here again is a standard figurine on a ceramic base fastened to a wooden base with an upright rest for books. For more details on the figurine itself, see Good Friends, Hum. 182. This pair (251 A&B) was first found in a U.S. catalog dated 1965 and sets are seen in TMK-3 through TMK-6, with the possibility that some very early ones might have been marked TMK-2. Since the figurine was restyled in the mid-1970s, the bookends with TMK-5 and 6 will also show the same more modern look and coloring.

251 B   She Loves Me,
She Loves Me Not, Bookend

Indicator	Size	Status	TMK-1	TMK-2	TMK-3	TMK-4	TMK-5	TMK-6
251/B	5"	P	—	?	P	P	P	P

The figurine of the boy picking petals from a daisy forms the other half of this set. The bookends are cataloged and sold as a set of two. For further details on this portion of the set see the description of the figurine itself, Hum. 174. This half of the set has also been restyled with the newer version looking directly down at the flower rather than with the straight-ahead stare of the earlier models.

251 A&B Good Friends, She Loves Me, *trademark unknown. Miller Collection.*

252 A&B Apple Tree Girl and Boy, *Bookends, TMK-5.*

252 A   Apple Tree Girl, Bookend

Indicator	Size	Status	TMK-1	TMK-2	TMK-3	TMK-4	TMK-5	TMK-6
252/A	5″	P	—	?	P	P	P	P

This bookend is essentially the figurine, Hum. 141/3/0 (the one version of the figurine that does not have a bird in the treetop), mounted permanently on a wooden base which is incised with all the identification marks. This set was issued about the middle of the 1960s and is the third and last of the three sets of bookends introduced at that time. It appears in the U.S. catalog for 1966. One report indicates that at least one pair of these is known with TMK-2, but this is an exception and would justify a premium of at least 50 percent. The rest have TMK-3 through TMK-6. For more details, refer to Hum. 141. This motif also appears in Table Lamp, Hum. 229 and the 1976 Annual Plate in bas-relief, Hum. 269.

252 B   Apple Tree Boy, Bookend

Indicator	Size	Status	TMK-1	TMK-2	TMK-3	TMK-4	TMK-5	TMK-6
252/B	5″	P	—	?	P	P	P	P

The figurine 142/3/0 is used for the second part of the Hum. 252 bookends. Whatever has been said about the introduction and trademarks of Apple Tree Girl is equally applicable to Apple Tree Boy. Refer to Hum. 142 for full information on the history of this motif. In addition, also see companion pieces in the 1977 Annual Plate, Hum. 270 and Table Lamp, Hum. 230.

253   Cancelled Number

Indicator	Size	Status	TMK-1	TMK-2	TMK-3	TMK-4	TMK-5	TMK-6
253	?	U	—	—	—	—	—	—

At first it was generally thought that this was a number never used by Goebel, but later research by Robert Miller and the factory indicate that it was assigned to the figure of a girl with a basket which may have been similar to Going to Grandma's, Hum. 52. There are no known samples at the factory or elsewhere. Our research shows no U.S. copyright.

254   Cancelled Number

Indicator	Size	Status	TMK-1	TMK-2	TMK-3	TMK-4	TMK-5	TMK-6
254	?	U	—	—	—	—	—	—

This classification originally meant that this number was never used and never would be used, but an intensive search by Robert Miller and factory personnel reveals that at one time it was assigned to a figure of a girl playing a mandolin, possibly like Happy Days, Hum. 150. Research in the U.S. Copyright Office reveals that Copyright GP146 was issued on August 22, 1963, and described as that of a girl on a base holding flowers.

255   Stitch in Time

255 Stitch in Time, *copyright 1963, TMK-5.*

Indicator	Size	Status	TMK-1	TMK-2	TMK-3	TMK-4	TMK-5	TMK-6
255	6¾″	P	—	—	P	P	P	P

This model is making her second appearance in the Hummel line. Originally, she appeared as one of the three School Girls, Hum. 177. Stitch in Time was copyrighted on August 22, 1963, as GF145 and appeared in U.S. catalogs by 1965. Hum. 255 has been reported only in TMK-3 through TMK-6; no TMK-2 examples known as yet. There are no significant variations in color or design; however, the 6¾″ height may vary slightly. *Zwei Rechts—Zwei Links,* German for "Two to the right — two to the left," is an active and more specific name for this determined knitter. Her third debut in the Hummel line occurs in Knitting Lesson, Hum. 256. This appears in the calendars for February, 1968, and January, 1975.

256   Knitting Lesson

Indicator	Size	Status	TMK-1	TMK-2	TMK-3	TMK-4	TMK-5	TMK-6
256	7½"	P	—	—	P	P	P	P

The little knitter from Hum. 255 has acquired a friend, and both are standing on a larger base. This is another exposure for the friend who has already appeared as one of the trio in School Girls, Hum. 177. The similarities between some figurines exemplify how one drawing of Sister Hummel's could be the inspiration for several figures. Hum. 256 was copyrighted in the U.S. as GF149 on October 9, 1963. It first appeared in a U.S. catalog the following year. The figurine is incised with the year of copyright, 1963. The German name of *Ob's gelingt* which asks, "Will it work?" is entirely different from its English name. To date, no unusual variation in this model has been reported. Examples are found with TMK-3 through TMK-6. The November, 1972, calendar page pictures this figurine.

256 Knitting Lesson, *copyright 1963, TMK-4.*

257   For Mother

Indicator	Size	Status	TMK-1	TMK-2	TMK-3	TMK-4	TMK-5	TMK-6
257	5"	P	—	—	P	P	P	P

This is one of the figurines introduced in the U.S. in 1964, the year of the New York World's Fair. Presumably the inspiration was to provide a companion piece for Hum. 87, For Father, who had been offering a stein of beer and a bunch of turnips since the 1950s. There was no record found of a U.S. copyright date. This motif was used as the illustration for the month of May in the 1973 calendar. It is found in TMK-3 through TMK-6. No major changes have been noted to date, but if an example with TMK-2 were found it would be exceptional. It might possibly be an early prototype valued at over $1,000.

257 For Mother, *copyright 1963, TMK-5.*

258   Which Hand?

Indicator	Size	Status	TMK-1	TMK-2	TMK-3	TMK-4	TMK-5	TMK-6
258	5½"	P	—	—	P	P	P	P

This model appeared earlier as the intent listener in Telling Her Secret, Hum. 196, and was first introduced in the U.S. about 1964-5. The U.S. copyright was issued on August 22, 1963, as registration GF147. This figurine is found in TMK-3, 4, 5, and 6 and is unverified in TMK-2. So far no major changes have been reported in style or color. The German name of *Rat mal!* translates to "Guess!" conveying the same idea. Graphics of the original work of Sister Hummel are available in postcard #5834 produced by Verlag Ars Sacra. The figurine appeared in the October, 1973, calendar.

258 Which Hand? *Copyright 1963, TMK-5.*

259   Cancelled Number

Indicator	Size	Status	TMK-1	TMK-2	TMK-3	TMK-4	TMK-5	TMK-6
259	?	U	—	—	—	—	—	—

Earlier publications referred to this number as one that had never been assigned and never would be used. Research of the factory records within the last few years has revealed that this number was assigned to the design "Girl with Accordion," similar to the restyled version of the girl in Birthday Serenade, Hum. 218. The project was cancelled in 1962. No known examples.

260 Nativity Set (Large)

Indicator	Size	Status	TMK-1	TMK-2	TMK-3	TMK-4	TMK-5	TMK-6
260 (17 pcs.)		P	—	—	?	P	P	P
260A	9¾″	P	—	—	?	P	P	P
B	11¾″	P	—	—	?	P	P	P
C	5¾″	P	—	—	?	P	P	P
D	5¼″	P	—	—	?	P	P	P
E	4¼″	P	—	—	?	P	P	P
F	6¼″	P	—	—	?	P	P	P
G	11¾″	P	—	—	?	P	P	P
H	3¾″	P	—	—	?	P	P	P
J	7″	P	—	—	?	P	P	P
K	5⅛″	P	—	—	?	P	P	P
L	7½″	P	—	—	?	P	P	P
M	11″	P	—	—	?	P	P	P
N	12¾″	P	—	—	?	P	P.	P
O	12″	P	—	—	?	P	P	P
P	9″	P	—	—	?	P	P	P
R	3¼″	P	—	—	?	P	P	P

This set is larger than Nativity Set, Hum. 214, and was not copyrighted until 1968 in the U.S. as GF500. Consisting of sixteen pieces, the figurines bear suffix letters from A through R. The pieces average about 50 percent larger than the earlier set, Hum. 214, and make an impressive arrangement at Christmas time. Due to inflation and the declining value of the dollar, retail price of this set has doubled in the last four years. It is not listed in all catalogs. Some dealers will break up sets so that collectors, without undue delay, can buy replacements for pieces damaged or missing. The complete list and specifications are entered above. One piece that causes some confusion among collectors is Hum. 260 F, We Congratulate. In the Nativity Set, the two figures are not on a base as they are in Hum. 220, the 4″ figurine. Furthermore, in Hum. 260 F the girl wears a garland of flowers in her hair.

260 A-R Large Nativity Set, TMK-5.

261   Angel Duet

Indicator	Size	Status	TMK-1	TMK-2	TMK-3	TMK-4	TMK-5	TMK-6
261	5″	P	—	—	—	P	P	P

This modified version of Hum. 193 (Candleholder) with the identical name of Angel Duet confuses many collectors. The differences are that in Hum. 261 the candle socket has been eliminated and the position of one angel's arm has changed. The angel on the viewer's right has his left hand holding the hymnbook and his right hand encircling the other angel's waist. In Hum. 193, the angel on the viewer's right does not hold the hymnbook but holds the candleholder in his left hand and rests his right arm on the other angel's left shoulder. One other noticeable difference between these two figurines is that Hum. 261 has sculptured hair, a characteristic style of the present master sculptor, Gerhard Skrobek.

261 **Angel Duet** *(see 193), TMK-5.*
Miller Collection.

262   Heavenly Lullaby

Indicator	Size	Status	TMK-1	TMK-2	TMK-3	TMK-4	TMK-5	TMK-6
262	5″	P	—	—	P	P	P	P

Here we have another example of a candleholder modified into a figurine using the same figures as Lullaby, Hum. 24. It is approximately the same size as the smaller Hum. 24/I which is 3½″ x 5″, but is incised with the copyright date of 1968 and was registered in the U.S. as GF551 on December 6 of the same year. It is found in limited quantities marked TMK-3 through TMK-6. The German name *Wiegenleid,* is simply "Lullaby." The 1962 calendar uses this figurine as the December illustration.

262 **Heavenly Lullaby,** *TMK-5.*

263   Merry Wanderer, Plaque

Indicator	Size	Status	TMK-1	TMK-2	TMK-3	TMK-4	TMK-5	TMK-6
263	5″	C	—	—	*	—	—	—

When the first edition of *Hummel Art* was published in 1978, the only information available was that the Goebel Company considered this a Closed Number which was never assigned and never would be used. In the interim, Robert Miller and the Goebel Company did further research and found that these numbers had been assigned to various designs for studies and samples. In the case of Hum. 263, the result was a style of wall plaques used by only one other unissued model, Hum. 294, Madonna and Child. Hum. 263 design was of the very popular Merry Wanderer for which two wall plaques already existed, Hum. 92 and Hum. 106. However, both Hum. 92 and Hum. 106 have frames. (Hum. 92 incorporated a ceramic, self-frame; Hum. 106 uses a wooden frame.) Hum. 263 is a bas-relief of the figure itself with a flat back with a slot for hanging. The only known example is a factory sample.

*Factory sample only.

264 Annual Plate, 1971, Heavenly Angel, *TMK-4. Courtesy W. Goebel Co.*

264 Reverse of 1971 Annual Plate. *"1871-1971.*
IN COMMEMORATION OF THE
100TH ANNIVERSARY OF W.
GOEBEL-HUMMELWERK. W.
GERMANY."
Courtesy W. Goebel Co.

264 Annual Plate, 1971, Heavenly Angel

Indicator	Size	Status	TMK-1	TMK-2	TMK-3	TMK-4	TMK-5	TMK-6
264	7½″	C	—	—	?	P	—	—

The Goebel Company completed its first century in business in 1971. In order to commemorate this event and to recognize the employees' contribution to its continued success, the company issued a special plate — a bas-relief design of Heavenly Angel matching the figurine, Hum. 21. On the back of the plate was an inscription acknowledging the employees' contribution to the Goebel Company. One of these was given to each person employed (several thousand in all). In addition, the plate without this special inscription was offered for general sale (issue price $25 in the U.S.) during that year and the mold destroyed at the end of the year. The number of plates made available matched only a fraction of the collectors who wanted a first issue of a continuing series. The obvious result was that the price zoomed in the secondary market and within a few years it had reached an asking price of $1,000 with the original box. (Today the empty box itself is quoted at about $30!) Most of the plates were transfer-marked with TMK-4. Another variation that year was the lack of mounting holes in the back of the plates shipped to England to take advantage of a lower duty that applied. Another plate first issued that year, but transfer-decorated with the Heavenly Angel design, was one introduced by Schmid Bros., Inc. The muted colors and lack of raised surfaces of the Heavenly Angel should make this difference quite apparent, even without a side-by-side comparison of the plates. A few Hum. 264 Heavenly Angel plates have been reported found with TMK-3 (Stylized Bee, One Line mark). Verified examples would bring a premium of about 25 percent over the price for the TMK-4 shown in the Price List. The plates received by each employee carried a special inscription. Reports of an occasional one of them being available have been received. A verified example of such "employee plate" would be valued about 50 percent more than the regular 1971 Annual Plate price shown in the Price List.

Three design studies of Annual Plate, 1971, Heavenly Angel, Hum. 264. Design on right was adopted. Factory samples courtesy W. Goebel Co.

Key to Symbols: A — Assigned; C — Cancelled; D — Discontinued; O — Open; P — Produced; R — Reissued;
(?) Examples Doubtful; (—) Examples Unlikely.

265 Annual Plate, 1972, Hear Ye, Hear Ye!

Indicator	Size	Status	TMK-1	TMK-2	TMK-3	TMK-4	TMK-5	TMK-6
265	7½″	C	—	—	—	P	P	—

The second annual issue is a bas-relief replica of the figurine of the same name, Hum. 15. The U.S. copyright is GF744 and was issued on July 15, 1971. This plate is also 7½″ in diameter and has the ring of embossed stars around the outside ege, a common design feature of this series. Since the plate's issue, the trademark was changed from TMK-4 to TMK-5, the Goebel Bee used until 1979. As a result, plates are found with either trademark, and the quantity produced of each is as much of a secret as the number of plates manufactured each year. The issue price was $38.

265 Annual Plate, 1972, Hear Ye, Hear Ye!, *TMK-4.*

266 Annual Plate, 1973, Globe Trotter

Indicator	Size	Status	TMK-1	TMK-2	TMK-3	TMK-4	TMK-5	TMK-6
266	7½″	C	—	—	—	—	P	—

The third Annual Plate, 1973, has the bas-relief replica of Globe Trotter, Hum. 79. One minor and unexplained variation is the fact that this plate is the only one to date that has only thirty-two stars in the identifying border. All other years have thirty-three stars. The U.S. Copyright, GF814, was issued on February 18, 1972. The issue price was $40. The vagaries of limited edition collecting are indicated by the fact that this plate sells for about one-fifth of the price of the first issue and about two to three times that of the second issue. Since the new TMK-5 (Goebel Bee mark) was introduced in 1972, this plate is found with both the previous TMK-4 and the newer TMK-5 marks. Both seem so evenly divided that no premium for either mark has been recorded.

266 Annual Plate, 1973, Globe Trotter, *TMK-5.*

267 Annual Plate, 1974, Goose Girl

Indicator	Size	Status	TMK-1	TMK-2	TMK-3	TMK-4	TMK-5	TMK-6
267	7½″	C	—	—	—	—	P	—

The Goose Girl figurine, Hum. 47, is one of the most identifiable and best known of all M. I. Hummel figurines, which is one of the reasons it was chosen for the cover of this book. The design on this plate is a bas-relief representation of the figurine. The U.S. Copyright, GF804, was registered on February 18, 1972. The issue price for a 1974 plate that year was $46. By this time the figurine associated with the design on the plate was becoming very hard to find, as many collectors were buying the figurine to mount in a shadow box frame with the plate itself.

267 Annual Plate, 1974, Goose Girl, *TMK-5.*

268 Annual Plate, 1975, Ride into Christmas

Indicator	Size	Status	TMK-1	TMK-2	TMK-3	TMK-4	TMK-5	TMK-6
268	7½″	C	—	—	—	—	P	—

This fifth Annual Plate utilizes the design of the original figurine by that name, Hum. 396, in bas-relief form, adding further demand to the scant supply of this figurine on the dealers' shelves and making Hum. 396 one of the top premium pieces produced. Strangely enough, research uncovered two copyrights for this plate. The first was filed on June 22, 1972, and the second one on November 19, 1973. It does raise the interesting possibility that two different design samples were made and one of them selected for production. One wonders where samples for this unissued design are located. Another opportunity for collectors may be waiting for discovery. The issue price of the plate for 1975 was $50.

Photographs courtesy W. Goebel Co.

268 Annual Plate, 1975, Ride into Christmas, *TMK-5.*

269 Annual Plate, 1976, Apple
Tree Girl, *TMK-5.*

270 Annual Plate, 1977, Apple
Tree Boy, *TMK-5.*

271 Annual Plate, 1978, Happy
Pastime, *TMK-5.*

272 Annual Plate, 1979, Singing
Lesson, *TMK-5.*

269 Annual Plate, 1976, Apple Tree Girl

Indicator	Size	Status	TMK-1	TMK-2	TMK-3	TMK-4	TMK-5	TMK-6
269	7½"	C	—	—	—	—	P	—

There is no doubt that Goebel was selecting popular subjects for the Annual Plates. Apple Tree Girl is another favorite that is almost synonymous with M. I. Hummel. The figurine from which the bas-relief was developed is Hum. 141, which is worth referring to for additional background. The U.S. Copyright, GF875, was registered on June 23, 1972. An almost unheard of exception in 1976 (especially with products from overseas),was that the issue price of the 1976 model was held at the same $50 level as the 1975 plate issue price. A picture of this plate is shown on the cover of the M. I. Hummel calendar for 1976. This calendar has been produced each year since 1952 by Goebel.

270 Annual Plate, 1977, Apple Tree Boy

Indicator	Size	Status	TMK-1	TMK-2	TMK-3	TMK-4	TMK-5	TMK-6
270	7½"	C	—	—	—	—	P	—

There was not the usual speculation on what the subject for this year would be. The safe bet turned out to be the expected Apple Tree Boy taken from the figurine of the same name, Hum. 142. The U.S. copyright for this model is GF876, also registered June 23, 1972. Robert Miller reports there was a variation in the plates for that year. At the last minute the design was slightly altered so that the boy's right sock was made higher than the left one. An early sample shows the left sock longer, with the shoes at a slightly different angle. How rare this plate is will be decided by the marketplace, as the quantity of the long left sock is unknown, and the number of interested persons is also unknown. While the issue price was increased to $65, it seemed no obstacle to collectors; many dealers were charging a premium for them even before the edition was closed.

271 Annual Plate, 1978, Happy Pastime

Indicator	Size	Status	TMK-1	TMK-2	TMK-3	TMK-4	TMK-5	TMK-6
271	7½"	C	—	—	—	—	P	—

The distribution of this plate caused problems. The consensus is that Goebel reduced the quantity of plates produced or was unable to expand production for the exploding public demand. They were in short supply all that year, and, because many collectors could not get one at the issue price of $65, or had to pay three times that amount, collectors became very unhappy. Some decided to sell their plate collections of past years and buy something else. The speculators had a major hand in escalating the price and preventing regular collectors from getting a plate at a fair price. Excessive demand for the companion figurine, Happy Pastime, Hum. 69, caused the price of this piece to orbit also. The U.S. copyright was registered as GF877 on June 23, 1972.

272 Annual Plate, 1979, Singing Lesson

Indicator	Size	Status	TMK-1	TMK-2	TMK-3	TMK-4	TMK-5	TMK-6
272	7½"	C	—	—	—	—	P	—

Alongside the 1978 Annual Plate, the 1979 Annual Plate composes an attractive, almost mirror image in design. Using the two corresponding

Photographs courtesy W. Goebel Co.

figurines, Hum. 69 and 63, one could create an effective display. The issue price that year was $90. The increase in price coupled with Goebel's expanded production before the end of the year satisfied the needs of most collectors without undue hunting or the payment of excessive premiums. The plate differs somewhat from the figurine, Hum. 63, and more closely follows Sister Hummel's original drawing. (Refer to Ars Sacra postcard #4949.) Hum. 272 was copyrighted in the U.S. on June 23, 1972, as number GF879.

273 Annual Plate, 1980, School Girl

Indicator	Size	Status	TMK-1	TMK-2	TMK-3	TMK-4	TMK-5	TMK-6
273	7½″	C	—	—	—	—	?	P

273 Annual Plate, 1980, School Girl, *TMK-6.*

Another Goebel selection that is near and dear to the hearts of many collectors. The increased price ($100 per plate), Goebel's expanded production, and the U.S. recession kept supply and demand more nearly in balance so that most collectors were able to buy their examples through regular channels at the suggested price. The matching figurine, School Girl, Hum. 81, provides an excellent companion display piece in a common deep frame or shelf. This plate along with many others was registered in the U.S. Copyright Office as GF878, on June 23, 1972.

274 Annual Plate, 1981, Umbrella Boy

Indicator	Size	Status	TMK-1	TMK-2	TMK-3	TMK-4	TMK-5	TMK-6
274	7½″	P	—	—	—	—	—	P

274 Annual Plate, 1981, Umbrella Boy, *TMK-6.*

Many collectors were guessing that the 1981 plate would be School Boy, Hum. 32, as a follow-up to School Girl in 1978. However, the better-known Umbrella Boy, Hum. 152/A, was selected for adaptation to the bas-relief of the plate. Due to a number of factors, the price has been held to $100. With sufficient production available, most collectors have been pleased to find their plates without too much difficulty at regular prices. The U.S. Copyright GF1079 was registered on November 19, 1973.

275 Annual Plate, 1982, Umbrella Girl

Indicator	Size	Status	TMK-1	TMK-2	TMK-3	TMK-4	TMK-5	TMK-6
275	7½″	A	—	—	—	—	—	?

275 Annual Plate, 1982, Umbrella Girl, *trademark unknown.*

In 1979, Goebel, in order to alleviate some of the speculation on and excessive demand for figurines that matched the annual plate, decided to pre-announce the heretofore closely guarded secret of what the subjects of future annual plates would be. Goebel announced the plate designs through the year 1986, which happens to be the last year for which U.S. copyrights have been filed.

276 Annual Plate, 1983, Postman

Indicator	Size	Status	TMK-1	TMK-2	TMK-3	TMK-4	TMK-5	TMK-6
276	7½″	A	—	—	—	—	—	?

The figurine of the same name, Hum. 119, has been used for this plate, but portrayed in bas-relief from an attractive side-view. Interestingly, this motif is placed with virtually no background detail, which is the way Sister Hummel's original drawing is done. Most plate figures sit or stand on grass, or at least on a more detailed background. The copyright registration number is GF1077, dated November 19, 1973.

276 Annual Plate, 1983, Postman, *trademark unknown.*

Photographs courtesy W. Goebel Co.

277 Annual Plate, 1984, Little
Helper, *trademark unknown.*

278 Annual Plate, 1985, Chick
Girl, *trademark unknown.*

279 Annual Plate, 1986,
Playmates, *trademark unknown.*

280 Anniversary Plate, 1975,
Stormy Weather, *trademark unknown.*

277 Annual Plate, 1984, Little Helper

Indicator	Size	Status	TMK-1	TMK-2	TMK-3	TMK-4	TMK-5	TMK-6
277	7½″	A	—	—	—	—	—	?

This bas-relief was derived from the figurine of the same name, Hum. 73. The most notable difference is that the basket has been filled with some appetizing fruit. Since its introduction in the late Forties or early Fifties, the figurine had, and still has, an empty basket. Sister Hummel's drawing shows round objects in the basket which are presumed to be eggs, as two chicks are shown nearby with portions of the shells. This plate, GF1076, is another of a group of seven plates copyrighted on the same day, November 11, 1973. Refer to Verlag Ars Sacra postcard #4642 which is an exact duplicate of the original drawing they own.

278 Annual Plate, 1985, Chick Girl

Indicator	Size	Status	TMK-1	TMK-2	TMK-3	TMK-4	TMK-5	TMK-6
278	7½″	A	—	—	—	—	—	?

The figurine derivative chosen for this plate is one that was first issued in the Thirties, Hum. 57. The figurine is sold in two sizes, and only the larger 4¼″ size has three chicks in the basket. The smaller size only has two, so there is a choice for those collectors who like to display the plate and the matching figurine together. Copyright GF1075, was issued on November 19, 1973, to cover this plate design.

279 Annual Plate, 1986, Playmates

Indicator	Size	Status	TMK-1	TMK-2	TMK-3	TMK-4	TMK-5	TMK-6
279	7½″	A	—	—	—	—	—	?

It is fitting that this subject follows the 1985 Chick Girl since they have been associated for years in the form of a pair of bookends, Hum. 61 A&B. These two plates mounted on a wall behind a table with these same bookends supporting this book and other Hummel publications would make an interesting arrangement. The plate is patterned after the figurine by the same name, Hum. 58; the plate motif follows the design in the larger of the two figurines, 58/I, as the rabbit in the back has both ears up. Again, there is a choice of different-sized figurines to use with the plate. This last plate in the pre-announced future issues was copyrighted on November 19, 1973, as GF1074.

280 Anniversary Plate, 1975, Stormy Weather

Indicator	Size	Status	TMK-1	TMK-2	TMK-3	TMK-4	TMK-5	TMK-6
280	10″	P	—	—	—	—	P	—

This plate, 10″ in diameter, was issued in addition to the Annual Plate as the first of a series. To date, the series consists of two plates issued at five-year intervals. The issue price of this first issue was $100; collectors liked the plate so well that the price in the secondary market reached a peak of about $375 within a year of issue. A comparison of this bas-relief with the figure by the same name, Hum. 71, will immediately indicate a drastic difference in the treatment of the children's expressions. In the figurine, the children appear to be slightly awed and fearful. In the Anniversary Plate, the expression is at the opposite end of the emotional rainbow. The sense of satisfaction and happiness is quite evident. Research indicates that Sister Hummel created two drawings involving these two children. Verlag Ars Sacra's postcard made from the other original drawing portrays the same obvious relief and joy that the storm was over. In fact, many people call the first drawing "Stormy" and the second one "Clearing." The copyright for this plate is GF1097 and was issued on September 5, 1974.

Photographs courtesy W. Goebel Co.

281   Anniversary Plate, 1980, Ring Around the Rosie

Indicator	Size	Status	TMK-1	TMK-2	TMK-3	TMK-4	TMK-5	TMK-6
281	10″	P	—	—	—	—	?	P

The reception of this plate was not quite as open-armed as the one for the first plate in the series. One factor was the issue price of $225 which had more than doubled in five years. Another factor may have been the public's 1980 deflationary mood. While the Anniversary Plate carries the same name as the figurine, Hum. 348, the question immediately arose of why there are only two girls dancing in the plate design while there are four girls in the figurine. Goebel explained that the original title of this plate was "Spring Dance" until at the last moment they realized that only one of the figurines on the plate was from Spring Dance, Hum. 353. The name was subsequently changed to Ring Around the Rosie.

281 Anniversary Plate, 1980, Ring Around the Rosie, *trademark unknown. Courtesy W. Goebel Co.*

282-299   Open Numbers

Indicator	Size	Status	TMK-1	TMK-2	TMK-3	TMK-4	TMK-5	TMK-6
282-299		O	—	—	—	—	—	?

Goebel declares an "Open Number" to mean: "An identification number, which in W. Goebel's numerical identification system has not yet been used, but which may be used to identify new 'M. I. Hummel' figurines as they are released in the future." It is important to remember that over twenty new figurines and articles were copyrighted in 1955 and were not introduced in the U.S. until 1971-1972. The last copyright issued to Goebel in the U.S., except for the plate copyrights, was for Hum. 262 in 1963. Hummel numbers starting with Hum. 264 and continuing through Hum. 280 are reserved for plates already issued or pre-announced. The nineteen Hummel numbers from 281 through 299 provide sufficient numbers to cover all the years to the year 2000 for the Annual and Anniversary Plate Series. Starting with Hum. 300, the next thirty-six numbers were all assigned by the year 1955 or 1956, and should carry copyright dates very close to those years. The German copyright date, probably used for incising, may well have preceded U.S. copyright registration by a year or so. From Hum. 337 through Hum. 350, all of the (U.S.) copyrights were registered in 1972, but most numbers up to 375 were registered no later than the mid-Sixties. Copyrights were found for Hummel numbers up through Hum. 396, Ride into Christmas. Nothing was found in the Hum. 400 series. Hum. 500 was registered on January 22, 1975, as GF1152 for a 1976 Mother's Day Plate entitled, "Flowers for Mother." It is important to re-emphasize that there is no fixed relationship between the incised copyright date and the date of issue. Other than Hum. 282-299, there remain only six "Open Numbers." These are Hums. 236, 244, 245, 397, and 398. Forty-two motifs between 300 and 399 are assigned to a number but not yet released.

300   Bird Watcher

Indicator	Size	Status	TMK-1	TMK-2	TMK-3	TMK-4	TMK-5	TMK-6
300	5″	P	—	—	—	—	P	P

Way back in 1956, a copyright was registered in the U.S. by the Goebel Company under the name of "Friend to Animals" which, as it turns out, was Gerhard Skrobek's first major assignment with the company in 1954. This particular work was assigned Hum. 233, but for some reason never was put into production and the number was cancelled. Twenty-four years later the same motif was released as Hum. 300. Between then and its release in the U.S. in 1979 as Bird Watcher, some restyling must have been done, for it has the deeply sculptured hair and other earmarks of the more recent work of Skrobek. Someplace along the line the name "Tenderness" was associated with it, but no written record of this name could be found. This small figurine had a suggested issue price of $90, but the demand was so great that within months some dealers were asking as much as $250 for it.

300 Bird Watcher, *issued 1979, TMK-5.*

301 Christmas Angel *(Assigned).*

302 Concentration *(Assigned). From #5332 courtesy Ars Sacra.*

303 Arithmetic Lesson *(Assigned). From #5338 courtesy Ars Sacra.*

301   Christmas Angel (Assigned Number)

Indicator	Size	Status	TMK-1	TMK-2	TMK-3	TMK-4	TMK-5	TMK-6
301	6¼″	A	—	—	—	—	—	?

When this piece was copyrighted in the U.S. in 1958, it was listed as "Delivery Angel with Basket." It has since been made known that Hum. 301 was sculpted in 1957 by Theodore R. Menzenbach, who was master sculptor in the 1950s prior to Skrobek, the present master sculptor. The Miller collection displayed a sample of this figurine which has a TMK-3 and is incised with the year 1957, in Eaton, Ohio, in 1980. Hum. 301 will be classed here as an Assigned Number which may be released at some unknown future date. A postcard #4779 has been published by Verlag Ars Sacra from the original drawing that is owned by them.

302   Concentration (Assigned Number)

Indicator	Size	Status	TMK-1	TMK-2	TMK-3	TMK-4	TMK-5	TMK-6
302	5″	A	—	—	—	—	—	?

Originally called "Do It Like Me" (Girl Knitting) when it was copyrighted in the U.S. on July 18, 1956, others referred to it as "Knit One, Purl One." The German name of *Wie macht sie das nur* translates as "How does she do it." When and how the final name, "Concentration," was decided upon is not known. This is the fourth time that this little knitter has appeared in the M. I. Hummel line. (See Hum. 255 for more information.) Hum. 302 will be classified as an Assigned Number at present and its status will be changed to "Produced" and "Priced" when and if it is offered for sale. It will carry the trademark in use at that time, but the chance of a sample being found with a TMK-2 or TMK-3 is always a possibility. Models for this figurine, the little knitter and the thoughtful boy, were taken from Ars Sacra drawings #5332 and #5338.

303   Arithmetic Lesson (Assigned Number)

Indicator	Size	Status	TMK-1	TMK-2	TMK-3	TMK-4	TMK-5	TMK-6
303	5¼″	A	—	—	—	—	—	?

This little girl and boy puzzling over a math problem appear to be a combination of the center boy from Hum. 170, School Boys, and the right-hand girl from Hum. 177, School Girls. It is unknown whether Sister Hummel composed such a drawing or whether it was contrived by the Goebel sculptor. This figurine was copyrighted in the U.S. on October 10, 1955, so any sample may carry a TMK-2. However, if Hum. 303 is issued in the future, it will carry the current trademark of that time. The German name for this future possibility is *Rechenstunde* which means the same as the English title. Postcards #5332 and #5333 by Verlag Ars Sacra may have been the inspiration for this studious pair.

304 The Artist

Indicator	Size	Status	TMK-1	TMK-2	TMK-3	TMK-4	TMK-5	TMK-6
304	5½"	P	—	—	P	P	P	P

While this figurine of a boy with a palette was only cataloged for sale in this country in 1971, it is incised with a 1955 copyright date and was registered in the U.S. Copyright Office in that year on October 20. This popular figurine has already appeared on two calendars, in 1977 on the cover and for April in 1973. The German name of *Kunstmaler* translates as "The Artist Painter." An unusual variation of this figurine was exhibited at the Eaton Festival in June, 1980. The figure was completely white except for painted eyes and lips. Could this have been a "lunchbox" sample for $500? Several other model numbers have also been exhibited or pictured that are only partially painted, but the story of their origin is still a mystery. Hum. 304 is found in TMK-3 through TMK-6. One authority considers TMK-4 to be scarce. An early sample with a TMK-2 would be a rare find. Postcard #567 has been published by Ars Sacra from the Sister Hummel drawing they own.

304 **The Artist**, *copyright 1955, TMK-5.*

305 The Builder

Indicator	Size	Status	TMK-1	TMK-2	TMK-3	TMK-4	TMK-5	TMK-6
305	5½"	—	—	—	P	P	P	P

This figurine of a mason or bricklayer is named more descriptively in German, *Der Schwerarbeiter,* or "The Heavy Worker." The figurine was copyrighted in the U.S. on June 24, 1955. In the catalogs available, this was first listed in 1965. In 1966, the catalog listed Hum. 305 at 5½" high for $16. Found in TMK-3 through TMK-6, there remains the unlikely possibility that this item will be discovered in TMK-2. Many early catalogs list only "Builder," as do some current catalogs. You will find both "Builder" and "The Builder," in the Alphabetical Index to minimize confusion. The Builder was used for August in the M. I. Hummel calendar for 1975. The location of the original drawing is undetermined at this time and no graphics have been found.

305 **The Builder**, *copyright 1955, TMK-5.*

306 Little Bookkeeper

Indicator	Size	Status	TMK-1	TMK-2	TMK-3	TMK-4	TMK-5	TMK-6
306	4¾"	P	—	*	P	P	P	P

The German name of *Stellvertretung,* the English for "Substitution," might more accurately describe what is going on with the Little Bookkeeper figurine, especially since there is another book on the floor. Could this be double-entry bookkeeping or keeping two sets of accounts? This is another motif that was copyrighted in the busy year of 1955 when it was registered in the U.S. on June 19. The copyright year is also incised on the base of the figure. It appeared in catalogs in this country in the early 1960s and is known with TMK-3 through TMK-6. Recently one example was found with a TMK-2, perhaps an early sample, valued in low four-digit figures. There is no record of any restyling or major variations in color or design to date. It has been used twice for calendars, in February, 1972, and in December, 1980, and for postcard #5439 by Ars Sacra.

*One example found.

306 **Little Bookkeeper**, *copyright 1955, TMK-5.*

307 Good Hunting, *copyright 1955,*
TMK-5.

308 Little Tailor *(new style), copyright*
1972, TMK-5.

309 With Loving Greetings
(Assigned). From #5202, courtesy Ars
Sacra.

307   Good Hunting

Indicator	Size	Status	TMK-1	TMK-2	TMK-3	TMK-4	TMK-5	TMK-6
307	5″	P	—	—	P	P	P	P

This little boy with field glasses overlooking his "rabbit prey" differs from a similar figurine, Sensitive Hunter, Hum. 6. In the latter case the hunter looks directly at the rabbit which is an unusual bright red. Hum. 307 is another of the introductions in the early 1960s and is available only in the 5″ size. Unimportant variations have been reported in TMK-3 through 6. The incised copyright goes back to the year 1955, the same year the copyright was registered in the U.S. Copyright Office on June 24. This could mean that samples were made at this time with TMK-2 and would be an interesting acquisition to any collector. This piece was used twice on calendars for September, 1971, and for October, 1978. The postcard of this is produced by Ars Sacra and is #5616. The name of this figurine in German is *Weidmannsheil,* meaning, "Good Sport."

308   Little Tailor

Indicator	Size	Status	TMK-1	TMK-2	TMK-3	TMK-4	TMK-5	TMK-6
308	5½″	P	—	—	—	P	P	P

This is one of over twenty figurines that were part of the 1955 all-out copyright effort by Goebel. Though the figurines were not introduced until 1972, the incised date sometimes confuses collectors into thinking that 1955 was the year of introduction. This piece is usually found with TMK-4 through TMK-6, although an unverified report was received of one with a TMK-3. The U.S. copyright records indicate that the figurine was restyled the same year it was introduced. In addition to the original date (June 24, 1955), a revision was registered on December 4, 1972. The restyled pieces are evinced by the typical, highly sculptured hair and textured finish that Skrobek, Geobel's master sculptor, uses. An impish grin now suits the tailor. Examples of this figurine before restyling are considered to be worth a premium according to an article by Robert Miller in the Eaton *Register-Herald* in 1980, perhaps as much as 200 percent. The current catalogs list this piece as 5½″ high, although variations from this size are known. See M. I. Hummel calendar for November, 1977, and Ars Sacra postcard #5770 for pictures.

309   With Loving Greetings
(Assigned Number)

Indicator	Size	Status	TMK-1	TMK-2	TMK-3	TMK-4	TMK-5	TMK-6
309	3¼″	A	—	—	—	—	—	?

This motif portrays a small boy on his knees with a square ink bottle with a brush in it next to him on the base. He is wearing an apron or smock and appears to be finger painting. While this was copyrighted under the name "Yours Very Truly" on June 24, 1955, it still remains held in abeyance as an Assigned Number which may be issued at some future date. The German name of *Ein dicker Gruss* is translated as "A Big Greeting." It is reported to have also been termed "Greetings From," with the original sample at 3¼″ high in Miller's *Supplement.* Sister Hummel's original drawing is owned by Verlag Ars Sacra who published postcard #5202 from it.

310 Searching Angel, Plaque

Indicator	Size	Status	TMK-1	TMK-2	TMK-3	TMK-4	TMK-5	TMK-6
310/A	4¼″	P	—	—	—	—	P	P

First introduced in the U.S. in January, 1979, catalogs, this kneeling angel on a cloud is found with only TMK-5 and TMK-6. In these catalogs and also in Canada, this plaque is listed as Hum. 310 A, indicating the possibility of a similar plaque being issued as Hum. 310 B with the angel facing to the viewer's right. Some of these pieces carry the artist's painted year, "79", and some do not. This artist's datemark, new in 1979, is favored by some collectors. This is another model that was copyrighted in the U.S. on October 20, 1955, and bears an incised "1955" on the back although it was issued in 1979. Miller reports this plaque as having been named "Angelic Concern" at one time. The present name in German is *Was ist denn do drunten los?* which translates into English as "What's happening down below?" Ars Sacra has published postcard #5914 from Sister Hummel's original drawing which they own.

310 Searching Angel, *Plaque, issued 1979, TMK-5.*

311 Kiss Me

Indicator	Size	Status	TMK-1	TMK-2	TMK-3	TMK-4	TMK-5	TMK-6
311	6″	P	—	—	P	P	P	P

When this very popular motif was designed and copyrighted in 1955 which is the date incised on the bottom, the doll wore socks. It was introduced in this form in the early 1960s with TMK-3 on the back. According to Miller, the figurine was restyled later in the decade at the request of the Siessen Convent to make the doll appear more "doll-like." At that time the socks on the doll were omitted. Examples of TMK-4 are found with and without socks; those examples with socks are worth premium prices valued at 50 percent over the ones shown in the Price List. The TMK-5 and TMK-6 are, of course, found without socks. The German name of *Hab'mich lieb!* means "Love Me!" This figurine appeared for the month of April in the 1974 M. I. Hummel calendar. The original drawing by Sister Hummel is reproduced by Ars Sacra as postcard #5670.

311 Kiss Me, *with socks, copyright 1955, TMK-5.*

312 Honey Lover (Assigned Number)

Indicator	Size	Status	TMK-1	TMK-2	TMK-3	TMK-4	TMK-5	TMK-6
312	3¾″	A	—	—	—	—	—	?

A seated boy, without the usual figurine base, apparently licking honey off his forefinger while grasping a large jar with his right hand, is terrified by a large honeybee. It was copyrighted in this country on July 18, 1955, under the assigned name of "Honey Licker" or *Honiglecker* in German. It is also reported to have been called "In the Jam Pot" at one time. This boy with the sweet tooth is scheduled for release on an as yet unannounced date. If it is released, it would be found only with the trademark current at that time, with the possible exception of one of the early sample pieces being found with a TMK-2. The original drawing by Sister Hummel is owned by Verlag Ars Sacra who have published postcard #5722 from the original.

312 Honey Lover *(Assigned). From #5722, courtesy Ars Sacra.*

133

313 Sunny Morning *(Assigned). From #5676, courtesy Ars Sacra.*

314 Confidentially *(new style), copyright 1972, TMK-5.*

315 Mountaineer, *copyright 1955, TMK-5.*

313   Sunny Morning (Assigned Number)

Indicator	Size	Status	TMK-1	TMK-2	TMK-3	TMK-4	TMK-5	TMK-6
313	3¾"	A	—	—	—	—	—	?

This baby in a crib in front of a fence with a huge overhanging sunflower blossom and blue bird perched nearby was assigned this number back in 1955 when it was registered in the U.S. Copyright Office as "Sunny Child." To date Hum. 313 has not been scheduled for release. When and if it is released, it will carry the trademark current at that time. The German name assigned to this piece is *Sonnenkind* which translates as "Sun Child." In Miller's *Supplement* he says it was also referred to as "Slumber Serenade." This is one case where Sister Hummel's usual background had to be worked into the three-dimensional version to make it a realistic adaptation. For exactly what this original drawing looks like see postcard #5676 by Ars Sacra.

314   Confidentially

Indicator	Size	Status	TMK-1	TMK-2	TMK-3	TMK-4	TMK-5	TMK-6
314	5½"	P	—	—	—	P	P	P

When this figurine, called *Zwiegespräch* in German, "Dialogue" in English, was designed and copyrighted in the U.S. on October 20, 1955, it was registered under the same English name it bears now. The original design was one of the ones shelved from 1955 until it was introduced in this country in 1972. In that version of the motif, the boy had no bow tie, his hair was smoother, and his features were paler and less detailed than in the modern design. In 1972, the year Hum. 314 was first available in the U.S., redesign Copyright GF1003 was filed on April 12 which added a bow tie on the boy, changed the design of the plant stand so that it now had a low step, and gave the "Skrobek" molded or sculptured look to the hair. One in the original early design was reported and priced at $1,500. Since more of these may be found, this price may be high. At present, no examples with TMK-3 have been reported, but TMK-4 through TMK-6 are available. One TMK-2 has been reported and valued in a low four-digit figure. The new design is well illustrated on the calendar for August, 1978. When introduced in 1972, the price was about $22 and in 1980 it was $85. Postcard #5555 published by Ars Sacra is an exact replica of the original drawing owned by them.

315   Mountaineer

Indicator	Size	Status	TMK-1	TMK-2	TMK-3	TMK-4	TMK-5	TMK-6
315	5"	P	—	—	P	P	P	P

This satisfied mountain climber who says in German, *I' hab's erreicht* ("I have achieved it"), is documented in TMK-3 through TMK-6 and first sold in the United States in 1964, the year of the World's Fair in New York. This piece found in any earlier mark would be an exception and worth a premium. Reports of a TMK-2 mark have not been sufficiently verified at this time. This is another of the group that was copyrighted in the U.S. in 1955 and is also incised on the base with this date. There have been no major variations in design, color, or size reported. A photograph of this piece was used for the month of July in the 1973 issue of the calendar published by Goebel. Postcards produced from the original art of Sister Hummel have been published by Ars Sacra as #5614. Prints and other graphics are also available.

316   Relaxation (Assigned Number)

Indicator	Size	Status	TMK-1	TMK-2	TMK-3	TMK-4	TMK-5	TMK-6
316	4″	A	—	—	—	—	—	?

Hum. 316 was registered on October 20, 1955, in the U.S. Copyright Office under the name *Sommerfrische,* which is incised on the piece itself and means "Summer Freshness." The figurine has also been referred to as "Nightly Ritual." This little boy in a rustic wooden tub embellished with typical M. I. Hummel touches of a sunflower, birds, and flowers is classed as an assigned number until it is approved for distribution at some future date. The German name for this unpublished edition is *Eine gute Erholung,* meaning, "A Good Recuperation." Postcard #5894 has been published by Verlag Ars Sacra as a replica of the original drawing they own by Sister Hummel.

316 Relaxation *(Assigned). From #5894, courtesy Ars Sacra.*

317   Not for You

Indicator	Size	Status	TMK-1	TMK-2	TMK-3	TMK-4	TMK-5	TMK-6
317	6″	P	—	—	P	P	P	P

The small dog begging for something concealed behind his master's back is found in TMK-3 through TMK-6. This favorite figurine of dog lovers could as well have been titled, "Speak, Speak Up" (if you want the surprise waiting for you). Some collectors match this piece with Which Hand?, Hum. 258, to make a similar pair. While this was copyrighted in the U.S. on July 11, 1955, the year incised on the base is 1957. It was listed in catalogs of the early 1960s as 5½″ high when it was introduced. Presently the specified catalog size is 6″ high. Therefore, variations in size can be expected. The German name for this model is *Nix für dich!* or "Nothing for you." No major variations in color or design are known. Sister Hummel's original drawing owned by Ars Sacra has been published by them as postcard #5196.

317 Not for You, *copyright 1955, TMK-5.*

318   Art Critic (Assigned Number)

Indicator	Size	Status	TMK-1	TMK-2	TMK-3	TMK-4	TMK-5	TMK-6
318	5½″	A	—	—	—	—	—	?

Copyrighted July 18, 1955, in the U.S. as Art Critic, this piece remains after twenty-five years an unproduced edition. The motif portrays a young boy with brush in his right hand studying a framed painting held in his left hand, with a blue bottle at his right foot. The assigned German name is *Der Kunstkritiker,* essentially the same as the English translation. When and if this will ever be produced for sale is unknown and until then it will be classified as an assigned number to be issued with the trademark that is being used at that time.

318 Art Critic *(Assigned). From #5672, courtesy Ars Sacra.*

319 **Doll Bath**, *copyright 1956, TMK-5.*

319   Doll Bath

Indicator	Size	Status	TMK-1	TMK-2	TMK-3	TMK-4	TMK-5	TMK-6
319	5″	P	—	—	P	P	P	P

A little girl bathing her doll is one of the very popular M. I. Hummel figurines which are not always available because of demand. In the past, premium prices were being asked in some markets. The base is incised with the copyright year of 1956 and the U.S. copyright is dated August 15, 1957, GP15386. It is found in catalogs of the early 1960s as being 5″ high and, as expected, is usually found with TMK-4 through TMK-6. A possible but unlikely occurrence would be an example with a TMK-2, which might indicate that it was an early sample from the mid-1950s. A picture of this was used in the calendar for the month of October, 1971. Postcards have been published by Verlag Emil Fink as #221 and also some larger graphics. The German name of *Puppen bad* is the same as the English.

320 **The Professor** *(Assigned). From #5729, courtesy Ars Sacra.*

320   The Professor (Assigned Number)

Indicator	Size	Status	TMK-1	TMK-2	TMK-3	TMK-4	TMK-5	TMK-6
320	5¾″	A	—	—	—	—	—	?

A U.S. copyright registered by Goebel on July 18, 1955, is listed as "The Professor." Samples may have been made for the registration and other approval purposes. There is one in the Goebel archives, 5¾″ high, which might well deserve the adjective "absent-minded" included in the title from the way this junior professor strolls along in deep concentration, hands behind his back. In the twenty-five years that have elapsed since the copyright date, he would seem to have had ample time to solve the world's problems. When and if he will ever be issued as an approved member in good standing of the M. I. Hummel entourage is not known. If and when this happens, he will no doubt be distinguished by the trademark in use at the time. Sister Hummel's original drawing of this motif is owned by Verlag Ars Sacra who have published an exact duplicate of the original drawing as postcard #5729.

321 **Wash Day**, *copyright 1957, TMK-4.*

321   Wash Day

Indicator	Size	Status	TMK-1	TMK-2	TMK-3	TMK-4	TMK-5	TMK-6
321	6″	P	—	—	P	P	P	P

At the Eaton Festival, Eaton, Ohio, in June, 1980, an interesting early study sample was displayed alongside the present design. This version, believed to have been designed by Unger in 1955, shows a sheet rather than a handkerchief reaching from the figure's extended hands to the basket. The present model, introduced in the early 1960s at about 6″ high, is holding a much smaller article, perhaps a kerchief. The U.S. copyright is dated July 18, 1956, GP15367, but production pieces are incised with the 1957 date. There is no information to date on whether or not any of these earlier variations with large sheets were made for sale. If one is found it would certainly fetch a nice premium, well up in the four-digit figures over the 1957 design found with TMK-3 through TMK-6. The current version has been used for the April pages in both 1972 and 1978 calendars. The German name for this motif is *Grosse Wäsche* or "Big Wash." The postcard, #5669, from the original drawing published by Verlag Ars Sacra interestingly pictures her fastening the last clothespin to hang a pair of pants on the line.

322 Little Pharmacist

Indicator	Size	Status	TMK-1	TMK-2	TMK-3	TMK-4	TMK-5	TMK-6
322	6″	P	—	—	?	P	P	P

Bearing an incised 1955 copyright date on the base, the same year as the U.S. copyright, this pharmacist figurine was listed in U.S. catalogs in the early 1960s in a 6″ size. The bottle he is holding has been found with different labels, the most common of which are "Vitamins" and the German word for castor oil, *Rizinusöl.* Any other factory-applied name would be considered very special with a value in the high hundreds. It is found with TMK-4 up to the current mark. Samples made in 1955, if found, would probably have TMK-2 and be considered premium examples valued in a low four-digit figure. Some variations in size have been noted, but no major changes in design or color have been reported. The German name, *Der Apotheker,* stands for "The Pharmacist." This motif has been published from the original drawing of Sister Hummel by Verlag Ars Sacra as postcard #5554. Pictures of the figurine itself appear in the calendars for the months of March in both 1971 and 1978.

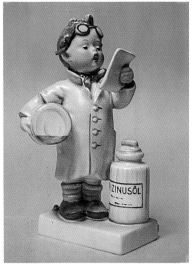

322 Little Pharmacist, *copyright 1955, TMK-5.*

323 Merry Christmas, Plaque

Indicator	Size	Status	TMK-1	TMK-2	TMK-3	TMK-4	TMK-5	TMK-6
323	5″	P	—	—	—	—	P	P

A small angel seated on a cloud holding a large candle with both hands was copyrighted in this country on October 7, 1955, and the plaques are incised on the back with the same year. The U.S. copyright lists the name as "Angel on Cloud" and the German name is *Frohe Weihnachten.* The 5″ plaque is found only with TMK-5 and TMK-6, since it was first introduced here in 1979. Some of the pieces may have the artist's date of "79" brushed on and some may not. As time elapses, a differential may be established in favor of one or the other. The original of this particular drawing is owned by Ars Sacra who published postcard #5905 from it.

323 Merry Christmas, *Plaque, copyright 1955, issued 1979, TMK-5.*

324 At the Fence (Assigned Number)

Indicator	Size	Status	TMK-1	TMK-2	TMK-3	TMK-4	TMK-5	TMK-6
324	4¾″	A	—	—	—	—	—	?

The July 18, 1956, copyright filed in the U.S. Copyright Office describes this as "figures at a fence." Apparently it was also referred to as "The Other Side of the Fence" and shows two young boys in back of a section of rail fence with a longhaired dachshund on the other side barking at them. This is enhanced by the usual Hummel touches of flowers and birds and is listed as an Assigned Number until and if it is released for production and sale at some time, when it will bear the current trademark. It will be released probably at 4¾″ high. The German name is *Am Zaun* which means the same in English. A sample is in the Goebel archives. Sketch at right indicates the general appearance of the existing prototype.

324 At the Fence (*Assigned*). *Artist's concept.*

325 Helping Mother *(Assigned).*
From #5438, courtesy Ars Sacra.

326 Being Punished *(Assigned).*
From #14646, courtesy Ars Sacra.

327 The Run-a-Way, *copyright 1972,*
TMK-5.

325 Helping Mother (Assigned Number)

Indicator	Size	Status	TMK-1	TMK-2	TMK-3	TMK-4	TMK-5	TMK-6
325	5"	A	—	—	—	—	—	?

When and if this little girl sewing at a table with a kitten at her feet ready to pounce on a ball of yarn is issued, it will be the second M. I. Hummel figurine to depict a cat in its design. It was also taken from the same original drawing of Sister Hummel as was Hum. 133, Mother's Helper. This figurine was registered in the U.S. Copyright Office on July 18, 1956. There is a sample in the Goebel archives, and possibly others were made for approval and copyright purposes. Any of these rarities that are discovered would probably carry a TMK-2 and be valued in the low four-digit figures. This remains an assigned number after twenty-four years and will remain so until Goebel releases it for production and distribution. It has been exhibited around the U.S. including the Old Chicago Show in 1979 and the 1980 Eaton Festival. The original English name was "Mother Said"; the German name, *Mutters grosse Stutze* translates as "Mother's big support." A postcard, #5438, is published by Ars Sacra.

326 Being Punished (Assigned Number)

Indicator	Size	Status	TMK-1	TMK-2	TMK-3	TMK-4	TMK-5	TMK-6
326	5"	A	—	—	—	—	—	?

The form of this piece is unique: it is designed so that it can be used either as a standing figurine or hung as a wall plaque by the hole in its flat back. This three-dimensional piece, 5" high, depicts a boy sitting in a corner for punishment while a skeptical cat looks up at him. This will be the third piece showing a cat, if it is ever released for production. It was copyrighted in 1956 with U.S. Copyright GF15360 and assigned under the same name. It has also been called "Naughty Boy," and the German name of *Junge im Karzer* translates as "Boy in Jail." A prototype piece that carried the TMK-2 has been exhibited several places, including the 1980 Eaton Festival. A postcard #14646, published from the original drawing, has been published by Verlag Ars Sacra, the owner. When and if this piece is ever released for production and distribution by Goebel it will probably carry the trademark current at the time. Any prototype found from 1956 with TMK-2 would be valued in the low four-digit figures.

327 The Run-a-Way

Indicator	Size	Status	TMK-1	TMK-2	TMK-3	TMK-4	TMK-5	TMK-6
327	5½"	P	—	—	—	P	P	P

This small fellow leaving home with his few belongings is known not only by this name but also as the "Happy Wanderer" from the German, *Der frohe Wanderer.* When it was first registered in the U.S. Copyright Office on July 18, 1956, as GP12635, it was called "Roving Song" and listed as 5¼" high. The piece is actually incised with the German copyright date of 1955 and is one of twenty-four motifs that were first available in this country in 1972 at $28.50. Not long after its release, Hum. 327 was restyled, as evinced by a revised U.S. copyright filed December 4, 1972, GF1004. The major visual differences are: the original model has articles protruding from the basket, the newer one does not; the old version has a gray hat and jacket, the present one has a green hat and blue jacket; the new one has the "Skrobek" hair and textured finish. The present models can also be distinguished by the incised 1972 copyright date. This piece is found in TMK-4 through TMK-6, except for an early prototype which had TMK-2 stamped on it. If another TMK-2 is ever found, it would be valued in the low four-digit figures. This motif was photographed for use in the 1978 calendar for the month of May. The postcard #14383 was published by Verlag Ars Sacra, owner of the original drawing.

328 Carnival

Indicator	Size	Status	TMK-1	TMK-2	TMK-3	TMK-4	TMK-5	TMK-6
328	6″	P	—	—	P	P	P	P

This "Mardi Gras" clown with the German name, *Fastnacht,* was registered in the U.S. Copyright Office as GP12636 on July 17, 1956. The catalogs indicate that this was available for sale in the U.S. in the early 1960s at 5½″ high and was incised with a 1955 copyright date. There are no major variations or restyling of the figurine and only a slight variation from the present cataloged size of 6″. An incised date of 1957 has been reported, although no U.S. record of registration has ever been found. If an early sample of this figurine is ever found with a TMK-2, it would be valued in the high hundreds or low four-digit figures. This appeared as the picture on the calendar for February, 1976. The postcard, #14245, and also some graphics were published by Ars Sacra. The original drawing owned by them shows another boy with a staff pictured on the right of Hum. 328.

328 Carnival, *copyright, 1957, TMK-4.*

329 Off to School (Assigned Number)

Indicator	Size	Status	TMK-1	TMK-2	TMK-3	TMK-4	TMK-5	TMK-6
329	5″	A	—	—	—	—	—	?

The July 18, 1956, U.S. copyright refers to two figures called "On Way to School," 5″ high. It was also referred to at one time as "Kindergarten Romance," and the German name of *Frisch gewagt,* translates as "Freshly dared is half won." Quite a selection of names for a piece that has never been produced and distributed, nor is it known if it ever will be. The boy appears similar to Hum. 82, School Boy, and the girl is carrying one of the ubiquitous German briefcases on her arm. If and when this is released, it will carry the trademark in use at the time. An early factory sample has been illustrated and if another is ever found, it should have TMK-2 and be valued in the mid four-digit figures. A postcard, #5221, has been published by Ars Sacra who own the original drawing.

329 Off to School *(Assigned). From #5221, courtesy Ars Sacra.*

330 Baking Day (Assigned Number)

Indicator	Size	Status	TMK-1	TMK-2	TMK-3	TMK-4	TMK-5	TMK-6
330	5¼″	A	—	—	—	—	—	?

This same name was used for the U.S. copyright which was registered on July 16, 1956. Apparently the figurine has also been referred to as "Kneading Dough." A picture of a factory sample has been published, and the piece is probably marked with a TMK-2; the figurine is 5¼″ high. If one of these became available for sale, it would be valued in the mid four-digit figures. This assigned number may or may not be approved for future production and, if so, it will probably be marked with the trademark in use at that time. The German name of *Die Bäckerin* translates as "The Baker Girl." The original drawing's location is undetermined at present and no graphics have been issued.

330 Baking Day *(Assigned). Artist's concept.*

331 Crossroads, *copyright 1955,*
TMK-5.

332 Soldier Boy, *copyright 1957,*
TMK-4.

333 Blessed Event, *copyright 1955,*
TMK-5.

331   Crossroads

Indicator	Size	Status	TMK-1	TMK-2	TMK-3	TMK-4	TMK-5	TMK-6
331	6¾"	P	—	—	—	P	P	P

This sculpture of two boys at a signpost is one of the group of twenty-four figures that was listed in the U.S. catalogs for the first time in 1972, even though the U.S. copyright was registered on July 16, 1956, using the same name for this 6¾" figurine. The pieces themselves are incised with the earlier (probably German) copyright date, 1955. This small tableau has an interesting and very scarce variation in design. When first issued, the boy with the slide trombone slung over his shoulder was carrying it with the mouthpiece at the top. This was altered so that all later pieces show the boy with the trombone reversed; that is, with the bell of the horn pointing upward. When this change was made, it was not recorded in the U.S. Copyright Office, but it must have occurred shortly after the original issue since very few of the early "mouthpiece up" versions are known. These command a premium price somewhere between the high three-digit and very low four-digit figures. Normally found with TMK-4 through TMK-6, an unverified report states that an example is known with TMK-3. If this piece is authenticated, it too would be in the same price range. An early example or prototype made in the mid-1950s, if ever available, would be a true collector's item, probably valued in the low four-digit figures. This motif was pictured in the M. I. Hummel calendar for September, 1977. The original drawing owned by Verlag Ars Sacra has been published as postcard #5551.

332   Soldier Boy

Indicator	Size	Status	TMK-1	TMK-2	TMK-3	TMK-4	TMK-5	TMK-6
332	6"	P	—	—	?	P	P	P

The first listings of this motif in early 1960 catalogs were as Soldier Boy, 5½" high. The U.S. copyright was registered in July, 1955, under the name of "Attention." The copyright date incised on the back of the early figurines is also 1955, although 1957 is also found incised on some. The trademarks reported range from TMK-4 through TMK-6. Any prototype with TMK-2 would be valued in the low four-digit figures. One rumor relates how this piece was actually produced before World War II but was suppressed by the regime because it was not exemplary of the Nazi soldier. To date there is more evidence to discredit this yarn than there is to support it; however, any verification in the form of an actual TMK-1 piece documented by when, where, and who purchased it would be welcomed. A slight change in the color of the insignia was made at an unspecified or unrecorded copyright date. The emblem on the soldier's cap was changed from a bright red to the present dark blue. The German name for this model is *Still gestanden!* for "At Attention." A postcard, #14868, was published by Ars Sacra from the original drawing which is owned by them.

333   Blessed Event

Indicator	Size	Status	TMK-1	TMK-2	TMK-3	TMK-4	TMK-5	TMK-6
333	5½"	P	—	?	?	P	P	P

While this is another one of the group introduced in the U.S. in 1964, the year of the New York World's Fair, the copyright goes back to July 18, 1956, as did many others. The U.S. registration number is GP12640. This is found with TMK-4 through TMK-6. The question mark in the table for TMK-2 indicates the possibility that one of the early prototype samples will turn up in the marketplace. If so, a TMK-2 should be valued in the low four-digit figures. Most catalogs have listed the height as it is now at 5½", although production procedures, no doubt, have resulted in minor variations. No major deviations in color or design have surfaced as yet, but somewhere out there is probably at least one interesting one waiting to be shared with other collectors. The postcard #5613 was published by Ars Sacra who also own the original drawing. The German name is *Das grosse Ereignis* for "The Big Event." The figurine is pictured on the M. I. Hummel calendar for February, 1973.

334 Homeward Bound

Indicator	Size	Status	TMK-1	TMK-2	TMK-3	TMK-4	TMK-5	TMK-6
334	5¼"	P	—	—	—	P	P	P

After being registered in the U.S. Copyright Office on July 17, 1956, as GP12642, this motif did not appear in the U.S. catalogs until 1971 with the 1956 or the earlier 1955 copyright date incised on the bottom. An important restyling occurred in 1975, but no record of it was found in the U.S. Copyright Office. The simulated tree stump (under the goat for strength) was removed and Skrobek gave the new model the textured finish and prominently sculptured hair characteristic of his work. The height has been listed as 5¼" with minor variations expected. Introduced in the early Seventies, Hum. 334 is found in TMK-4 through TMK-6, with the possibility of one of the early samples with the TMK-2 reaching collectors' hands for a low four-digit figure. The early ones with the support under the goat are worth premium prices, about double the figures shown on the Price List for TMK-5, which reflects the market value of the new style. The German name of *Heimkehr vom Felde* stands for "Return Home from the Fields," which is nearly the title used for the U.S. copyright of "Return from the Field." A good picture of this model is found on the calendar for August, 1973. Postcard #5773 was published by Ars Sacra from the original drawing which is owned by them.

334 Homeward Bound, *copyright 1956, TMK-5. New style.*

335 Lucky Boy (Assigned Number)

Indicator	Size	Status	TMK-1	TMK-2	TMK-3	TMK-4	TMK-5	TMK-6
335	5¾"	A	—	—	—	—	—	?

This little boy holding a pig in his right arm and grasping a folded umbrella in his left hand was copyrighted in the U.S. as GP12643 on July 18, 1956, using this name. One publication states that the name, "Fair Prizes," was the original name. The German name of *Der Glücksbub* means the same as the English one. Early samples for study, approval, and copyright purposes would have been marked with TMK-2. One of these is in the factory archives and if any more appear in the future they would be valued in the mid four-digit figures. This assigned number may or may not be released for production at some future date. When and if this happens, the pieces may be incised with a 1956 date but the trademark will be the one in use at that time. Postcard #4641 has been published from the original by Verlag Ars Sacra from the original drawing.

335 Lucky Boy *(Assigned.) From #4641, courtesy Ars Sacra.*

336 Close Harmony

Indicator	Size	Status	TMK-1	TMK-2	TMK-3	TMK-4	TMK-5	TMK-6
336	5½"	P	—	—	P	P	P	P

First cataloged in the early 1960s U.S. catalogs at 5½" high, it is still specified at that same height although small variations may be encountered. Collectors have found several different copyright dates (1955, 1956, and 1957) incised on the bottom. The actual U.S. Copyright, GP12644, was registered on July 17, 1956, under the name of "Birthday Serenade," which had already been assigned to Hum. 218. This is still the name given in the German, *Geburtstagsständchen.* At some unknown time, figures were changed and "modernized" in what appears to be the Skrobek style. There is no record in the U.S. Copyright Office of this change. Essentially, the diamond printed dress of the taller girl now appears to be diamond quilted. In the early models, the socks of each girl were even. Now the larger girl's right stocking is higher than the left, and the smaller girl's left stocking is higher than the right. This piece is found in TMK-3 through TMK-6. No graphics have been located; the July, 1972, calendar page pictures the figurine.

336 Close Harmony, *copyright 1956, trademark unknown.*

337 Cinderella, *eyes down, copyright 1975, TMK-5.*

337   Cinderella

Indicator	Size	Status	TMK-1	TMK-2	TMK-3	TMK-4	TMK-5	TMK-6
337	4½″	P	—	—	—	P	P	P

This girl feeding doves from a bowl was copyrighted on April 4, 1961, at 4¼″ high, but the figures are incised on the bottom with a 1956 date. Shortly after the introduction here in 1972, it was restyled and another copyright was issued in the U.S. Copyright Office as GF1005 on December 4, 1972. The main deviation in the older version is that the girl is looking up or almost straight ahead, whereas in the present version the girl is looking down. In the present model the girl's bangs and skirt are textured, a la Skrobek. Any early examples with open eyes (up) would be worth 50 percent more than Price List values. TMK-4 and TMK-5 values in the Price List are for closed eyes (down). This figure was used as the illustration for the June, 1978, calendar page. No postcards or other graphics have been found and the location of the original drawing is unknown. The German name *Aschenputtel* is the same as the English, "Cinderella."

338 Birthday Cake, *candleholder (Assigned). TMK-2, Miller Collection.*

338   Birthday Cake, Candleholder (Assigned Number)

Indicator	Size	Status	TMK-1	TMK-2	TMK-3	TMK-4	TMK-5	TMK-6
338	3¾″	A	—	*	—	—	—	?

This small girl with the Dutch bob is holding a large cake with an oversized red candle in it. The piece might be issued without candle. This was copyrighted in the U.S. as GP12645 on July 18, 1956, but has not yet been released for sale. An early prototype of this motif with TMK-2 has been exhibited by Robert Miller at the Old Chicago Show in 1978 and the Eaton Festival in 1980. If another one of these should ever become available it would probably have a value in the mid four-digit range. The German name, *Der Gerburtstagskuchen,* is the same as the English. This Assigned Number may or may not be released for production and distribution at some future date. If it is released, it would be incised with a 1955 or 1956 copyright date on the bottom and labeled with the trademark that is current at the time of issue. Ars Sacra published postcard #5604 from the original drawing they own.

*Prototype in Miller Collection.

339 Behave *(Assigned). From #14303, courtesy Ars Sacra.*

339   Behave (Assigned Number)

Indicator	Size	Status	TMK-1	TMK-2	TMK-3	TMK-4	TMK-5	TMK-6
339	5½″	A	—	—	—	—	—	?

This was called "Be Good" when copyrighted in the U.S. on July 17, 1956. Another publication states that at one time during the development it was called "Walking her Dog." The company has now assigned the design of this little girl admonishing her rambunctious dachshund to Hum. 339. When and if it will ever be released for production and sale is unknown. If this does happen, it will no doubt carry either a 1955 or 1956 copyright date incised on the bottom and a transfer label that reflects the trademark that is current at that time. At least one TMK-2 is in existence which has a value in the low four-digit range. Whether or not any more were made will be determined in years to come. The German name is *Wir gehen Spazieren,* which translates as "We're going for a walk." Postcard #14303 has been published by Ars Sacra, the owner of the original drawing.

340 Letter to Santa Claus

Indicator	Size	Status	TMK-1	TMK-2	TMK-3	TMK-4	TMK-5	TMK-6
340	7¼″	P	—	—	?	P	P	P

If the name of this motif had been translated directly from the German, *Brief ans Christkind,* it would have been called "Letter to the Christ Child." However, it was registered as "Letter to Santa Claus" in the U.S. Copyright Office on August 15, 1957, GF15361. At 7¼″ the height remains the specified size to the present, with possible small variations in production pieces. This piece is found with several different incised copyright dates approximating the mid-1950s. It was first available in the U.S. in the very early 1970s with a TMK-4 mark. The most important differences apparent in the redesign (which was not found registered in the U.S. Copyright Office) are that present models have red snow pants and dark blue knitted caps with matching mufflers. They also have all the characteristics of Skrobek's modeling such as the rougher, textured surfaces of the clothing. In the original models, the snow pants matched the light colored coat and stocking cap with background of light gray. A red stamp was also added to the new envelope. The revised version is found in TMK-5 and TMK-6. An older prototype would have been stamped with a TMK-2, although TMK-3 pieces have been reported. A picture of this figurine was appropriately used in the Hummel calendar for the month of December, 1973. Postcard #14266 was published by Ars Sacra from their original drawing.

340 Letter to Santa Claus, *new style,* TMK-4.

341 Birthday Present (Assigned Number)

Indicator	Size	Status	TMK-1	TMK-2	TMK-3	TMK-4	TMK-5	TMK-6
341	5¼″	A	—	—	—	—	—	?

The figure of this small girl with bobbed hair stands holding a plant of unknown botanical name. This 5¼″ figurine was registered in the U.S. Copyright Office on July 18, 1956, as GP12647. A picture of this motif has been published in Miller's *Supplement* to the book *HUMMEL,* so at least one sample exists. If someone is fortunate to locate another, it probably would be a prototype stamped TMK-2 and incised with the year 1955 or 1956. It would be valued in the higher four-digit figures and would undoubtedly be the showpiece of any collection. When and if this model is ever approved for production and sale, it would probably have the same incised copyright date but be labeled with the trademark current at time of issue. The German name for this assigned design is *Das Geburtstagsgeschenk,* having the same meaning as the English name. Ars Sacra postcard, #5604, from their original drawing, pictures this gift-bearer in the right foreground.

341 Birthday Present *(Assigned).* From #5604 *courtesy Ars Sacra.*

342 Mischief Maker

Indicator	Size	Status	TMK-1	TMK-2	TMK-3	TMK-4	TMK-5	TMK-6
342	5″	P	—	—	—	P	P	P

Reports of this model being incised with copyright dates of 1958 and 1960 are somewhat earlier than the date on the registry in the U.S. Copyright Office, which is April 12, 1961, GP28612. It was first listed for sale at 5″ high in the U.S. 1972 catalogs, priced at $28.50, and has been found identified with TMK-4 through TMK-6. It would be possible that earlier prototype pieces would have a TMK-2 or 3. A verified prototype would be valued in the higher four-digit figures. No important variations in design or color have been reported. The German name for this figurine, *Der Störenfried,* is essentially the same as the English one. A picture of this motif appears in the calendar for July, 1977. A postcard, #5328, was published by Ars Sacra who own the original drawing.

342 Mischief Maker, *copyright 1960,* TMK-5.

343 Christmas Song (*Assigned*). *From #5258 courtesy Ars Sacra.*

343   Christmas Song (Assigned Number)

Indicator	Size	Status	TMK-1	TMK-2	TMK-3	TMK-4	TMK-5	TMK-6
343	6½″	A	—	—	—	—	—	?

This was registered as "Angel with Stave," GP15366, 6½″ high, in the U.S. Copyright Office on August 15, 1957. Factory records indicate that at one stage of the development the piece was also called "Singing Angel." This small figure is portrayed wide-eyed and singing while holding a star on a staff in the left hand and a four-sided lantern in the right one. At least one factory sample is known and may well be a TMK-2, probably with an incised copyright date from the mid-Fifties. If someone, through a stroke of good fortune, should acquire another authentic prototype, it would have a value in the mid four-digit figures. When and if this motif is ever approved for production, it will probably have the same original copyright date, but will be marked with the trademark that is current at that time. The German name of *Weihnachtslied* translates to the same in English. The original drawing by Sister Hummel is owned by Ars Sacra who have published postcard #5258 from it.

344 Feathered Friends, *copyright 1965, TMK-5.*

344   Feathered Friends

Indicator	Size	Status	TMK-1	TMK-2	TMK-3	TMK-4	TMK-5	TMK-6
344	4¾″	P	—	—	—	P	P	P

The German name of *Schwanenteich* roughly translates as "Swan Pond." However, when it was copyrighted in the U.S. on July 18, 1957, as GP15365, this figure carried the above name, "Feathered Friends." It has been listed in the U.S. catalogs since 1972 for $27.50 at either 4½″ or 4¾″ high and incised with a 1956 copyright date on the base. The fact that it is found with TMK-4 through TMK-6 indicates it was probably produced before 1972 when TMK-5 was introduced. An early sample reported by one collector has a 1956 copyright date and also a TMK-2. This piece, probably one of the approval samples or small test lots, was insured for $2,000. No major revisions in design or color have been reported, although this does not preclude the discovery of an interesting variation. A picture of this motif was used for the month of June in the 1977 calendar. Postcard #5620 has been published by Verlag Ars Sacra who own the original drawing.

345 A Fair Measure, *eyes down, copyright 1972, TMK-5.*

345   A Fair Measure

Indicator	Size	Status	TMK-1	TMK-2	TMK-3	TMK-4	TMK-5	TMK-6
345	5½″	P	—	—	—	P	P	P

When this was issued in Germany it was, and still is, called *Der Kaufmann* or "The Merchant." It was registered using its English name in this country on August 15, 1957, as GP16362, 5½″ high. It was not until 1972 that this piece was cataloged and sold in the U.S. for about $27. Soon after the introduction in the U.S., it was completely restyled in the "Skrobek manner" with sculptured hair and textured or modeled clothing. The important difference is that in the new 1972 version the boy is looking down at the container on the scale instead of looking over the container with a rather fixed stare. For convenience the early one is called "Open Eyes" and is scarce enough to command a price in the mid-hundreds. The new version is called "Closed Eyes" and follows the prices shown in the Price List. This model has been produced for sale in TMK-4 through TMK-6, except for the prototypes or approval samples, which if found with TMK-2 would be valued in the low four-digit figures. This piece was pictured for the month of November in the 1980 calendar. The original drawing by Sister Hummel has not been located and no graphics made from it have been found.

346 Smart Little Sister

Indicator	Size	Status	TMK-1	TMK-2	TMK-3	TMK-4	TMK-5	TMK-6
346	4¾"	P	—	—	P	P	P	P

This motif was actually registered as GP1536, 4¾" high, on August 15, 1957, and appears in the U.S. catalogs about five years later incised with the year 1956 on the bottom. It carried a TMK-3 with minor variations in height, ranging from 4¼" to 4¾" high. It has been available since that time and therefore is also found in TMK-4, 5, and 6. To date, no prototype examples or early samples marked with TMK-2 have been reported, even though such an unusual find is a possibility and would be valued in the very high four digits. No significant changes in color or design, which might also be valued highly, have been reported. The German name, *Das kluge Schwesterlein* translates roughly, "The Clever Little Sister." This figurine was illustrated in the calendar for May, 1971, and on the cover of the 1980 edition. This photograph is a fine, close-up example of the intricate sculpturing style used by Gerhard Skrobek, Goebel's master modeler. The trefoil leaf design in the girl's apron is a welcome change from the usual polka dot on so many others. The original drawing is owned by Ars Sacra and was published by them as postcard #5902.

346 Smart Little Sister, *copyright 1956, TMK-5.*

347 Adventure Bound

Indicator	Size	Status	TMK-1	TMK-2	TMK-3	TMK-4	TMK-5	TMK-6
347	7½"	P	—	*	—	P	P	P

This outsized, action-packed, impressive sculpture of seven boys is known in Germany as *Die sieben Schaben*, or "The Seven Swabians." It was copyrighted in the U.S. on October 4, 1957 (GP15364), under "Adventure Bound," with 1957 incised on the bottom of the figurine. The factory records show that this figurine, adapted from Sister Hummel's original drawing now owned by Ars Sacra, was sculpted by Theodore R. Menzenbach, who was Goebel's master modeler at that time. It takes an artist a full day to decorate this one piece. Listed for the first time in U.S. catalogs in 1971, it is normally found marked only with TMK-4, 5, or 6. A few early samples or prototype pieces have been discovered which are valued in the mid four-digit range. This made the cover of the calendar for 1973. Postcard #14239, from the original drawing, has been issued by Ars Sacra.

*Prototype in Miller Collection.

347 Adventure Bound, *copyright 1957, TMK-5.*

348 Ring Around the Rosie

Indicator	Size	Status	TMK-1	TMK-2	TMK-3	TMK-4	TMK-5	TMK-6
348	6¾"	P	—	—	P	P	P	P

This large, 6¾" high group of four girls first appeared in U.S. catalogs in the early Sixties, but carried the incised copyright date of 1957, the same year it was registered in the U.S. Copyright Office as GP15548. There was no record of a later copyright found even though there are stories of some examples existing with a 1972 incised copyright date. None have been verified as yet. In 1969, the suggested price for this piece was listed in U.S. catalogs at $100 and it was marked with TMK-3. Currently, the specified height is 6¾". One early sample piece with TMK-2 has been reported and is valued in the low four-digit figures. The German *Ringelreihen* translates the same as the English name. The original drawing by Sister Hummel is owned by Verlag Ars Sacra from which postcard #5619 has been produced. A modification of this design depicting only the small girl in front with the brown dress and the girl to her immediate left is the bas-relief on the 1980 Anniversary Plate, Hum. 201, named, also, "Ring Around the Rosie."

348 Ring Around the Rosie, *copyright 1957, TMK-5.*

349 The Florist *(Assigned). From #4774 courtesy Ars Sacra.*

350 On Holiday *(Assigned). From #14467, courtesy Ars Sacra.*

351 The Botanist *(Assigned). From #5860, courtesy Ars Sacra.*

349 The Florist (Assigned Number)

Indicator	Size	Status	TMK-1	TMK-2	TMK-3	TMK-4	TMK-5	TMK-6
349	7¼″	A	—	—	—	—	—	?

This figure of a young, aproned child intently studying a red blossom similar to the several growing on the base was registered as "Boy with Flowers," 7¼″ high, GP28615, in the U.S. Copyright Office on April 21, 1961. A picture of a factory prototype has been published in Miller's *Supplement to HUMMEL* book; the piece is probably incised with a copyright date of 1961. If a sample similar to that is found before the figure is released, it would probably be marked with TMK-3 and be valued in the mid four-digit figures. When and if this motif is ever approved for production and sale, it will probably have the same incised copyright but will be identified by the current trademark in use at the time. The German name for this assigned model is *Der Blumenfreund* which means "The Flower Friend (Lover)." Postcard #4774 has been published by Ars Sacra from their original drawing.

350 On Holiday (Assigned Number)

Indicator	Size	Status	TMK-1	TMK-2	TMK-3	TMK-4	TMK-5	TMK-6
350	4¼″	A	—	—	—	—	—	?

A search of the files indicates that on September 9, 1965, Goebel filed a copyright GF294 for Hum. 350, described as "Girl with Umbrella and Basket." Further research by Robert Miller and the Goebel factory turned up a prototype of this motif that for unknown reasons has never been issued. At one time it was also called "Holiday Shopper"; the German name, *Zum Festtag*, would translate as "For the Holiday." The prototype model shows a small 4¼″ figure standing bright-eyed and attentive, holding a rolled umbrella stafflike in her right hand, an empty basket draped over her left arm, with a bouquet of flowers tucked in the crook of that arm. This unissued pattern is probably incised with the copyright year of 1964 or 1965 along with either TMK-3 or TMK-4. If another prototype example should ever become available, it would be valued in the mid four-digit figures. When and if issued, the trademark should correspond to the one in use at that time. A postcard, #702, has been published by Verlag Emil Fink who own the original drawing. This girl is the one on the right of Ars Sacra postcard #14467.

351 The Botanist (Assigned Number)

Indicator	Size	Status	TMK-1	TMK-2	TMK-3	TMK-4	TMK-5	TMK-6
351	4″	A	—	—	—	—	—	?

This Hummel number appears to have been assigned to the adaptation of one of Sister Hummel's original drawings depicting a seated girl, 4″ high, studying a scarce gentian blue flower held in her hand, apparently after fashioning some of them into the garland she is wearing around her head. A pert little blue bird perched on a small stump at her right seems to be talking directly to her. The adaptation was registered in the U.S. Copyright Office on May 30, 1972 with the unimaginative name of "Girl Holding Flowers." Fortunately, a prototype was located in the Goebel factory archives as described above, but for some reason it has remained in a state of suspension. When and if the company decides to release this figurine for sale to the public, it will probably be incised with the copyright date of 1972 and carry the company logo then in use. If some collector is fortunate enough to acquire one of the unissued samples, it would be valued in the mid four-digit figures. The German name assigned to this motif is *Enzian-Mädchen* or "Girl with Gentian Flowers." Ars Sacra own the original drawing and have produced an exact replica as postcard #5860.

352   Sweet Greetings (Assigned Number)

Indicator	Size	Status	TMK-1	TMK-2	TMK-3	TMK-4	TMK-5	TMK-6
352	4¼"	A	—	—	—	—	—	?

Another one of the series of figurines that has been assigned a number but never released, Hum. 352 was registered in the U.S. Copyright Office as GF291 on September 9, 1965, and briefly described in the document by the name, "Girl Standing by Fence." Further investigation by Robert Miller with the help of the Goebel Company uncovered a model of this piece in the company archives. The prototype shows a small, 4¼" girl standing in front of a rail fence holding a large red heart in front of her with both hands. A mascot bird perched on the post at her right seems to be chirping instructions to her vehemently. It is likely that this piece is incised with the 1965 copyright date and marked with either TMK-3 or TMK-4. If another authenticated sample were ever found it would be valued in the mid four-digit range. When and if the Goebel Company decides to reclassify this from an "Assigned Number" to join the hundreds of other pieces currently offered for sale, these production pieces, while marked with the same copyright year, would be labeled with the current company trademark in use at that time. The German name, *Ein süsser Gruss* means essentially the same as the English one. The central figure in the original drawing published by Ars Sacra, postcard #5835, was probably the inspiration for this figurine.

352 Sweet Greetings *(Assigned).* *From #5835, courtesy Ars Sacra.*

353   Spring Dance

Indicator	Size	Status	TMK-1	TMK-2	TMK-3	TMK-4	TMK-5	TMK-6
353/0	5¼"	R	—	—	?	?	R	R
/I	6¾"	P	—	—	P	P	P	P

This attractive and highly desirable motif has the distinction of being the only Hummel article issued in two sizes since the Hum. 225 Table Lamp, Just Resting. Some collectors will pay more for the small 5¼" size than they will pay for the larger 6¾" size because the small size was produced in very limited quantities until it was reissued in 1978. No record has yet been found of any examples incised with only the whole number 353 and no size indicator. About a year after this piece was registered in the U.S. Copyright Office as GF148, "Spring Dance," on August 22, 1963, it was available for sale in the U.S. with the copyright year 1963 incised on the base, 7" high, for $33. The German name used at that time was *Frühlingstanz* and the model number incised on the base was 353/I. No record was found in searching the available catalogs of any listing of the smaller 353/0 until it was reissued in 1978-79 for $100. The resale price soared to $400 within months of its reissue. A picture of this figurine appears for the month of September in the 1972 issue of the Hummel calendar. The design of this piece with two figures is suggestive of the four-figured Ring Around the Rosie, Hum. 348 and the 1980 Anniversary Plate, Hum. 281. The present German name is *Sommertanz* which translates as "Summer Dance." No original drawing has been located nor have any graphics.

353/0 Spring Dance, *reissued in 1978, TMK-5.*

354 A   Angel with Lantern, Holy Water Font, (Assigned Number)

Indicator	Size	Status	TMK-1	TMK-2	TMK-3	TMK-4	TMK-5	TMK-6
354A	5″	A	—	—	—	—	—	?

354 A Angel with Lantern, *Holy Water Font, (Assigned). Artist's concept.*

354 B   Angel with Trumpet, Holy Water Font, (Assigned Number)

Indicator	Size	Status	TMK-1	TMK-2	TMK-3	TMK-4	TMK-5	TMK-6
354B	5″	A	—	—	—	—	—	?

354 B Angel with Trumpet, *Holy Water Font, (Assigned). Artist's concept.*

354 C   Angel with Bird and Cross, Holy Water Font, (Assigned Number)

Indicator	Size	Status	TMK-1	TMK-2	TMK-3	TMK-4	TMK-5	TMK-6
354C	5″	A	—	—	—	—	—	?

In the first edition of *HUMMEL* by Eric Ehrmann, this number was listed as a Closed Number, one that was never used and never would be used. Further research by Robert Miller and the factory disclosed a trinity of font prototypes which are aptly described by the above names and assigned to this number until they are authorized for production or abandoned altogether. The abstract of the U.S. copyright may be incomplete as it shows only that Hum. 354 was registered as GP28607 on April 21, 1961, with the name assigned as "Kneeling Angel with Horn." If a collector is of the opinion that she or he has discovered one or all three of these, the pieces should meet the triple test of being incised with the facsimile signature on the back, a model number of 354A, B, or C also incised on the back at the top, and a motif on the front that matches the name. It should also have an incised copyright date on the back of about 1961 and either a TMK-3 or TMK-4 company mark. Any one example found fulfilling these requirements would be valued from the high hundreds to a thousand dollars. Refer to Hum. 357, 358, and 359 for somewhat similar figurines.

354 C Angel with Bird and Cross, *Holy Water Font, (Assigned). Artist's concept.*

355 Autumn Harvest

Indicator	Size	Status	TMK-1	TMK-2	TMK-3	TMK-4	TMK-5	TMK-6
355	4¾"	P	—	—	—	P	P	P

This little girl with basket of ripe apples and bouquet of flowers is reminiscent of little Red Riding Hood without the hooded cape. The figurine is known in German as *Herbstsegen* or "Fall Blessings." Registration of this design is dated April 9, 1964, in the U.S. Copyright Office, and production pieces are incised to this day with that date on the bottom. The specified height has varied from 4¾" to 5" high. Since the early prototypes the design may have been altered slightly so that the hair is more accentuated by a "wiped," two-tone finish, which leaves a lighter color as a highlight. A picture of this figurine was used for the month of October in the calendar of 1977. The introduction price of this figurine was $22.50 in 1972. Examples are found in TMK-4, 5, and 6. A piece with TMK-3 would be quite unusual. This appears to have been adapted from an original drawing owned by Ars Sacra that has a lamb and a pennant topped by a cross in the girl's basket instead of the fruit shown in the figurine basket. See postcard #5205 published by Ars Sacra for an exact replica of the original Sister Hummel drawing.

355 Autumn Harvest, *copyright 1964, TMK-5.*

356 Gay Adventure

Indicator	Size	Status	TMK-1	TMK-2	TMK-3	TMK-4	TMK-5	TMK-6
356	5"	P	—	—	—	P	P	P

While this figurine, which in several ways is reminiscent of Hum. 327, The Run-a-Way, was first cataloged in the U.S. in 1972 along with about twenty other new ones, it had been copyrighted only the year before in the U.S. on December 3 as GF770. The figurine is incised on the bottom with the same copyright date of 1971 and has been cataloged over the years ranging from 4¾" to the current 5" high. This piece also shows the influence of master modeler Gerhard Skrobek in the hair and in the finish. It is found with TMK-4, 5, and 6. It is unlikely because of the late copyright date that even a prototype, if found, would have any earlier mark. The German name of *Frohes Wandern* translates as "Happy Wandering." One publication mentions that this was also called "Joyful Adventure" at one time. It was used as the illustration for September in the 1978 calendar. The original drawing is owned by Verlag Ars Sacra, and graphics from this were produced by them as postcards #14905 and #5607.

356 Gay Adventure, *copyright 1971, TMK-5.*

357 Guiding Angel

Indicator	Size	Status	TMK-1	TMK-2	TMK-3	TMK-4	TMK-5	TMK-6
357	2¾"	P	—	—	—	P	P	P

This kneeling angel with a lantern in her right hand was copyrighted as a figurine, GP28613, on April 21, 1961, and was one of the large group of over twenty new motifs cataloged in the U.S. for the first time in 1972. At that time it was listed for $11 and the suggested price has increased almost 300 percent since then. The incised copyright date on the bottom of each piece is 1960. This may have been visualized as a set similar to the three unissued fonts, Hum. 354 A, 354 B, and 354 C. This particular angel seems to have features in common with Hum. 354 A, called Angel with Lantern. One U.S. catalog has merely listed 357, 358, and 359 as "Angels Assorted," 2¾" high. No record has been found of graphics produced or of the original drawing by Sister Hummel. The German name of *Kniender Engel mit Laterne* is very descriptive of this piece and translates as "Kneeling Angel with Lantern."

357 Guiding Angel, *copyright 1960, TMK-5.*

358 Shining Light, *TMK-5.*

358 Shining Light

Indicator	Size	Status	TMK-1	TMK-2	TMK-3	TMK-4	TMK-5	TMK-6
358	2¾"	P	—	—	—	P	P	P

As previously mentioned, this piece apparently was thought of as one of a set and was so listed in some catalogs. Therefore, the historical information for this narrative is identical with Hum. 357. This piece, as with the other similar ones, is found in TMK-4, 5, and 6. If a prototype or early sample were found it might well carry the earlier TMK-3 identification and therefore be a premium piece valued at several hundred dollars. The German name of *Kniender Engel mit Kerze* is descriptive of the figure and translates as "Kneeling Angel with Candle." This item differs considerably from Hum. 354 C. No record of the original painting or graphics has been found to date.

359 Tuneful Angel, *TMK-5.*

359 Tuneful Angel

Indicator	Size	Status	TMK-1	TMK-2	TMK-3	TMK-4	TMK-5	TMK-6
359	2¾"	P	—	—	—	P	P	P

This figurine seems to have quite a bit in common with the font, Hum. 354 B, Angel with Trumpet. It also was listed in some catalogs, together with the two preceding figurines, as "Angels Three, Assorted," 2¾" high. Most of the historical information on this piece is identical to Hum. 358, which should be referred to for more information. The German name *Kniender Engel mit Trompete* translates as "Kneeling Angel with Trumpet." Some collectors see some similarity between this and the other angels with trumpet or horn, such as the best known one, Joyous News, Hum. 27.

360/A Boy and Girl, Wall Vase

Indicator	Size	Status	TMK-1	TMK-2	TMK-3	TMK-4	TMK-5	TMK-6
360/A	6"	R	—	—	P	—	R	R

An unproductive search of the available catalogs during the Sixties and Seventies discloses no record of this piece, even though it is known with TMK-3. It was not until 1978 that this was reissued and listed in the German and Canadian catalogs along with more than forty pieces reintroduced that year. In 1979 it was listed in the U.S. catalogs at $50 and promptly escalated about 300 percent in price in the secondary market, which was about half the price of rare TMK-3 examples. These premiums may be highly dependent on the future production of the Goebel Company. This design as a wall vase was registered in the U.S. Copyright Office on December 10, 1958, as GP20105. All production examples since that time have been incised with the 1958 copyright date. This would indicate that if an example were ever found with a TMK-2, it originally might have been a prototype piece or sample used for copyright or other purposes. Since Hum. 360/A, 360/B, and 360/C were all registered at the same time, it does not seem likely that Hum. 360/A was ever issued as 360 only (without suffix). Some collectors have questioned whether or not Hum. 360/B and 360/C were added to production later than Hum. 360/A. This does not seem to be the case. So far no TMK-4 example has been reported. Location of original drawing is undetermined.

360/A Boy and Girl, *Wall Vase, reissue, c. 1958, TMK-5.*

360/B Boy, Wall Vase

Indicator	Size	Status	TMK-1	TMK-2	TMK-3	TMK-4	TMK-5	TMK-6
360/B	6″	R	—	—	P	—	R	R

As mentioned under 360/A, to which one should refer for complete detail, this motif of the boy only was copyrighted at the same time, December 10, 1958, as GP20106, and its availability over the years is just as obscure. The relatively few examples that have been found all carry the TMK-3 and to date none with TMK-4 has been reported. This was reintroduced in 1978-79 at the same price of $50 and did a similar upward spiral in the secondary market, where prices may or may not remain, depending on the quantity produced by Goebel in the years to come. No original drawing has been found that would show what 360/A and its two counterparts were derived from. The German name for this piece and the two others is the same as the English.

360/B Boy, *Wall Vase, reissue, copyright 1958, TMK-5.*

360/C Girl, Wall Vase

Indicator	Size	Status	TMK-1	TMK-2	TMK-3	TMK-4	TMK-5	TMK-6
360/C	6″	R	—	—	P	—	R	R

The story of the last of the three related vases, 6″ high, is fully covered in the information about Hum. 360/A and Hum. 360/B. Their careers from the copyright date of December 10, 1958, show a remarkable parallel as to events, trademarks, scarcity, and suggested retail price. They do differ, as reference to the Price List will indicate, in valuations in the secondary market. As might be expected, the wall vase with both the boy and the girl in the motif commands a higher price than either of the other two with single figures.

360/C Girl, *Wall Vase, reissue, copyright 1958, TMK-5. Courtesy W. Goebel Co.*

361 Favorite Pet

Indicator	Size	Status	TMK-1	TMK-2	TMK-3	TMK-4	TMK-5	TMK-6
361	4¼″	P	—	—	P	P	P	P

The three-dimensional adaptation of the kneeling girl with a basket on her right arm giving full attention to a spring lamb was copyrighted in the U.S. on April 21, 1961, as GP28611 under the above name. The copyright that is incised on the production pieces is 1960, probably the year of the German copyright. It was listed in the U.S. catalogs in 1964. One noteworthy item is the wide range and variety of sizes that were specified in the catalogs. The early ones in the mid-Sixties listed this as 5″ high. In the later years of that decade, there was a listing at 4½″ high, and in the Seventies, as now, it was listed as 4¼″ high. It is found with TMK-3, 4, 5, and 6. Any premium for the larger pieces is reflected in the Price List for the earlier trademarks. As with so many others, the German name of *Ostergruss* or "Easter Greeting" is unrelated to the name used in the U.S. of "Favorite Pet." An illustration of this figurine was used for the month of March in the calendar for 1973. The original drawing by Sister Hummel is owned by Verlag Ars Sacra, from which graphics were published as postcard #5326.

361 Favorite Pet, *copyright 1960, TMK-5.*

362 I Forgot *(Assigned). From #4639 courtesy Ars Sacra.*

363 Big Housecleaning, *copyright 1960, TMK-5.*

364 Supreme Protection, *Madonna (Assigned). From #219, courtesy Emil Fink.*

362   I Forgot (Assigned Number)

Indicator	Size	Status	TMK-1	TMK-2	TMK-3	TMK-4	TMK-5	TMK-6
362	5½″	A	—	—	—	—	—	?

The name "I Forgot" assigned to Hum. 362 had not yet been assigned when the copyright was issued in the U.S. on April 21, 1961, as it was merely described as "Girl with Basket and Doll." Several years ago this number was listed as an Open Number, meaning that at the time it had not been used or assigned to any design but might be used in the future. Due to more research by Robert Miller and Goebel, a prototype was found in the company archives which shows a pensive girl holding a limp, "jester" type rag doll in her right hand and a wicker basket over her left arm. If and when this piece is ever issued it will probably be incised with a 1960 or 1961 copyright date and will carry the trademark currently in use at that time. The original by Sister Hummel is owned by Ars Sacra, from which a postcard #4639 was made. The German name, *Ich hab's vergessen,* means "I Have Forgotten."

363   Big Housecleaning

Indicator	Size	Status	TMK-1	TMK-2	TMK-3	TMK-4	TMK-5	TMK-6
363	4″	P	—	—	—	P	P	P

This diligent girl on her knees hard at work scrubbing the floor was registered in the U.S. on April 21, 1961. It was cataloged for the first time in the U.S. in 1972 at 4″ high. At that time the retail price was $28.50 with TMK-3 insignia and incised with a 1960 copyright year. If a collector is fortunate enough to obtain a verified early sample or prototype, it would be valued in the low four-digit figures. An action-packed picture of this motif was used for the month of March in the 1977 Hummel calendar showing thick suds on the floor and in her bucket. The German name *Grossreinemachen,* means "Big Cleaning" in English. The original drawing by Sister Hummel is unlocated as are any graphics.

364   Supreme Protection, Madonna (Assigned Number)

Indicator	Size	Status	TMK-1	TMK-2	TMK-3	TMK-4	TMK-5	TMK-6
364	8¾″	A	—	—	—	—	—	?

This number was listed a few years ago as a number that had never been assigned to any design but might be assigned in the future. Since then, some intensive research by Robert Miller and the Goebel Company revealed that this number had been assigned to a figurine adapted from a work of Sister Hummel and copyrighted in the U.S. on April 9, 1964, as GF208, "Madonna and Child." This standing Madonna with the Child resting on her left arm is gowned in a blue robe resembling that of the Flower Madonna, Hum. 10, in overall impression. Hum. 364, however, has a mantle with six-pointed stars versus the star formed of five dots in Hum. 10. The under robe is in a rich gold with intricate embossings. She wears a jeweled crown topped with a cross. The Child also wears a jeweled crown and ornate robe. When and if this design is released for production and sale it should be incised with a copyright date of 1963 or 1964 and have the trademark that is in use by Goebel at that time. Any prototype or early sample discovered would probably have either a TMK-3 or TMK-4 and would be valued in the mid four-digit figures. The German name, *Schutzmantel-Madonna* means "Protected Cloak Madonna." Verlag Emil Fink owner of the original has published postcard #219 from it.

365   Littlest Angel (Assigned Number)

Indicator	Size	Status	TMK-1	TMK-2	TMK-3	TMK-4	TMK-5	TMK-6
365	2½″	A	—	—	—	—	—	?

This is another unissued prototype discovered in Goebel's archives. It had been assigned to this number which previously was designated as a number that had never been used. This sculpture of a 2½″ seated figure with close-cropped hair resembles a life study of a small baby to which are attached wings that look more like the gossamer wings of a bee rather than those composed of a series of individual feathers. It appears to be the very antithesis of Sister Hummel's work except for some actual portraits she did of young children on special request of parents. This has all the appearances of a parody rather than a serious, allegorical work. The German name, *'s Hummele,* ("It's a Bumblebee") may indicate her intention to portray a human child as having "busy bee" characteristics. The English name "Littlest Angel" is bland and rather humorless compared to the German name. This was copyrighted in the U.S. on April 9, 1964, and any sample made at that time would likely be incised with TMK-3 or TMK-4. If this piece is released for production and sale it would carry the same incised copyright date and the trademark that is currently used at that time. Verlag Ars Sacra, owner of her original drawing, used it to publish postcard #5725.

365 Littlest Angel *(Assigned). From #5725, courtesy Emil Fink.*

366   Flying Angel

Indicator	Size	Status	TMK-1	TMK-2	TMK-3	TMK-4	TMK-5	TMK-6
366/C	3½″	P	—	—	?	P	P	P
/W	3½″	P	—	—	?	P	P	P

A 1972 addition to the small Nativity Set, Hum. 214 was previously copyrighted on April 6, 1964, under the same name, and production pieces are incised with that copyright year. It is found in TMK-3, 4, 5, and 6 and is available in both full color and overglaze white. A combination of the German name, *Hängeengel,* meaning "Hanging Angel" and the English name, "Flying Angel," makes an excellent description. It is an angel designed to be hung at the top of the stable, thereby creating an impression of a flying angel. Only 3½″ long, its principal use is in the Nativity Set, but it could be used equally well as an ornament to hang on the Christmas tree in either color or white. The original drawing of this motif is owned by Ars Sacra who published a postcard #4933.

366 Flying Angel, *copyright 1964, TMK-5.*

367   Busy Student

Indicator	Size	Status	TMK-1	TMK-2	TMK-3	TMK-4	TMK-5	TMK-6
367	4½″	P	—	—	P	P	P	P

This studious girl was not copyrighted until October 14, 1967, in the U.S., even though 1963 is the copyright year incised on the base. That is an unusually long interval between the two dates. The sizes have been cataloged from 5″ high in a 1966 issue to 4¼″ which is the current specification. Notice the similarity between this motif and the girl in Smart Little Sister, Hum. 346. Everything, including the unusual trefoil design in her apron and the hair style, is the same except for variations in coloring. This piece was first sold in this country in 1964 and is found in TMK-3 through TMK-6 with the incised copyright year of 1963. No major variations in color or design have been reported to date. The German name of *Musterschülerin* translates as "Model Pupil." An excellent picture of the figure is used in the 1973 calendar for the month of September (naturally, the beginning month for school). This was extracted from an original drawing used for Smart Little Sister, Hum. 346 figurine, as can be seen in postcard #5902 published by Verlag Ars Sacra.

367 Busy Student, *copyright 1963, TMK-5.*

368 Lute Song *(Assigned). Artist's concept.*

368   Lute Song (Assigned Number)

Indicator	Size	Status	TMK-1	TMK-2	TMK-3	TMK-4	TMK-5	TMK-6
368	5"	A	—	—	—	—	—	?

When this was first registered in the U.S. Copyright Office on October 14, 1967, it was described as "Small Girl with Banjo, 5 inches high." When the first edition of *HUMMEL* by Eric Ehrmann was published by Portfolio Press in 1976, Hum. 368 was listed as an "Open Number," one that had never been assigned, but might be assigned at some future date. Research since 1976 has revealed that a copyright had been issued in the U.S. Later, Robert Miller and the Goebel Company found a prototype in the company archives which verified this. Lute Song appears to be identical to one of the Close Harmony pair, Hum. 336, except for coloring and some details. The German name, *Lautenspiel,* translates as "Lute Play." When and if this is issued in the future, it will probably be incised with the German copyright year which may be earlier than 1967, and will be labeled with the trademark that is current at that time. Any prototype found before then would have a value in the mid four-digit figures.

369 Follow the Leader, *copyright 1964, TMK-5.*

369   Follow the Leader

Indicator	Size	Status	TMK-1	TMK-2	TMK-3	TMK-4	TMK-5	TMK-6
369	7"	P	—	—	P	P	P	P

This very popular figurine of three beaming children standing in close order with an inquisitive puppy bringing up the rear was one of the large group of twenty-four new models cataloged for sale in the U.S. in 1972. The suggested retail price was $110, which has since increased over 300 percent. There is a three-year lag between the date it was copyrighted in the U.S. (1967) and the year (1964) that is incised on the base, which is probably the year it was copyrighted in Germany. It is found with TMK-3, 4, 5, and 6. If an early prototype or copyright sample reached the market and was fully authenticated it would be valued in the low four-digit figures and might have the earlier TMK-3. An excellent picture of this group in a natuaralized setting appears on the cover of the 1978 calendar. The original drawing by Sister Hummel from which this three-dimensional adaptation was derived is owned by Ars Sacra. Postcard #5918 has been published by them from the original. The German name, *Mach mit,* has the same meaning as "Follow the Leader."

370 Companions *(Assigned). From #207, courtesy Emil Fink.*

370   Companions (Assigned Number)

Indicator	Size	Status	TMK-1	TMK-2	TMK-3	TMK-4	TMK-5	TMK-6
370	4½"	A	—	—	—	—	—	?

A few years ago nothing was believed to have been designed with this number. The U.S. Copyright Office records indicated otherwise. On September 9, 1965, registration number GF290 issued to Goebel described Hum. 370 as "Two Boys, One with Basket." Later Robert Miller and the Goebel Company found this to be the case by locating a prototype with this number, 4½" high, in the company archives. Records indicated that this had been modeled by Gerhard Skrobek in 1964 after a drawing by Sister Hummel called "Brotherly Love." The German name of *Gratulanten-Muttertag,* meaning "Happy Mother's Day," is similar to the next number, 371, Daddy's Girls, which leads to the conclusion that, being designed and copyrighted at the same time, they were visualized as a similar pair of figurines. When and if this model is issued in the future, it will be incised with either a copyright date of 1964 or 1965 and marked with TMK-3 or possibly TMK-4. If another sample should appear before then and is properly authenticated, it would be valued in the low four-digit figures. Verlag Emil Fink owns the original and has published postcard #207 and print #112.

371 Daddy's Girls (Assigned Number)

Indicator	Size	Status	TMK-1	TMK-2	TMK-3	TMK-4	TMK-5	TMK-6
371	4½″	A	—	—	—	—	—	?

The history of this unissued but potential figurine parallels almost exactly that of the preceding item, Hum. 370, Companions, as it is believed to have been intended as one of two figurines that would make an interesting pair. In fact, in German, each one has a similar name, *Gratulanten-Muttertag,* or "Congratulants, Mother's Day" for Hum. 370 and *Gratulanten-Vatertag,* or "Congratulants, Father's Day" for Hum. 371. Refer to Hum. 370 for dates and other pertinent information on marks and availability. The original drawing of both of these pairs is now owned by Verlag Emil Fink and graphics have been published by them in the form of postcard #208 and print #113.

371 Daddy's Girl's (*Assigned*). From #208, *courtesy Emil Fink.*

372 Blessed Mother, Madonna (Assigned Number)

Indicator	Size	Status	TMK-1	TMK-2	TMK-3	TMK-4	TMK-5	TMK-6
372	10¼″	A	—	—	—	—	—	?

Originally in 1976 this was listed as a number that had never been assigned or used but might be used in the future. Shortly thereafter, a search of the U.S. copyright records indicated that Hum. 372 was registered on September 9, 1965, as a figurine described as "Standing Madonna with Child," 10½″ high. A later search of Goebel Company archives confirmed this to be the case, and a prototype of the figurine was found with the record that it had been done by the present master modeler, Gerhard Skrobek. This tall, slender madonna is somewhat in the manner of Hum. 45 and Hum. 46, Madonna with Halo and Madonna without Halo, respectively. The major differences are that in this sculpture the pale blue robe covers her head as well as the rest of her body, and she is holding the Child chin-high with both hands straight in front of her. When and if this model is released for production and sale it will be incised with either a 1964 or 1965 corpyright date and will be identified with the trademark currently in use at that time. If another sample of this figure is found prior to that time, it will no doubt have a TMK-3 or TMK-4 as the company identification and be valued between one and two thousand dollars. Verlag Ars Sacra own the original and have used it to publish postcard #5062.

372 Blessed Mother (*Assigned*). From #5062, *courtesy Ars Sacra.*

373 Just Fishing (Assigned Number)

Indicator	Size	Status	TMK-1	TMK-2	TMK-3	TMK-4	TMK-5	TMK-6
373	4½″	A	—	—	—	—	—	?

In an early book on Hummel figurines published in 1976, this number was listed as a number that had not been used or assigned to any model but might be used in the future. Later that same year a record in variance with this statement was found in the U.S. Copyright Office. A copyright was registered by Goebel on September 9, 1965, as GF292 and described as Hum. 373, "Boy Fishing," 4½″ high. Research since then uncovered an actual sample model in the Goebel Company's archives that had, in fact, been sculpted the year before by Gerhard Skrobek, their master modeler. The figure appears to be a variation of a drawing of Sister Hummel's which shows a boy sitting on the bank but with a different catch than the shoe. Ars Sacra published postcard #5548 from the original drawing. In German the name is *Der Fischer* meaning "The Fisherman." When and if this design is released for public sale, it probably will be incised with either a 1964 or 1965 copyright date on the base and the current trademark then in use. If another sample of this motif should be found before then it may have either TMK-3 or TMK-4 on the base and be valued in the low four-digit figures.

373 Just Fishing (*Assigned*). From #5548, *courtesy Ars Sacra.*

374 Lost Stocking

Indicator	Size	Status	TMK-1	TMK-2	TMK-3	TMK-4	TMK-5	TMK-6
374	4½"	P	—	—	—	P	P	P

Not only has this boy lost his stocking but his left shoe is also missing. This piece was one of five new designs registered in the U.S. Copyright Office on September 9, 1965. It was listed by the above name as GR293, 4½" high. Examples are incised 1965. It was first found in a 1972 catalog. The current price is about three times what it was in 1972. It has been reported with TMK-3 through TMK-6. To date there have been no significant variations in size, color, or design reported, although there may have been some. The original drawing of this motif by Sister Hummel has not been located to date and neither have the graphics, if any. The German name of *Hab mein Strumpf verloren* translates as "Lost My Stocking."

374 Lost Stocking, *copyright 1965, TMK-5.*

375 Morning Stroll *(Assigned). From #14285, courtesy Ars Sacra.*

375 Morning Stroll (Assigned Number)

Indicator	Size	Status	TMK-1	TMK-2	TMK-3	TMK-4	TMK-5	TMK-6
375	4¼"	A	—	—	—	—	—	?

For some time published information indicated that this number had not been used by the Goebel Company for a specific figurine, but might be used at some later date. Further investigation revealed that this was not the case, as a copyright had been registered in the U.S. Copyright Office on September 9, 1965; the piece being described as Hum. 375, "Girl with doll carriage and dog," GF287. Still later an actual example was found in the Goebel archives indicating that the name "Morning Stroll" had been assigned as the tentative name; the height was listed as 4¼", and the sculptor was Gerhard Skrobek. The scene is similar to Hum. 67, Doll Mother, but with a differently designed carriage with a playful dachshund added in the foreground. When and if this motif is issued, it will no doubt be incised with either 1964 or 1965 as the copyright year, and the trademark will be TMK-6 or a later one in the series. The German name for this is *Ausfahrt* which means "Stroll." Any authentic prototype would be valued in the low four-digit range. Postcard #14285 has been published from the original drawing by Ars Sacra who own the drawing.

376 Little Nurse (Assigned Number)

Indicator	Size	Status	TMK-1	TMK-2	TMK-3	TMK-4	TMK-5	TMK-6
376	4"	A	—	—	—	—	—	?

On page 45 of a small book published by Verlag Ars Sacra entitled *Sonntagsbüchlein*, there is a picture of a drawing by Sister Hummel showing a small angel advising a young boy about his bandaged finger and the danger of using a knife. A copyright found registered on May 30, 1972, as Hum. 375, "A little girl dressed as a nurse," seemed to have little in common with the picture in the book. Later research by Robert Miller and the Goebel Company found a prototype of this supposedly "Open Number." In this prototype, the same little boy as in the book is sitting on the stool, but instead of an angel, a girl dressed in a gray nurse's uniform wearing a white headband with a red cross is admonishing the injured boy to be more cautious the next time. The company records reveal that this was originally called "First Aid" and was sculpted by Gerhard Skrobek in 1965. The German name is *Hänsel, merk dir das* which translates as "Hansel, remember that!" If someone were fortunate enough to acquire a sample before release, it would be valued in the mid four-digit range.

376 Little Nurse *(Assigned). Courtesy Ars Sacra.*

377 Bashful

Indicator	Size	Status	TMK-1	TMK-2	TMK-3	TMK-4	TMK-5	TMK-6
377	4¾″	P	—	—	—	P	P	P

While the bottom of this figurine is incised with a 1966 copyright date, it was not copyrighted in this country until December, 1971, using the above name. It was first listed for sale in distributors' catalogs for 1972. Since 1973, when the price was $20, the suggested retail price has increased by about 350 percent. This was one of the group of twenty-four new figurines introduced for the first time in the U.S. in 1972. This little girl with the basket behind her has the German name of *Vergissmeinnicht* meaning "Forget me not." It is only found with TMK-4, 5, or 6. If an early sample of the prototype became available, which is very unlikely, it might be marked with the earlier TMK-3. So far there have been no major changes in the 4¾″ height, the colors, or the design. The original drawing owned by Ars Sacra was used by them to publish postcard #5203 as an exact duplicate.

377 Bashful, *copyright 1966, TMK-5.*

378 Easter Greetings

Indicator	Size	Status	TMK-1	TMK-2	TMK-3	TMK-4	TMK-5	TMK-6
378	5¼″	P	—	—	—	P	P	P

This young boy dressed up in his Easter finery with a basket of yellow chicks on his left arm was first registered in this country on December 3, 1971, under the same name. The German name of *Ostergruss* appears to be identical to the English one. The figurine is incised with the 1971 copyright date on the underside of the base. In 1972 this motif first appeared for sale over here at a suggested retail price of $24. The following year it had only increased to $25.50, but with inflation escalating and the dollar dropping, the price has increased over 300 percent since it was issued. Essentially there have been no important deviations in the 5¼″ height, the colors, or design reported. It is found with TMK-3, 4, 5, or 6. A picture of this figurine was used for the month of March in the 1980 calendar. The original drawing is owned by Ars Sacra who has published postcard #5206 as an exact replica of the original.

378 Easter Greetings, *TMK-5.*

379 Don't Be Shy (Assigned Number)

Indicator	Size	Status	TMK-1	TMK-2	TMK-3	TMK-4	TMK-5	TMK-6
379	4½″	A	—	—	—	—	—	?

This is another number that was thought at first not to have been assigned to any motif but reserved for use at some future date. The copyright record found in 1976 indicated differently, as it listed this number already registered in the U.S. as GF833 on May 30, 1972, and described it as "Little girl feeding a bird on a fence," 4½″ high. In Robert Miller's *Supplement* to the book *HUMMEL,* he states that this was assigned as early as 1966 when Gerhard Skrobek sculpted the model. It depicts a small girl with kerchief on her head standing in front of a section of a split rail fence, feeding a bird on the fence, and holding a flower in the crook of her left arm. If and when this piece is released for production and sale, it will probably be incised with a copyright date of 1966 and be identified by the trademark being used by Goebel at release time. Any other early samples that might surface from some unexpected source would probably have either a TMK-3 or TMK-4 and would be valued in the low to mid four-digit figure range. The original drawing of this subject by Sister Hummel is owned by Verlag Emil Fink who produces postcard #698 as an exact replica. The German name of *Da, nimm's doch* means "Here, take it."

379 Don't Be Shy *(Assigned). From #698, courtesy Emil Fink.*

380 Daisies Don't Tell, *TMK-6, courtesy Goebel Collectors' Club.*

380 Daisies Don't Tell (Assigned Number)

Indicator	Size	Status	TMK-1	TMK-2	TMK-3	TMK-4	TMK-5	TMK-6
380	4½″	P	—	—	—	—	—	P

This exclusive design for fifth year members of the Goebel Collectors' Club was designed by Goebel's master sculptor Gerhard Skrobek in 1966 from an original drawing by Sister Hummel now owned and published by Ars Sacra as #5790. It was not registered in the U.S. Copyright Office until 1972 at which time it was described as "Little girl pulling daisies." The German name, *Er liebt mich,* translates as "He Loves Me" and suggests that this will be an interesting companion piece to Hum. 174, She Loves Me, She Loves Me Not. The purchase of this figurine will be limited to new or renewal memberships in the Goebel Collectors' Club starting in June, 1981, and ending the last of May, 1982. It will have an inscription on the back indicating that this is for the exclusive purchase of collectors holding fifth year memberships in the Club. It can only be obtained by submitting a redemption card received with the membership card to an authorized Hummel dealer. It may take the dealer several weeks to redeem your card for the figurine which is priced at $80 in the United States and $95 in Canada.

381 Flower Vendor

Indicator	Size	Status	TMK-1	TMK-2	TMK-3	TMK-4	TMK-5	TMK-6
381	5¼″	P	—	—	—	P	P	P

This 5¼″ boy with a staff in his right hand and what appears to be a surprisingly heavy load of flowers in the basket on his back was copyrighted in the U.S. on December 3, 1971, which is the same year that is incised on the underneath side of the base. The following year, 1972, it was cataloged for sale in this country for $24 and the 1973 catalog lists it as an even 5″ high at a suggested retail price of $35, about one-third of the present price. This is found marked with either TMK-4, 5, or 6 and to date no major variations in color or design have been reported. A picture of this motif was used for the month of May in the calendar for 1977. The original drawing is owned by Ars Sacra who publish it as postcard #5197. The German name of *Zum Blumenmarkt* translates as "To the Flower Market."

381 Flower Vendor, *copyright 1971, TMK-5.*

382 Visiting an Invalid

Indicator	Size	Status	TMK-1	TMK-2	TMK-3	TMK-4	TMK-5	TMK-6
382	5″	P	—	—	—	P	P	P

This is still another motif that was copyrighted on December 3, 1971, and registered in the U.S. Copyright Office as GE769 with the same name as above, 5″ high. The same year is incised on the underneath side of the base indicating the year of the copyright. The very next year it was offered for sale in a 1972 distributor's catalog. This little girl strides along carrying a basket with a bottle in it accompanied by the little bird which has become almost as much of an M. I. Hummel symbol as the small button-type flowers used in so many designs. The German name for this model is *Krankenbesuch* and translates as "Visit to a Patient." It is identified with either TMK-4, 5, or 6. A picture of this figurine was used for the month of January for the 1977 calendar. So far there have been no important changes in size, color, or design reported, but there may be some out there worth writing about. The original drawing is owned by Verlag Emil Fink, from which a graphic was published by them as postcard #810.

382 Visiting an Invalid, *copyright 1971, TMK-5.*

383　Going Home (Assigned Number)

Indicator	Size	Status	TMK-1	TMK-2	TMK-3	TMK-4	TMK-5	TMK-6
383	4¼″	A	—	—	—	—	—	?

Several years ago, this was one of the series of numbers that were termed "Open Numbers" with no design assigned. Research has disclosed that a copyright had been filed in the U.S., and a prototype model and records were located at the factory. In the copyright registered on May 30, 1972, the model was described as "little boy and girl travelers," while the factory records indicated it had been tentatively called "Fancy Free," perhaps when it was designed in 1966 by Gerhard Skrobek. The German name of *Wanderfreunde* means "Wandering Friends." This 4½″ figure of a boy with a staff in his right hand is trudging along with a kerchiefed girl clutching a bag and two flowers in her left hand. When and if this motif is ever for sale, it will probably be incised with the 1966 copyright date and be identified with the trademark in use by the company at release time. Any other sample which might show up of this pair would be considered very rare and collectible. It would be valued in the mid four-digit figures. Ars Sacra own the original drawing and have published postcard #5836 as an exact replica.

383 Going Home *(Assigned). From #5836, courtesy Ars Sacra.*

384　Easter Time

Indicator	Size	Status	TMK-1	TMK-2	TMK-3	TMK-4	TMK-5	TMK-6
384	4″	P	—	—	—	P	P	P

The German name for this pair of girls with two rabbits is *Osterfreunde* which means "Easter Playmates," suggesting the possibility that this might have been intended as a companion figurine to the boy with three rabbits called (just) Playmates, Hum. 58. However, Easter Time was used when the copyright was registered in the U.S. on December 3, 1971, as GF767, 4″ high. The same year is found incised on the underside of the base as the copyright year. The U.S. catalogs for 1972 list this motif for the first time at a suggested retail price of $27.50, which is about one-quarter of the list price as this is written. It is found with TMK-4, 5, or 6. This was the model for a picture used in the calendar for April, 1977. The original drawing by Sister Hummel from which this was adapted is owned by Verlag Emil Fink who has published it as postcard #652.

384 Easter Time, *TMK-5.*

385　Chicken-Licken

Indicator	Size	Status	TMK-1	TMK-2	TMK-3	TMK-4	TMK-5	TMK-6
385	4¾″	P	—	—	—	P	P	P

This figurine of the girl holding a basket of chicks in front of her is also called "Chicken Liesl" which is the translation of the German, *Kükenliesl*. However, Chicken-Licken was the name under which the copyright was registered in the U.S. on December 3, 1971, 4¾″ high. This same year, 1971, is also incised on the underside of the base of production models to indicate the copyright year. It is found identified by the last three trademarks in use at presstime, TMK-4, 5, or 6. It is possible, but improbable, that one with an earlier mark might be found which might indicate that the prototype examples were made earlier than 1971. To date there has been no indication that there are any variations of this motif in color, size, or design which would be worth a premium over regular models. The M. I. Hummel calendar for July, 1980, shows an interesting photograph of this motif. It not only is pictured in a naturalized setting disguising the base, but a special model must have been made up for that purpose, as the clothing shows very pronounced texturing and the hair is highly sculptured. It appears to have been made by Gerhard Skrobek. The first U.S. catalog to list this piece for sale is the 1972 issue which listed it as $28.50, 4¾″ high. The original drawing is owned by Ars Sacra and a graphic has been published by them as postcard #5833.

385 Chicken-Licken, *TMK-5.*

386 On Secret Path

Indicator	Size	Status	TMK-1	TMK-2	TMK-3	TMK-4	TMK-5	TMK-6
386	5¼"	P	—	—	—	P	P	P

This inspiration for Sister Hummel's original drawing was her brother, Adolf. One night he was especially weary after working a part-time job, and he fell asleep in a neighbor's haystack on the way home, only to awake around midnight. He was pictured by his sister hurrying home with hay trailing from under his arms. The crickets were probably added for luck, to forestall or to ease the spanking he was sure to get for such a tardy arrival. The sculpture was registered in the U.S. Copyright Office as GF763 on December 3, 1971, 5¼" high. The underside of the base is incised with that date to indicate the year it was copyrighted. The following year, 1972, it was listed in the U.S. catalogs for the first time for about $27. It is found identified with either TMK-4, 5, or 6 with no major variations. The picture of the model is used for the month of August in the 1976 calendar. The German name, *Auf heimlichen Wegen,* translates the same in English. It is thought that Sister Hummel did two duplicate originals of this particular motif; one now owned by Ars Sacra who have published postcard #14249, and one by Fink published as #697. In 1977 Schmid Brothers issued an annual plate, bell, and music box, as well as a stained glass circular plaque with this motif, which they call "Moonlight Return." In 1980 they produced a limited edition of large prints at $150 each, each one autographed by Sister Hummel's brother Adolf.

386 On Secret Path, *TMK-5.*

387 Valentine Gift

Indicator	Size	Status	TMK-1	TMK-2	TMK-3	TMK-4	TMK-5	TMK-6
387	5¼"	P	—	—	—	P	P	—

This figurine is a very special Limited Edition. The number produced will not exceed one for each first-year member of the Goebel's Collectors' Club. (For more information on the Club see page 241.) Each first-year member was issued a redemption card with his/her membership card. The card could be redeemed for this figurine by presenting it to any authorized M. I. Hummel dealer, together with $45. The Goebel Club says the membership was "over one hundred thousand" at that time. The number of members who have redeemed their cards is not generally known. Despite that figure, there are many times that number who want the figurine, with the result that it has been resold for five to eight times the issue price. There is no assurance of what price these will trade for in the future.

The design was registered in the U.S. Copyright Office on May 30, 1972, as GF829, 5¼" high. The inscription on the heart the girl is holding says in German, *i hab di gern,* which translates as "I love you very much." This same year, 1972, is incised on the underside of the base for the copyright year and also appears on the blue transfer label which reads: "Exclusive Special Edition No. 1 for Members of the Goebel Collectors' Club," along with TMK-5 and the artist's insignia. The 1972 date should not be confused with the issue date of 1977, the year the Collectors' Club was formed. A postcard, #5940, was published by Ars Sacra who own the original drawing.

387 Valentine Gift, *Limited Edition,* *TMK-5.*

388 Little Band, Candleholder

Indicator	Size	Status	TMK-1	TMK-2	TMK-3	TMK-4	TMK-5	TMK-6
388	3"	P	—	—	—	P	P	P

On October 16, 1968, a series of five copyrights was issued in the U.S. using three different, seated figurines, individually or collectively, as Hum. 388 through 392. This particular piece shows the three figures seated on a 4¾" in diameter round base with a candle socket in the center. The 1968 copyright date is incised on the underside of the base. It is only found with TMK-4, 5, or 6, and the date it was first offered for sale is not definite in the available catalogs. By 1973 the whole series from Hum. 388 through Hum. 392 was cataloged for sale. In 1973 this candleholder was listed for $38, and in the 1980 catalog it was listed for $100.

388 Little Band, *Candleholder,* *TMK-5.*

388/M   Little Band, Music Box-Candleholder

Indicator	Size	Status	TMK-1	TMK-2	TMK-3	TMK-4	TMK-5	TMK-6
388/M	3″	P	—	—	—	P	P	P

This combination consists of Hum. 388 Candleholder mounted as a cover on a wooden music box purchased from another source. A variety of tunes have been reported as being issued, but no particular song is known to command a premium to date. The 1968 copyright date is incised on the base on this article as it was on the preceding one. The three figures, either individually or collectively, have not been identified in Sister Hummel's drawings and the graphics published from them. Some individual drawings of children with musical instruments bear a resemblance to these three.

388/M Little Band, *Music Box, Candleholder, TMK-5. Dous Collection.*

389   Girl with Sheet Music

Indicator	Size	Status	TMK-1	TMK-2	TMK-3	TMK-4	TMK-5	TMK-6
389	2½″	P	—	—	—	P	P	P

This is the 2½″ figure that comprises one of the three pieces mounted on the two previous Hummel numbers. As stated, this was registered in the United States in 1968, which is the date incised on the bottom. This also is known in TMK-4, 5, and 6, and was probably issued in the early Seventies. In some catalogs this piece and Hum. 390 and Hum. 391 are listed as "Children Trio" and sold by the set or individually as Girl with Sheet Music, Boy with Accordion, and Girl with Trumpet. To clarify the names, these three pieces as a set are listed in the Alphabetical Index as Children Trio (B) to distinguish this one from another three-piece set called Children Trio (A) (Hum. 239 A, Hum. 239 B, and Hum. 239 C). The German name of *Mädchen mit Notenblatt* is the same as the English name.

389 Girl with Sheet Music, *foil label, TMK-5.*

390   Boy with Accordion

Indicator	Size	Status	TMK-1	TMK-2	TMK-3	TMK-4	TMK-5	TMK-6
390	2½″	P	—	—	—	P	P	P

This second individual piece of the trio is also 2½″ high and also may be sold as part of Children Trio (B) or individually. The incised copyright date is 1968, the same as the year of registry in the U.S. To date, no special variations in this or any other member of the trio have been reported, and the only three marks found are TMK-4, 5, and 6. The German name, *Junge mit Bandoneon,* is the same as the English one. Due to the small size of figures such as these, the marking may be indistinct or in some cases the form or kind may be altered to suit conditions.

390 Boy with Accordion, *foil label, TMK-5.*

391   Girl with Trumpet

Indicator	Size	Status	TMK-1	TMK-2	TMK-3	TMK-4	TMK-5	TMK-6
391	2½″	P	—	—	—	P	P	P

The third seated figure with her knees drawn up is 2½″ high and is identified with an incised 1968 on the bottom representing the year it was copyrighted. In addition, it is found identified as TMK-4, 5, or 6. With this small trio the M. I. Hummel signature is small and sometimes faint due to uneven surfaces to which it is applied. These have been identified with an aluminum foil label imprinted with the trademark, which is necessary because there is insufficient room on the base. The German name, *Mädchen mit Trompete,* is the same as the English one.

391 Girl with Trumpet, *foil label, TMK-5.*

392 Little Band

Indicator	Size	Status	TMK-1	TMK-2	TMK-3	TMK-4	TMK-5	TMK-6
392	3″	P	—	—	—	P	P	P

Once again the three figures in this series of arrangements are mounted on a common circular base. The only difference between this one and the first one, Hum. 388, is there is no candle socket in Hum. 392 so, therefore, it is classed as a figurine and not a candleholder. Both versions are cataloged under their respective categories and sell for the same price. This is also incised 1968 on the base, representing the copyright year, and is found in TMK-4, 5, or 6. No important variations in style or color have been reported to date.

392 Little Band, *on base, TMK-5.*

392/M Little Band, Music Box

Indicator	Size	Status	TMK-1	TMK-2	TMK-3	TMK-4	TMK-5	TMK-6
392/M	3″	P	—	—	—	P	P	P

The difference between this box and Hum. 338/M is the absence of a candle socket in this model. The other statements that apply to Hum. 338/M are applicable here. The German name of *Kindergruppe auf Musikwerk* translates as "Group of Children on Music Box." The original drawings of these children have not been located and no graphics by either Ars Sacra or Emil Fink have been found.

392/M Little Band, *Music Box, copyright 1964, TMK-4.*

393 Dove, *Holy Water Font (Assigned). From #5916, courtesy Ars Sacra.*

393 Dove, Holy Water Font (Assigned Number)

Indicator	Size	Status	TMK-1	TMK-2	TMK-3	TMK-4	TMK-5	TMK-6
393	4¼″	A	—	—	—	—	—	?

This was formerly thought to have been an Open Number, one that had not been used for a design. A search of the company archives in the last few years revealed that this number had been assigned to a holy water font designed by Gerhard Skrobek in 1968. However, there was no record found of the registration of the design in the U.S. Copyright Office. This raises the question of whether or not this will be offered for sale at some future time. A prototype of this piece is pictured in Robert Miller's *Supplement* to the original *HUMMEL* book. The dove is the religious representation of the Holy Spirit and the words on the banner are *Komm Heiliger Geist* for "Come Holy Ghost." The German title of *Weihkessel, Taube* is essentially the same as the English name. Postcard #5916 is a reproduction of the original drawing owned by Ars Sacra.

394   Timid Little Sister (Assigned Number)

Indicator	Size	Status	TMK-1	TMK-2	TMK-3	TMK-4	TMK-5	TMK-6
394	6½″	A	—	—	—	—	—	?

This figurine might become another addition for frog lovers when and if it is released for sale. It could be added to the ranks of the other two, Hum. 201, Retreat to Safety and Hum. 219, Little Velma. Until fairly recently this number had been classed as an Open Number, not yet assigned to any design, but research by several persons found that a copyright had been registered by Goebel in the U.S. Copyright Office on July 21, 1972, as GF881, 6½″ high. It was described as "a little boy and girl looking at a frog." A couple years ago a prototype was located in the factory archives with related records that verified the first bit of information. According to these records, the piece was designed by Gerhard Skrobek in 1972 so, when and if issued, it is likely to carry that year incised on the bottom as the copyright year. The German name, *Das angstliche Schwesterlein,* translates essentially the same as the name in English and does not recognize the presence of the boy, either. The original drawing is probably owned by Emil Fink who published postcard #206 which resembles the boy and girl but without the frog.

394 Timid Little Sister *(Assigned).* *From #206, courtesy Emil Fink.*

395   Shepherd Boy (Assigned Number)

Indicator	Size	Status	TMK-1	TMK-2	TMK-3	TMK-4	TMK-5	TMK-6
395	6″	A	—	—	—	—	—	?

An early book on M. I. Hummels in 1976 listed Hum. 395 as an Open Number meaning that there had been no design assigned to this number but one might be assigned later. Research by this author of the U.S. Copyright files unearthed different facts. A figurine described as "A little boy with a lamb by a fence," 6″ high, had been registered as number GF828 on May 30, 1972. Later, a search by Robert Miller and the Goebel Company located the prototype that had been called "Young Shepherd" and which had been designed in 1972 by Gerhard Skrobek. If by chance another sample piece is found, it would be valued in the mid four-digit figures. The name used in Germany for this figurine is *Hirtenbub* which means "Young Shepherd." The original drawing of this motif by Sister Hummel has not been found, nor have any graphics been located.

395 Shepherd Boy *(Assigned).* *Artist's concept.*

396   Ride into Christmas

Indicator	Size	Status	TMK-1	TMK-2	TMK-3	TMK-4	TMK-5	TMK-6
396	5¾″	P	—	—	—	P	P	P

According to Goebel Company records, this figurine was adapted from Sister Hummel's drawing by Gerhard Skrobek in 1970. The following year, this action-packed figure of a boy sliding downhill was registered in the U.S. Copyright Office as GF762 under the same name, 5¾″ high, on December 3, 1971. A year later, in 1972, it was found listed in U.S. catalogs at a suggested price of $48.50. The list price in 1980 was over seven times the issue price. These production examples were incised with the 1971 copyright date on the underside of the base and have been identified since issue by TMK-4, 5, or 6. While this figurine has always been popular, the demand really escalated when the same motif, executed in bas-relief, was used for the fifth Annual Plate, Hum. 268, in 1972. As with similar issues, many collectors arrange the figurine and plate together in a shadow box frame for a very effective display. With the huge demand, the asking price for this figurine far exceeded the suggested retail price. Depending on where and when one was located, the asking price or auction bid was often several times the current list price. With

396 Ride into Christmas, *copyright 1971, TMK-5.*

the supply increased and the slowdown in the economy, there is a much better chance of buying one of these for approximately the suggested retail price. The German name for this piece is *Fahrt in die Weihnacht,* which translates about the same as the English name. The original drawing is owned by Verlag Ars Sacra in Munich, and they have published this print as a greeting card, #5898. The Hummel calendar for December, 1976, has a picture of this figurine that might make an interesting companion piece for the plate.

397　Open Number

Indicator	Size	Status	TMK-1	TMK-2	TMK-3	TMK-4	TMK-5	TMK-6
397		O						

According to the information available from the Goebel Company, this number has not been assigned to any Hummel design, and therefore it is being listed as one which is open and may or may not be assigned to a new product adapted from one of Sister Hummel's drawings. The last search of the U.S. copyrights did not produce any subject registered with this number.

398　Open Number

Indicator	Size	Status	TMK-1	TMK-2	TMK-3	TMK-4	TMK-5	TMK-6
398		O						

Robert Miller noted there is no information available on this number, so presumably it has yet to be assigned to a specific Hummel motif. For this reason it has been listed as an open number, which may or may not be used to adapt one of Sister Hummel's drawings to a new three-dimensional article by the Goebel Company. A recent search of the U.S. Copyright records also shows that no motif has been registered for this number.

399　Valentine Joy

Indicator	Size	Status	TMK-1	TMK-2	TMK-3	TMK-4	TMK-5	TMK-6
399	5¼″	P	—	—	—	—	?	P

In previous publications this number was also listed as an Open Number similar to Hum. 397 and Hum. 398. In 1980 it was announced that this number and name would be issued as the fourth special Limited Edition sold only to members of the Goebel Collectors' Club. The piece may be purchased when they present the redemption card issued to them with their 1980 membership card (sometime between June 1, 1980 and May 31, 1981). The list price for this figurine is $95 in the United States and $105 in Canada. The first three Limited Editions varied widely in the types of article and the designs. The first was the figurine, Valentine Gift, Hum. 387, in 1977; the second was a round plaque, Smiling Through, Hum. 690, in 1978; and the third one, in 1979, was the hand-colored bust of Sister M. I. Hummel, HU-2C. This fourth issue, Hum. 399, reverts not only to the figurine classification, but it is practically the twin of the first issue. However, the German inscription on the heart of Valentine Joy is a somewhat more restrained Valentine greeting (*I mag di,* meaning, "I Like You"), compared to "I Love You Very Much" for Hum. 387. It is also the same size and bears the same special notation on the back. No registration of this number and assigned motif was found in U.S. copyright records. The original drawing by Sister Hummel is owned by Verlag Ars Sacra who produce exact replicas of it as postcard #5939.

400-499

Nothing was registered in the U.S. Copyright Office through 1977 for any of these numbers.

500-599

A few years ago, many rumors were traveling from city to city, country to country about a Goebel Mother's Day plate series. The phenomenal success of

399 **Valentine Joy,** *Goebel Collectors' Club Limited Edition. Dous Collection.*

399 **Valentine Joy** *base showing TMK-6 and artist year-date.*

the Goebel's Annual Plates and the Mother's Day plates of other producers, starting in 1969 with Bing and Grondahl, indicated the introduction of such a series as a strong possibility. To date, none of these rumors has become an actuality, but an indication of serious consideration is evidenced by a copyright for Hum. 500 on January 1, 1975, GF1152, with a tentative description of Mother's Day plate, "Flowers for Mother." The Goebel Company has made no known official statement about whether this series is still under consideration. Of course, if any prototypes of early study samples ever surfaced they would surely exceed the price of the famous 1971 Annual Plate by several times.

In the same series, the records show that Hum. 501, 4, 5, 6, 7, and 8 were listed as portraying busts of boys and girls (possibly derived from some of the life study portraiture Sister Hummel did of young children on commission). This entry was dated May 19, 1951, almost twenty-five years prior to the Hum. 500 registry. The status of these Hummel numbers is obscure.

690 Smiling Through, *Plaque, Limited Edition, Goebel Collectors' Club, 1978-1979, TMK-5. Courtesy Goebel Collectors' Club.*

690   Smiling Through, Plaque

Indicator	Size	Status	TMK-1	TMK-2	TMK-3	TMK-4	TMK-5	TMK-6
690	5¾"	P	—	—	—	—	P	—

This circular, bas-relief plaque, 5¾" in diameter, is based on an original drawing of Sister Hummel's which is now owned by Verlag Ars Sacra. They have published graphic #5832 from the original. This plaque was selected for the second Limited Edition exclusively for members of the Goebel's Collectors' Club in 1978. It is labeled with an overglaze blue transfer label reading as follows: "Exclusive Special Edition No. 2, Hum 690 For Members of the Goebel Collectors' Club." The artist's initials and the TMK-5 transfer label are above "W. Germany, 1978." The plaque can be displayed on an easel or mounted in a frame and hung on the wall. At first the Club offered a personalized frame with member's name for this purpose, but, at the request of Hummel dealers, the offer was withdrawn shortly thereafter. The issue price was $50 plus the member's redemption card presented to an authorized Hummel dealer. This plaque has not been as popular as the first issue, which is true of many similar limited edition series. It is offered for sale in the secondary market at the range indicated in the Price List. This is the first piece to be numbered in the 600 series by Goebel, which indicates the likelihood of additional articles with these higher numbers.

700   Annual Bell, Let's Sing, 1978

Indicator	Size	Status	TMK-1	TMK-2	TMK-3	TMK-4	TMK-5	TMK-6
700	6"	P	—	—	—	—	P	—

A first issue of a series of bells about 6" high in bas-relief was exciting news. The raised design used was the same as the motif of the figurine, Let's Sing, Hum. 110, which should be referred to for information on the history. The bird on the bell is on the opposite side from that on the figurine. On the reverse side, not shown, the year of issue, 1978, is embossed and highlighted in red. The reception of this piece (first issued at a list price of $50, and later in the year at $55) by collectors and speculators was phenomenal. By June of 1978, sales in the secondary market at $300 were not uncommon. As the Price List shows, the current market price is considerably less, or roughly double the issue price. The future course of the price will depend on a continued strong demand and on how many are still "under the counter or under the bed." This action is rather typical of many first year issues of limited edition items, such as the 1971 Hummel Plate, Hum. 264, the first Lalique plate in 1965, and the Wedgwood first issue of 1968. Many Hummel collectors were upset because they could not buy either the plate or bell for 1978. According to some dealers, this resulted in collectors giving up. Some sold the plates they had accumulated to buy other limited series that were less volatile and more available. The inside of the bell contains a blue transfer label overglaze with the following: "First Edition, Annual Bell, Hum 700, Handcrafted." It also had the TMK-5 mark, with W. Germany, and 1977 as the copyright year as well as the usual artist mark. This was the first use of the 700 series by Goebel for M.I. Hummel articles.

700 Let's Sing, *First Annual Hummel Bell, 1978, TMK-5. Courtesy Goebel Collectors' Club.*

701 **Farewell,** *Second Annual Hummel Bell, 1979, TMK-5. Courtesy Goebel Collectors' Club.*

702 **Thoughtful,** *Third Annual Hummel Bell, 1980, TMK-6. Courtesy Goebel Collectors' Club.*

703 **In Tune,** *Fourth Annual Hummel Bell, 1981, TMK-6. Courtesy Goebel Collectors' Club.*

701   Annual Bell, Farewell, 1979

Indicator	Size	Status	TMK-1	TMK-2	TMK-3	TMK-4	TMK-5	TMK-6
701	6¼″	P	—	—	—	—	P	—

This bas-relief is the same motif used for the figurine of the same name, Hum. 65, which should be referred to for background. The inscriptions on this Second Annual Bell and the red embossed year, 1979, follow the same pattern as described before for the first issue, Hum. 700. The issue price of this bell was $70, and due to the increased production effort on the part of the Goebel Company, plus possibly less demand, Hum. 701 was readily available to all who wanted it. By 1980 this bell could be obtained on the secondary market for considerably *less* than issue price. This may prove that not all limited editions move in an upward spiral that outpaces inflation, especially in a recessionary climate.

702   Annual Bell, Thoughtful, 1980

Indicator	Size	Status	TMK-1	TMK-2	TMK-3	TMK-4	TMK-5	TMK-6
702	6¼″	P	—	—	—	—	?	P

This third bell issue has no real counterpart as a figurine. It is obviously closely related to Hum. 14 A, the boy figure of the pair of bookends, Bookworm, 14 A and B. The boy was never produced as a separate figurine, but the girl is available as a figurine in two sizes, Hum. 3 at 5½″ and Hum. 8 at 4″ high. Occasionally an odd, separate boy bookend, Hum. 14 A, is found, but it can easily be distinguished from a figurine by its flat back and stoppered hole in the bottom for adding sand. A comparison between Hum. 14 A and the bas-relief on the bell will disclose a much larger book, different placement of the legs, an added scarf, and a change in hair styling on the bell rendition. This 1980 bell was issued at a list price of $85 and was readily available at list or, in some instances, below list in that deflated year. This bas-relief was adapted from Sister Hummel's drawing that has been published as postcard #14265 by Verlag Ars Sacra who own the original creation.

703   Annual Bell, In Tune, 1981

Indicator	Size	Status	TMK-1	TMK-2	TMK-3	TMK-4	TMK-5	TMK-6
703	6¼″	P	—	—	—	—	—	P

The subject of the fourth Annual Bell, In Tune, was adapted from Sister Hummel's original drawing which was published by Ars Sacra as graphic #5896. For some unknown reason, the Goebel Company does not pre-announce the motifs to be used on bells of future years as they have done with plates. This gives collectors the opportunity to match wits with each other and Goebel in a guessing contest. What seems to be a consensus of eligible candidates is as follows, but not necessarily in the order they may appear.

Name	Hum. No.
Joyful	53
Good Friends	182
Latest News	184
Little Bookkeeper	306
Cinderella	337
Smart Little Sister	346
Favorite Pet	361
Big Housecleaning	363
Busy Student	367

Nominations are open for which of these it will be each year, including ones not on the list, and will gladly be received and entered in the "computer," but it will be impossible to "make book" for the readers who want to place bets instead of names.

Other Hummel Numerical Series

Research of the U.S. Copyright records several years ago revealed some large gaps in numbers above Hum. 399. This may have been due to the Goebel Company's having assigned specific lines or designs to various numerical series. Possibly it could be due to a change in company policy that resulted when it became no longer necessary to register designs in this country because of the terms of the International Copyright Convention. Signers of this convention, of which West Germany is one of the parties, agree to honor all copyrights registered in other member countries. What information is available for plaques, dolls, and International Figurines follows in numerical order up to Hum. 2000.

800-999 International M. I. Hummel Figurines

So far any information on these two hundred numbers is restricted to about two dozen designs. The initial credit belongs to the sharp-eyed "picker" in a Budapest flea market in 1976, who either realized some unusual looking figurines in folk costumes were M. I. Hummel figurines or had the innate "sixth sense," that most successful scouts and pickers are endowed with. In either case, the chance to make a small, quick profit was the motivation for gambling on them for quick resale to a dealer in Austria. Indefinite rumors that an antique dealer owned some unusual figurines in Rumania prevailed in the Seventies, but it took the positive persistence of a full blooded collector-detective, Robert L. Miller, to convert rumor into fact. Having finally acquired eight figurines in Eastern European costumes, all signed M.J.Hummel, he obtained the permission of the Goebel Company to search their archives. This resulted in the unearthing of the "Rip Van Winkles," asleep for over thirty years in the Goebel factory, which are illustrated here. This research also indicated that in about 1940 Goebel explored the possibility of producing the irresistible Hummel children in the native costumes of other European countries besides Germany. They commissioned Sister Hummel to make the

Top:

(L to R) *Bulgarian. 808; Bulgarian, 811; Swedish, 824; Swedish, 825; Swedish, 825. All copyrighted 1940, courtesy W. Goebel Co.*

Bottom:

(L to R) *Serbian, 812; Serbian, 968; Serbian, 813; Serbian, 904; Serbian, 947. All copyrighted 1940, courtesy W. Goebel Co.*

(L to R) Czech, 842; Czech, 841. Both copyrighted 1940, courtesy W. Goebel Co.

drawings from which Möller and Unger, their two master modelers, sculpted the figurines illustrated. It was not clear if any of these were ever sold, and, of course, the project was abandoned shortly thereafter because World War II started. Some of these are unique and have no counterparts in the original "German" series, such as Hum. 810 and 811, which are posed in a folk dance position. Other International ones, for example, Hum. 947, "Goose Girl," have easily recognized counterparts (Hum. 47, Goose Girl). Are there more of these extremely rare examples to be found?

One incident may be a clue. In June of 1979, a young couple in Chicago stopped where this author was signing books and answering questions. The woman described a piece she had purchased as a young Italian girl when she visited Yugoslavia years previously. Fortunately her husband had the equivalent of a "ten-thousand-word" description in the form of excellent colored slides. Viewing these immediately revealed that what she was describing was an International Serbian Goose Girl, Hum. 947, valued in five figures. To date, it is perhaps the only perfect one known. Pictures were not available from this stunned couple until they had their treasure safely stored in the bank vault and fully insured. One interesting detail is the form of the model number incised on the bottom. It is 947/0. Can there be more models, more examples of the same models, or even more sizes of Hum. 947/0? Only time and the persistence of dedicated collector-detectives will come up with the answers.

Serbian figurine, 812, copyrighted 1940, courtesy W. Goebel Co.

(L to R) Slav, 831; Slav, 832; Slav, 833. All copyrighted 1940, courtesy W. Goebel Co.

(L to R) Bulgarian, 810; Bulgarian, 809; Bulgarian, 810; Bulgarian, Bulgarian, 806. All copyrighted 1940, courtesy W. Goebel Co.

(L) Base of Bulgarian figurine, 808, showing Incised Crown, stamped Full Bee TMK-2, and incised Germany. (R) Base of Bulgarian, 806, with Bulgarian identification at top and bottom.

(L to R) Hungarian, 852; Hungarian, 853; Hungarian, 852. All copyrighted 1940, courtesy W. Goebel Co.

1000-2000   M. I. Hummel Dolls

Indicator	Size	Status	TMK-1	TMK-2	TMK-3	TMK-4	TMK-5	TMK-6

Only recently in reviewing older research records was it realized that some of the Hummel dolls which are described and illustrated in Chapter 4, had left their imprint in the records of the U.S. Copyright Office. The first entry was on March 1, 1953, a year or so after Goebel had switched from a composition body and molded rubber head (issued about 1950) to an all-rubber doll made in their own factory. These had hand-painted faces and carefully tailored clothes. On January 3, 1953, Hum. 1809, "Peterle"; 1810, "Rosl"; 1811, "Mirel"; and 1812, "Franel" were registered. Fourteen years later, two registrations indicated that the well-known change from the unreliable rubber to the flesh tone vinyl plastic was made. The names of Hum. 1802 and 1803 listed on February 2, 1967, recorded as GF440 and GF450, were "Boy with Wicker Basket on Back" and "Girl with Broom," molded of plastic.

HU-1 M. I. Hummel Bust, *old style, incised "Hu-1, 1965," approximately 15" high, TMK-4.*

Non M. I. Hummel Items

HU-1 Sister M. I. Hummel Bust

Indicator	Size	Status	TMK-1	TMK-2	TMK-3	TMK-4	TMK-5	TMK-6
HU-1	15"	D	—	—	—	P	—	—

While this and the next two items are included here, they are not the result of a work of art by Sister M. I. Hummel, herself, but rather the work of one of Goebel's master modelers, Gerhard Skrobek, who created this one in 1965. This large, 15" head-and-shoulder bust in white bisque finish was first issued in the mid-1960s with the TMK-4 mark. The model number HU-1 is also incised on these examples. When these were discontinued is not a matter of published record, but two facts are evident: there are relatively few of these pieces available, and then only at premium prices, as indicated in the separate Price List.

HU-2(w) M. I. Hummel Bust, *incised "HU-2," TMK-5.*

For more information and background on other Goebel products that might be misinterpreted as adaptations of Sister Hummel's work, see the chapter of this book entitled, "Goebel — Not Hummel," page 182.

HU-2(w) Sister M. I. Hummel Bust (white)

Indicator	Size	Status	TMK-1	TMK-2	TMK-3	TMK-4	TMK-5	TMK-6
HU-2(w)	5"	D	—	—	—	P	P	—

This appears to be a 5" scaled-down model of HU-1. It was sculpted by Gerhard Skrobek in 1967 and carries that date and "Skrobek" incised on the rear of the base. On the front of the base, the facsimile signature *M.J.Hummel* is incised. The underside is incised with the model number HU-2 and the blue TMK-5 transfer label. There is no copyright date. The first listing was found in a U.S. distributor's catalog for 1977 at a list price of $15 and again in the 1978 issue at $17. Since these were available for such a short period, prices reached as high as $75 in the secondary market. It was omitted from the 1979 issue and superseded by the colored bust described next.

HU-2(c) Sister M. I. Hummel Bust (color)

Indicator	Size	Status	TMK-1	TMK-2	TMK-3	TMK-4	TMK-5	TMK-6
HU-2(c)	5"	D	—	—	—	—	P	—

This is the same 5" bust as the one above, HU-2(w), except that it is in lifelike colors which were specially selected by Gunther Newbauer, Goebel's chief master painter. This is an exclusive Limited Edition available only to third year members of the Goebel Collectors' Club (May, 1979 to May, 1980) upon presentation of a special redemption card and payment to an authorized Hummel dealer. The issue price was $75 in the U.S. and $85 in Canada. When first issued, quotations in the secondary market were above the issue price, but apparently the 1980 recession eliminated any premium.

HU-2(c) M. I. Hummel Bust, *Limited Edition, Goebel Collectors' Club. Incised "HU-2, 1967," and "Skrobek, 1967." Courtesy W. Goebel Co.*

For Father, Hum. 87. Left: TMK-1 with light brown turnips. Right: TMK-3A with orange turnips, very scarce. Grande Collection.

Vacation Time, Plaque, Hum. 125. Variation with six uprights in fence made prior to TMK-3. Scarce. Janet Hoppa Collection.

Band Leader, Hum. 129, trademark unknown. Unusual example with music upside-down. Profitt Collection.

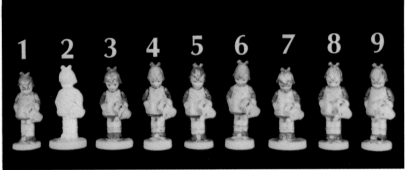

Little Gardener, Hum. 74. Note color variations, change of base from oval to round, and various sizes. Left to right: (1) TMK-1C. (2) Very rare overglaze white, no marks. (3) TMK-2A. (4) TMK-2B. (5) TMK-2D. (6) TMK-2, divided base. (7) TMK-3B. (8) TMK-3B. (9) TMK-3B. Grande Collection

Bird Duet, Hum. 169, examples demonstrating variations in placement of wings, baton, and color differences. Left to right: (1) TMK-3. (2) TMK-3. (3) TMK-5. (4) TMK-2E. (5) TMK-2. (6) TMK-2. (7) TMK-2. Grande Collection.

Silent Night Candleholder, Hum. 54, extremely rare with black child. Note shoes. Hum. 31 has no shoes. TMK-2B. Mary Mullen Collection. Photograph: Caroline Delevitt.

3 *Valuing M.I. Hummel and Goebel Figurines*

Merry Wanderer, Hum. 7, marked TMK-1 and 7/I. Note double-tiered base.

Variations, Deviations, Scarcities, and Rarities

The manufacture of M.I. Hummel figurines is a hand operation based on methods which evolved long before the Industrial Revolution or today's mass production techniques. Since they are not only handmade, but also hand painted, variations and deviations from standard plus restyling and redesigns abound, resulting in a field day for collectors of these figurines. Collectors of many other articles have only pattern and size as variables to choose from. In M.I. Hummel figurines, there are not only different motifs, but there are differences in any one motif. There are many standard sizes for some of the models coupled to innumerable deviations from each of the standards.

Older methods of molding were inexact. Each successive casting might be slightly larger than the preceding one due to absorbed moisture. Styles in design and color shifted over the years. New master modelers took the place of the original ones. Each new artist produced "master models" which varied from that of his predecessor. Variation built on variation, deviation piled on deviation, producing an incalculable number of combinations and permutations. What a fine hunting ground for avid collectors. They can find big ones, little ones, eyes open, eyes closed, socks on, one sock on, no socks. There is something for everyone. Collectors revel in the opportunity to have something that is different than anyone else's or at least different than almost anyone else's.

Congratulations, Hum. 17, TMK-1D, with no socks. Newer models have socks. Current mark restyled with textured finish. Thomas Carr Collection.

The photographs and the life history of the various models point out the actual specifics. For example, the collector can choose from a minimum of fourteen or more official and unofficial sizes of Merry Wanderer, Hum. 7 and Hum. 11. Some of them differ from all the rest because of the number of buttons on the vest, the marking on the bottom, or because of the coloring, styling, double base, single base, copyright dates, and six possible trademarks. Collecting variations in just one model like Merry Wanderer can be a mathematician's headache or a collector's dream. There are several hundred more models that offer similar challenges.

With all of these "acres of diamonds" abounding in scarce and rare M.I. Hummel figurines, how does an average collector go about judging the importance of examples that are in his or her collection? How can one distinguish the ridiculous from the sublime, the important from the nonentity? The best way is to study both the Current Price List and the "Numerical List of Hummel Figurines" which contain the photograph,

Birthday Serenade, Table Lamp, Hum. 234, TMK-2 with boy playing horn, girl playing accordion. Private collection.

Cross with Doves, Font, Hum. 77. Only example known, so at this time must be considered unique. Private Collection.

Serbian Goose Girl, Hum. 947, formerly unique, now considered extremely rare. Private Collection.

Little Velma, Hum. 219, TMK-2. Once believed never produced by Goebel. Very few examples known, so it is considered extremely rare. Dous Collection.

history, production record, and most important variations of all Hummel figurines. Between these two sources a good idea of the scarcity of an example should be apparent.

A question often asked is what is meant by rare, by scarce, and other related terms as applied to Hummels. One way to understand the terms is to start with the highest category. Most collectors agree that a one of a kind or a "unique" example is the scarcest of all examples. In 1979, readers called to the attention of this author two pieces that illustrate this category of "unique." One was Hum. 77, Cross with Doves, which was reported as a number that was never used by Goebel and of which no pieces had been made. A reader dispelled this myth by sending pictures to prove the existence of the only piece known at this time. Cross with Doves readily falls into the "unique" category.

Another case was a perfect example of Hum. 947/0, Goose Girl in Serbian costume. At the time the photographs were inspected, only an imperfect factory sample was known. The perfect piece, being the only one in that condition, was considered "unique."

How is the value determined on such unusual pieces? It could be determined by a qualified appraiser, by selling the example at auction, or by offering it to well-known collectors with the understanding it would be sold at the highest offer received. In the case of the Serbian Goose Girl, Hum. 947, an appraisal indicated the probable value would range from $12,000 to $18,000. It is understood to have been insured for $25,000 and offered for sale at this figure. One collector submitted a $15,000 bid which was refused. Within a year, the collector who made the offer was fortunate to find another perfect piece in Europe at a much more attractive price. What is the original piece worth now? Depending on the very limited market for such a piece, it might fetch $8,000 to $12,000, since it is no longer "unique" but now "extremely rare."

For the next step down the ladder, many people use the term "extremely rare," usually meaning in Hummel collecting that perhaps from two to ten pieces may ultimately be available. Little Velma (Girl with Frog), Hum. 219/2/0, was thought to be "unique" when discovered, but, now, perhaps five examples are known with the possibility of yet a few more to be discovered. In the class of "very rare," a consensus might estimate about ten to fifty examples extant, but here the difference in opinion diverges; especially between those who own one and those who want to buy one.

The class "rare" is so often overused in conversations, catalogs, and auctions, that it is applied to cases where there could be an unlimited number of examples existing that have not been reported. It should properly apply to cases where the expected total ranges from fifty to one hundred pieces. Proceeding down the scale of importance to "very scarce," and where the actual quantity and potential market are at best good guesses, a total of one hundred to one thousand examples might fit this term. "Scarce," itself, is a modest term for advertising copy writers, and collectors probably hope their example is one in a thousand to one in five thousand. The very bottom of the pyramid would be covered by the term "uncommon," which could encompass a quantity of, perhaps, five thousand or more. Would the 1971 Annual Plate, Heavenly Angel, Hum. 264, be considered "uncommon," or further up the scale? Perhaps a better term for a large, unknown quantity such as this might be "high priced." Anyone with sufficient capital can locate one or more on very short notice, and if they offer over the current market price they might be swamped.

When all is said and done, the above classifications and the quantities that might qualify for the terms are pure speculation, since the price in each and every case is determined by the amount that an equally informed buyer and seller will mutually agree to in an exchange of ownership. As pointed out several times in other sections of this book, trying to be too exact in pinpointing a price can be difficult. The further up the rarity scale the example is, the truer the statement is.

The number of well-publicized variations in styling, color, and limited production pieces probably ranges between one and two hundred that are visibly recognizable to a large enough group of normal Hummel collectors to be attractive and interesting. This excludes the innumerable variations in sizes, trademark idiosyncracies, and minor deviations in assembly and painting that are interesting and which are worth a small premium to a limited number of collectors. The premiums paid for any example that deviates from standard are affected by a number of variables such as the popularity of the model under consideration plus conditions that would also affect the price of any standard issue such as the time, place, and persons involved. There is no science involved in premiums for variations and deviations, but there is the law of supply and demand.

Most of the known variations, deviations, and limited production models have been described previously in outlining the history of each model number in numerical sequence. In some cases only the rarity is illustrated and known. To further illustrate some of the various types and degrees of unusualness, pictures in this section have been selected and identified by a short description underneath. The values of unusual examples may be included in the Current Price List or in the history of each model. The use of the Current Price List without consulting the background information can lead to an incorrect assessment on either the high or low side. Use the big book and the Price List as an inseparable pair in researching the unusual pieces and their value.

Heavenly Angel, Hum. 264, 1971 First Annual Plate is hard to categorize. Certainly qualifies as high-priced.

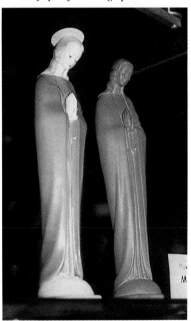

(L) Madonna with Halo, 45/I, rare, with purple robe. (R) Madonna without Halo, Hum. 46/I, in terra-cotta body. Photographed at the Eaton Festival, 1980.

Angel with Yellow Bird, Font, Hum. 167. Old model, TMK-2, with hole in back for hanging. New ones have hole in top. S. Adlis Collection

Hello, Hum. 124. (L to R) (1) 124/0, TMK-3B; (2) 124/0, TMK-3B with color variation in pants; (3) 124/I, TMK-5 (reissue); (4) 124/0, TMK-2; (5) 124/I, TMK-2; (6) 124 (only), TMK-2. Last three are all hollow molds. Grande Collection.

Little Bookkeeper, Hum. 306. Prototype model of figure first issued in 1971 with TMK-4. This very rare piece marked with TMK-2. Copyrighted by Goebel in 1955. Wilgus Collection.

Prayer Before Battle, Hum. 20 with different marks. (L to R) (1) TMK-3; (2) TMK-1A; (3) TMK-2B; (4) TMK-2B. Grande Collection.

Angel at Prayer, Font, Hum. 91B, TMK-1. Early model with no halo and mounting hole in back.

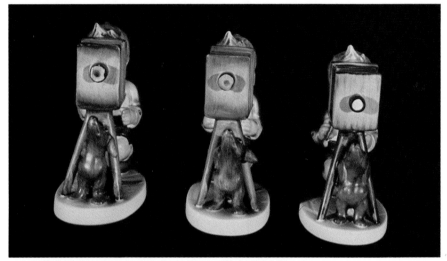

Photographer, Hum. 178. (L) TMK-2. (C) TMK-3A. (R) TMK-5. Note differences in camera front, legs, dogs, ears, and colors. Grande Collection.

Goose Girl, Hum. 47, with very scarce "blade of grass" between geese; 5¼" high, 47/0, TMK-1. Dous Collection.

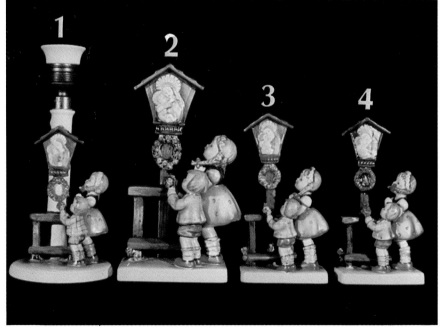

Adoration, Hum. 23, and Shrine Table Lamp, Hum. 100, extremely rare. (L to R): (1) 100, TMK-1D; (2) 23/III; (3) TMK-5; (4) 23/I, TMK-2; (5) 23/I, TMK-1A. Grande Collection.

Candlelight, Candleholder, Hum. 192.
(L) TMK-2 with long candle socket
reaching base, discontinued style, scarce.
(R) TMK-3 with short candle socket with
candle. Both 1948 copyright dates.
Grande Collection.

Easter Time, Hum. 384. (L) TMK-5 with unusual unpainted face.
(R) TMK-5 with standard finish. Grande Collection.

Meditation, Hum. 13, showing size, style, basket, and mark variations. (L to R) (1) 13/5, TMK-5; (2) 13/II, TMK-5; (3) 13/0,
TMK-2; (4) 13/0, TMK-2; (5) 13/0, TMK-3; (6) 15/0, TMK-3B; (7) 13/0, TMK-3B; (8) 13/0, TMK-4. Note full basket of flowers in
13/5; others empty. Model 13/2/0 (not shown) has partial basket of flowers. Grande Collection.

Skier, Hum. 59, TMK-3, slightly oversize, with original wooden skis, fiber disks.

Begging His Share, Hum. 9. **(L)** TMK-4, 5½″ high, solid cake. **(R)** Rare, oversize, 7″ high, with candle socket.

Forest Shrine, Hum. 183, TMK-2, 9″ high. Discontinued and rare.

A Fair Measure, Hum. 345. **(L)** TMK-5 with 1972 copyright date incised, divided base. **(R)** TMK-5 with 1955 copyright date incised, doughnut base, old style, smaller, smoother finish, weights reversed and eyes up, scoop on container. Grande Collection.

The Run-a-Way, Hum. 327. Two styles produced. **(L)** TMK-5 with 1955 copyright date, old style. **(R)** TMK-5 with 1972 copyright date, redesigned with changed basket design, hat, feather, and colors. Grande Collection.

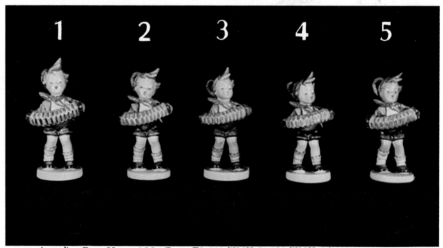

Accordion Boy, Hum. 185. **(L to R)** (1) TMK-2; (2) TMK-1A; (3) TMK-2; (4) TMK-3; (5) TMK-2D. Note hair and face differences. Grande Collection.

Spring Cheer, Hum. 72. **(L)** TMK-2 with yellow dress and no flowers in right hand. **(C)** TMK-3B, green dress and no flowers in right hand; very scarce. **(R)** TMK-3C, new mold, green dress, with flowers in left hand. Szynkiewicz Collection.

Volunteers, Hum. 50. **(L)** 50/I, TMK-3. **(R)** 50/I, TMK-5 (reissued in 1978). Grande Collection.

Lost Sheep, Hum. 68. **(L)** TMK-2 with dark brown pants. **(R)** TMK-2 (later) with green gray pants. Current models restyled with gray green pants, textured finish. Grande Collection.

Heavenly Protection, Hum. 88, TMK-2, 9" high.

Little Fiddler, Hum. 2 and 4, showing variations in sizes, colors, and designs. (1) 2/3, TMK-2; (2) 2/2, TMK-2; (3) 2/1. TMK-2; (4) 2/0, TMK-1; (5) 4, TMK-2; (6) 4, TMK-1 (USZ); (7) 4, TMK-2; (8) 4, TMK-2; (9) 4, TMK-3C. Grande Collection.

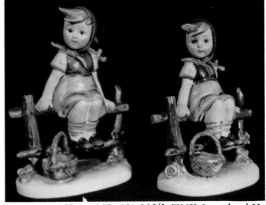

Just Resting, Hum. 112. (1) 112/I, TMK-2, replaced Hum. 112, TMK-1, when small size (112/3/0) was introduced. Note differences. Lipowski Collection.

Reinstated M.I. Hummel Figurines

Since the first ten or more M.I. Hummel models were issued in 1935, more than four hundred other models or sizes have been added. Many of these have been cataloged and produced continually since the date they were first introduced. Other models or model/sizes have been dropped from the catalogs for various reasons. Some have not been available in the U.S. primary market for many years.

For several models, their day in the sun was so brief that very few examples have surfaced. Less than five examples have been found of such discontinued figurines as Hum. 151, Seated Madonna in brown. Over the years, most of these discontinued models or sizes have become scarce, highly prized, and highly priced specimens. Some have changed owners at more than $10,000.

In 1977 rumors were circulating that forty or fifty presently uncataloged items would be reinstated and offered for sale once more in the primary market at prices consistent with other comparable pieces (many at $100 or less). The Canadian and German catalogs for 1978 announced the availability of most of the rumored pieces in very limited quantities compared to the potential demand. Most of these quickly found their way into the secondary market in the U.S. at premiums of from 100 to 500 percent over issued price. In 1979 and 1980, essentially the same reissues were made available to U.S. dealers. Reissues, Reintroductions, or Reinstatements are identified in the production chart accompanying the photograph and history of each model by the letter "R" in the Status column and the same designation in the Current Price List.

Spring Dance, Hum. 353/0 was first introduced in 1964, but so few pieces were ever made that it has been a high-priced rarity, selling for over $1,000. In 1979, it was reissued in the U.S. for $100. Immediately, dealers bid this price up so that, overnight, customers were having to pay more than $400 dollars for it. This happened to many others, such as Whitsuntide, Hum. 163, and included some that were reissued with the old TMK-3 instead of TMK-5 or 6. While these prices were skyrocketing, the prices of the original old rare ones were either stationary or slipping backward. Collectors had quickly discovered they could buy almost exact duplicates of old rarities for a fraction of the price. Sure, the trademark was different, but this did not show in the collectors' display cabinets. When every Teresa, Diane, and Harriet have new reissues in their collections, will Penelope still feel ecstatic about the one she paid more than ten times as much for because it was a rare collector's prize at one time?

The answer seems to lie with Goebel. If all the old rare models or sizes are reissued in identical design and large quantities, collectors might decide to cash in their collections. Some Hummel collectors did cash in their plate collections when they could not find the 1978 plate and bell except at a premium of three to five times suggested retail. On the other hand, if discontinued rarities were reissued with noticeable changes that did not affect their aesthetic appearance, marked "reissued" with the year, and in a pre-announced limited quantity, some collectors said they

Three examples of Whitsuntide, Hum. 163. Left: TMK-1A. Center: TMK-2A. Right: Reissue with no candle, smaller clock face, and shorter height. Grande Collection.

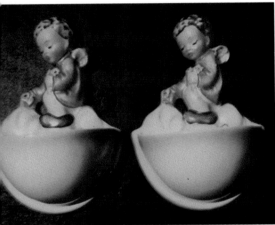

Angel Cloud, Font, Hum. 206. Left: TMK-4 with 1949 copyright date. Right: Reissue marked TMK-5 with 1949 copyright date. Dous Collection.

Auf Wiedersehen, Hum. 153. Left: TMK-2, boy with green hat, discontinued design and very scarce. Right: Also marked TMK-2, restyled version, boy without hat. Reissued in 1978 and will be found with TMK-5 or 6. Grande Collection.

might have the opposite reactions. They would be pleased to have the opportunity to buy previously unattainable or unaffordable models which might themselves appreciate in years to come.

With collectors having to guess the future course of reissues, prices are likely to gyrate within very wide extremes for both original rarities and the reissues that have made them not so rare. With no indication that reissues will not continue to be produced in abundance, there seems to be little incentive for collectors to buy these reissues with the idea that they are likely to become scarce themselves. Some collectors who own original early models of these rarities are considering selling them if they can break even.

Collectors should be acutely aware of differences between reissues and their earlier, rare counterparts. One obvious difference is the trademark. Reissues should have TMK-5 or 6 on the bottom (with rare exceptions), and be priced in line with the prices shown for these two marks in the Current Price List. Physical differences exist between some of the models with older marks and the reissues. At present, a complete list of differences between each of the reissues and the older versions has not been finished, but representative examples are in the following list.

Not everyone agrees on what has been reintroduced and what has not. A fairly good concensus of what was added to the U.S. catalog in 1978, after having been absent for one or many years, follows. These new entries may be referred to variously as reissues, reinstatements, or reintroductions. In this book the terms are used interchangeably and are represented in all lists by the letter "R".

Distinguishing a reissue from one of the more valuable and older "cousins" is difficult. In all cases, examples of Hummel numbers with TMK-5 or TMK-6 are reissues, and are marked so. Unfortunately there are exceptions. Several reinstated motifs have been found with the older TMK-3 (in the case of Whitsuntide) or TMK-4. In addition to the usual trademark difference, some have other distinguishing features. Most of these differences are not apparent unless you have an older model for comparison. Whatever information is available at this time is shown under remarks.

Note: Minor differences in color, mold, or assembly may not be significant or consistent from piece to piece and from older marks to TMK-5 or 6.

Waiter, Hum. 154. Left: Reissue with TMK-5. Center: TMK-3, marked 154. (decimal). Right: TMK-1, with gray pants, scarce. Grande Collection.

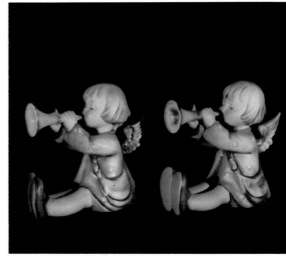

Joyous News, Hum. 27. Left: 27/III, TMK-1. Right: 27/III, TMK-2. Both are rare with these marks. Reissued in 1978 with TMK-5 or 6. Grande Collection.

Happy Days, Hum. 150. Left, Hum. 150/0, 5½" high, marked TMK-2, with girl's head in normal position. Right: Hum 150/0, 5½" high, marked TMK-2, with head turned to her left, unusual variation. Reissued in 1978 without flowers on base, with TMK-5 or 6. G. Peters Collection.

Reinstated M.I. Hummel Figurines

Number Size Mark	Name	Difference from Older Issues
2/III	LITTLE FIDDLER	TMK-5 or 6. Possibly restyling.
3/III	BOOK WORM	TMK-5 or 6. Side by side, restyling.
7/III	MERRY WANDERER	TMK-5 or 6. Possibly restyling.
13/II	MEDITATION	TMK-5 or 6. No flowers in basket.
13/III	MEDITATION	TMK-5 or 6. Possibly Restyling.
24/III	Lullaby, CAN	TMK-5 or 6.
27/III	Joyous News, CAN	TMK-5 or 6. Possibly Restyling.
48/II	Madonna, MAD	TMK-5 or 6.
49/I	TO MARKET	TMK-5 or 6. Some are 49 (only) not 49/I.
50/0	VOLUNTEERS	TMK-5 or 6.
50/I	VOLUNTEERS	TMK-5 or 6. Some older ones larger.
51/I	VILLAGE BOY	TMK-5 or 6. Cross strap narrower.
52/I	GOING TO GRANDMA'S	TMK-5 or 6. Spoon darker brown, not touching.
82/II	SCHOOL BOY	TMK-5 or 6.
83	ANGEL SERENADE	TMK-5 or 6. Side-by-side comparison.
84/V	WORSHIP	TMK-5 or 6. M.I. Hummel on back of shrine.
113	HEAVENLY SONG	TMK-5 or 6. Discontinued again, Feb., 1981.
124/I	HELLO	TMK-5 or 6. Brown pants.
139	Flitting Butterfly, PLQ	TMK-5 or 6. Baby's head against frame.
143/I	BOOTS	TMK-5 or 6. ½″ smaller than some.
150/0	HAPPY DAYS	TMK-5 or 6. Old ones all solid base.
150/I	HAPPY DAYS	TMK-5 or 6. Boys scarf has red dots.
151	Madonna, MAD	TMK-5 or 6. Very similar.
153/I	AUF WIEDERSEHEN	TMK-5 or 6. Side-by-side comparison.
154/I	WAITER	TMK-5 or 6.
163	WHITSUNTIDE	TMK-5 or 6. ½″ shorter. Clock face smaller.
165	Swaying Lullaby, PLQ	TMK-5 or 6. Side-by-side comparison.
168	Standing Boy, PLQ	TMK-5 or 6. M.I. Hummel incised on back.
176/I	HAPPY BIRTHDAY	TMK-5 or 6. Cake surface bumpy, not swirled.
180	Tuneful Goodnight, PLQ	TMK-5 or 6. Side-by-side comparison.
1833	FOREST SHRINE	TMK-5 or 6. Side-by-side comparison.
196/I	TELLING HER SECRET	TMK-5 or 6.
206	Angel Cloud, HWF	TMK-5 or 6. Has 1949 incised copyright date.
218/0	BIRTHDAY SERENADE	TMK-5 or 6.
224/II	Wayside Harmony, TLP	TMK-5 or 6. Side-by-side comparison.
225/I	Just Resting, TLP	TMK-5 or 6.
231	Birthday Serenade, TLP	TMK-5 or 6.
232	Happy Days, TLP	TMK-5 or 6.
234	Birthday Serenade, TLP	TMK-5 or 6.
235	Happy Days, TLP	TMK-5 or 6.
353/0	SPRING DANCE	TMK-5 or 6.
360/A	Wall Vase, Boy & Girl, WV	TMK-5 or 6. Incised only 1958.
360/B	Wall Vase, Boy, WV	TMK-5 or 6. Incised with only 1958.
360/C	Wall Vase, Girl, WV	TMK-5 or 6. Incised with only 1958.

It will pay collectors to be especially well informed when buying old examples. Also, be sure of the reliability of the source, as there is always the remote possibility that the marks on some reissues may have been altered in order to secure the higher price that older marks would command at an auction.

Pricing M.I. Hummel Figurines

The prices shown in the separate Current Price List are the most up-to-date available. It is published as a supplement to *Hummel Art II* for that reason. *Hummel Art II* is a complete, basic reference for Hummel collectors. The separate, Current Price List, revised annually, will furnish collectors with prices and trends in the collecting marketplace current for that year. It has the additional capabilities of being used as a perpetual inventory, an appraisal list for insurance purposes, and as a traveling companion to take along in your pocket or purse when you buy. For more information on these uses, refer to "Protecting Hummel Art: Appraising and Insuring."

Drawing #14838 courtesy Ars Sacra.

The prices shown in the Price List have been selected from a huge bank of actual market data obtained by the author from auctions, sales, dealers' lists, and advertisements. They represent more than 20,000 bits of information that have been color-coded and plotted so that the variations for any one model number, size, variation, and trademark can be analyzed. The color code permits weighting the data according to the reliability of the source from which it was received and the type of transaction.

From these distributions of data, the most representative figure for a given model/size and trademark is determined. It is a matter of judgment. It is not any one price, the highest price, the lowest, the average, or the medium. It is what appears to be the most likely price at which you could buy that particular model, size, and trademarked figurine from a knowledgeable and reliable dealer. It represents the fair market value and a realistic insurable value for which a replacement could be obtained in case of loss or breakage.

Drawing #5617 courtesy Ars Sacra.

While the figure on the Price List is shown as an actual dollar value, in practice it is a position in the actual range of prices that could be encountered. The low end of the implied range in each dollar figure may be as low as 50 percent below the printed guide price and go up to as high as 25 percent more than that figure. This is mentioned to put into perspective two frequent occurrences. If a collection is liquidated, it would be unrealistic to expect to receive the prices shown in the guide. Liquidations involve expenses, commissions, advertising, and a reasonable profit for the agent. If you sell or liquidate a lot by yourself, the expenses may not be as high, but you will likely have a great deal more personal time involved and still not have as big a net return. The 25 percent premium over the published price seems like a reasonable ceiling to the implied range and represents what sometimes is paid by a buyer for a popular piece in order to get it at once without any wait, delay, effort, or expense.

The prices in the Price List are for the "normal" or "standard" designs, sizes, and trademarks. Because of the great number of variations from the norm, it is essential that guide prices be adjusted as indicated in the section of Hummel Art II entitled, "Photographs, History, and Production Records of the Collection," starting on page 34. Anyone contemplating appraising, selling, or buying Hummel

Drawing #5771 courtesy Ars Sacra.

Angel kneeling in prayer, marked HE 1/0, TMK-2, 3½" high, is a Goebel, not Hummel figurine. Note resemblance to angel on left in Angelic Song, Hum. 144, pictured below.

Angelic Song, Hum. 144, is a genuine M.I. Hummel with incised facsimile signature on back. Dous Collection.

Infant of Krumbad, Hum. 78/III, TMK-3, 5½" high, showing incised facsimile signature of M.I. Hummel as it appears on genuine Hummel figurines.

figurines would be doing themselves a disservice by not applying the information contained in that important section when arriving at a fair and proper price. Exceptions to the guide prices in the Price List abound.

The Price List has question marks (?) and dashes (—) in some columns which indicate the uncertainty or improbability of a motif existing in that mode. On the other hand, the history of the motif in *Hummel Art II* will usually indicate a certain broad price range to use in the eventuality of its being found (such as "low four-digit figures"). There are no allowances in the guide prices for variations of sizes. Some differences above or below those shown deserve a premium which may vary depending on the model and the amount. Some general comments are contained in *Hummel Art II* on premiums for size variation. For those many models that are known to exist in two different styles, sometimes with the same trademark, the case histories will give further pointers as to whether or not such variances are included in the Current Price List.

An important consideration in pricing M.I. Hummel figurines is to refrain from reading too much into slight differences in decoration or placement. A true variation should be an easily recognized deviation from what might be termed the "standard" for that Hummel number. A few auctioneers and collectors tend to place overemphasis on details that are minor in nature and do not merit a premium from the published price. On the other hand there are some buyers who overemphasize minute deficiencies or differences in order to downgrade a given example.

Most important of all is to use the guide price as the starting point in considering a number of variables which could cause the piece to deviate from the published price — much more or much less. Such factors as those mentioned above plus the place of sale, the time of sale (boom times vs. depressed economic conditions), the effect of reissues, and the number of interested buyers. (At an auction there have to be at least two buyers who want the figurine enough to pay the Price List guide price.) Hopefully, there will be several present who have been waiting for months on end to find just such an example and have come prepared to pay 50 or 100 percent more than expected — or, even better — don't consider price an obstacle. If you have a copy of *Hummel Art I* it will pay to reread the article, "Price Guides Can Help," on page 33.

Goebel — Not Hummel Figurines

About one out of every three letters from readers expresses concern that they have been unable to identify a "Hummel" they own because it was not included in *Hummel Art I*. This recent letter, which is typical, reads: "Dear Mr. Hotchkiss, Your book 'HUMMEL ART' is wonderful. Not only are the photos beautiful, but your organization of material makes it a joy to read, and easy to look up data. I am writing because one of the Hummels I have is not listed in your book. This is a small angel with the Full Bee trademark (TMK-2) in blue and is incised HE 1/0,

3½″ high. Is there some reason this Hummel was omitted from your book? Please tell us what information you have on this Hummel."

The reason the piece was not listed in the first book is because it is NOT A HUMMEL. With so many readers confused on such a small percentage of their decorative art, this section was written to accomplish two objectives. First, to restate for emphasis what has already been discussed earlier — *all authentic M.I. Hummel figurines are made by Goebel, but all Goebel products are not Hummels.* The trademarks on the bottom of items made by Goebel identify them only as the maker but give no indication as to what artist created the original art. The six Goebel trademarks shown in this book on page 18 have been used by Goebel from 1935 to the present to identify that they were made by them regardless of who created the design.

All figurines and related articles that were adapted by Goebel from the original drawings made by Sister M.I. Hummel are incised somewhere on each piece with M.J.Hummel. . If this signature is missing, the odds are better than 10,000 to 1 that the article is not a genuine M.I. Hummel. Refer to chapter, "Identifying M.I. Hummel Figurines," for more information and possible exceptions. The confusion stems from two sources. Some collectors acquired the habit of reading the Goebel trademark as "Hummel." From World War II until 1979, the Goebel trademark included a symbol made up of a bumblebee flying through the letter "V". The letter "V" stands for the German word "Verkäufs-gesellschaft," meaning distributing company. In German the word *hummel* means bumblebee; translation: "Hummel Distributing Company." In the early years, only this symbol was used. The name Goebel did not appear. Anyone purchasing a figurine with only this symbol would say it was a Hummel. In 1972, this symbol was combined with the word Goebel to minimize the confusion, and beginning in 1979, only the name Goebel appears as the trademark on M.I. Hummel articles as well as every other item of decorative art made by Goebel.

Artists commissioned by Goebel and some of Goebel's own artist/sculptors have created figures that might easily confuse many collectors (especially when the only mark on the bottom is the Full Bee, TMK-2 that practically says "Hummel Distributing Company"). To illustrate this possibility, the angel on the left is a figurine incised 144 on the back plus a Bee trademark and incised M.J.Hummel. . The one on the right is marked HE 1/0 with only a Bee trademark and a similar star design in the robe. To further bewilder a collector, some M.I. Hummels such as Hum. 214/C are too small to receive the impression of the facsimile signature clearly or at all.

The second objective of this section is to provide collectors with more information on what the marks on other Goebel products mean so they can identify and appreciate what they own. It was originally intended to list all of the other artists who created art forms for Goebel along with the corresponding code letters used with the model number on the bottom of each piece. The collectors owning decorative art made by Goebel but not M.I. Hummel would then be able to identify their property. The Goebel Collectors' Club said this was not practical as there

*Madonna in Prayer, plaque, HM-66 with TMK-1 and copyright year of 1935. HM meaning "Holy Madonna," created and sculpted by one of Goebel staff artists. Is **not** an authentic M.I. Hummel figurine.*

Nativity set, HX-257 with Goebel trademark, has each piece incised HX-257 A through H. Whittaker Collection.

Left: Friar Tuck Monk, incised M 41/B, originated by Goebel's staff sculptors in many similar forms. Right: Cloaked Angel with Lantern, incised Rob 412, from a drawing by artist Janet Robson, and adapted as a figurine by one of Goebel's sculptors. Gullo Collection.

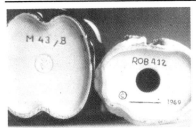

Left: Friar Tuck showing incised (and filled) number M 43 B to designate the model, and TMK-2B stamped in an incised circle. No manufacturer's name, trademark insignia or year. Right: Angel by Janet Robson, showing incised (and filled) model number ROB 412, plus copyright insignia, registered by W. Goebel in 1959 along with TMK-3, with W. Germany as the country of origin.

Beehive, incised SD-26, to indicate this was designed by one of Goebel's artist/sculptors, and not by Sister M.I. Hummel.

Walt Disney characters, designed by Walt Disney in the 1930s and adapted to figurines by Goebel sculptors. B. Phillips Collection.

were too many names involved, so what follows is a sampling of the code letters most likely to appear along with the name of the artist they represent. Perhaps the Club will be able to provide this information about all Goebel products in the future. In the meantime, puzzled collectors may be able to identify ones that are not shown here by writing to the Club. See page 241 for information on the Club and the address.

The code letters used on most Goebel decorative art indicate the artist who created the original art. Some of this art originated from artist/ sculptors who were on the Goebel Company staff. Some of the better known ones from the early days are Arthur Möller and Reinhold Unger who not only interpreted the original Sister Hummel drawings as figurines but also created many art forms from their own imagination. Later Theo Menzenbach, Gerhard Bachmann, and Gerhard Skrobek, the present master sculptor, continued to adapt the work of other artists as well as to create works of their own.

Much of the work done by the Goebel Company artist/sculptors was religiously oriented. Production pieces made from such are identified by two incised letters before the incised model number. The first letter is usually "H" which stands for the German word, *heilige,* which means holy. The second letter indicates specifically or generally which religious figure is represented. A partial list is: HM for Holy Madonna; HJ for Jesus; HE for Holy Angel; and HX for supplemental religious figures. (For example: HX is the prefix used for the camels in the various nativity sets). HX82 (A through L) is a nativity set modeled by Reinhold Unger in 1938 that collectors may mistake for Hum. 214. HX-82 may be found with a Sacrart name added by a distributor. HX 257 is another non-Hummel set.

Secular work created by Goebel's "in house" artist/sculptors are incised with many different single and double letters preceding the model number. Unfortunately, there is no way of easily associating such series with a specific sculptor's name at this time. For example, the well-known Friar Tuck series may have "S", "T", and other single letters in front of the model number even though originated by staff sculptor Theo Menzenbach. ZV indicates a series of table decorations done by Schnetter depicting birds, while FT is used on a series done by Unger in the 1930s. GF stands for a group of figurines done by an "in house" sculptor, which were further marked in an oval design "Kinderland-Handpainted." FF is not the initials of an artist but was the prefix used at one time for a series of Figurines of Fräuleins. ZT was used as a prefix on functional table decorations and XF was for miscellaneous articles. SD is another "in house" series of which SD-26 is a hive-shaped bank with several bees on the sides as contrasted to KT730/A-to-F, a six-piece Bee Orchestra. More time and research may eventually answer all of the collectors' questions about Goebel's non-Hummel products, but to sum up, no M.J.Hummel — no Hummel.

The work created for Goebel by freelance artists on a commission or license arrangement is identified on the final product by incising several letters of the artist's name before the model number. For example, the pieces based on the art of Walt Disney are identified by an incised DIS followed by the incised model number. Typical of this large group are ROB for Janet Robson, SPO for Maria Spötl, GRA for Hilda Gray, TSCH for G. Tschirnich in 1956, and ROCK for Norman Rockwell figures (1962-9). The present Co-Boy line was designed by Hans Welling and is marked WELL on the bottom. The Chimney Sweeps, often confused with the M.I. Hummel figure of the same name, were originated by Arthur Möller in the Thirties and many of them are preceded by the letters KF. For example, one well-known one is KF-38. The new Amerikids, recently designed by Harry Holt, are marked Holt on the bottom. The popular and extensive Goebel Wild Life series was created by Goebel's master sculptors, Skrobek and Bachman, and are prefixed with the letters CV in front of the model number. BYJ is incised on Goebel's line of Red Heads designed by Charlot Byj. The Blumenkinder figurines were adapted from original drawings by the well-known artist Lore, and the pieces are incised with her full name in front of the model number; i.e., Barefoot Boy is incised LORE 229 on the bottom of each example. HAHN 502 is the complete name/number of the artist who designed a series, one figure of which depicts a man and woman dancing. The word "Sacrart" appears on some non-Hummel items made by Goebel to indicate that such figures were produced in cooperation with a German publisher of religious art.

It is impractical to include a complete current price list for the hundreds of designs of non-Hummel items produced by Goebel. For collectors owning one or more of the Goebel-Not Hummel pieces who want to include them in their insurance policy, a fair replacement value would be the price they originally paid for them within the past few years, plus an allowance of perhaps 10 percent for inflation for each year since purchase. Those who have had such pieces for as long as fifteen years will find that the current replacement price is about three times what they cost in the mid-Sixties.

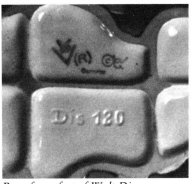

Base of one of set of Walt Disney figurines, shows incised model number prefixed by first three letters in his last name. Shows TMK-2B followed by "R" for registered, and © "WG" monogram for W. Goebel, and Germany for country of origin.

Female bust by artist G. Tschirnich; incised on back TSCH 4-B with TMK-3, © by Goebel 1956, followed by Western Germany.

Base of standing angel candleholder pictured left. Incised "Spötl, III/49," with Incised Crown, stamped Full Bee, TMK-2, stamped black Germany.

Angel candleholders designed by Maria Spötl. Seated angel marked on base with stamped Full Bee, TMK-2, Incised Crown, stamped black Germany. Fletcher Collection.

"His First Smoke" adapted by a Goebel sculptor from a similar drawing by Norman Rockwell between 1962 and 1969. Incised "ROCK" followed by model number.

4 *Artistic Derivatives of Original Hummel Art*

Hummel Dolls by Goebel

In the past three years, bits and pieces of new information have been carefully cataloged to be interwoven with previous research so that this book would contain new facts, faces, and figures. In assembling this information, it becomes quite obvious that there is still much, much more material waiting to be mined from the archives of the Goebel Company, the museum in Neustadt, the Goebel doll factory, old catalogs, the doll collection in the Hummel home in Massing, and from collectors.

While Goebel had made ceramic doll parts as early as the 1870s, as reported in *Hummel Art I,* it was not until eighty years later that the Goebel sculptors/artists, Arthur Möller and Reinhold Unger designed the first M.I. Hummel dolls adapted from Sister Hummel's drawings. The very first were produced in 1950 with a rubber head molded by Goebel and a composition body which was made by a supplier. By 1952, the entire doll was assembled from molded rubber — head, body, arms, and legs. These were painted with a flesh tone paint and dressed in authentic, handmade Bavarian costumes to match their counterparts in M.I. Hummel figurines.

A small section of an early catalog from the 1950s that is reproduced here indicates that at that time there were eight models offered in the 10″ size for about $5 in U.S. currency, and a 16½″ version available for about $10.50. The earlier half-rubber doll was still listed in the larger 13¾″ size for about $9. Another early doll not previously recorded was patterned after Hear Ye, Hear Ye!, Hum. 15 figurine, but had "Nacht Wachter, Original M.I. Hummel" listed on the triangular green name tag and was incised on the back of the head with TMK-2 (Full Bee) with model number 1719. This was sent in by a reader from Baltimore, Maryland.

Unfortunately, these dolls were "adorable but not durable" to quote from an article in the Goebel Collectors' Club *Insights,* vol. 4, no. 1. In some cases, the rubber not only deteriorated but almost disintegrated so that arms, legs, and faces creased and cracked due to some chemical inbalance in the rubber compound or an interaction between the paint and rubber. Some dolls from this period have survived in fine condition to this day, while a companion piece purchased at the same time may be completely deformed and collapsed.

Surviving examples in near perfect condition should be treated with tender loving care. While there is no assurance that a now satisfactory example will not suffer the same fate, its stability will be improved by keeping it in a cool, dry place and, especially, by protecting it from

Early china half-figure made by Goebel for pincushion. From the collection of Eleanor Lar Rieu. Courtesy of Frieda Marion.

Hummeldolls rubber, closed (can be undressed and dressed, head and arms movable):			
	Size 26 cm	42 cm rubber ′	42 cm half rubber
	DM 20.—	42.—	35.—
Nr. 1: GRETL, girl with basket und flowers			
Nr. 2: SEPPL, boy with shorts and Bavarian hat			
Nr. 3: BERTL, girl with basket			
Nr. 4: HANSL, boy with stick and shorts and red head-cloth			
Nr. 5: LIESL, knitting girl			
Nr. 6: MAX, long trousers with stick, without hat			
Nr. 7: Strolling along, Little wanderer like figurine Nr. 05			
Nr. 8: Chimney-sweep			

Reprint from Goebel catalog, c. 1952, listing M.I. Hummel all rubber and half rubber dolls. The U.S. price of the dolls is about one-fourth of the prices shown. The heights of the dolls were 10½″, 16½″, and 13¾.

Opposite page: Reproduction of Sister Hummel drawing printed, published, and copyrighted in the U.S. in 1943 by Ars Sacra, Herbert Dubler, Inc., New York. Print is titled, "Want Some?" Cataloged as #5196 and currently available from Ars Sacra. Was adapted by Goebel for figurine, Not for You, Hum. 317. Williams Collection.

A page from a 1963 Goebel catalog illustrating vinyl dolls produced at that time.

Current M.I. Hummel dolls produced by Goebel. All are 10¼" high.

bright sunlight. Several doll hospitals consider these damaged rubber dolls as irreparable basket cases, but not one very dedicated collector. Her sentimental attachment to Gretl inspired her to restore it as a display-worthy companion for her perfect rubber Hansl twin doll. She did this by first disassembling the parts and stuffing them with wet sawdust used on some types of dolls. The next day she removed all the damp stuffing and replaced it with dry material. This procedure removed all the creases. After doing the same to the head and arms, she reassembled the parts and then wrote the author to ask what to do to fill in the cracks in the paint coating. The suggestion was made to use the new elastic glazing compound or the silicone rubber used to caulk around bathtubs, and, after that, to touch up the piece with matching rubber-based paint. Following the suggestion, this innovative collector succeeded in restoring her Gretl doll which had been believed to be beyond salvage.

After this unhappy experience with rubber, Goebel developed an all vinyl plastic doll with naturally luminous flesh tones so that only detail decorating was necessary. These dolls, first produced about 1963, if subjected to normal use, are still found in excellent condition. A catalog dated 1963 and reproduced on page 188 shows that the line has been expanded from the original eight to a total of nineteen different models, all of which were numbered in the 1700 series. These were identified as the rubber ones were, with M.J.Hummel incised and filled in with white on the nape of the neck, along with the model number and TMK-3 (Stylized Bee) mark. The body was also trademarked, and each doll had a triangular fiber tag hung on the arm which also bore the trademark and incised facsimile signature.

From the mid-Sixties on, the history of Hummel dolls becomes blurred in regard to what was retained, added, or deleted in the line. The records in the U.S. Copyright Office indicate that at least two or more designs were copyrighted on February 2, 1967, as model numbers 1802 and 1803, rather than in the 1700 series. They were respectively described as Boy with Wicker Basket on His Back and Girl with a Broom. During the 1960s the dolls were dressed in Bavarian costumes patterned after specific M.I. Hummel figurines. However, with few exceptions they were given only a boy's name or a girl's name and not the occupational or situation name of the corresponding figurine. For example, Felix, Hum. 1708 is costumed similarly to Hum. 12, the Chimney Sweep figurine, except for the broad-brimmed hat. Other versions of this doll have been seen wearing the comparable skullcap of the figurine. The dolls, Wanderbub, Hum. 1707 and Puppenmütterchen, Hum. 1725, have situation names similar to the figurines.

By 1976 Goebel no longer distributed dolls through their authorized distributors and dealers in the United States. Another importer, Reeves International, Inc., of 1107 Broadway, New York City 10010, did have Hansl, Gretl, Tinder Boy, Travelling Boy, Goose Girl, and Alpine Boy available through their own dealers, a few of whom are listed under "Sources." These retailed at that time for around $30 to $40. A small number of Hummel figurine dealers imported their own dolls directly from Germany. Some dealers are still doing this, so there is a price differential among dealers that may be worth exploring.

The 1976 line consisted of six 10″ dolls and six 8″ dolls. When the 8″ dolls were added is not known. The catalog numbers used for both the 8″ and the 10″ sizes were different than the ones used before. The new 8″ dolls are Vroni, Rudi, Seppl, Mariandl, Jacki, and Rosl. In 1980, there were three more 10″ dolls, but none of the 8″ size remained in the line. By this time, Goebel was once more distributing dolls through its own distributors and authorized M.I. Hummel dealers. The list price for the dolls ranged from $70 to $75, a price approaching the secondary market price of old dolls. Some dealers importing dolls sold them for less than this. The nine dolls in 1980 were Hansl, Gretl, Wanderbub, Gänseliesl, Strickliesl, Radi-Bub, Rosl, Peterle, and Felix.

The secondary market in previously owned M.I. Hummel dolls is small in comparison to the activity in older M.I. Hummel figurines. In fact there is so little action that the prices are flexible and fluctuate within broad limits. Some dealers occasionally have one of the rubber dolls of the 1950s in fine condition for $150 to $200. The later vinyl dolls are not traded enough to have very exact prices but are usually available from $50 to $100 depending on the size and model. The 10″ size is represented by these prices. Many of these are the ones that were selling in the Seventies for about $30.

Goebel M.I. Hummel Calendars

Do you have a Mercedes appetite, a Volkswagen income, and a love of Hummels? Maybe your yen could be satisfied by collecting the M.I. Hummel calendars published by Goebel every year since 1951. Each one has thirteen color photographs of different figurines suitable for framing. The price per picture for the current year is only about $.30 each. Many of these have special appeal because of the beautiful settings and scenery such as created for Telling Her Secret, Hum. 196, used for the month of January in the 1980 edition. The individual pictures are about 7″ by 9″ and can also be used to set off the matching figurine, bell, or plate in a shadow box.

The older editions from the 1950s and the 1960s are collectors' items in themselves. In the first edition of this book, the illustrations did not include those for the first two years and 1955. Now, through the courtesy of Robert L. Miller, of Eaton, Ohio, the German editions for 1951, 1952, and the English edition for 1955 can be shown. The U.S. editions originated in 1952 using the 1951 German calendar pictures and continued to lag by one year until the 1975 German edition showed the Annual Plate for that year. The U.S. edition had to use the next year's plate in 1976. They then resumed as before, the German edition pictures being used for the U.S. calendar for the following year — like shooting two birds with one picture.

The prices of the older calendars vary drastically, ranging as high as $100 for the very first issues in mint condition down to about $60 for the later 1950s editions. Early 1960s start at about $60, diminishing to $30 at the end of the decade. The 1970 calendars bring prices as high as $50 for the 1970 issue to $5 or $6 for the last few years. These general prices are an extreme over-simplification, as some years are much preferred because of high artistic merit. Other years are out of line because more collectors want them than there are copies readily available. Flea market

M.I. Hummel calendar series originated with publication of the German edition for the year 1951. First English version was printed for the year 1952. Miller Collection.

Second German edition of M.I. Hummel calendar for 1952. Miller Collection.

English, 1954, Heavenly Protection. (Called Guardian Angel in 1950.)

"HUMMEL"-CALENDAR 1955

Fourth English edition of M.I. Hummel calendar for the year 1955. Miller Collection.

shoppers, country auction buffs, or garage sale browsers should buy at a fraction of these prices when one or two odd issues appear.

The Goebel calendars illustrate M.I. Hummel figurines only. For calendars that illustrate a great variety of her original drawings, refer to the section on graphic Hummel art for more details on calendars produced by Ars Sacra and Emil Fink that are faithful reproductions of her original drawings. These also make interesting backgrounds for displaying figurines. If one of the older calendars cannot be located, both of these publishers have wall-sized prints for sale which can be used for the same purpose.

English, 1956, Candlelight.

English, 1957, School Girls.

English, 1959, Meditation.

English, 1960, Stormy Weather.

English, 1961, BookWorm.

English, 1962, Flower Madonna.

190

English, 1963, Telling Her Secret.

English, 1964, Serenade.

English, 1965, Goose Girl.

English 1966, Spring Dance.

English, 1967, School Girls.

English, 1968, Duet.

English, 1969, Mail Is Here.

English, 1970, Ring Around the Rosie.

English, 1971, To Market.

»HUMMEL«-CALENDAR 1972

English, 1972, Stormy Weather (close-up).

»HUMMEL«-FIGURINES-CALENDAR 1973

English, 1973, Adventure Bound.

»HUMMEL«-FIGURINES-CALENDAR 1974

English, 1974, Umbrella Boy.

»HUMMEL«-FIGURINES - CALENDAR 1975

English, 1975, Happy Days.

M.J. Hummel Figurines-Calendar 1976

English, 1976, Apple Tree Girl.

M.J. Hummel Figuren-Kalender 1977

German, 1977, Follow the Leader.

M.J. Hummel Figurines-Calendar 1978

English, 1978, Follow the Leader.

M.J. Hummel Figurines Calendar 1980

English, 1980, Smart Little Sister.

M.J. Hummel Figurines-Calendar 1981

English, 1981, School Girl.

Berta Hummel Art
by Schmid Bros., Inc.

Lovable, serene, innocent are adjectives frequently used by collectors to describe Hummel art. The person responsible for introducing the magic appeal of this art into the United States was a young man who saw some figurines at a fair in Germany in 1935. The man was John G. Schmid, son of Paul Schmid, who was the founder of the present Schmid Brothers, Incorporated. He recalls: "I remember turning down the figurines the first time I saw them but something kept pulling me back to them. I placed an order for one dozen of the six I saw. My father was horrified. He thought we would never sell seventy-two figurines. After all, it was the middle of the Depression." The retail price at that time averaged about two dollars each. In a recent letter to the author, Schmid, who is now retired, said: "Originally we bought the Hummel Madonna, the Good Shepherd, and several others that were religiously oriented, but then we bought the children."

For a number of years Schmid Brothers, Inc. were the exclusive importer of M.I. Hummel figurines into this country, except for a man by the name of Matthew Smith in the West who bought some later. When Ebling & Reuss, who were importers of other products made by Goebel, saw the increasing success of Hummel figurines, they requested and were granted a second distributorship. About 1968 Goebel terminated their relationship with Schmid Brothers as a distributor and set up their own subsidiary called Hummelwerk, the successor corporation of the original Herbert Dubler, Incorporated, of New York (see for more details). This separation initiated legal action that is reported to have resulted in a substantial settlement to Schmid Brothers, Inc.

In 1968, Schmid imported a wide range of Hummel articles using lithographs of Sister Hummel's original drawings for decoration. These were obtained from the publishers of her work in Germany. In 1971 they issued the first of a limited edition series of Christmas plates with a transfer of a Sister Hummel drawing called "Angel with Candle." Goebel also inaugurated the first of a series of annual plates that same year with a bas-relief design taken from the same Sister Hummel original which they named Heavenly Angel, the same as the figurine, Hum. 21, which they produced.

This simultaneous introduction of two plates done from identical original art precipitated several lawsuits that finally ended with the German Supreme Court ruling that Viktoria Hummel, Berta's surviving mother, was entitled to the reproduction rights of all of Berta Hummel's creative work executed before she entered the Franciscan Order in Seissen in 1931. The convent retained the reproduction rights to her works done as a Franciscan nun until her death in 1946. (This ruling was made on February 22, 1974, as recorded in the publication NJW, 1974, pages 904-907.)

Schmid refers to the products they are licensed by Mrs. Viktoria Hummel to make as "Sister Berta Hummel items" as compared to the license Goebel has from the convent to use the art of Sister Maria

At the Hummel family home in Massing, West Germany, Mrs. Viktoria Hummel, the artist's mother, reminisces with Paul Schmid III, president of Schmid Bros., Inc., as they share one of Berta Hummel's scrapbooks.

Heavenly Angel, Hum. 264, First Annual Plate by Goebel. Bas-relief design features bright, hand-painted colors.

Angel with Candle, 1971 Christmas Plate by Schmid Bros., Inc., has transfer-printed design in soft, muted colors similar to original drawing.

PAST ISSUES

Schmid Christmas Plate Series Depicting the Authentic Art of Sister Berta Hummel

1971 "Angel with Candle"
©Schmid Bros., Inc. 1970

1972 "Angel with Flute"
©Schmid Bros., Inc. 1971

1973 "Nativity"
©Schmid Bros., Inc. 1972

1974 "The Guardian Angel"
©Schmid Bros., Inc. 1973

1975 "Christmas Child"
©Schmid Bros., Inc. 1974

1976 "Sacred Journey"
©Schmid Bros., Inc. 1975

1977 "Herald Angel"
©Schmid Bros., Inc. 1976

1978 "Heavenly Trio"
©Schmid Bros., Inc. 1977

1979 "Starlight Angel"
©Schmid Bros., Inc. 1978

1980 "Parade into Toyland"
© Schmid Bros., Inc. 1979

Schmid Mother's Day Plate Series Depicting the Authentic Art of Sister Berta Hummel

1972 "Playing Hookey"
©Schmid Bros., Inc. 1971

1973 "The Little Fisherman"
©Schmid Bros., Inc. 1972

1974 "The Bumblebee"
©Schmid Bros., Inc. 1973

1975 "Message of Love"
©Schmid Bros., Inc. 1974

1976 "Devotion for Mothers"
©Schmid Bros., Inc. 1975

1977 "Moonlight Return"
©Schmid Bros., Inc. 1976

1978 "Afternoon Stroll"
©Schmid Bros., Inc. 1977

1979 "Cherub's Gift"
©Schmid Bros., Inc. 1978

1980 "Mother's Little Helper"
© Schmid Bros., Inc. 1979

1981 "Playtime"
© Schmid Bros., Inc. 1980

Schmid Christmas Bell Series Depicting the Authentic Art of Sister Berta Hummel

1972 "Angel with Flute"
©Schmid Bros., Inc. 1971

1973 "Nativity"
©Schmid Bros., Inc. 1972

1974 "The Guardian Angel"
©Schmid Bros., Inc. 1973

1975 "Christmas Child"
©Schmid Bros., Inc. 1974

1976 "Sacred Journey"
©Schmid Bros., Inc. 1975

1977 "Herald Angel"
©Schmid Bros., Inc. 1976

1978 "Heavenly Trio"
©Schmid Bros., Inc. 1977

1979 "Starlight Angel"
©Schmid Bros., Inc. 1978

1980 Parade into Toyland
© Schmid Bros., Inc. 1979

Schmid Mother's Day Bell Series Depicting the Authentic Art of Sister Berta Hummel

1976 "Devotion for Mothers"
©Schmid Bros., Inc. 1975

1977 "Moonlight Return"
©Schmid Bros., Inc. 1976

1978 "Afternoon Stroll"
©Schmid Bros., Inc. 1977

1979 "Cherub's Gift"
©Schmid Bros., Inc. 1978

1980 "Mother's Little Helper"
© Schmid Bros., Inc. 1979

177294

1981 "Playtime"
© Schmid Bros., Inc. 1980

1981 "Christmas Bell"
© Schmid Bros., Inc. 1980

Innocentia Hummel work for M.I. Hummel figurines and related articles. The M.J.Hummel facsimile signature has been registered for the exclusive use on Goebel products adapted from her work.

Schmid has continued issuing Christmas plates since the first issue in 1971. A year later in 1972, Schmid introduced their first edition of a Berta Hummel Mother's Day Plate called "Playing Hookey." The best known of this series is the 1977 plate, "Moonlight Return," which is the same as the M.I. Hummel figurine, Hum. 386, On Secret Path. The story behind this design is told in detail with the history of the figurine on page 160. Schmid issues each year, in addition to these two limited editions, related items with the same motif such as children's cups, Christmas tree ornaments, candles, and bells, each with the current year date on them. All of these are lithographic reproductions of Berta Hummel's work before she entered the convent. Also worth the attention of collectors are single or short series editions such as the Tranquility plates accented in twenty-four karat gold in an edition of 15,000 and issued at $250 each. A faceted French crystal paperweight having a bas-relief sulphide bust of Sister Hummel on a blue background was another limited edition issued at $150 in 1978.

Schmid Bros. annual Christmas plate, 1981, "A Time to Remember."

Acclaimed by many as one of Schmid's most important contributions is the recent organization of a traveling exhibit consisting of forty examples of young Berta's art known as "The Formation of an Artist: The Early Works of Berta Hummel." This exhibit premiered at the University of Notre Dame on July 10, 1980. The U.S. tour terminates at Virginia Polytechnic Institute on April 25, 1982. The remaining locations and dates of the exhibit are listed later in this book. A color catalog of the exhibit illustrating each of the forty works contains a description and critical assessment of each one. The accompanying essay by the renowned art connoisseur and author, Dr. James S. Plaut, will also be of major interest to Hummel collectors. The catalogs are available at the exhibits and in stores in soft cover version for $5 and hardbound for $27.50. Each one is a treasure of information about the art of Berta Hummel.

Limited Edition Plate, "Tranquility," by Schmid Bros., Inc., hand-painted on fine porcelain, with issue price of $250.

Concurrent with the exhibit, Schmid Brothers issued two limited edition lithographs. One edition of only 525 copies is the self-portrait of Berta Hummel made from the original in the exhibit and priced at $125. The second lithograph edition is one of 900 of the original drawing called *Moonlight Return* (see picture of 1977 Mother's Day Plate), at the issue price of $150. This work was inspired by an episode in her brother Adolf's life and has also been issued by Goebel as a figurine, On Secret Path, Hum. 386. Adolf has personally autographed each print in the edition.

In past years Schmid has produced numerous other decorative art items using lithographs or decalcomania transfers made directly from original Hummel drawings. Several series of small plaques have been produced as open editions, of which some are now closed. Other items have been musical key chains, regular music boxes, musical jewel boxes, and a wide range of motifs on candles, some of which are dated and some

Schmid Bros., Inc., Berta Hummel Limited Editions for 1976. Bell matches motif of Christmas Plate for that year.

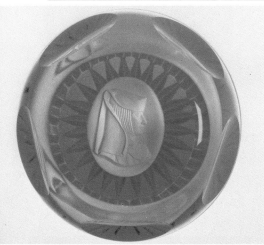

Visage French sulphide paperweight, sequentially numbered 1-400. Pictured with box autographed by Adolph, Berta Hummel's brother. Issued by Schmid Bros., Inc., at $150.

Hummel keychain music boxes, each playing a different tune, by Schmid Bros., Inc.

Hummel trinket boxes offered by Schmid Bros., Inc., with a choice of six different Hummel drawings.

set in musical candleholders. These have a wide appeal to a segment of Hummel collectors as evidenced by the increasing competition for them when they surface in the secondary market.

One reason for the increased interest is their potential to make any Hummel collection not only more interesting but also more artistic. Candles can be effectively displayed, especially during the holiday season, with suitable paintings, prints, figurines, tree ornaments, or nativity sets that are also derivatives of Berta Hummel's creativity.

One unusual collectible consisting of a complete coffee service for four was recently acquired by Heidi Poag. This was made in Germany and distributed in this country by Schmid for several years in the early Seventies. Such a set can be used effectively by itself or in combination with some other form of Hummel art. This is suggested in the accompanying photograph of the coffee service with the figurine, Run-a-Way, Hum. 327, standing next to a matching plate. A similar arrangement would make quite a conversation piece for any gathering of dedicated Hummel enthusiasts.

Prices of many Berta Hummel editions by Schmid Bros., Inc., may be found in *Plate Collector* magazine once a month. The secondary market for other articles is rapidly developing. For the present, the approximate list price of the novelty items should be used. For the decorative art, an increase over purchase price of from 10 to 15 percent per year would be realistic for insurance purposes.

Heart-shaped musical jewelry boxes, satin-lined, with Berta Hummel motifs on lids, by Schmid Bros., Inc.

Photographs: Schmid Bros., Inc.

Oval boxes featuring decoupaged Berta Hummel drawings, by Schmid Bros., Inc.

060-003
6 Assorted 6¾" H.
2-3/8" Dia.

060-005
4 Assorted 15" H.
2-3/4" Dia.

060-004
6 Assorted 5¾" H.
2-7/8" Dia.

647-131
Candleholder 3 5/8" Dia.
060-004 Candle 5¾" H.

Three sizes of candles decorated with Berta Hummel drawings. Candleholder is available for smallest size. All by Schmid Bros., Inc.

391-349
Musical Candleholder tune "Speak Softly" 3½" Dia.
060-002 Candle 6½" H.

060-002
12 Assorted 6½" H.
1-7/8" Dia.

647-130
Candleholder 3¾" Dia.
060-002 Candle 6½" H.

060-001
12 Assorted 4½" H.
1-7/8" Dia.

391-348
Musical Candleholder tune "Edelweiss" 3½" Dia.
060-001 Candle 4½" H.

©Schmid Bros. 1973

Candles decorated with Berta Hummel art and three types of candleholders (one musical) by Schmid Bros., Inc.

Coffee service for four, made in Germany and distributed by Schmid Bros., Inc., is decorated with transfer-printed Berta Hummel drawings. Figurine, The Run-a-Way, Hum. 327, is posed next to matching plate. Heidi Poage Collection.

Photographs: Schmid Bros., Inc.

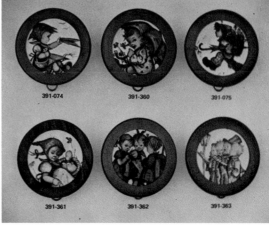

391-074   391-360   391-075

391-361   391-362   391-363

Part of the series of Sister Berta Hummel plaques from Schmid Bros., Inc.

Graphic Hummel Art by Ars Sacra and Emil Fink

In 1931, when the artistic talent of Berta Hummel was ripe for world recognition, the world was suffering in the throes of the worst depression of the twentieth century. It seems remarkable that such an inauspicious time for any artist could actually prove to be a very promising one for Berta Hummel.

It seems even more amazing that her work would gain worldwide recognition, especially since Berta, an acclaimed master pupil at the Fine Arts Academy in Munich, chose to enter a secluded Franciscan convent in Siessen immediately after graduation. But, paradoxically, although the artist, herself, renounced the world in assuming her vows, her art was never destined to be restrained behind convent walls. For even in the tranquility of the mother house, the great gift of Sister Maria Innocentia was perceived and given every encouragement.

Berta Hummel had an abundance of ability. Even as a child, no scrap of paper, no blackboard at school, not even her father's business papers were safe from her sketching. She had a magic pencil and brush tuned with the necessary creative insight to capture the essence of fun, frolic, awe, or fear in the everyday life of little children.

Even a depressed economy did not interfere with the first publication of Berta Hummel's paintings and drawings. New findings, published here for the first time of the close relationship between Ars Sacra and Berta Hummel, reveal how simply it all started.

At the beginning of March, 1933, the publishing company of Ars Sacra received a brief note from the convent at Siessen saying, "Enclosed please find three proof-sheets of the newest sketches of our young artist B. Hummel. We beg to inquire whether and under what conditions an edition of devout pictures in black, and later on in color, would be possible."

This contact sparked Ars Sacra's interest. They immediately recognized that the pictures sent had "very estimable qualities" and "would certainly appeal to the public and would soon be popular." This spark subsequently led to the creation of three separate contracts, with varying rights, between Ars Sacra and Berta Hummel and her convent over the ensuing years.

The relationship between Ars Sacra and Berta Hummel was one of mutual confidence. Ars Sacra pledged "to promote the original work of the artist on a large scale," while Berta sent a steady stream of original drawings. Letters that traveled between the convent and the publishing house numbered almost fifty in one year's time.

A special friendship developed between Berta and Mrs. Maximilianne Müller, co-founder of the publishing company Ars Sacra, Joseph Müller, who sent letters of inspiration and suggestions of new themes to the artist. Sometimes, upon receiving such a letter, Berta would promptly

Earliest published Hummel children. First printed by Ars Sacra in February, 1934, as postcards in rotogravure. First drawing published was one of the Sacred Heart of Jesus as a small print in October, 1933, by four-color letterpress.

A sampling of the several hundred different postcards that have been produced directly from Hummel original drawings owned by Ars Sacra.

go to her easel and sketch the desired subject. When Mrs. Müller suggested that she draw a "little sweep," she was told the next day that the "little sweep" was already on the easel in the form of a charcoal drawing.

At Mrs. Müller's invitation, Berta made several trips to the publishing company in Munich and also frequented the Art Academy which was just up the road from Ars Sacra. These meetings were spent discussing originals for approval and means to enhance reproduction and colors of other works.

One such suggestion on the part of Ars Sacra was to urge Berta to do her pictures uniformly, in a smaller size. Berta, however, had her own reasons for doing large-scale drawings and simply explained to Ars Sacra, "I have done some funny things but in a large size because I can set about it better this way."

By 1934, Emil Fink, Berta's second publisher, had the foresight to copyright selected drawings of Berta's convent work. He combined Berta's sketches with Margarete Seemann's poems into a volume entitled *The Hummel Book.* Soon after the publication of the book and after taking her final religious vows, Sister Hummel resumed studies at the Art Academy to expand her artistic training.

Weakened by the first signs of the disease, tuberculosis, Sister Hummel returned to the convent in 1936 to recover from her illness. Frequent correspondence from Ars Sacra informed her of the great approval her work was receiving. One such letter read, "We have received a great number of favorable reviews" (in newspapers and periodicals).

Another letter brought word to Sister Hummel that Ars Sacra was in need of more original drawings, for there was now a strong demand for Hummel art. She found herself with too much to do, and very little time to do it in. She was caught between the limitations of her illness and the demands for her religious art for the convent and her drawings of the children for Ars Sacra. The nun humbly replied to Ars Sacra saying, "Frankly, I am pleased with your request and I should like to start at once, if only I had the time." Another evidence of mounting pressure is noticeable in the rare letter written by Sister Hummel on October 18, 1939, reproduced here.

Drawing #14674 courtesy Ars Sacra.

Drawing #5616 courtesy Ars Sacra.

Drawing #5547 courtesy Ars Sacra.

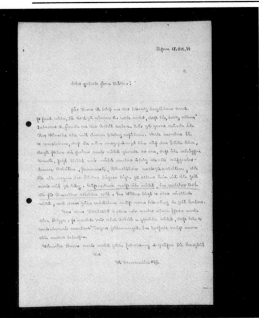

A copy of one of the very few letters hand-written by Sister Hummel to her publisher. Usually all correspondence was taken care of by another member of the Siessen Community.

Insignia used by Ars Sacra on their reproductions of Hummel drawings.

International copyright insignia to identify products with registered copyrights.

Insignia used by Verlag Emil Fink on their reproductions of Hummel drawings.

Siessen, October 18th, 1939

Dear Mrs. Müller,

I have been most grateful for your kind letter from Switzerland. I am glad to know that you are there and, which is even more, that you have found interest and joy in your work after all. I wish with all my heart I could fulfill your desires all at once. But you will understand, however, that I am exhausted now after having finished the book; in addition to this I could not gather so much fresh strength during the holidays. Now there is nothing left to do but make up for the work, liturgical garments, altar-paintings, which I put off because of the book. On top of that, time goes by too quickly. Moreover, I don't know what kind of work I shall do for America. So, I am really not wanting in determination; if one wants to create something good, one needs to have vigour and time.

We have neither got a sketch nor a photograph of the frontispiece. There was plenty of work to do about it, and, for the lack of time, I don't believe I would be able to do it again. In case of need one has to manage otherwise.

I really wish that you may enjoy your time of recovery and remain very truly

Yours

M. Innocentia
O.S. Fr.

Prior to the impending war, Ars Sacra published a very fine book entitled, *Hui, die Hummel* ("Oh! the Hummel"), an edition which gave a full survey of the work of the artist. But due to Hitler's warped view of religion and Ars Sacra's religious programs, the book was subsequently banned in Germany. It was since republished in 1972 by Ars Sacra in English and is now titled *The Hummel.*

Meanwhile, the menacing clouds of the Nazi regime and the years of the Second World War were to loom over the work of Sister Hummel. The publishing house of Ars Sacra (or Sacred Art) was considered a thorn in the side of Hitler. They were forced to freeze the publication of Hummel art in Germany, as only enough paper for the export market was allocated to them with which to earn export credits. The Nazis also viciously attacked the art of Sister Hummel in newspaper columns and reviews all over the country.

Although the printing of Hummel pictures in Germany was banned for a time, Ars Sacra continued to give orders to the artist to proceed with her drawings. For, as Mrs. Müller explained, "In these sad times, one has a longing for the gay Hummel cards which can even bring a smile to a depressed person." Sister Hummel vowed to continue doing her very best for Ars Sacra. However, it was not long before she had to abandon her promises to them. During the terrible war year of 1944, her illness steadily worsened until, in November of 1946, the patient, the Sister, and the artist gave back her soul to God.

The Ars Sacra publishing plant was bombed during the war with the loss of some original Hummel drawings. Also the company could not meet the demand for Hummel art during the first period after the war because the military government did not lift the publishing ban on religious materials until 1948.

From then on Ars Sacra has continued to publish and promote the artist's work. Ars Sacra now administers the artistic heritage of Sister Hummel through postcards, note cards, posters, small pictures of saints, books, and calendars. There are perhaps one thousand drawings by Sister Hummel of which five hundred may be of broad interest to the public. Ars Sacra has rights to more than three-hundred fifty of "her best work up to the end of her creativity."

The convent, although it was often bare of Sister Hummel's originals, has assembled about fifty to one hundred of her drawings in a new museum. Some of her drawings are owned by individual collectors. Her work done prior to entering the convent is still with her family, with all rights reserved to Schmid Bros., Inc., the original importer of Hummel figurines to the United States.

Direct copy of original Sister Hummel drawing published by Ars Sacra as #5619. Courtesy Ars Sacra.

Until recently the distribution of Hummel prints, pictures, cards, and calendars has not been widespread in the United States. Basic changes are now in progress at Ars Sacra that will expand the distribution of Hummel art in this country. Currently their products are available through Jacques Nauer, a great-grandson of Josef Müller, the founder of Verlag Ars Sacra in 1896. Nauer is presently in charge of franchising and licensing the distribution of Ars Sacra Hummel art in the United States. His brother, Marcel Nauer, is in charge of the company in Munich.

Within a few years, not only will the two-dimensional reproductions be more readily available but, according to reliable sources, it seems likely that Ars Sacra's complete collection of original drawings will be on permanent display for the public in a new art museum which will probably be located somewhere in the Midwest.

M.I. Hummel figurine made from the sculpture created by Gerhard Skrobek in 1957. Issued by Goebel as Ring Around the Rosie, Hum. 348.

There appears to be little doubt that in the next five to ten years more and more collectors will acquire prints as part of their Hummel art collections. This will give figurine collectors the opportunity to compare Sister Hummel's original drawings to the three-dimensional figurines. In some cases, the similarity is striking; in others the two-dimensional art contains something that had to be sacrificed for practical reproduction into three-dimensional figures.

Most of the Ars Sacra prints from Hummel originals are available in all formats such as fine arts postcards, small Hummel pictures in the 2¾″ by 4¼″ size, and the larger Hummel wall pictures with sheet sizes of 7¾″ by 11¾″ and 9¾″ by 14¼″. The postcards cost around $.50 and the small pictures are sold by the hundred for about $10. The wall picture prices depend on the size of the work, with the largest costing about $20 to $25 unmounted and unframed, and up to $50 to $100 mounted and framed. *The Hummel* book in English costs about $15.

Direct copy of original Sister Hummel drawing published by Ars Sacra as #5233. Courtesy Ars Sacra.

M.I. Hummel figurine made from sculpture created by Goebel artist and issued as For Father, Hum. 87.

Emil Fink postcard, #651, inspiration for Skrobek-designed Hum. 380, Daisies Don't Tell. Courtesy Emil Fink.

Greeting cards on paper and silk range from $.80 to $1.25. The first annual limited edition wall hanging shown here sells for $35 and can be obtained from Hingham Collectables. (See "Services.")

Further information may be found by writing to the Verlag Ars Sacra U.S. address which is included in "Services" in the back of this book. Emil Fink, who was mentioned earlier as the publisher of another book of Sister Hummel's drawings in color with poems by the late Margarete Seemann, also produces other two-dimensional Hummel art. They publish fine arts postcards and various-sized prints and lithographs but from a smaller library of less than one hundred drawings to which they have the publication rights. Many of the subjects in the drawings are produced in the full figure, but some are cropped or reduced to produce a close-up image of the face or point of interest. One report indicates that Verlag Emil Fink became involved in publishing Hummel originals because a daughter in the Fink family attended the Munich Art Academy at the same time as Berta Hummel. It was believed to be through this friendship that they acquired at least some, if not all, of the works that they publish.

While their products are available in this country, it is on a limited basis. Mr. Richard Scheible, presently in charge of this company, gave us the name of one distributor, Marcel Schurman Company, but Schurman did not have a list of the items they distributed or names of the retail outlets where they could be obtained available for this author. Apparently the most popular item is their book, *The Hummel Book,* with fifty-two Hummel pictures in monochrome and polychrome and poems by Margarete Seemann. The first English edition of this was published in 1950 and it has been in print ever since. Not mentioned before is a postcard calendar they publish each year similar to that issued by Ars Sacra. The prices for their products are comparable to those mentioned previously for Ars Sacra.

Most of the work published by Ars Sacra and Emil Fink can be identified by the different insignia used by each company. These two insignias are reproduced on the preceding page for the benefit of collectors. They are also accompanied by the international copyright symbol. The Hummel signature does not appear on every product, as some of them have been reduced or "cropped" which blocks out the signature that appeared on the original.

In the secondary market, the large wall prints framed and in good condition bring $50 to $75, depending on the size and the subject. The prints of children are usually the most sought after. The smaller prints, especially unframed, and the postcards usually bring somewhat less than their original cost in the secondary market. So do the calendars, but it is likely that the older ones will be in more demand as a result of the increased interest in the Goebel M.I. Hummel calendars. The ones from Ars Sacra and Emil Fink are a good source of subjects for framing examples of her original concepts.

Some Ars Sacra Products Which Will Be Available in the U.S.

One of a series of souvenir spoons. Each spoon has a different Hummel motif on the handle, available from Ars Sacra.

An array of large decorative candles, each with a different Hummel motif.

Close-up of package wrapped in Hummel gift wrap paper with string name tag.

Large calendar, 10½" by 16". Left: First issue. Right: 1981 issue. Printed in three languages on heavy stock. Twelve suitable-for-framing prints.

An assortment of jigsaw puzzles with various Hummel motifs.

Six books in German, each illustrated with Hummel drawings.

First limited edition canvas wall hanging calendar, published in an edition of 15.000, 16" by 21", and distributed by Hingham Collectables. From a Hummel original drawing owned by Ars Sacra.

Replica of Sister Hummel's original drawing which has been chosen as the center motif for the 1982 limited edition canvas calendar distributed by Hingham Collectables. The title is, "They're for Mom's Pie." Courtesy Ars Sacra.

Small calendar, 4¼" by 6½", printed in four languages. Left: First issue, 1946. Right: 1980 issue. Contains twelve reproductions of original Hummel drawings.

Needlework, Other Hummel Art Forms

Other Hummel art can mostly be classified as decorative, useful, or functional. A large proportion of it is produced by using the prints published from the original Hummel drawings by Verlag Ars Sacra and the smaller collection owned by Verlag Emil Fink. The prints, which vary in dimensions from wallet size to large wall pictures, are applied by decoupage method to music boxes, clocks, plaques, and tabletop boxes of various shapes and uses. Perhaps the next most numerous adaptations of Hummel art are made by applying decalcomania transfers to decorative and functional items such as tableware, thimbles, mugs, glassware, bells, and any other articles currently in vogue. Goebel turned out some 8″ by 10″ plaques using prints applied to wood grain hardboard in the 1960s. The section on Berta Hummel items includes many more examples of decoupage and decal transfers by Schmid. Herbert Hermann has two unique vases decorated with custom adaptations of the original Hummel drawing for Heavenly Angel (also known as Angel with Candle), which apparently are the only prototypes known and valued in the high hundreds.

Collectors who may wish to decorate plain articles of their own choice can do so by using the prints for decoupage. There are a number of instruction books written on this craft, and various sized prints can be obtained from sources listed in the back of this book. At present there is no retail source for decal transfers, although the method is not complicated. In addition to prints or transfers for decorating other objects, Hummel art is also found in needlework, jewelry, glass, and cast metals.

Happy are the Hummel collectors who can handle a needle with skill. They now have the opportunity to create their own personal examples of Hummel art. A few years ago Paragon Needlecraft of New York City obtained a license from Ars Sacra of Munich, Germany, to produce needlework kits using exact copies of Sister Hummel's original drawings which Ars Sacra own. All of these are designs that appear in prints and M.I. Hummel figurine forms.

The first kits announced a few years ago were designed for the cross-stitch. The basic kit consists of a finely woven piece of homespun made from a combination of polyester and cotton yarns on which is stamped an exact replica of an original Hummel drawing such as Apple Tree Girl, Hum. 141. The finished sizes vary from 9″ by 12″ to 11″ by 14″ in oval and circular shapes. The required amount of each color embroidery thread, needle, and easy-to-follow instructions accompany the stitch diagrams. Kits are available with and without frames.

Since the initial introduction. some designs have been added and some discontinued. There are about twenty-five different ones in all. Recently kits using crewel embroidery stitches have been added and so has the currently popular latch hook kit which includes 5 mesh convas with the required amount of yarn for each color cut to the proper length. The special latch hook is also included. Some of these are for wall hangings up to 16″ by 27″. A list of the various designs currently cataloged is shown.

Assorted pictures, 4″ by 5″ and 4″ by 6″, framed.

Musical bookends and cube by Schmid Bros., Inc.

Paragon Kit #0464, Telling Her Secret.

Paragon base fabric and yarn for kit #0464.

Hummel Stitchery Designs

Pattern Names	Cross-Stitch	Crewel	Embroidery	Latch Hook	Equiv. Hum. No.
Umbrella Children (Sun)		+	*		280
Umbrella Children (Rain)		+	*		71
Mother Swan	*	+	*	*	344
Birdwatching	*	+	*	*	300
Little Friends		+	*		348
Farm Boy		+	*		64
Farm Girl		+	*		199
Boy with Bird		+	*		63
Telling Her Secret		+	*		196
Apple Tree Boy	*	+		*	142
Apple Tree Girl	*	+		*	141
Peasant Boy		+	*	*	16
Peasant Girl		+	*	*	96
Mother's Helper		+			133
Booklore		+	*		306
Chick Girl, Pillow		+			57
Playmates, Pillow		+			58
Apple Tree Children, Bell-Pull		+	*		141-2
Spring Frog			*		201
Baby Chicks			*		None
Laundry Day			*		321
Lots of Luck			*		None
Not a Care in the World			*		69
Holiday Angel			*		None
Kneeling Angels			*		193

Sizes of above kits vary. Cross-stitch and crewel sets are 10″ round, 12″ round, 9″ by 12″, and 11″ by 14″, depending on the model number. Latch hook designs range from 11″ by 14″ to 16″ by 27″.

*Paragon Needlecraft designs   + Jenson (Denmark) designs

The kits currently sold with the frame vary in price depending on the size and type of material and stitch. The range is from about $10 to as high as $60 for the larger latch hook designs. Most good local craft shops should have some or all of the designs available. If they don't, they may be willing to order what you want. For those readers who may not live near such a specialized shop, Paragon Needlecraft supplied the name of one dealer who handles orders by direct mail. Another mail order dealer who advertised in *Women's Day* magazine, Oct. 14, 1980, listed two latch hook designs of Peasant Girl (#9310K) and Peasant Boy (#9311K) wall hangings, finished sizes of 16″ by 27″ for $29.98, plus $2.25 for postage and handling. See "Needlecraft Sources" for names and addresses.

One overseas mail order dealer of limited edition plates and figurines also advertised eighteen stitchery designs. Of particular interest to collectors with limited time or interest in needlework is the availability of done-in-Denmark, completely hand-finished pictures all framed and

Finished design from Paragon Kit #0932, Not a Care in the World.

Peasant Girl, Paragon #8036 and Peasant Boy, Paragon #8037. Cross-stitched and framed in antique walnut frames with gold liners by Nancy Townsend.

Apple Tree Boy, Paragon #8032 and Apple Tree Girl, Paragon #8031. Cross-stitched designs with frames. Joan H. Welch Collection.

Chick Girl, similar to Hum. 57, done in crewel embroidery from a kit by Mrs. Paul Ziegelmair.

Little Goat Herder, similar to Hum. 200, done in crewel embroidery from a kit by Mrs Paul Ziegelmair.

Meditation, similar to Hum. 13, needlepoint designed and executed by Barbara Barr from Emil Fink graphic #201.

pillows all ready for filling. These, being classed as works of art, come through U.S. Customs duty-free. Surface mail charges are included in the price listed and air mail delivery is 5 percent of the cost of the completed framed design.

One other alternative is available to a minority of Hummel enthusiasts. Those with sufficient artistic ability can create a design on the fabric directly from one of the color postcards of Sister Hummel's original drawings for execution in some form of stitchery such as needlepoint. The accompanying photograph shows the superb work of Barbara Barr who used a Hummel postcard to sketch her own original on fabric, selected the colors, and did the needlepoint. Illustrated are two of the many Hummel motifs she has stitched from graphics of original Hummel drawings.

The opportunities for self-expression through Hummel needlework are varied and challenging. The kits provide a do-it-by-number method which is easily mastered. Starting with just a postcard as a guide requires an artistic eye and skilled hand. The end results properly framed can make interesting companions when displayed with matching M.I. Hummel figurines.

From time to time some manufacturers have produced jewelry items such as pins and pendants using various Hummel designs. One extensive collection of thirty or forty brooches was assembled after a methodical search of the secondary market over a period of years. A variety of metals and finishes were found, including white metal, bronze finish, copper finish, and some sterling silver. After many blind alleys, we accidentally found the source of this jewelry while seated at breakfast next to a salesman of religious articles. The company is named Creed, designers and manufacturer of religious "Masterpieces, Jewelry, and Gifts." Mr. John P. Creed, President, told us that these brooches were made years ago in the "Hummel-manner." He could not recall any of the details except that the line was discontinued and the remaining inventory was scrapped to reclaim the silver content. No pictures, lists, or catalogs survived. Anyone having such a catalog would be doing a real service to collectors by sending it to us for publication.

A unique wood carving of exceptional high quality was hand-carved by a Creed artist in the form of a box surmounted by a replica of the Merry Wanderer figurine, Hum. 7. This was hand-carved and finished from one solid block of cherry wood as a presentation piece which anyone would be proud to own. If readers know of any wood carvings in the form of Hummel figures, the author would like the details, as rumors persist of some having been made in the Philippines and in Europe.

A piece of jewelry advertised in 1979 in bas-relief antique silver or brass finish for $12.50 was a replica of Umbrella Boy, Hum. 152A, about 2″ by 2″ square, which had been produced by making a mold from an older example which possibly may have been done by Creed. According to the producer, these were well received but were discontinued at the request of an attorney of the Goebel Company.

Another line of Hummel jewelry is called Hum-Bee and was introduced by Tandem Expressions of Torrance, California, a few years ago. These are all made of 14 karat gold, so the prices are constantly fluctuating. Charms in the form of a bumblebee are available plain or with diamonds, rubies, and sapphire gems. These same designs may be purchased as stickpins or tie tacs for a slight additional charge. The bumblebees are also produced as pierced earrings. We have also seen some fine, custom-made "Bee" jewelry that a well-known dealer wears which were gifts from her husband and which any Hummel connoisseur would appreciate.

Photographs of a number of different three-dimensional figurines cast in metal have been sent in by their owners for comment. These examples are in bronze, brass, or white metal and were never available in large quantities — at least in this country. One was in the style of the "Dentist Dodger" made by Herbert Dubler, Inc., during WWII and probably was cast by making a mold of the original figurine. In general these would not have a wide appeal because of their quality, lack of detail, and the distracting highlights from the shiny metal surface. However, they do represent interesting examples of another form of Hummel art.

The only glass Hummel-like figurine that has been inspected is in the form of the Goose Girl, Hum. 47. The illustration shown here is the rarest ruby color and is from the Grande Collection. At first these were thought to have been made very recently in Czechoslovakia, but the research of an inquisitive glass columnist unearthed the full story which appeared in her column, "Gwen's Glassline," in the April 18, 1980, issue of *Glass Review* magazine. Apparently these were made as early as 1930 and again produced in the 1960s in 6″ and 8″ high models by the L.E. Smith Glass Company. The assorted colors are crystal (water white) in shiny and matte finish, amber, green, blue, ruby, and amberina. Eileen Grande, owner of several differently colored ones, was thoughtful enough to pass this information along to share with you. In the secondary market examples bring about $20 for the crystal ones and range from there to about double for the ruby examples.

Playmates, similar to Hum. 58, needlepoint designed and executed by Barbara Barr from Ars Sacra graphic #4950.

Amberina glass Goose Girl, similar to Hum. 47, made by L.E. Smith Glass Company in several colors. Collection of Eileen Grande.

Hum-Bee Jewelry 14 karat gold charms, pins, and earrings by Tandem Expressions.

Hummel brooches made by Creed. Now discontinued.

5 *Other Adaptations of Hummel Art*

Reproductions of Original Hummel Art

Depending on the expert, estimates of the quantity of drawings done by Sister M. I. Hummel during her short life vary from less than one thousand to less than two thousand. Whatever the correct figure is, that is the maximum number of originals in existence. Every other one of the millions of items of Hummel art is a reproduction in one form or another, or possibly a fake. Every lithograph, figurine, box, bell, or bangle is another example of a superior, average, or mediocre reproduction of one of her originals.

Most collectors seem to consider a reproduction as something inferior, undesirable, or even having the taint of being dishonest. This is understandable. It is hard to persuade a Tiffany collector who has paid several hundred thousand dollars for a rare lamp that a three-hundred dollar reproduction of the same lamp is anything desirable. Frederick Carder, the founder of Steuben Glass used to say that when Carnival Glass, "the poor man's Tiffany," became available at prices that the masses could afford, the wealthier classes put their Tiffany, Steuben, and Lalique art glass in the attic.

This is not necessarily always the case. There are good reproductions. There are average reproductions. There are mediocre to terrible reproductions. The handmade copies of some of the fine early American Chippendale furniture, crafted in Williamsburg by original methods of construction, are very highly prized and highly priced reproductions. The fifteenth century etchings made by Durer are reproductions from his original engraved plate. They are also highly sought after copies or reproductions.

If it were not for the good and excellent lithographic reproductions made by the millions today, most of us would not be able to enjoy the fine or decorative arts at a modest price. If there had been no excellent graphic and ceramic reproductions of Sister Hummel's work, it is unlikely that anyone would be reading this page. One of Sister Hummel's expressed desires was to have inexpensive, quality reproductions made of her work, so, regardless of economic status, everyone could afford copies to enjoy and cherish. This objective has been attained by the fine lithographs made by Emil Fink and Ars Sacra who have been publishers of her work for almost fifty years, by figurines produced by Goebel, and by her decorative art first introduced into this country by Schmid.

From the tone of the letters received from readers, it would appear that Hummel collectors do not think of the aforementioned graphics or

Hummel-like lithograph, copyrighted 1972 by Donald Art Co., Inc., New York. Is numbered 1909 with artist signature, "Bukal." Note bees.

Friedel figurine in style of Sensitive Hunter, Hum. 6. Made in Japan, imported from Germany.

Hannel figurine, hand-carved in West Germany, "Bunny's Breakfast," limited edition.

Opposite page: Napco, Hummel-like figurines, 11"high, designed by Herman Newhauser; molded and decorated in Japan.

Goose girl, Arnart 22/620, 4¾" high, Japan, c. 1976.

April Showers, Napco C8747, 7" high, Japan, c. 1976.

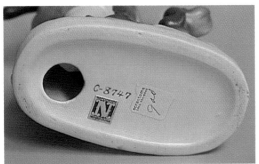

Base of Napco April Showers showing foil label.

M. I. Hummel figurines as reproductions. Rather, it is some of the Hummel-like or Hummel-inspired copies which do not do justice to the feeling, sensitivity and innocence of her original work that they regard as inferior reproductions. The purpose of this section is to familiarize collectors with some of the lesser known Hummel art that falls in the average and below average categories of reproductions that may detract from rather than enhance the enjoyment of Hummel art.

During World War II, two different companies produced a limited number and quantity of motifs as figurines. These two are the Beswick Company of England and the Herbert Dubler Co., Inc., of New York City. While there are still links missing in the historical chain of events that connects Beswick and Dubler to Hummel art, it appears that both were initiated as a legitimate effort to fill the void left by embargoes and the severing of communications created by the war. More details on both of these efforts, as well as photographs of the figurines, follow this examination of Hummel reproductions.

Arnart and Napco Figurines

Currently among the suppliers of Hummel-like or Hummel-inspired art, are two importers, Arnart Imports of New York City and National Potteries of Cleveland, who are importers of figurines from Japan. These figurines appear to have been inspired by Hummel art. The Arnart Company's "Original Child Life Series" was designed by Eric Stauffer. Some of these are identified with only the current Arnart crown. Earlier ones are backstamped with the same crown superimposed over "Arnart Fifth Ave.—handpainted" with the model number below. Some examples are stamped only "designed by Eric Stauffer" above two crossed arrows with the points down. While the appeal or the quality of this line is not as high as that of M.I. Hummel figurines, neither are the prices. Comparable examples are about one-fourth to one-eighth the price of Hummels.

The trade name the National Potteries uses is a contraction, NAPCO, on their line of "Our Children" figures, with some designed in various situations and costumes that are Hummel-like, and many others that have no Hummel parallels. This extensive and varied line was designed by Herman Newhauser. They are molded and decorated to his specifications in Japan. The history of the markings on these figurines has not been documented, but many have a foil lable with a large letter "N" filling all but the border. The model number that is also on the bottom has the prefix letter "C" followed by a four digit number like the photograph of the base of April Showers on this page. This would be the only way of tying the product to the manufacturer if the label were removed. There is not always a country of origin showing. These are in about the same price range and quality as the Arnart pieces, but seem to have more appeal and variety at very modest prices.

Other examples of Hummel-like or Hummel-inspired figures illustrated in this section are two relatively new introductions. The Hannel carved wooden figure is more like Hummel in name and price than in appearance and is mentioned here more as a matter of record than for its being of Hummel inspiration. The other line is Friedel. They are not very common, and little is known of their origin. It would appear that they are imported from Germany but molded and decorated in Japan. There are at least two different backstamp decals used. Both are over-glaze and have the word "Friedel" at the top. Under the name, both styles say "Registered Trademark—Handpainted." Some are in English and some in German. The prices are about one-tenth those of comparable M.I. Hummel figurines. There is no secondary market for any of these miscellaneous reproductions — probably because they are readily available in gift shops. Most would sell at auctions for about their retail price or below, except for those marked "Made in Occupied Japan." Any article marked "Made in Occupied Japan" is collectible because of that mark and not because they appear Hummel-like.

The oldest documented Hummel-like reproduction is a piece sent in only recently by a reader who had purchased it in 1937. The whole problem of fakes and frauds seems to enter the Hummel collector's world in the secondary market through lack of knowledge on the part of both the buyer and the seller, or through the intent of a seller who deliberately misrepresents an Arnart, NAPCO, or other Hummel-like figurine as a genuine Hummel. At that time the reproduction becomes a fake Hummel figurine and a fraud has been commited.

Earliest known reproduction of M. I. Hummel figurine received as a wedding present in 1937 in Seattle. Used since then to hold cook books. No identifying marks.

"Our Children Series" by Napco, National Potteries, Cleveland, Ohio. Designed by Herman Newhauser in extensive variety of subjects and sizes up to 11" high. Made in Japan. Identified by Napco logo and series number on bottom.

6 asstd.   C-8795   4-3/4" H

6 asstd.   C-8749   5-3/4" H   32/2   NAPCOWARE

"Hummel" Figurines by Dubler and Beswick

During the years of World War II hostilities, prior trade agreements and copyright restrictions were suspended between the warring factions. In this "all's fair in love and war" situation, Herbert Dubler, Inc., in New York and the Beswick Company in England initiated the production of their own versions of M.I. Hummel figurines. Although these "Hummel" figurines made by other than the Goebel Company are considered by some sources to be fakes, others are more inclined to regard them as interesting variations inspired by the art of Sister M.I. Hummel.

The firm of Herbert Dubler, Inc., of New York City produced (or at least sold under their name and label) a series of Hummel figurines of inferior material and workmanship that were unquestionably identifiable as being adaptations from original drawings of Sister M. I. Hummel. They were described on the label on the bottom as being "Authentic Hummel Figurines, Produced by Ars Sacra, U.S.A."

The history of this firm was fully researched and reported in *Hummel Art I.* It was founded by Herbert Dubler, a member of the family that operated Verlag Ars Sacra, Joseph Müller in Munich that was the first to produce Hummel graphics. He sold the U.S. distributorship and name, in about 1939, to some New Yorkers and went back to Germany.

Severing all connections with Herbert Dubler, the new owners continued to sell Hummel graphics. Of course these or the figurines were not available in this country once the U.S. was at war with Germany. About 1940, the New York company made arrangements to produce figurines and obtained U.S. copyrights as illustrated and marked on this page. In their brochure they claimed to have copyrighted some twenty or more adaptations of Sister Hummel's original works and that, furthermore, they were paying royalties to the "Franciscan Convents" in this country as Goebel did to the Seissen Convent in Germany.

Before making judgment as to authenticity or duplicity, many questions need answering. Did Goebel have full copyright protection of the U.S. Copyright Office for all these designs? Were they in the public domain so that anyone was entitled to use them? During wartime, are the rules different, such as the expropriation of foreign subsidiaries that was known to have occurred? What constitutes an infringement during wartime? Did the Dubler firm intend to sell their figurines as products identical to the ones made by Goebel and thus mislead the American public? There are no real answers to date. It seems the decision of authenticity or spuriousness is a moot question and perhaps academic. The Dubler firm, through a series of incorporations about 1968, has since become Hummelwerk, a distributing subsidiary owned by the Goebel Company who is, of course, the sole licensed producer of M.I. Hummel figurines.

This is where the subject wound up three years ago, but since then the English "Hummels" produced during the same intervening wartime

Unnamed Dubler plaque, 4" by 5", New York, 1942-45. Similar to Vacation Time, Hum. 152.

Unnumbered Dubler plaque, c. 1942. Similar to Brother, Hum. 95.

Label used on Dubler figurines. Made in U.S. about 1940-42.

years have made their appearance. Piece by piece, examples of figurines marked M.I. Hummel manufactured by Beswick of England have been discovered in the last three years. At least eleven designs were produced, as shown on the accompanying list. This firm was absorbed by the well known Royal Doulton Company who has many other more important problems than trying to find the historical records of the original Beswick Company.

However, from what information is available, there appears to be some parallels with Dubler; supply lines severed by the war, no moral obligation to honor any rights of a present enemy, and continuing demand for figurines. No evidence has been found to date that royalties were paid to any Franciscan convent.

The Beswick figurines, as can be seen by comparison with the Dubler photographs, are of better material (porcelain or bone china versus plaster of paris for the Dublers). The Beswick modeler produced adaptations resembling the Goebel figures more closely, but they are obviously from a distinctly different modeler's hand. Neither the Dubler nor the Beswick figures were made by using a Goebel figurine to create production molds. In this respect, each Beswick and Dubler figurine would be considered an original work of art created by a professional sculptor and derived directly from one of Sister Hummel's original drawings. This is exactly how Goebel classifies their M.I. Hummel figurines for U.S. Customs purposes — a work of art.

Beswick Figurines

903	Trumpet Boy	December, 1940
904	Book Worm	December, 1940
905	Goose Girl	December, 1940
906	Strolling Along	January, 1941
907	Unknown Name	January, 1941
908	Stormy Weather	January, 1941
909	Unknown Name	January, 1941
910	Meditation	January, 1941
911	Max & Moritz	February, 1941
912	Farm Boy	March, 1941
913	Globe Trotter	March, 1941
914	Shepherd's Boy	March, 1941

See accompanying illustration of how the bases of 910 and 914 are marked with incised model number, the Beswick logo, and "copyright" — "Hummel Studios." They are also signed in black with an imperfect facsimile of the M.I. Hummel signature, but not incised as are the Goebel M.I. Hummels.

Imitation "M.I. Hummel" signature on base of Beswick, 914.

Beswick figurine, Stormy Weather, 908. Made in England, c. 1941. Similar to Stormy Weather, Hum. 71. Miller Collection.

Pages from a Dubler catalog issued about 1942 showing some of the figurines which had been copyrighted in the U.S.

Beswick figurines, Shepherd's Boy, 914 and Meditation, 910. Made in England, c. 1941. Similar to Shepherd's Boy, Hum. 64 and Meditation, Hum. 13. Courtesy of Coventry Antiques.

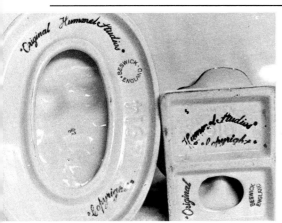

Bases of Beswick figures incised 914 and 910, with "Original Hummel Studios" and "Copyright" in script; stamped "Beswick England" (in circle).

Beswick figurine, Trumpet Boy, 903. Made in England, c. 1941. Similar to Trumpet Boy, Hum. 97. Miller Collection.

Baby in a Basket, Mel 6, modeled by Arthur Möller in 1945. Discontinued in 1962. TMK-1A, USZ. Coventry Antiques.

The Beswick case is probably best summarized by a letter to this author dated April, 1980, from Paul Atterbury, Historical Advisor to the Royal Doulton Group, which reads in part:

> I think it is completely inaccurate to refer to them as fakes because as you say in your second paragraph, a fake is by definition something made to deceive. As all these were clearly marked both Beswick and Hummel, there can have been no attempt to deceive. Unfortunately we have no records of this period of production beyond the designs in the pattern book, which you have seen, and so I have not been able to establish any of the details of the original production agreement. Certainly we have no records of either royalty arrangements or permission to reproduce being granted by any authority here or abroad. However, I am sure that we would not have produced the figures without some such agreement.

> Everybody I have talked to here believes, as you seem to, that the figures were produced by Beswick in an attempt to fill a gap in the market caused by the inevitable interruption in trade with Germany during the war. At that time the English manufacturers were given government instructions to find as many export orders as they could in order to bring foreign currency into the country, and so I think it is likely that Beswick were simply trying to capture a part of the Hummel market in America, while Goebel themselves were unable to exploit it.

Since the law and fair play in the U.S. assumes any entity whose motives or actions have been challenged to be innocent until proved right or wrong, it seems advisable to await more information before classifying Dubler and Beswick Hummel figurines as fakes or deceptions done deliberately in order to obtain unlawful gain.

Are Dubler and Beswick figurines collectible? Apparently enough collectors think so to form a modest-to-active demand in the secondary market. The Dubler figurines, depending on the model and the conditions of sale have a relatively low value — probably due to greater supply available and the comparably inferior quality. Prices range from $20 to $50 unless an uninformed flea market vendor has one for sale at a lower price. The Beswicks are a different story. Very few have been found. The quality is superior to the Dublers, with the result that the only two sold at public auction prior to this publication fetched $4,000 for the pair. The numbers of these two are B (for Beswick) 914 — "Johnny Had a Little Lamb" (like Hum. 64, Shepherd's Boy) and B 910 — "Lucky Letter" (like Hum. 13, Meditation). The way they are signed is illustrated and described. The only other one publicly exhibited is in the Robert Miller collection in Eaton, Ohio, and is B 908 (no coined name) and similar to Hum. 71, Stormy Weather.

Mel Figurines

Hummel collecting is rich in dividends derived from the constant stream of surprising new discoveries, exceptions to the normal, variations, rarities, and just plain new historical background about the hobby. A good example is the discovery a few years ago of some figurines that looked exactly like regular M. I. Hummels. However, these did not carry the stamp of authentication in the form of the incised facsimile signature, and, furthermore, they had an unfamiliar incised numbering system that was related to the word Mel. They were marked Mel 1, Mel

2, and Mel 3. Especially baffling, they appeared to be almost identical to the Advent Candlestick Group of Children — Girl with Nosegay, Hum. 115; Girl with Fir Tree, Hum. 116; and Boy with Horse, Hum. 117.

The well-known collector, dealer, and Hummel columnist, Pat Arbenz, acquired these as well as Mel 6, which does not resemble any other M. I. Hummel issued to date. These were like "burrs under a saddle" to any Hummel expert of Pat's stature. Not being one to surmise or guess, he went straight to the top of the Goebel organization for answers.

Dieter Schneider, the U.S. Managing Director of the Goebel Company replied to Arbenz in a letter reprinted in the February issue of the *Plate Collector* magazine that a total of eight Mel models, ranging from 1 through 8, had been designed from M. I. Hummel drawings by Arthur Möller and Reinhold Unger from 1939 to 1948. They were not marketed as genuine M. I. Hummel figurines because of the approval clause of their contract with Sister Hummel and the Franciscan Convent at Siessen. This implies that either these were not submitted for approval or that approval was not given. Since all approved master models were assigned one of the Hummel series of numbers, they decided to indicate that these were deviations from normal procedure by using the last three letters of the Hummel name (Mel), and by omitting the incised facsimile signature.

This was changed years later in the Sixties when Mel 1, 2, and 3 were remodeled by Gerhard Skrobek, the present master modeler, and approved by the convent. They were then released as Hum. 115, 116, 117 and are now listed as either Advent Candlestick Group or Christmas Angels in a set of three consisting of Girl with Nosegay, Hum. 115; Girl with Fir Tree, Hum. 116; and Boy with Horse, Hum. 117.

What about the other Mel numbers, 4, 5, 6, 7, and 8? Previously only Mel 6, a small candy or dresser box, had been identified. But, just as this book was going to press, the author was able to document the exciting discovery of a new Mel figurine, Mel 7, which is pictured for the first time in print at right. Mel 7 was released around 1947 and was adapted from an unknown drawing by Sister Hummel. This small figurine must certainly be categorized as unique at this time, with a value in the very high hundreds.

In the past few years, there have been a few other examples of Mels 1, 2, 3, and 6 offered for sale. They are in the larger collections now. The selling range has been in the low- to mid-hundred figures. Discovery of a previously unknown one in the series could well be worth more than twice the present range due to rarity and novelty.

Baby in a Basket marked Mel 6, TMK-1A, U.S. Zone. DeCenzo Collection.

Most recently discovered Mel 7, small dresser box with winged child adorning lid of basket. Sprague Collection.

Mel 7, with lid removed, showing base with incised Mel 7, incised TMK-1, and stamped US Zone Germany in black.

6 *Buying and Selling Hummel Art*

How to Buy Hummel Figurines

It is two o'clock in the afternoon of Friday, December 8, 1978, at Crowley's Macomb Mall store in Detroit. A crowd of at least one hundred persons has gathered drawn by a rumor that some Hummel figurines had just arrived and would be sold on a first come (to get a number) basis at regular retail prices. With about twenty figurines available, there was a one in five chance of getting one, and a twenty-to-one shot it might be a piece the buyer already had. This type of excess demand was not exceptional that year. Crowds, three and four deep, ganged up at counters and booths at the mere suspicion that figurines would be on sale. Price was a secondary consideration. One dealer in June of 1978 sold twenty 1978 bells at $300 each in the first four hours the Eaton Festival was open. The list price was $55, about one-fifth of what some frustrated collectors were willing to pay. Obviously this is not the ideal way to buy Hummel figurines, Hummel art, or any type collectible. It is reminiscent of the rampant speculation that crashed the stock market about forty years ago and which burst the tulip bubble in Holland in the nineteenth century.

Drawing #5774 courtesy Ars Sacra.

Fortunately conditions since then have normalized considerably. It is no longer a sellers' market, In 1980, as an example, there were about half the pages of advertising per issue in one large national magazine for collectors' items as compared to pages in 1978-79. At the same time buyers cannot always get what they want, when they want it, or at the suggested list price. It might be termed a selective market. If you are in the right place at the right time, and if you want what is there, you are fortunate. Naturally there is still plenty of dissatisfaction with both the quantity and the price.

Due to the manner in which Hummel figurines are made (in batches), and the way they are distributed (by allocation), buying in the primary market still presents problems for many collectors, but not as many as were prevalent in 1978. With over 400 model/sizes cataloged, only a fraction of these are in production on any given day. Limited shipments to dealers may contain only motifs recently produced, and sometimes more than one of the same model and size are received.

Collectors should bear in mind three axioms which apply to buying Hummel art or to purchasing almost any collectible.

Buy the book before you buy the figurine. The more you know, the more you will appreciate what you are buying and the better your chances will be of receiving good value.

Know your dealer. Reputable dealers have the welfare of the collector at heart and will continue to treat him as a valued customer through good

Drawing #5773 courtesy Ars Sacra.

times and bad. Some maintain "want lists" for their customers. Others, however, are still charging 50 percent over Goebel's suggested selling prices to any unwary customers they find. While this may be legal, it hardly seems the height of ethical conduct. The list of dealers in the back of this book hopefully has been screened of any such dealers. Dealers do exist who pay a premium in order to obtain a wide selection for their extensive customer list. Many augment their domestic allocations by purchasing figurines in Germany at list prices, paying the packing, shipping, and duty on these. In order to survive they have to mark these up above suggested U.S. prices, but not 50 percent. Their customers know that they are getting preferred service for the premium price.

Santa Claus does not sell Hummel figurines. What you get is closely related to what you pay, with few exceptions.

Drawing #14262 courtesy Ars Sacra.

The above axioms also apply to the secondary or "after" market which deals in previously owned Hummel figurines. Some dealers with very large inventories carry both new and previously owned items for their advanced collectors. It is especially important for the collector to have done his or her homework when buying in this market. Greater knowledge will pay big dividends in better buys and fewer mistakes to live with. Such knowledge and experience is also required when buying at auctions, flea markets, or garage sales where the sellers may know very little about the history, condition, or true value of their merchandise. Airport gift shops usually have the highest prices. In 1980 prices in many such shops were 100 percent more than suggested list price.

Drawing #14287 courtesy Ars Sacra.

Buying at auction or other secondary outlets should be undertaken only after some experience with Hummel art and auction procedures have been acquired. Other helpful published material is listed in the Bibliography. Several basic principles are essential for successful bidding at auctions.

- Don't bid on *any* article that you have not thoroughly inspected before the sale.
- Read and/or listen carefully to the terms and conditions of the auction.
- Set your top price at the time you inspect the article and stick to that figure.
- As a successful bidder, carefully re-inspect the article you now own before leaving the sale.

Auctions are frequently very good places where the experienced or advanced collector can buy successfully and where the uninitiated and uninformed can learn fast, sometimes with regret. Many auctioneers accept mail or phone bids if you cannot attend in person.

Buying by mail broadens the chances of finding what you want but entails some additional risks, which should be allowed for. Many persons are shy about buying by mail for fear of getting a poor bargain. However, there are many reputable dealers who combine their retail store operations with mail-order businesses. They value their good local reputation too highly to risk any problems with the U.S. Postal Service or the publisher who carries their ad.

Drawing #14288 courtesy Ars Sacra.

Drawing #5612 courtesy Ars Sacra.

Drawing #5011 courtesy Ars Sacra.

Drawing #5918 courtesy Ars Sacra.

It is prudent to stick with ads in the large national magazines, at least at the start, or with dealers who place large display ads. The mail orders dealers listed in the back of this book have helped thousands of collectors for many years. There should be no problems with any of them. If one occurs, the author would like to know all the details. The mail order buyer should always reserve the right of refusal with refund of the full purchase price if inspection reveals the items do not match the descriptions in the advertisement or satisfy the buyer's personal standards. It is wise to make this a condition of the sale when placing the order.

In summary, the person looking for one particular Hummel figurine for himself may have difficulty locating exactly the model he wants at the normal retail price. The casual buyer of Hummel art looking for a gift for collector-friends or relatives who does not know the market may encounter problems in locating a suitable gift at retail prices. By using the names of the dealers listed in the back of this book, the novice or uninformed buyer will have a good advantage in finding a wide selection at a fair price. Of course, these are not the only dealers in the country maintaining large inventories or selling at fair prices. There are thousands of reliable dealers in the U.S. who have just what you want. It will also pay to ask your friends for advice in locating the ones nearby. If you still cannot find a dealer in your area, the Goebel Collectors' Club or one of the three Goebel distributors in the U.S. should be able to offer some names of helpful dealers near you.

How to Sell Hummel Figurines

When Mary Nash received her check from the auctioneer in Groveland who sold her collection the week before, she was dismayed. The check was for $5,145, a little more than half of the $9,075 which she had them insured for on her fine arts policy. She recalled that the auctioneer *did* say that a commission of 25 percent of the sales total would be deducted for selling the collection of forty-eight pieces. Allowing for that, she figured she should have received about $6,806 if they sold for the insured valued. Before challenging the amount she decided to study the individual sales figures.

When Mary compared some of individual auction prices with the prices the same pieces were listed for in her insurance policy, she was completely mystified by the lack of relationship between the two sets of figures. Her Flower Madonna, Hum. 10, was insured for $100 but sold for only $30. Angelic Prayer, Hum. 91A, brought $30 at the auction but had been insured for $50. She did manage a smile when she saw that Ride into Christmas, Hum. 396, which she remembered buying in 1972 for $48.50, brought $360 at the auction and had been insured for only $200.

She immediately called Colonel Bob Fraser her auctioneer for an explanation of the large discrepancy between what she received and what she thought they were worth. The Colonel explained that the gross return amounted to $7,260 or about 80 percent of the insured value. He considered 80 percent an above-average return from an outdoor auction in inclement weather. "Furthermore," he added, "If it had not been for three dealers who attended the auction, the total would have been much less." It seemed that most of the crowd had come to buy the household furnishings, and only a few of them bid when the Hummels were sold. He also reminded her that she had agreed to share the advertising expense of the auction which amounted to $300. Therefore, the 25 percent commission and the advertising expense came to $2,100, which left a net payment of $5,145.

"Well," she worried, "I understand the amount better now but I still don't understand why the prices were so much over or under the individual insurance value prices." "Mrs. Nash," the Colonel replied, "When you have sold everything from cattle and farm machinery to Haviland china and Hummel figurines, as I have for twenty years, you learn a lot about the eccentricities of auction buyers. If there is only one person in the crowd who really wants the article being sold, it will be knocked down for less than it is worth. On the other hand, if there are two or more who came to the auction solely to buy a special piece, you may realize considerably more than the 'store' price." Colonel Bob went on to elaborate, "You remember that little figure of the boy sliding downhill? (Hum. 396.) You should know that, before the auction, three different women wanted to know when that piece was going to be sold, and they all examined it very carefully." One told him she had been trying to get that model for three years. "I don't know what you had it insured for, but I do know what they paid was more than 'store' price by a long shot, just by the way they kept trying to raise their own bids. My guess is that had your collection been sold somewhere other than at a small, outdoor rural auction you would have done much better."

As you can conclude from the above incident, selling a Hummel collection may be disappointing. There are other ways of selling — many of which can also be as disappointing, frustrating, and downright hard work. Whether the collection is large or small, any method has advantages and disadvantages. All have varying degrees of risk involved as pertains to what amount you will receive. This cannot be accurately forecast. An outline of different ways collectors can sell their Hummel art follows, along with some pros and cons.

·ZWIEGESPRÄCH·

Drawing #5555 courtesy Ars Sacra.

Sell Directly to Another Local Collector.
Often brings the best price but chances of finding one who wants exactly what you are selling are slim.

Advertising the Collection Locally.
Will probably result in lots of calls or visits. Many of them will be dealers offering less than retail prices and plenty of curious "lookers." This involves lots of personal time and some risk of theft.

Give the Collection to a Local Dealer on Consignment.
Requires little effort for the owner but may take months or years to sell the whole collection. The dealer will want from 10 to 20 percent for selling them. Any loss or damage will be your responsibility.

Advertise Nationally in Publications Such as *The Antique Trader, Collectors' News* or *The Plate Collector.*

Thousands of collectors will see the offer, even some who may pay full book prices. Requires much effort, letter writing, packing, and some returned items.

Advertise in the Hummel Collectors' Club Newsletter.

One of the dividends of membership in this worthwhile club is the opportunity to list, free of charge, any Hummels you wish to buy or sell. Furthermore, Dorothy Dous the founder will act as intermediary, if necessary, to see that both parties receive fair treatment without revealing their identity.

Answer Want Ads in National Magazines.

Usually the advertiser will receive low offers unless the article offered is a very rare and unusual piece. The potential buyer may send all or some pieces back for a refund because they did not come up to his or her standards. Damages in shipping are a real risk for those inexperienced in guessing how far the U.S. Postal Service will drop their best efforts in protective packing.

Call or Visit Dealers at a Local Show.

It is often possible to obtain more than one offer and to sell for cash to the highest bidder immediately. The collector may not strike "pay dirt" on the first attempt.

Sell at Auctions.

This is the fastest way of selling everything in a collection for cash, and probably has the highest risk, pricewise, but requires the least personal effort on the part of the owner. Can be very rewarding if sold in the auction market which includes mail bids and which has a large following of Hummel collectors.

Drawing #5109 courtesy Ars Sacra.

Many Hummel collectors have disposed of their collections in an entirely different and gratifying manner. They have given their collection away. What daughter would not cherish all or her share of figurines her mother had affectionately collected over the years and which represented so many pleasant family remembrances during her life? What friend or neighbor who had always enjoyed hearing about each acquisition would not welcome one or more examples as an enduring memento of friendship or neighborliness?

In addition to these personal gifts to friends and relatives, it is not unusual for a collector to give a small or even very large collection to his or her favorite charity. While the charity may not be interested in displaying it, they will appreciate the proceeds derived from its sale. The donor is entitled to a charitable deduction on his next tax return. This is normally equal to the fair market value at the time the gift was made. Therefore, in an indirect way, the owner does benefit financially from a tax deduction while giving a helping hand to those who help others.

Drawing #5111 courtesy Ars Sacra.

The explosive increase in public-owned collections, restorations, and museums offers still another alternative to having to sell a Hummel collection. Since most of these public institutions are certified as non-profit corporations, the value of the gift will be tax deductible, the same as for a charitable organization. Some of these not-for-profit corporations will reserve the right to sell some or all of the collection to purchase other exhibits that they might have a greater need for at some future date.

The numerous means of disposing of a Hummel art collection listed here should be varied enough so that collectors can choose the one best suited to their needs and circumstances. Parting with a collection that has been carefully built up over many years deserves the same thoughtful attention that the acquisition received. Others who have had this experience are a good source of valuable information, as is the Bibliography in the back of this book.

Hummel Art As An Investment

At a recent seminar, a lady asked the two questions that are frequently posed by letter writers. "Should I sell my 1971 M. I. Hummel plate now before the price drops any lower than $800?" "Should I buy a 1971 plate box for $40 to enhance the possibility of getting more money for it?" Sister Hummel's fondest hope was that her art would and could be enjoyed by everyone. She entertained no thought of personal gain. As a nun rigorously observing the vow of poverty, she no doubt would be horrified if she had had any idea that her art was being purchased as a means to make the owner richer in dollars — not in satisfaction. The reply to the lady that she should buy a plate because she liked it, and that if she no longer cared for it she should sell it or give it away might have seemed abrupt. She should have bought art for art's sake. Bought because she liked what she saw. Bought because it gave her a sense of satisfaction and pleasure.

During the Seventies the idea of buying Hummel art for enjoyment became confused or commingled with the idea that it was a sure way to make money. With prices of Hummel art and most other collectibles escalating to undreamed of heights it was difficult for people to submerge the monetary aspect and to buy strictly for aesthetic reasons. However, one group of buyers was not so confused. This was a group of investor/speculators who kept only one objective paramount in their minds. That objective was to make money fast. They did not necessarily know or care what Hummel art was. They bought only if they thought

An ad in The Antique Trader *by an individual desiring to sell the items listed. Information on figurines does not indicate the TMK for each figurine.*

A sample free ad available to members of the Hummel Collectors' Club from a recent issue of the club's newsletter. Note the complete information.

(11)

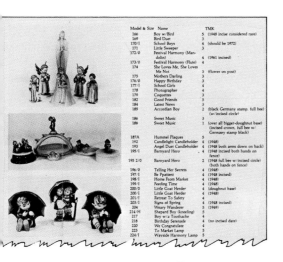

A partial page from an excellent auction catalog of a fine collection of 260 Hummels sold by Douglas Galleries, Auctioneers and Appraisers. Route #5 Deerfield, Massachusetts.

Auction action at the recent Hummel Festival in Eaton, Ohio. Kramer and Kramer were the auctioneers.

trading Hummel art would make money faster than any other method. The result was an artificial market consisting of bonafide collectors *and* speculators competing with each other for a limited supply of figurines, plates, bells, or other Hummel articles. There was one big difference between the two groups. Collectors wanted only one example of what appealed to them. Well-loaded speculators, taking all they could get their hands on, stashed them under the counter, in the attic, and under the bed until the prices went up. But, as the *Art & Antique* magazine editor said to his readers, "That which is appreciated by the collector may not always appreciate in value enough to satisfy the investor." The appreciation of Hummel art can never depreciate. Martin T. Sosnoff in *Forbes Magazine,* April 30, 1979, said, "When banks are selling stocks to buy objets d'art for their clientele you know that the bottom of the market cycle for stocks is close at hand," and the collecting boom is ready for a pause to catch its breath.

Now that the Eighties have arrived and the supply of many figurines and other Hummel articles has been increased, there seems to be a small leak in the inflation balloon which has slowed the sensational rise. In some cases a descent of some magnitude may be seen, especially in the secondary market. The phenomenal forty times increase in the original $25 price of the 1971 Annual Plate is now more than likely a thirty times increase. The 1979 plate is selling below issue price. Those collectors who bought the 1971 plate when it was issued can feel doubly fortunate. They have had ten years to enjoy the beautiful bas-relief of Sister Hummel's Heavenly Angel with the knowledge that, if they should decide to sell it, they would be very likely to get more than they paid for it. How *much* more remains to be seen and is not of upmost concern to the true collector. Past experience indicates a different course; many devotees of Hummel art will probably never sell their collections. Most of them know of relatives or friends who would be delighted to receive their collections. Their Hummel art gifts will go on giving pleasure for years to come.

History may repeat itself, first with demand exceeding the supply, when true collectors are joined by investor/speculators to drive prices artificially high, followed by the investors abandoning the field about the time the supply has been increased. When that happens, Hummel collectors will have a better chance to buy what they like when they like, and at reasonable prices. Later, if the value rises to more than they originally paid, it will be appreciated. Even if the future price is less than the purchase price, the difference will be compensated many times over by the many years of enjoyment. One truism appears to be that collectors who buy because Hummel art pleases their eye almost invariably wind up with monetary dividends plus artistic dividends.

7 *Enjoying Hummel Art*

Hummel Collectors' Club

The two women pictured here, Dorothy Dous and her daughter, Tammy, have probably given a helping hand to more Hummel collectors than any other two persons involved in this absorbing hobby — and with big smiles, as pictured. They are able to do this through the Hummel Collectors' Club which they organized some years ago for the sole purpose of researching and collecting information to pass along to members in a quarterly newsletter. Their only interest is Hummel collecting and collectors. Morning, noon, and night they find time to help others who have a problem or question about Hummels.

For example, suppose you want to sell some Hummels you no longer want. As a member of the Club you can tell them what you have to sell, and at what prices, and they take over from there. The Club's *Newsletter* will carry your listing with a code number, so you won't be bothered with phone calls, or, worse, by underworld characters who seek your address to help themselves to whatever you have, for free.

The Club will forward the replies addressed to your code number to you for acceptance or rejection of the offers to buy. In reverse, if you want to buy a figurine you've been unable to get, be it a new one or a rare old one, just send a letter to Dorothy or Tammy and your wants will be made known to all the Club members. But, suppose you are a new collector just learning the ropes and you don't feel confident buying from an unknown person who might send you something that is not perfect? In this case Dorothy will act as intermediary. Any figurine you intend to purchase can be sent directly to her for inspection before she turns your money over to the seller.

Dorothy Dous, founder of the Hummel Collectors' Club and her daughter Tammy.

A unique, unheard of, service is the Club's spare parts bank for collectors. Suppose you had the misfortune to drop a Merry Wanderer, Hum. 7/0, and a broken portion of the umbrella was lost. The Club's bank may have the same model, but it is a "basket case" (too far gone to repair), but the umbrella is intact. You are welcome to the part necessary to have yours restored, and it may be that Dorothy knows several reliable sources who could perform the restoration. (If not, consult the list later in this book.) Donations of damaged figurines to the bank are always welcome from members and non-members.

In recent past issues of the *Newsletter* the editors have published a list of models which are known to exist with Crown marks. They also have printed a comparison of the reinstated pieces with the older models so members will be able to distinguish one from the other.

News about forthcoming releases, fair prices, price trends, worthwhile upcoming shows, auctions, and festivals are other featured topics of interest. If a member has a problem not previously covered in a *Newsletter* on which he or she needs competent counsel, Dorothy or Tammy will probably be able to help. Send them enough information (including good pictures) and a self-addressed, stamped envelope.

By this time those not already familiar with the Hummel Collectors' Club, are thinking, "It sounds good, but how can I afford to belong to a club that has so many advantages?" That is not the question. the question is how can you afford *not* to belong to a club like this for only $15 a year?

Those collectors who would like more details or a sample copy of a *Newsletter,* if available, should write directly to the Hummel Collectors' Club, Box 257, Yardley, Pennsylvania 19067.

Goebel Collectors' Club

If big is better, then this club has to be good. Its publications keep over two hundred thousand members abreast of changes and developments in the multifaceted Goebel product lines, of which one is M. I. Hummel figurines. In addition to figurines based on Sister Hummel's art, Goebel produces lines created by such artists as Charlot Byj, Janet Robson, Hans Welling, Harry Holt, and Islo Ispanky, plus many creations by Goebel's own staff sculptors. Possession of a Club membership is the only way to secure the special limited editions made available on a yearly basis exclusively to members. A membership guarantees a warm reception at the headquarters in Tarrytown, New York, where there is an extensive display of all current company products and changing exhibits of some of the discontinued or closed editions. A free lunch is another "perk" for members who have an occasion to visit the factory in Rödental, Germany, where they can see a few steps in making M. I. Hummel figurines demonstrated in a special room for tourists. Membership is an automatic way of getting four prepaid issues of *Insights,* the Club's quarterly publication, which covers new products and educational articles on existing lines. The Club is not the place to buy any Goebel products, including M. I. Hummel figurines. It does not sell anything directly to its members except the annual membership which currently is $15 a year.

This bisque plaque is issued to new members of the Goebel Collectors' Club at the time they join. It measures about 4" in diameter.

Typical membership card, lower right, and the redemption card that accompanies it, upper left.

The special editions that are sponsored by the Club are available only through one of Goebel's authorized dealers upon presentation of a redemption card. So far the Club has sponsored five special editions of M. I. Hummel items and one or more other company products. For the year 1977-1978 the Special Limited Edition was the figurine, Valentine Gift, Hum. 387. In 1978-1979 it was a plaque, Smiling Through, Hum. 690. The next one, in 1979-1980, was a Hummel-related item in the form of a small colored bust of Sister Hummel, HU-2C. For 1980-1981, the Club issued redemption cards for another Hummel figurine, Valentine Joy, Hum. 399. For 1981-82, Daisies Don't Tell, Hum. 380, will be the special limited edition.

The Goebel Collectors' Club will continue to be valuable to collectors of Hummel art as long as the Club's efforts and publications remain predominately devoted to subjects and service that are of interest to collectors of M.I. Hummel figurines and plates.

Exhibits and Museums

At present there are a number of places where collectors can view various examples of Hummel art and, especially, M.I. Hummel figurines. Some of the largest and best collections are exhibited for public view only occasionally. Hummel displays open to the public on a continuing basis are:

The Goebel Factory in Rödental, West Germany. In the entrance area a large display of the current line of M.I. Hummel figurines is tastefully and artistically arranged along with other Goebel products. None of their archival specimens are on permanent display, but hopefully they will be placed in a more convenient location in the future. At times some items of the archival figurines issued and unissued have been displayed at festivals, especially the one in Eaton, Ohio, which is held thesecond weekend in June.

The Goebel Collectors' Club headquarters in Tarrytown is located in a large, old home. The first floor has been remodeled into display rooms for Goebel products, the most extensive of which are the M.I. Hummel figurines. From time to time, interesting prototypes or design studies from the factory in Germany are displayed. For example, one absorbing presentation in 1979 featured more than twenty International Figurines which were designed before World War II with the thought of issuing M.I. Hummels in the folk costumes of other European countries. These are pictured in this book in the numerical section, 800-900 numbers.

Caravelle Hotel Exhibit. The owner, Don Stephens, has put together what may be the second largest collection of Hummel figurines in this country. Many of these, including some of the very rare numbers such as Hum. 54 with Black Child, are displayed in the lobby of the hotel in Rosemont, Illinois, which is less than five minutes from O'Hare Airport in Chicago. In addition to this, some Hummels may be on display at other locations in Rosemont. A call to the hotel will advise you where and when others may be seen.

Wisconsin Memorial Park. A small collection of thirty-two examples may be seen in the Great Memorial Hall, along with other art valued at more than one million dollars that is displayed at North 132nd and Capitol Drive, Brookfield, Wisconsin.

Dealers' Exhibits. Some of the most educational displays open to the public are actually found in the shops of many of the large specialist dealers in M.I. Hummel figurines. A few of these are listed in this book under "Dealers, U.S.A." Some of these dealers also own private collections which any advanced collector would be privileged to see and to hear about firsthand from the owner.

Private Collections. Some of the large private collections in this country are open at times by special invitation to other advanced

Drawing #5554 courtesy Ars Sacra.

Drawing #5162 courtesy Ars Sacra.

Drawing #14386 courtesy Ars Sacra.

collectors. Any of these are superior to any museum display that now exists.

The Franciscan Convent in Siessen, West Germany. In 1979 a new museum was opened which displays a diverse sampling of Sister Hummel's drawings, many never published, and features the only sculpture done by her. While this is open to the public, prior arrangements should be made by tourists.

Berta Hummel Traveling Exhibit. Already covered in this book is the exhibit named "Berta Hummel: The Formation of an Artist" comprised of forty works that she completed between her twelfth and twenty-first years. This exhibit first opened in the fall of 1980. The locations the exhibit will visit in the last half of 1981 and early 1982 are shown on page 243. Catalogs are available which show an illustration of each work of art, its background, and critical assessment by Dr. Plaut.

Future Permanent Exhibits or Museums. Authoritative sources have indicated that in the years to come there will be a permanent display of the collection of Robert and Ruth Miller in Eaton, Ohio, their home town, which should eclipse anything on view today. Another concept in the very formative stages is for a museum located, possibly, in the Midwest, which would become the permanent repository of the entire collection of almost four hundred Sister Hummel drawings owned by Verlag Ars Sacra of Munich. Another possibility is that the diverse collection now housed in the Hummel family home in Massing may sometime be placed on public display along with the important memorabilia intimately connected with the short but productive life of their daughter Berta.

Festivals

Eaton Hummel Festival, Eaton, Ohio, which has been held for the past several years during the second weekend in June, is the scene of the largest festival devoted exclusively to Hummel art. Ten to twenty thousand people will converge on this small Ohio town to view the latest discoveries in Hummel art acquired by Robert and Ruth Miller and to buy Hummel figurines and other derivatives of her art from thirty to fifty specialist dealers from all over the United States. On that weekend several million dollars worth of figurines are on view, many of which are for sale. In addition, the Goebel Company has set up some interesting displays and demonstrations. Motion pictures of how the figurines are made are shown, and seminars are held to answer questions posed by collectors. On Saturday night a large auction is held which is known to have run for six or more hours. The net proceeds of this community effort go for improvements to the educational system of the town. Reservations for rooms are at a premium, so advance booking is essential. There is ample parking space for those who have mobile sleeping equipment.

German Alps Festival, Hunter, New York. For a number of

Main gate, German Alps Festival, Hunter, N.Y.

Collectors waiting in line to buy Hummel figurines at the German Alps Festival. Photograph: James Coyne.

View from ski lift, German Alps Festival. Photograph: James Coyne.

years Don Conover has put on a ten-day festival that outshines anything of this kind known to the author. In the past few years an important sidelight has been the special showing of Hummels for sale with demonstrations, seminars, and motion pictures, all specially arranged by the Goebel Company. With the huge crowds that attend, rooms are at a premium, and the proprietor of one motel must have been a New York City taxi driver. It is best to stay out of the immediate area or overnight in the camping grounds.

Typical dealer's display, Eaton Festival. Courtesy Camines.

Seminars and Illustrated Lectures

The only regularly scheduled seminars are those held at the Eaton (Ohio) Hummel Festival the second weekend in June. At these, Robert L. Miller and usually Dieter E. Schneider, U.S. Managing Agent for Goebel, lead a question and answer session on each of the two days of the festival for all interested. These are informative for the average collector and sometimes cover insights or ideas that have not been previously published.

There are many other qualified advanced collectors who conduct seminars, on request, for special gatherings of clubs or national meetings. Some of these experts are, in addition to Miller, Patrick Arbenz, Rue Dee Marker, Dorothy Dous, Eileen Grande, and this author. These may be formal talks illustrated with slides or actual figurines. Other meetings are identification sessions or a combination of both when collectors bring pieces from their own collections, for identification or for more information. For specific details, write directly to the above individuals. Their addresses are listed in the back of this book.

The Goebel Collectors' Club has an excellent new color sound movie (1980) narrated by Joan Ostroff, Vice-president of the Club, telling how Goebel products are made and which includes many scenes and comments about M.I. Hummel figurines. Ostroff and Jim Lerner, another Vice-president, as well as other Goebel personnel conduct seminars and show the movie by request of various groups. More information can be obtained about these services by writing directly to the Club in Tarrytown. See "Collectors' Guide" for address.

Hummel Look-Alike Contest

In addition to sponsoring the Goebel Collectors' Club, W. Goebel Porzellanfabrik of West Germany has sponsored a Hummel Figurine Look-Alike Contest for many years. The contestants are children from two to eight years old posed and costumed as much like Hummel figurines as possible. The winners are chosen from photographs submitted to the company. Entry blanks may be obtained from Hummel dealers, and there is no fee for entering. Prizes can be as much as $1,000 in cash and a portrait of the winner.

Hummel Look-Alike Contest winner costumed and posed as a live replica of figurine Big Housecleaning, Hum. 363.

8 *Protecting Hummel Art*

Appraising and Insuring

A casual glance at a few recent headlines should provide reason enough for concern and action: "Armed Robbers Clean Out $30,000 Hummel Collection in Daylight Getaway" (Indiana); "Early Morning Burglary of Hummels and Collectibles Estimated at $116,000" (California); "$200,000 Loss of Hummels Attributed to Professional Ring" (Pennsylvania).

Talks with hundreds of Hummel owners indicate that not one out of ten realizes the true value of his or her collection at today's prices. One woman brought three pieces in for indentification which her son had purchased in Germany years ago. Two of them were worth $2,500 each, and the third was estimated at $750. Thirty-three figurines listed in a letter originally cost the owner less than $100 but now have a value of $9,500. These collectors and thousands of others are subject to loss or damage with little or no chance of compensation because they are not properly insured. Other collections are underinsured because the owners are using the price list for just-purchased figurines. Hummel figurines purchased twenty-five or more years ago are worth several times the price of similar new ones. Too many people rely on their homeowners' policy which is limited and indefinite. It does not cover breakage or appreciation in value of works of art such as Hummels.

This book makes it easy not only to find out what your Hummels are worth, but also how to get them properly insured against most risks and perils at modest rates. All that is necessary is to read and follow the simplified procedure outlined next.

First, obtain your own personal copy of *Hummel Art II* with the separate Price List for the *present year*. First, take time to read the book to expand your knowledge about your collection. You will learn to recognize unusual variations that can bring large premium prices. In this context the Price List will be a more accurate guide.

Next, take one piece at a time and examine it for model and size number, as well as trademark. Make sure that it is incised M.I. Hummel. Then locate the corresponding number and size mark on the Price List which is in numerical order. Follow across that line until you come to the column that has the trademark at the top which matches the piece in hand. Box in the dollar amount shown under the trademark and opposite the correct model and size marks.

As an example, suppose you have a small girl with a book bag strapped on her back carrying a basket. Looking on the bottom of the figurine you find the number 81/0 incised there. Turn to number 81 in *Hummel Art II* and you will find the figure is named School Girl.

Opposite page: Book Worm, Hum. 3, 5½" high, TMK-5, adapted in 1935 by Arthur Möller, Goebel master sculptor.

Compare the picture to your example and read the adjacent history. Then study the trademark that is also on the bottom to decide which one of the six trademark groups shown on page 18 resembles the one on your figurine. Suppose it turns out to be the Full Bee, TMK-2. Under the heading, TMK-2, the value for 81/0 is listed at $140. When you recall buying that twenty-five years ago in Gimbels for $4.50, it may take a moment to get over the shock.

By continuing through the collection in this manner, you may come to one that has no dollar figure for your combination of model and mark. You may be able to approximate it by comparing it to others of the same size and mark. Another method is to average the prices on either side of it. If you happen to have 50/2/0, Volunteers, with Crown TMK-1, you will find only a question mark(?). Notice that this size is about half the value of the larger size in comparable marks. Take one-half of $350 (50/0, TMK-1) and the resulting $175 will be a close approximation.

When you have all of your collection evaluated, add all the boxed figures to find the total amount of insurance needed for a fine arts policy or personal article floater to your homeowners' policy. This will provide an authentic list to discuss with your insurance agent. Until the publication of *Hummel Art II,* the only way to obtain a fine arts policy or personal article floater was to have each item valued by an approved appraiser. Such appraisals cost from $40 to $100 per hour. A $5,000 collection might cost from $100 to $200 for an appraisal. There was no such thing as an acceptable, do-it-yourself evaluation for insurance purposes.

Prior to publishing this book, an extensive questionnaire was sent to over one hundred insurance companies to determine whether or not they would accept the latest current prices as authoritative values for which they would settle in case of a loss. The results were surprising. Many of the biggest companies said they would welcome such authoritative published figures as the basis for writing either a fine arts policy or a personal article floater.

Drawing #5769 courtesy Ars Sacra.

These special policies list the value of each piece in an attached schedule (in this case a photocopy of the table with boxed in figures). The company and the insured agree that the stated price in the schedule will be paid in case of a justifiable claim. Many said they would accept such schedules prepared by the owner as long as he used the *latest* current values published with *Hummel Art II.* Others said this would be sufficient for most collections valued under $20,000. Above that, they would probably require a review by another knowledgeable dealer or appraiser. Many said they would like their companies' names listed in *Hummel Art II.* All of them emphasized the necessity of contacting their local offices, NOT THE HOME OFFICE, by using the Yellow Pages in the local phone directory. Some of the companies who will accept owners' appraisal based on *Hummel Art II* values are Travelers, Aetna, Continental Group of Companies, Hartford Insurance Group, St. Paul Fire and Marine, Liberty Mutual, and some other smaller ones.

Finally, to complete your do-it-yourself appraisal, have three photocopies made of your inventory list. The insurance agent will want one photocopy to include in the policy, another copy should be kept in your safety deposit box, and the third can be used as a quick reference to what you now own. Underlining your future wants will make it a valuable buying guide and "hint" list.

Your policy on Hummel figurines should contain the important breakage coverage clause which costs slightly more. Some policies may automatically cover any new purchases you make during the life of the contract. There is usually a limit, such as a specific dollar amount or a percentage of the policy total. Policies have been reported that cover any part of the collection while it is in transit or on exhibit. Collectors should discuss their specific needs with the local agent. Sometimes it is necessary to shop around to find the policy that meets every requirement. There are a number of firms that specialize in fine arts policies for large collections, dealers, galleries, and institutions. Whether or not the agent suggests or requires it, it is also an excellent idea to photograph the complete collection. This will serve as a valuable visual record and authenticate the existence of the collection.

A helpful aid to photographing figurines is a publication called, "Photos Help When Disaster Strikes." This can be obtained from the Eastman Kodak Company, Dept. 841, Publication AM-4, 343 State Street, Rochester, New York 14650, at no cost. Send a self-addressed envelope (no return postage required) with your request.

In the event you have some figurines for which you cannot assign a value or in case your agent wants the list reviewed by a recognized fine arts appraiser, Hotchkiss Associates, members of the Appraisers Association of America, may be able to assist. You can get further information by writing to them at P.O. Box 463, Sanibel, Florida 33957.

Safeguarding Hummel Art

Some of the larger Hummel dealers and collectors have found it advisable to have two strings in their protection "bow." The first and foremost string being insurance that will cover all hazards. (A new simplified way of securing this preferred type of insurance that most collectors do not have is fully covered under Appraising and Insuring Hummel Art, page 229.)

For the second string, a number of alternatives interwoven with an insurance program are possible. They can be a simple do-it-yourself program of any one or all of the following. 1. Lock your doors at all times, even when you are there. A $30,000 Hummel holdup happened less than a year ago at five o'clock in the afternoon. Both husband and wife were at home and, after being bound up, watched the robbers remove their collection. 2. Change existing locks so that every door has a good and adequate deadbolt. 3. Install chain doorstops, together with a peephole in the door to preview all callers. 4. Keep all windows locked with adequate fasteners. 5. Use timers to light up your home when you are out. Many leave a radio tuned to talk shows or turn on a recorder playing loud conversations. 6. Install outside floodlights at the corners of the buildings and keep shrubbery trimmed low. 7. Invest a dollar for three adhesive-backed labels for door entrances that say "This Property

Custom made, floor-to-ceiling built-in cabinet safely displays owners' extensive Hummel collection behind plate glass. Lighting from fixtures mounted in top of cabinet filters through adjustable glass shelves attractively illuminating display from ceiling to floor of owners' dining room. Grande Collection.

Closer view of dining room display cabinet. Note Infant of Krumbad, Hum. 78, in eight variations, sizes. Grande Collection.

Focal point of this large kitchen is floor-to-ceiling lighted cabinet occupying one wall. Easily viewed Hummel collection is protected from breakage or dust by plate glass. Grande Collection.

Is Protected by The National Alarm Service," then hope that all the uninvited guests that call are amateurs. To sum up — lock up and light up.

Statistics show that the suburbs are accounting for a greater and greater percentage of breakins and thefts. The chance of recovery of the stolen items is now down around 5 percent. Other areas and types of business have been faced with even more severe harassment and have developed methods of defense. Among those that are prime targets are banks, service stations, and jewelry stores. Jewelry store problems probably come closer to those of the collector. In fact, some jewelry stores carry M.I. Hummel figurines. Not every reader has the need or could afford the expense of the sophisticated systems some of these stores install. Between these top-of-the-line systems and the do-it-yourself programs there exists an almost infinite number of alarm devices and systems that can be adapted to fit every need and budget. However, all experts seem to agree that there is no protective system that can provide absolute safety from theft.

Alarm systems used by businesses and homes fall into roughly four classifications: local, direct connect, monitoring stations, and on site stations. Briefly, most local systems are self-contained ultrasonic units that give off an alarm inside or outside the house if the protected area is entered. Several well known ones are plug-in devices such as the ones sold by 3M that looks like a book and the Master Lock, Ultrason-II that looks like a stereo speaker. The cost is in the range of $200, and more than one unit will usually be required. The direct connect system may be ultrasonic or a combination of "triggers" all designed to automatically notify the police. These may range from $500 to several thousand dollars.

The monitoring station installations can include all of the above plus much more, such as video scanning and even picture-taking. The distinguishing feature is that all alarms go first to a central office of the installer of the protection system. These use their parent company names like Honeywell, Westinghouse, and others. All include a monthly service charge. These are extensive and expensive installations. Their effectiveness varies depending on basic design and the way the alarms are handled at the central office. In one case the central office received an alert late at night. Rather than send qualified personnel or the police to investigate, they called the nextdoor neighbor, a widow, and asked her to go over to see if everything was all right.

To sum up, jewelry stores never depend on just prevention or detection but combine these with an insurance package that will protect them to the extent each store believes it needs and can afford. The collector can use any from the above array that gives him peace of mind — and, remember, in case of a break-in, DON'T RESIST.

Repairing Hummel Art

Collectors of Hummel art as a group would be classed as perfectionists. They not only insist on an article that appeals to them but they also

Drawing #5898 courtesy Ars Sacra.

want it to be of highest quality without blemishes or imperfections. Unfortunately most Hummel art, and especially M.I. Hummel figurines, is fragile even though made of the highest grade ceramics. To capture the true beauty and feeling of one of Sister Hummel's drawings, it is necessary to have features such as locks of hair, fingers, extended arms, or other accessories protruding so that even a slight blow or small drop could cause a fracture. Prints, dolls, decoupage items, or original paintings by Sister Hummel have their own risks of damage.

Any damage to a Hummel is a first class tragedy to the owners whether self-inflicted or caused by some other action. Their grief is not only due to the loss of value but more likely stems from feelings of attachment and sentiment. A fine old example handed down through the family, one purchased on a special trip, an important anniversary gift, a remembrance sent home by a son or daughter on duty in Germany are examples that may be treasured for far more than the dollar value. Here economics and eventual resale price are of little consequence.

Fortunately most types of damage can be repaired and replaced so well, if done professionally, that even the owner cannot distinguish any visible evidence of the figurine having been mended or restored. Unless the owner has some aptitude, training, and experience in ceramic repairing along with access to the proper equipment and material, he is advised not to attempt even minor repairs. The do-it-yourself enthusiast whose repertoire is limited to making mends with Elmer's glue will usually wind up with a mismatched break and evidences of excess dried glue. A professional's work will show no line where the break is, and he uses advanced adhesives that are stronger than the ceramic itself.

Drawing #4780 courtesy Ars Sacra.

This does not mean that all minor defects have to be done by an experienced professional. There are plenty of ceramic repair hobbyists who are capable of correcting most damage cases, especially those with an artistic eye for blending and matching colors. Today there are some excellent ceramic repair kits containing air-dry materials that do not require a kiln. For those who are interested in doing this type of exacting work it is highly recommended that one of the good books on repairing be studied as a first step. Several are listed in the Bibliography.

The vast majority of Hummel collectors will be better off locating a professional who will produce an indistinguishable correction. Some are listed in the back of this book. One of these listed added a missing arm to one of the author's figurines by sculpting a duplicate using a picture as a guide and decorating it to exactly match the original shattered one. Twenty years later the repair is still invisible.

Since there are as many various levels of repairers as there are automobile mechanics, collectors should make sure of the qualifications prior to having the work done. The author's personal experience with the names listed under Repairers is limited to only one. Others may be as good or better. If you don't know a repairer or someone who has had good results with one, you can call almost any high-grade china shop, gallery, or museum for the names of some they have used successfully.

Expert repairs are expensive, but an estimate of what the actual cost

Drawing #14259 courtesy Ars Sacra.

Drawing #5615 courtesy Ars Sacra.

Drawing #14412 courtesy Ars Sacra.

Drawing #5334 courtesy Ars Sacra.

will be can be had ahead of time. For collectors who have to send work out of town, most repair shops, if asked, will send an estimate on receipt of the object and hold it until the price is accepted or rejected. See *Hummel Art I* on how to pack for shipment and what means of shipment to use.

Good repairers are also very busy, so an advance estimate of time required, as well as cost, is a good idea. Many need weeks or months to finish an assignment. This may be an indication that you have selected an expert. The cost of repairing a large quantity of pieces is not justified economically. It does not pay to buy damaged figurines with the idea of having a specialist repair them so they can be sold at a profit. Personal attachment, association, or sentiment do justify restoring all but inexpensive examples.

With such high grade materials and workmanship available for mending and decorating, how does the average collector who prefers older pieces keep from buying a repaired piece at perfect piece prices? One sure but difficult way is to become an expert on repairs or, better yet, know someone who is. If you have a very reliable dealer you probably have the best assurance of not being duped. Most dependable dealers are more worried about selling something that is not perfect than most collectors are about buying it. The dealer has built an impeccable reputation and guards it jealously.

Buying at auctions, garage sales, and flea markets is different. At auctions you buy "where is, as is," meaning you buy it like it is. The responsibility is yours, and, once a defective piece is purchased, there may be no recourse after the hammer falls. Specialized Hummel auctioneers (see "Services, Auctioneers") take great pains to clean, examine, and even test each and every piece prior to auctioneering it off. Any errors by these experts are those of omission and not commission. Today it is very difficult to detect and announce all imperfections. If a buyer discovers a piece is defective that was sold as perfect, most auctioneers will refund the price if the discovery is made within a few days — especially if the collector is well known to the auctioneer.

A classic example happened recently when an advanced Hummel collector purchased an old Ring Around the Rosie, Hum.348, for well over $1,000 at an out of town auction. The following Monday the auctioneer received a call from her saying that she was surprised that he had not cataloged the piece as having had two of the girls' heads reattached. She said "black light" (ultraviolet) light examination showed this to be the case. Astounded that he had missed this in the same type of examination, he told her to return it for a full refund. On receipt, he could find nothing that looked like a repair of the heads of the two girls. He decided to go one step further and use the "ultimate" examination, a technique used on multimillion dollar Rembrandt oil paintings. He arranged for an X-ray examination by a professional laboratory. The report of this sophisticated technique was that the two heads in question showed no evidence of having been repaired — but the heads of the other two had been broken off at one time and reset.

The moral of the story is twofold. Black light is no longer an infallible examination means, as was once thought. This is principally because many of the new paints floresce so much like the finish used by the manufacturer that repairs are no longer distinguishable by black light. The second point is that an excellent professional repair may be so well done it cannot be seen under magnified visual examination. The above example is a one-in-a-million exception and should not unnerve the beginner into complete inaction and loss of confidence.

Should there be any skepticism concerning the authenticity or condition of a high-priced figurine, it is good business practice to request a written statement on the bill of sale when buying from an unknown source. It should contain words to the effect that the article is perfect as described, and, if found not to be, it may be returned for a full refund within a reasonable time (five to twenty days). Where it is necessary to buy figurines by mail this statement is practically mandatory and will not be resented by reliable dealers.

How much are damaged or repaired pieces of Hummel art worth? An oversimplified answer is about one-half the values shown on the separate Price List for this book. This applies to inconspicuous flakes, minor paint chips, or excellent professional repair. When the damage is as extensive, in the form of unrepaired bad breaks or, especially, missing parts, the value is closer to 10 percent of the price guide figures.

Drawing #14385 courtesy Ars Sacra.

The other extreme for defective examples applies when a unique (one-of-a-kind) piece with some minor damage is sold. Most collectors and museums accept it. They have no choice. Museums, especially, seem willing to make exceptions for extremely rare pieces. They feel a real obligation to preserve and display the whole or entire scope of an art, craft, or whatever their specialty. Did the Vatican scrap Michelangelo's, Pieta because some unbalanced individual used a sledge hammer on it? Of course not. Did the Corning Museum of Glass display only the fragments of the world-famous Venetian Dragon Stem Goblet after the flood had subsided? Not at all. These cases looked hopeless. Today, after scientists and expert artisans teamed up to develop new products and techniques for repair and restoration, these priceless items are again available for public education and enjoyment. In many cases the damage is invisible to an unaided eye. The same principles apply to Hummel art. The greater the rarity of an item, the greater the time and money that will be spent restoring its imperfections. The value of such items will approach the value of a similar perfect piece, but it must be a rare example.

One offbeat Hummel collection consists of nothing but imperfect pieces. By judicious selection and placement, this collection looks perfectly normal. It made it possible for one collector to own a collection that would otherwise have been financially unattainable. The enjoyment in this case must certainly come from the decorative qualities of figurines, as the market value of the pieces is of no consequence.

Drawing #14409 courtesy Ars Sacra.

Finally, for those collectors who have "basket cases" that are not worth repairing, the Hummel Collectors' Club (see on page 223) has a spare parts bank that makes a good repository for badly smashed pieces until another collector is in trouble and has a need for a replacement arm,

Drawing #5791 courtesy Ars Sacra.

Drawing #5792 courtesy Ars Sacra.

Drawing #5795 courtesy Ars Sacra.

leg, or head. This is only one of the helping hands that Dottie and Bob Dous extend to members of the club they founded.

Next to figurines, perhaps dolls are the most subject to damage, especially since they are made to be played with and not just for display. As doll collectors know, there are many fine doll hospitals. If there is not one near you, there are some as near as your mailbox (look *in Hobbies Magazine*). The owners of these hospitals have a deep attachment for dolls and usually do a superb job of repair, including providing new eyes, wigs, and new outfits.

As for remaining Hummel art, prints, pictures, and cards are the most numerous. The repair of prints, paintings, and pictures is a highly specialized craft. Tears, rips, and yellowing of the paper can be restored by experts if the original piece is valuable — as it would certainly be if you were fortunate enough to own an original signed M.I. Hummel. Damaged frames, mats, or glass can be repaired by any good picture framing company in the larger cities or by the owner.

Other articles using Hummel art such as boxes, bells, plates, eggs, candles, and other decorative art can be restored if worthwhile by specialists in the materials used. At present, most of these items would not be worth repairing, except for sentiment, since replacements can be bought for less than the cost of any major repair.

Cleaning

Sometimes the Hummel figurine children need a bath just as any real life children, but not because of playing in mud puddles, sliding in wet grass, or being stuck up with bubble gum. Thankfully, the frequency is also much less. M.I. Hummel figurines that have been exposed on a mantel or open display shelves over the years, even with normal dusting, need freshening up. The time will depend on the type and amount of airborne dirt, smoke, and fumes.

Even some new Hummel figurines that are purchased in Germany will need washing. These figurines distributed in Germany are wrapped at the factory in what appears to be a gray packing tissue made of regenerated newsprint which frequently leaves smudges on the figurine's face. The figurine you unpack may make your hands look as though you have thumbed through all the pages of the Sunday edition of the paper. Some meticulous dealers and collectors make it a standard practice to wash all figurines that arrive in this tissue. The question is not whether figurines ever require washing, but rather how to do it without damaging the color or finish and without breakage.

Obviously, the easy out of using an automatic dishwasher is not recommended for fragile ceramic pieces. The Goebel Collectors' Club *Insights* for Fall-Winter, 1979, vol. 3, no. 3 suggested the following procedure. "First line your sink with an absorbent towel, rubber mat, or something similar to insure against chipping. Next, fill the sink with tepid water and a mild soap solution and dip your figurines gently (and individually). Never put them under running water, for a sudden gush from the spout could easily knock this fragile item out of your hands.

Rinse in the same way. A cotton swab, soft artist's brush, or even a soft toothbrush could be used gently for those hard-to-reach areas. Line your drainboard, or similar flat surface, with a soft cloth and let your figurines air dry. You could, of course, towel them dry very carefully, but the less handling the better."

Dorothy Dous, who issues the Hummel Collectors' Club *Newsletter,* has probably cleaned more figurines than 99 percent of the dealers and collectors of Hummel art. She suggests a somewhat stronger detergent for figurines purchased in the secondary market such as auctions and private sales. She recommends Top Job, Grease Relief, Janitor in a Drum, or similar heavy detergent and has found that they will not harm old Hummel figurines but will leave them super clean. The stronger detergents have the added potential to loosen or remove any area that has been "touched up" over the years.

Drawing #14741 courtesy Ars Sacra.

One way to minimize the effort of cleaning and risk of damage is to keep your collection displayed under glass in one of the ways mentioned in this book in the section on Displaying, page 242. Some collectors who store their collection in this manner feel that the only care necessary is a very occasional wiping with a treated cleaning cloth or professional tack rag. When under glass and cleaned with a dry cloth right on location the possibility of breakage is greatly minimized. For mothers of active children at the "let's see, feel, taste, and touch" age, such secure display is almost mandatory for peace of mind.

Now that some sales of original drawings by Sister Hummel are being reported, the best suggestion for cleaning such an original art, or even some of her other graphics, is DON'T. This is the province of the professional as are repairs and most framing. The Hummel prints applied by decoupage to many articles such as boxes and plaques should need only a damp cloth to remove any surface dust or grime. Needlework done by any stitch is much better off framed behind glass in order to maintain the original, like-new, look. However, many needleworkers would rather not mount behind glass because of reflections and so wait until professional cleaning is necessary.

Drawing #5793 courtesy Ars Sacra.

Photographing Hummel Art

Photography itself is a challenging hobby just as collecting Hummel art is. Those fortunate enough to enjoy both of these hobbies are almost certain to have excellent individual pictures of each piece in their collection. Taking pictures of small collectibles such as figurines, coins, stamps, and miniatures is known as tabletop photography, a very descriptive name since a table is the easiest place to photograph small items.

To the majority of Hummel collectors, taking pictures of their own collection will sound like a great chore and an unnecessary expense, at least until misfortune hits. While the Internal Revenue rules allow a deduction for an uninsured casualty loss, the amount of the loss allowed depends on having pictures of whatever was lost, strayed, or stolen.

Without any pictures taken before, the claim could be disallowed. Some insurance companies also require photographs and encourage them. If a loss is sustained, photos are a great benefit in getting a fair settlement from an adjuster under the common homeowner's policy. For the preferred fine art policies, they are a great backup and many insurance companies insist on pictures as well as the priced inventory schedule on which any future claims will be settled.

Once a collector has photographs, he or she will marvel at their many uses. They are great to take on trips and to club meetings to show others without the risk of loss or damage to the articles themselves. They actually serve the same purpose as Grandma's "brag book," to show off the adopted Hummel children. If there is an occasion to sell some by mail, good color photographs are almost a necessity, especially if there are variations from standard that are important.

Fine quality, individual color photographs of each piece in the collection can consume a great deal of time, and can be expensive to have them taken professionally. When four hundred color pictures were required to illustrate the pieces of Hummel art in *Hummel Art I,* a quotation was obtained from one commercial studio in Rochester, New York. If the figurines were packed and brought to the studio the price quoted was $25 for each one, making an astronomical total of $10,000. Needless to say, some intensive shopping around turned out to be very worthwhile. Most of the pictures you see in this book were taken right in the home with no risk of packing and transporting for two round trips. The photographer was Mary McCarthy, a freelance expert who specialized in wedding photography. By using a highly standardized setup with the author and the owners of the collection (not named for security reasons) as assistants, the cost, including the film, was less than $2 per item.

The setup we employed is explained here so that the interested reader has one suggested course to follow. A supply of light blue paper was used to form a curved background so that no horizontal line would show. The camera was a 35mm single lens reflex of recent design. This was mounted on a tripod to eliminate any possibility of movement. A strobe light bounced off an aluminized umbrella provided diffused, soft lighting without deep shadows, adding more of a three-dimensional effect.

A trial roll was run and processed to determine the best exposure range. When the final shooting was done, two exposures were made of each figurine, one at the indicated exposure and one a half stop overexposed so that the printer could have a choice. The slide film used was Kodachrome, 64 speed, because of the high color saturation in the finished transparencies. For those continually photographing tabletop articles like figurines, a light box can be constructed that makes setting up unnecessary. This can be made portable to take along on trips.

No doubt many collectors stopped reading the above because of the complexity of operation. For them, inexpensive snapshot cameras, similar to recent miniature pocket instantamatic cameras in the 110 size, or the instant color print cameras may suffice. Excellent pictures can be obtained by setting a figurine on a table very near a window or on an open porch as shown in the sketch. A plain color skirt, robe, or other fabric will cover any distracting background. Bright daylight, not direct sunlight, coming in the window or porch can be balanced by putting a piece of white cardboard to reflect light onto the shadow side as shown in the diagram.

Most inexpensive cameras will take clear pictures as close as three feet from the object. At that distance, the camera will probably include an area of about 20″ by 24″. For an inventory, arrange a number of figurines in rows on temporary supports in order to photograph a group and fill the picture area. If the camera is moved the least bit or is too close the picture will be fuzzy. For individual pictures that will be larger and show more detail, a closeup lens is available for some makes. This inexpensive attachment is well worth the small investment. With the closeup lens, good pictures can be made of the marks on the bottom of the figurine. The new 400 speed color film, for prints or slides, is ideal for this window lighting.

Flash photos using flashbulbs or electronic flash is a quick way of taking shots when you want them and where you see them. The lighting is flat (shows less modeling) and bright reflective surfaces like glass or polished metal or wood will reflect the flash causing the picture to flare or be fuzzy. By moving to one side and taking the picture at an angle most of this can be prevented. If the articles are in a cabinet, open the doors and, if the background is shiny, shoot at an angle. The Kodak and Polaroid instant cameras take immediately available pictures with and without flash. The Polaroid SX-70 is excellent for individual pictures as you can focus through the lens within about 18″ of the object, giving a picture area of only 8″ by 8″. A close-up attachment is available that gives still greater enlargement. It is especially useful for photos of the marks on the bottom of the figurines.

An excellent publication entitled, "Photos Help When Disaster Strikes" gives much more useful information. It covers ideas for photographing all of your personal or real property. This can be obtained from the Eastman Kodak Company, Department 841, Publication AM-4, 343 State St., Rochester, New York 14650 at no cost. Include a self-addressed envelope (no return postage required) with your request.

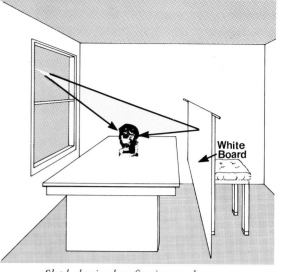

Sketch showing how figurines can be photographed with an inexpensive snapshot camera. Camera can usually be brought to within three feet of subject.

9 Collectors' Guide to Services

The purpose of listing these names and addresses in this book is to make it easier for collectors to locate sources that have been found helpful and reliable by other Hummel collectors. By no means is this an all-inclusive list. There are hundreds who are as competent, or moreso, in solving your problems. Those on this list have no association with the author, nor did they pay any fee for being listed. Some sources are known that did not qualify for listing. It is up to the readers to establish for themselves the adequacy of these names to render the service they wish at the prices they are willing to pay. If any of these sources do not measure up to your standards, we would appreciate receiving the details, but under no circumstances can we assume any liability.

Appraisers The Appraisers Association of America is the largest specialized group of personal property appraisers with members in most cities around the country. They will give you the name of ones who may be nearby who are specially qualified to help. The trust officers of local banks will also know personal property appraisers who should have the knowledge and background to render good service. With this book you can do the appraisal yourself or lend the appraiser the book to simplify his job.

> Appraisers Association of America
> 60 East 42nd St.,
> New York, NY 10017

Auctioneers Listed are a few of many auctioneers who have conducted specialized Hummel auctions. There are many more distributed all over the country that can do an equally fine disposal. Almost all auctioneers, including the ones below, are skilled in auctioning a great variety of personal property and have a large local or even national following. If one of the auctioneers listed is not near you, use the Yellow Pages of your telephone book for names, watch the paper for those frequently conducting sales, or talk to trust officers at local banks who have a good knowledge of area auctioneers.

> Douglas Galleries
> Route 5,
> S. Deerfield, MA 01373
>
> Du Mouchelle Art Galleries
> 409 E. Jefferson Ave.,
> Detroit, MI 48226
>
> Good Friend Associates
> M. L. Sone Auctioneer
> 1009 Chestnut St.,
> Newton, MA 02164
>
> Ken Hornberger
> Rt. 4, Box 140
> Lawrence, KS 66044

> Kramer and Kramer
> 108 E. Main St.,
> Eaton, OH 45320
>
> Lufkins
> 4301 Cat Mountain Dr.
> Austin, TX 78731
> Auctions by mail, twice a year
>
> Pace Auctions
> 1591 Elmwood,
> Des Plaines, IL 60016
>
> Adam A. Weschler & Son
> 905-9 E Street, N.W.,
> Washington, DC 20004

Drawing #5673 courtesy Ars Sacra.

Drawing #14118 courtesy Ars Sacra.

Drawing #5679 courtesy Ars Sacra.

Clubs The two principal clubs of interest to Hummel collectors have been thoroughly discussed in this book. In addition to their names and address given below there are other local clubs which are impractical to list in a book like this. To find out if there is a local Goebel Collectors' Club near you write to the address given below.

Goebel Collectors' Club
105 White Plains Road
Tarrytown, NY 10591

Hummel Collectors' Club
PO Box 247
Yardley, PA 10591

Dealers, U.S.A. Those listed are only a sampling of the thousands of authorized dealers selling M.I. Hummel figurines. Most of the ones listed are those who have above-average knowledge and inventories of M.I. Hummel articles. Many of them are specialists in mail orders. If you do not know one or more dealers in your area, you can get information about them by writing to one of the three distributors of Goebel products listed in this section. If you are a member of the Goebel Collectors' Club, they will be able to make some suggestions. A small percentage of Hummel dealers price figurines by "what the traffic will bear," especially airport shops. Avoid them. You now have the Current Price List to Hummel Art to satisfy yourself that you are paying fair prices.

ABC Gift Shop
8849 McGaughey Road
Indianapolis, IN
Mail order, calendars, buys
old figurines

Dorothy Marie Anthony,
1818 E. Atlantic St.,
Philadelphia, PA 19134
Mail order only

Beru's, Inc.
10051 West Washington St.,
Indianapolis, IN 46229
Mail order. Does not buy
from collectors

Mel Brown,
1353 N. State St.,
Chicago, Il

Brumelda
PO Box 5007
Million Hills, CA 91345
Mail order

Cameo Gift Shop
22 N. Main St.,
Chagrin Falls, OH 44022

Camines Collectibles
402 Appalachian Dr.,
Boone, NC 28607

Carol's Gifts
17601 South Pioneer Blvd.,
Artesia, CA 90701
Mail order

Chaikalena
1206 West 38th St. at "26 Doors"
Austin, TX 78705
Large retail display

Clark China and Gift Gallery
73 Westfield Ave.,
Clark, NJ 07066

Coventry Collectables
PO Box 316
Bolton, MA 01740
Mail order, buys from collectors

Dorothy Dous
1261 University Dr. PO Box 257
Yardley, PA 19067
Mail order. Extensive inventory,
buys from collectors

Dorothy's Treasures
1512 Est 54 Place
Tulson, OK 74105
Mail order

The Gallery
Gifts and Graphic Arts
3954 West 69th Terrace
Prairie Village, KS 66208

German Alps Store
Main St.
Hunter, NY 12442

Eileen Grande
12 Iroquois Dr.,
Saratoga Springs, NY 12866
Extensive inventory. Mail order

Grandma's Gallery Inc.
12957 Gulf Blvd., E.
Madeira Beach, FL 33708

Sam F. Jackson
417 University Blvd.,
Tuscaloosa, AL 35401

JuDee Kay's
PO Box 292
Bremen, IN 46506
Extensive inventory, old and new
figurines. Buys from collectors

Ruth Laudien
432 Palmetto Dr.,
Lake Park, FL 33403

Leo's Jewelry and Gifts
34900 Michigan Ave.,
Wayne, MI 48148
Extensive inventory of old and new figurines.
Buys from collectors

The Lion's Den
Fontans Shopping Center
PO 35663, Tulsa, OK 74135
Buys and sells, mail order

Maxine's Gift and Collectors Gallery
7144 University Ave.
Des Moines, IA 50311

Miller's Supermarket
Eaton, OH 45320
Extensive inventory of new
and old figurines

Misty's Gallery
Pat Arbenz, owner
228 Fry Blvd.,
Sierra Vista, AZ 85635
Large inventory of new and old
figurines, mail order

My Grandfather's Shop
2415 Ennals Ave.
Wheaton, NY 20902
Buy and sell old and new
figurines. Handle mail
orders.

The Old World
The Quadrangle
2800 Routh
Houston, TX 75201

Plate Collector's Exchange
478 Ward St. Ext.,
Wallingford, CT 06492

Donna L. Pokorn
Rt. 2, 2050z
Chickamaya Lane,
Long Grove, IL 60047

Rankins
512 Scott Drive,
Green Bay, WI 54303

Scottsdale East
8011 East Roosevelt
Scottsdale, AZ 85257
Mail order

Serendipity Shop
1203 Old Town in the Village
5500 Grenville Ave.
Dallas, TX 75206
Extensive inventory of figurines, dolls,
cards and other Hummelania

Shirley Ann-Tiques
3820 S. Union St.,
Independence, MO 64055

Shirley Niz
2 Carriage Lane
Lemont, IL 60521

Margie Simpson
PO Box 520113
Miami, FL 33152
Sells old and new figurines

Tiffany's Treasures, Ltd.
14019 Midland Road
Poway, CA 92064

Pat Upton
Woodhollow Court
Syosset, NY 11791

Bronner's
Christmas Wonderland
25 Christmas Lane
Frankenmuth, MI 48734
One of largest dealers —
new Hummels. Mail orders.

Dealers, Foreign As in the United States, there are many fine dealers in Canada and Europe. Only a few that the author has had personal experience with are listed. Members of the Goebel Collectors' Club who are traveling outside the U.S. can get the names of dealers in the larger cities they will be visiting by contacting the Club.

City Gavacenter
Frederiksberggade 2
Copenhagen 1459, Denmark

Dave L. C. Carson, Mail order
22 Monclaire Ave.,
Moncton, NB,
Canada E1E-IT8

Harry's Gift Shop, Mail order
675 Kaiserlautern
5-11 Mannheimer Strasse
West Germany

Lucette
Postfach 1169, Mail order
6367 Karbon
West Germany

L. Ostermayer, mail order
33-37 Konigstrasse
8500 Nurenberg
West Germany

McIntosh Watts
193 Sparks St.,
Ottawa, Ont. K1P 5B9
Canada

Rob McIntosh China Shop
1 Water St., S.E.
Cornwall, Ont. K6H 6MF

Phil Jost,
6533 Bacharach/Rhein
P.O. Box 88,
West Germany

Decorating and Display The effectiveness with which your collection of Hummel art is presented is a major factor in the enjoyment that you and others receive from it. Some collectors approach the problem by soliciting professional help the same as they do in decorating a home or office. Others obtain satisfaction in using their own artistic ideas. The *Plate Collector* Magazine has many fine articles and suggestions for accomplishing this goal. This section is not designed to suggest how but merely to list some sources of equipment and materials that others have used effectively in accomplishing innovative treatments of their collections. One truism seems to be that the results are proportional to the time and effort devoted to planning and executing the display and not necessarily related to the financial outlay.

Atkins and Merrill, Inc.
Electro Products Division
1 Etna Road
Lebanon, NH
for display lighting

Bard Products, Inc.
1825 Willow Rd.
Northfield, IL 60093

C.E. Morgan Building Products,
Division
601 Oregon Street,
Oshkosh, WI
For display cabinets and materials.
Write for information

Century Display Manufacturing Corp.
11602 West King Street
Franklin Park, IL 60131

Conco Industries, Inc.
43 Water Street
West Haven, CT
For display cabinets

Fetzer's
PO Drawer 486,
Salt Lake City, UT
For large display cases

Hamlin-Overton Frame Company, Inc.
125 Elkenburg Street
South Haven, MI 49090
Frames that hold plates safely

Howard Displays, Inc.
500 10th Avenue
New York, NY
For display cabinets

Kotler Picture Frame and Moulding
300 North Oakeley Blvd.,
Chicago, IL
Write for information concerning shadow
boxes and frames for plates

M and R Specialties
Dept. C, Box 34,
Bensenville, IL 60106
Shadow boxes, shelves, bases, plate frames.
Illustrated catalog

Reflector Hardware Corporation
1450 North 25th Avenue
Melrose Park, IL 60160
For special display lighting

Reliance Picture Frame Company
250 Fifth Avenue
New York, NY

Syroco Division
Syracuse, NY 13201
For display cabinets

Tall Emporium Products, Inc.
Keystone Park
Emporium, PA
For display lighting

Exhibits and Festivals The two principal festivals and their dates have been covered rather completely earlier in this book. Those who have not attended will most likely be pleasantly impressed and become repeat customers. As this hobby progresses there will be many more opportunities such as these developing. One that for the present is temporary in nature is the traveling museum exhibit previously mentioned. Listed below are the remaining opportunities to see this worthwhile introduction to Hummel art.

Drawing #4776 courtesy Ars Sacra.

The Formation of an Artist
The Early Works of Berta Hummel

*Sunset Center
Carmel, California
(January 10-February 8, 1981)*

*Augusta Richmond County
Museum
Augusta, Georgia
(February 28-March 29, 1981)*

*Central Missouri State
University Museum
Warrensburg, Missouri
(April 18-May 17, 1981)*

*Alford House
Anderson Fine Arts Center
Anderson, Indiana
(June 6-July 5, 1981)*

*California State Polytechnic
University Library
Pomona, California
(July 25-August 23, 1981)*

*McMillan Memorial Library
Wisconsin Rapids, Wisconsin
(September 12-October 11, 1981)*

*California State College Library
San Bernardino, California
(October 31-November 29, 1981)*

*Lauren Rogers Library
and Museum of Art
Laurel, Mississippi
(December 19-January 17,1982)*

*Washington County
Museum of Fine Arts
Hagerstown, Maryland
(February 6-March 7, 1982)*

*Virginia Polytechnic Institute
Blacksburg, Virginia
(March 27-April 25, 1982)*

Drawing #5670 courtesy Ars Sacra.

Insurance There are many insurance companies that write fine arts policies. The names listed here are some of those that have indicated to the author that most of their local agents will accept the prices on the separate Price List with this book as the basis for such a policy. Do not contact the home office. Look for the local representatives of these and other companies in the Yellow Pages of the phone directory. It may pay to shop around if your own agent is unable to help you, as prices and types of coverage vary.

Aetna Insurance Company
Chubb & Company
Continental Insurance Company
Government Employees Insurance Co
Hanover Insurance
Hartford Insurance Group
Liberty Mutual
St. Paul Fire & Marine
Traveler's Insurance Corporation

Fine Arts Insurance Specialists

Flather and Company, Inc.
888 17th Street, N.W.
Washington, DC 20006
Specializing in fine arts insurance.
Write for information

Insurance Information Institute
110 William Street,
New York, NY 10038

Drawing #5669 courtesy Ars Sacra.

Lampshades

Hartville Collectibles
788 Edison St. N.W.
Hartville, OH 46632

Miniatures Many creative Hummel collectors have taken a page from

Drawing #14676 courtesy Ars Sacra.

doll collector books by arranging one or more related M.I. Hummel figurines in a natural setting by making use of the extensive background and accessory miniatures that are available. The furniture and accessories are scaled so that one inch of miniature articles is the equivalent to one foot in real life, which is an ideal proportion for Hummel figurines. Some of the annual M.I. Hummel calendars are done in a manner which may trigger still other scenes and situations. Ride into Christmas, Hum. 396, Letter to Santa, Hum. 340, March Winds, Hum. 43, and Skier, Hum. 59 could all be combined into a suitable outdoor diorama, while a formal living room in miniature would be an ideal setting for a musical with Band Leader, Hum. 129, leading several figures with stringed or wind instruments. Nativity Sets, of course, are already designed for the mantel or tabletop during the holidays. Many small figurines can be suitably teamed with an array of kitchen miniatures that are available. Some of these might be Baker, Hum. 128, Little Sweeper, Hum. 171, and Not for You, Hum. 317. How about Mail Coach, Hum. 226 and Auf Wiedersehen coupled in an outdoor diorama?

Aztec Imports
4273 Fenn Rd.,
Medina, OH 44256
Extensive catalog, 1″ to 1′

Chestnut Hill Studio
Box 907
Taylors, SC 29867
1″ to 1′ scale.
All furnishings

Paragon Needlecraft, Distributors
230 Fifth Ave.,
New York, NY 10001
Kits with matching frames for crewel embroidery of Hummel children. At local needlework stores or departments, or write for nearest dealer

Ars Editions, Inc.
(formerly Ars Sacra)
P.O. Box 121, Massapequa Park,
NY 11762
Complete full-color catalog, $4.50

Europe Import Company
13525 Gratiot
Detroit, MI 48205

Brookstone Company
125 Vose Farm Road
Peterborough, NH 03458
Marking and other special purpose tools

Dreml Manufacturing Company
Department 350
Racine, WI 53406
Engraving tools

L. Kummbrow
16460 Wagonwheel Dr.,
Riverside, CA 92506
½″ to 1″ scale.
Toys, Tiffany windows, glass, furniture, houses

Masterpiece Miniatures
Box 9,
Belle Haven, VA 23306
1″ to 1′ scale.
Period furniture, drapes, carpets

Needlework

Retail Sources by Mail:

Aa Hykdgaard Hebseb ApS
21 Store Stranstraede
DK-1255 Copenhagen, K
Denmark

Prints and Postcards

Emil Fink Verlag
15 Heidenhofstrafse
7 Stuttgart,
West Germany.
Write for catalog.
Prints are also available

Geme Art Gallery
6234 N.E. Glisan
Portland, OR 97213

Protection Equipment*

Electronics Corporation of America
Photoswitch Division
3 Memorial Drive,
Cambridge, MA
For electronic security systems

GBC Closed Circuit TV Corp.
74 Fifth Avenue
New York, NY 10011
Magnavox wireless burglar alarms and other alarm systems.
Write for information

The Miniature Mart
1807 Octavia St.
San Francisco, CA 94109

Miniature Silver
317 South Prospect,
Park Ridge, IL 60068
1/12″ scale

The American Needlewoman
3806 Alta Mesa Blvd
Fort Worth, TX 76133

WD Hummel Kits
Box 5442
Hicksville, NY 11861

Hingham Collectables
P.O. Box 182
Hingham, MA 02043
Wall hangings and Hummel graphics.

The Lion's Den
P.O. Box 341774
Miami, FL 33134
Hummel postcards, prints

Mosler Safe Company
1561 Grand Blvd.,
Hamilton, OH 45012
Safes for storing valuables

Napko Security Systems, Inc.
6 Di Tomas Court
Copiaque, NY 11726

Nu Tone Division
Madison and Red Bank Road
Cincinnati, OH 45227
Write for security systems information

Potter Electric Signal Company
2083 Craig Road,
St. Louis, MO 63141
For security and alarm systems

Qualified Security Specialists, Inc.
Distributors of Qunaar Security Systems
1559 Monroe Ave.
Rochester, NY 14618

Simms and Associates
Art and Museum Consultants
18311 S.W. 95th Court
Miami, FL 33157

3-M Company
Security Systems
3-M Center
St. Paul, MN 55101
Write for information about their
special Intruder Alarm

United Security Products, Inc.
PO Drawer 2428
Dublin, CA
Security systems for protecting your
Hummels

Westminster Collectibles
6186 Skyline Drive
East Lansing, MI 48823
Sell an "Invisible Marking Pen Kit"
Read under black light

*Please refer to the section on safeguarding your collection for more information. New equipment and devices are being introduced almost daily so the above information is only a sample of what was available when this book was published.

Repairs*

Antique Restoration
1001 Hight Street,
Burlington, NJ 08016

Anything Antiques and Art Restoration
770 Harrison Street,
San Francisco, CA 94107

Rose Behar
2404 University Street
Houston, TX

Berkley, Inc.
2011 Hermitage Ave.
Wheaton, MD 20902

Butterfly Shoppe Studio
637 Livernois
Ferndale, MI

Veronica Burns Art Ltd.
2210 Stonecroft Street
Grafton, WI 53024

Cordier's Fine Arts
1619 South La Cienega Blvd.
Los Angeles, CA
Restorers of ceramics and other fine
decorative arts

Craftsmen's Guild
1938 Portland Blvd.
Portland, OR 97217

Harry A. Eberhardt and Son, since 1888
2010 Walnut St.
Philadelphia, PA 19103
Will repair porcelain figures. Gives
estimates on repairs of items sent by mail

Hess Repairs
200 Park Avenue South
New York, NY 10003
Repairs porcelain, china, etc.

Old World Restoration, Inc.
705 Wooster Pike, Rt. 50
Terrace Park, OH 45174

Restorations Unlimited
2800 Rt. 205c, Quadrangle
Dallas, TX 75201

Sierra Studios
P.O. 1005
Oak Park, IL 60304
Porcelain, china repair.
Specialize in mail order repair work

Simms and Associates
Art and Museum Consultants
18311 S.W. 95th Court
Miami, FL 33157

Donna M. Towle
Chestnut Street Antiques
1009 Chestnut Street
Newton Upper Falls, MA 02164

Tristan's Restorations,
Ark Road,
Mt. Holly, NJ 08060

Vipro Ltd.
10220 Royal Drive,
St. Louis, MO

Daniel Zalles,
580 Sutter Street,
San Francisco, CA

*Most restorers take weeks or months to complete repair orders because the good ones are very busy.

Books on Repairs

Cross, Rena. *China Repair and Restoration.* Drake Publishing Company, New York City, 1973.

Encyclopedia of Antique Restoration and Maintenance. Clarkson N. Potter, New York City, 1974

Grotz, George. *The Antique Restorer's Handbook.* Doubleday, New York.

Porter, Arthur, ed. *Directory of Art and Antique Restoration.* 465 California Street, San Francisco, California 94104.

Yates, Raymond. *How to Restore Bric-a-Brac and Small Antiques.* Harper and Row, New York, 1953.

Drawing #14675 courtesy Ars Sacra.

Appendix

History of the W. Goebel Company

The Goebel factory began its career by producing slate pencils, blackboards, and marbles in 1871. Franz Detleff Goebel and his son William had wanted to produce porcelain and, nine years after its inception, the F. and W. Goebel Factory boasted a porcelain kiln. Production of practical items such as dinnerware, beer steins, and coffee sets began, in addition to the production of bisque dolls' heads. The third generation of Goebels introduced earthenware to the line in 1926. This expansion provided Goebel employees with nine years of experience and expertise with the earthenware body before the factory began to produce M.I. Hummel figurines.

In 1935, Arthur Möller, then a Goebel sculptor, picked up a book of Sister Maria Innocentia's sketches and created the first three-dimensional figurines adapted from her drawings. Charmed with the results, Goebel executives approached Sister Hummel and the Siessen Convent for permission to produce a small line of M.I. Hummel figurines to sell.

The agreement and royalty arrangement drawn between the Goebel Factory and the Siessen Convent stipulated that the convent had the right to prior approval of any M.I. Hummel prototype, and that Goebel would pay the convent a royalty on all Hummel figurines produced. The first figurines were introduced at the Leipzig Trade Fair in 1935. This feat was to change the course of Goebel history.

During World War II, German exports were cut off to major outlets.

W. Goebel factory in Rödental, West Germany. Courtesy of Busharts.

Master model used for making working molds.

Goebel master sculptor, Gerhard Skrobek applies finishing touches to model of Merry Wanderer, Hum. 7. Note Sister Hummel's drawing in background.

Consequently, Goebel centered its efforts on the domestic products. Some reliable sources claim that certain of the M.I. Hummel figurines were censored for their content. One can readily understand why highly religious pieces might be disfavored by the Nazi government.

After the war, production soared and M.I. Hummel figurines were again a favorite in the export market. American G.I.'s stationed in the Coburg region in the final stages of the war were particularly attracted to the figurines. These G.I.'s were a major factor in spreading the popularity of M.I. Hummel figurines to the United States and Canada.

Today, one-hundred ten years and five generations later, Wilhelm Goebel heads a company producing a wide range of fine, decorative, and useful art products. Included are articles made of several types of ceramics, glass, and plastic. These are manufactured in a number of plants in Germany and one in the United States. Thousands of highly skilled artists and craftsmen are employed to create, produce, and distribute a continually growing stream of articles besides the M.I. Hummel articles so intimately associated with Goebel's history since 1935. Dieter E. Schneider, U.S. Managing Director of W. Goebel, is responsible for all of the varied enterprises carried on in this country.

Steps in Making Hummel Figurines

To make one Hummel figurine from an original drawing of Sister Hummel's is simple if you are endowed with a talent most of us do not have. To make hundreds and thousands of the same motif requires the same sculpting skill as to make one, but the rest of the process, even though ages old, is not so simple. It requires many combined skills, technical knowhow, sophisticated equipment, quality controls, time, and very special materials.

The best way to appreciate the skills and technology employed is to have a personally conducted tour of the factory, but this is no longer possible. The second best way is to see a new color motion picture of the important parts of the process and to listen carefully to the excellent narration by Joan Ostroff, Executive Vice-President of the Goebel Collectors' Club. The least dramatic and less visual method is to continue to read what follows.

For one or one thousand figurines, the sculptor, such as Gerhard Skrobek the present master sculptor, must first model a three-dimensional version of Sister Hummel's original drawing using a special compound which is pliable enough to work and yet maintains the finest of details. The completed model is then submitted for approval by the Franciscan Convent in Siessen before production can begin. With approval in hand, the sculptor then starts to undo what he has so painstakingly created. He cuts the original sculpture into as many pieces as are required to make a faithful reproduction of the master by using two-part plaster molds. Some intricate designs may require cutting the model into as many as thirty pieces and then making a master mold from each one of the component parts. The master molds are carefully preserved and reserved to make the working molds used for regular production pieces.

Demonstration of how two part molds are filled.

Removing a "green" part from half of a working mold.

Production workplace for assembling Umbrella Girl, Hum. 152 B. Photograph by G. Bushart.

Assembling parts (garnishing) for Follow the Leader, Hum. 369.

Parts loaded on truck for firing in continuous electric kiln. Photograph by G. Bushart.

A corner of the decorating room and individual workplaces. Photograph by G. Bushart.

Starting with a production mold for each individual piece of the complete figure, the molds are filled with a thin liquid about the consistency of cream, which it resembles. Actually it is a compound of finely ground clay, kaolin, feldspar, and many other small but important additives combined with enough water to bring the mixture to the specified viscosity. The end result, called "slip" by the trade, is poured into the top of the closed, two-piece mold until it is completely full. The mold is made of a porous material which starts to absorb the water in the slip immediately. As the water is absorbed, a solid coating begins to form on the interior walls of the mold. The longer the slip is allowed to stand, the thicker will be the deposit. After a carefully timed interval, the remaining slip is poured out of the mold which is then opened and the hollow deposit removed. In this stage the piece is solid enough to maintain the shape imposed by the contour of the mold.

After all the parts of the future figurine have been cast in the above manner, and the "greenware" has been allowed to air dry for a period of time, a craftsman ("garnisher") assembles all of the component parts by using the same slip as a bonding agent for each piece. The alignment of each part is critically important to produce an exact copy of the master model. In addition to assembling, the garnisher also smooths out any imperfections that may have occurred in molding or assembly so that the completed object appears to have been made in one hollow piece. He also pierces a small hole or two in inconspicuous places to prevent the figure from exploding from entrapped steam formed in the kiln.

The "duplicate original" is now ready for the curing process which is performed by loading similar pieces on a flat surface or pallet and, as is necessary in some cases, adding supports so that the piece will not sag out of shape in the intense heat of the electric oven or kiln. Today the modern kilns are continuous so that the pallets move slowly at a predetermined speed through various temperature zones to bring the pieces up to optimum baking temperatures and then very gradually to cool them to about room temperature.

Before anything more is done the pieces are carefully inspected and the imperfect ones, which sometimes are a significant percentage of the total, have to be discarded. Those that pass are dipped in another type of slip to seal the bisque and provide a smooth surface for decorating. This solution imparts a blue gray appearance to the figurine which disappears in the next trip through the kiln where it is fired at very high temperatures. This makes the glaze coating glass-hard and completely bonded to the body. Again there is a careful inspection to remove the imperfect ones from the ones that will pass to the final decoration department.

It has been reported that over four hundred persons are involved in the most intricate, exacting operations of all — the decorating. A four- to five-year apprenticeship is required to acquire the necessary skill for some of these operations. A single figurine is not completely painted by one person. Painting is performed in stages requiring different levels of artistry and ability which is partially demonstrated in photograph at left. This also permits a thorough setting of the various colors that are blended and mixed by each individual artist from a master palette of carefully selected and controlled colors. The final decorating is to the face which requires artists of the highest skill to impart the proper flesh tones and facial details. If one person were to paint the complete figurine, some models would take a whole day to complete. This gives an indication of the concerned care used by these decorators, and also some indication of why figurines cost as much as they do. The skill of the final artist is recognized by allowing that person to place their initial or symbol on the base of the figure, permanently attesting to the identity of the final decorator.

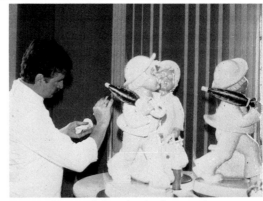

Close-up of decorating in demonstration room. Merry Wanderer, 7/X.

Starting on a pilot basis in 1979, these final artists placed their personal letter or symbol on the bottom and added the date, '79, immediately following their mark. The procedure was approved and has now been expanded until all pieces leaving the factory today (not necessarily off the dealers' shelves) should have this significant date adjacent to the artist's mark. Collectors welcome this innovation. In the years to come there will be no question about the year a piece was completed, which is an important premium factor in buying or selling older figurines in the secondary market. Until recently collectors had to depend on the Goebel trademark (TMK) to get a rough and varying approximation of the date the piece was made. It is now well established that many of the early trademarks were used sooner than generally assumed. Also there is significant overlapping of trademarks during the transition to a new emblem. It is possible that in years to come artist-dated pieces, especially those done in the years 1979 and 1980, could command a premium over ones with the same trademark but lacking the artist-year mark. Only time holds the answer to this supposition.

Goebel master painter applies final details to Goose Girl, Hum. 47, at Eaton Festival.

The final firing is done to set the colors as an integral part of the figure and to make them essentially immune to fading, normal wear, or water. With the introduction of new developments in organic finishes in the last several decades, the new colors will retain their original luster and brilliance in the same manner that automobile finishes have markedly improved during the same period.

With the final firing complete, the last and most critical inspection is performed to eliminate flawed pieces overlooked in previous inspections and to remove any that are substandard due to painting or final firing. Those that pass are packed for export in a molded styrene inner pack, cartoned, and labeled. These for sale in Germany are wrapped in a gray tissue and excelsior cushioning material before cartoning and labeling.

Finished figurine, Merry Wanderer, 7/X and standard M.I. Hummel color scale.

Bibliography

Drawing #5942 courtesy Ars Sacra.

Drawing #5945 courtesy Ars Sacra.

Books

Anderton, Johanna. *Twentieth Century Dolls,* North Kansas City, Mo.: Athena Publishing Co., 1971.

Angione, Genevieve. *All Bisque and Half Bisque Dolls.* New York: Thomas Nelson, Inc., 1969.

The Antique Trader Weekly editors. "Hummel Update: More Details Presented on These Popular Collectibles," by Claudia Frech. "Hummels, Facts and Fiction," by Allen J.F. Von Geisler. *Annual of Articles on Antiques for 1974.* Dubuque, Ia.: Babka Publishing Co., 1974

The Antique Trader Weekly editors. "Research Done on Hummels" and "The Goebel Company and Its Other Products," by Claudia Frech. "More Info on Hummels," by Claudia Frech. *Annual of Articles on Antiques for 1973.* Dubuque, Ia.: Babka Publishing Co., 1973.

The Antique Trader Weekly editors. "Trash or Treasure — Hummels," by Philip DeVilbiss. "Hummel Collector Shares Knowledge," by Claudia Frech. *Annual of Articles on Antiques for 1972.* Dubuque, Ia.: Babka Publishing Co., 1972.

Bartels, Nadja, and McKinven, John G., editors. *The Bradford Book of Collectors' Plates 1976.* New York: McGraw Hill Book Co., 1977.

Coleman, Dorothy. *Collectors Encyclopedia of Dolls.* New York: Crown Publishers.

Ehrmann, Eric. *Hummel, The Complete Collector's Guide and Illustrated Reference.* 2nd ed. Huntington, N.Y.: Portfolio Press Corp., 1979.

Grotz, George. *The Antique Restorer's Handbook.* Garden City, N.Y.: Doubleday and Co., 1976.

Hotchkiss, John F. *Hummel Art,* Des Moines, Ia.: Wallace-Homestead Book Co. Out of print.

Hotchkiss, John F. *Hummel Art Supplement, 1979.* Out of print.

Hotchkiss, John F. *Hummel Art Supplement, 1980.* Out of print.

Hudgeons, Thos. II, editor. *Hummel Plates and Figurines.* House of Collectibles, 1980.

Hummel, Berta. *The Hummel Book.* 17th ed. translated by Lola Ch. Eytel. Stuttgart, Germany: Emil Fink, Verlag, 1973.

Johl, Janet Pagter. *Your Dolls and Mine.* New York: Linquist Publishers, 1952.

Larney, Judith. *Restoring Ceramics.* Cincinnati, Ohio: Watson/Guptill, 1975.

Luckey, Carl. *Hummel Figurines and Plates,* 3rd ed.   : Books Americana,

Marion, Frieda. *China Half-Figures Called Pincushion Dolls.* Newburyport, Mass.: J. Palmer Publishers, 1974.

McGrath, Lee Pariz. *Housekeeping with Antiques.* New York: Dodd, Mead & Co., pp. 137-156.

Wiegand, Sister, OSF, *Sketch Me.* Eaton, Ohio: Robert Miller, 1979.

The Hummel, Drawings by Berta Hummel with Light Verse. Munich, West Germany: Verlag Ars Sacra, Josef Muller, 1972.

Yates, Raymond F. *How to Restore China, Bric-A-Brac and Small Antiques.* New York: Gramercy Publishing Co., 1953.

Drawing #5943 courtesy Ars Sacra.

Periodicals

Allison, Grace. "W. Goebel Porzellanfabrik Commemorates Our 200th Birthday."
National Antiques Review, August 1976, pp. 20-21.

Arbenz, Pat. "Hummel Facts by Arbenz." *Plate Collector,* July 1976 to present.

Arbenz, Pat. "Collectors' Showcase" monthly feature, *Plate Collector,* October 15,
1980, p. 52.

Christensen, G. "Decorating Unlimited." *Plate Collector,* February 1978, p. 60.

Eschenbach, Virginia. "The Merry Wanderer," *Antique Trader Weekly,* September
15, 1976, pp. 78-79.

Fisback, Linda Ellis. *"The Great Frame Up,"* Plate Collector, Nov. 15, 1980,
p. 23.

Lasher, Faith B. "Hummels or Goebels?," *Saters Antique News,* January 7, 1977,
p. 20.

Miller, Robert L. Quarterly column on Hummels in *Collector Editions.*

Miller, Robert L. Monthly column in *Collector News* on Hummels.

Miller, Robert L. "Recent Rare 'Finds' Enhance Hummel Collecting," *Antique
Trader,* March 2, 1977, pp. 24-25.

Miller, Robert L. "Millers Uncover Extraordinary Hungarian Figurines," *Acquire,*
March 1977, pp. 42-43.

Monaghan, Nancy. "They Aren't Antiques but Cherubic Hummels Are Prized By
Collectors," *Times Union* (Rochester, N.Y.), February 28, 1977, 3rd section,
p. 2.

Pfuhl, Nalten "Hummel Wealth Awarded to German Convent." Translated by
John Woesner, *Tri-State Trader,* May 18, 1974.

Roye, Josephine S. "Berta Hummel's Figurines." *Sater's Antique News,* May 4,
1973, pp. 8-9.

Staff Written, "Hummel Collecting, Part 1, Berta's Early Life," *Acquire,* July
1975, pp. 43-44.

Staff Written, "Hummel Dolls." *Tri-State Trader,* September 13, 1975.

Staff Written. "The Millers' Hummel Collection." *Acquire,* May, 1976, p. 9.

Staff Written. "Trouble at Hummel," *Newsweek,* July 17, 1972, p. 65.

Witt, Louise Schaub. "Along the Collector's Line," *Collector's News,* September
1973, p. 32.

Drawing #5206 courtesy Ars Sacra.

Other Sources

Brown, Alex, information on English Hummels.

Collectors' News, July, 1978, "Goebel's Answer to 1978 Hummel Prices and
Shortages."

Dous, Dorothy. Hummel Collectors' Club *Newsletter.* Yardley, Pa., November
1976.

Dous, Dorothy. International Goebel Collectors' Club Newsletter. Yardley, Pa.
April 1975-July 1976.

Golden, Colo. August 22, 1978. Rare "Little Fiddler Plaque" #107 reported.
Letter #1.

Gwen's Glassline by Gwen Shumpert, "Glass Hummel." (Produced by the L.E.
Smith Glass Company), *Glass Review,* April 1980, p. 10.

Huber, Clayton, Hummel catalogs from the 1950s.

Lancaster, New York. Reported in reader letter #22, Madonna, Hum. 46,
September 23, 1978, terra-cotta Hummel figurines reported.

The Plate Collector, September, 1978, Naled requested Goebel to withdraw the frame offer presented in the Goebel Collectors' News, Spring/Summer, 1978.

Poag, Heidi, correspondence on Hummels, 1979-1980.

Schmid Newsletter, May/June, 1978. The thrust of the newsletter is: "Schmid and Hummel; a long lasting friendship." Photos of Adolph Hummel (brother) and Viktoria Hummel (mother).

Wall Street Journal, August 8, 1978. "Hummel Figures, the Very Image of Innocence, Mask a Nasty Battle — Goebel vs Schmid."

Public Documents

Germany, German Supreme Court. February 22, 1974, as published in *Neue Juristische Wochenschrift* (NJW) 1974, pp. 904-907.

Germany, Lower court decision. 1952 decision published in *Neue Juristische Wochenschrift* (NJW), 1952, pp. 784-785. In German.

State of New York, Department of State, Division of Corporations and State Records, Certificate of Incorporation of Herbert Dubler, Inc., pursuant to Article 2 of the Stock Corporation Law.

United States, Department of Commerce, Bureau of the Census, Foreign Trade Division. Extracts from FT 246, U.S. *Imports for Consumption.* Calendar Years 1971-1975. Presenting date on U.S. Imports of Ceramic Figures.

United States Department of Commerce, Bureau of the Census, Foreign Trade Division. Extracts from IM 146, U.S. Imports for Consumption. Cumulative, January-Septembver 1976. Presenting data on U.S. Imports of ceramic figures.

About the Author

For several years John F. Hotchkiss has been a resident Fellow at the Rochester (New York) Museum of Arts and Science Center as a result of his specialized knowledge of antiques, and especially glass, in which he has had an interest for over forty years.

During the last twenty years he has produced a number of books, such as *Art Glass Handbook, Carder's Steuben Glass, Cut Glass Handbook,* and a *Bottle Collector's Handbook.* This last book was co-authored with his daughter, Joan Welch. He also wrote *Limited Edition Collectibles,* the first comprehensive book on this subject.

After retiring as superintendent of an Eastman Kodak Company manufacturing division, he lectured on antiques and collectibles on three world cruises, at which time he became interested in the Hummel figurines he had been buying for his daughters. After three years of research, he wrote the first complete book on Hummel art in 1978 and followed with *Supplements* in 1979 and 1980.

In addition, Mr. Hotchkiss appraises antiques and collections for insurance and estate purposes under the auspices of Hotchkiss Associates. He is a member of the Appraisers Association of America. In this one-thousand-member organization, he is the only member listed as specializing in the appraising of Hummel art at the present time.

A native of Geneseo, New York, he is a graduate of Carnegie-Mellon University in Pittsburgh and a past president of their alumni federation. He and his wife, Fidelis, live in Sanibel, Florida, but spend the summer months in Rochester, New York.

—Alice Walsh